Communications in Computer and Information Science 2775

Rationale

The CCIS series is devoted to the publication of proceedings of computer science conferences. Its aim is to efficiently disseminate original research results in informatics in printed and electronic form. While the focus is on publication of peer-reviewed full papers presenting mature work, inclusion of reviewed short papers reporting on work in progress is welcome, too. Besides globally relevant meetings with internationally representative program committees guaranteeing a strict peer-reviewing and paper selection process, conferences run by societies or of high regional or national relevance are also considered for publication.

Topics

The topical scope of CCIS spans the entire spectrum of informatics ranging from foundational topics in the theory of computing to information and communications science and technology and a broad variety of interdisciplinary application fields.

Information for Volume Editors and Authors

Publication in CCIS is free of charge. No royalties are paid, however, we offer registered conference participants temporary free access to the online version of the conference proceedings on SpringerLink (http://link.springer.com) by means of an http referrer from the conference website and/or a number of complimentary printed copies, as specified in the official acceptance email of the event.

CCIS proceedings can be published in time for distribution at conferences or as post-proceedings, and delivered in the form of printed books and/or electronically as USBs and/or e-content licenses for accessing proceedings at SpringerLink. Furthermore, CCIS proceedings are included in the CCIS electronic book series hosted in the SpringerLink digital library at http://link.springer.com/bookseries/7899. Conferences publishing in CCIS are allowed to use our online conference service (Meteor) for managing the whole proceedings lifecycle (from submission and reviewing to preparing for publication) free of charge.

Publication process

The language of publication is exclusively English. Authors publishing in CCIS have to sign the Springer CCIS copyright transfer form, however, they are free to use their material published in CCIS for substantially changed, more elaborate subsequent publications elsewhere. For the preparation of the camera-ready papers/files, authors have to strictly adhere to the Springer CCIS Authors' Instructions and are strongly encouraged to use the CCIS LaTeX style files or templates.

Abstracting/Indexing

CCIS is abstracted/indexed in DBLP, Google Scholar, EI-Compendex, Mathematical Reviews, SCImago, Scopus. CCIS volumes are also submitted for the inclusion in ISI Proceedings.

How to start

To start the evaluation of your proposal for inclusion in the CCIS series, please send an e-mail to ccis@springer.com

Xiao Ding · Yongquan Dong
Editors

Computational Linguistics and Natural Language Processing

Second International Conference, CLNLP 2025
Suzhou, China, July 18–20 2025
Revised Selected Papers

Springer

Editors
Xiao Ding
Harbin Institute of Technology
Harbin, China

Yongquan Dong
Jiangsu Normal University
Xuzhou, China

ISSN 1865-0929 ISSN 1865-0937 (electronic)
Communications in Computer and Information Science
ISBN 978-981-95-4787-6 ISBN 978-981-95-4788-3 (eBook)
https://doi.org/10.1007/978-981-95-4788-3

This Springer imprint is published by the registered company Springer Nature Singapore Pte Ltd.
The registered company address is: 152 Beach Road, #21-01/04 Gateway East, Singapore 189721, Singapore

Preface

The 2nd International Conference on Computational Linguistics and Natural Language Processing (CLNLP 2025) was held in Suzhou, China from July 18–20, 2025. It was organized by Suzhou University of Science and Technology and Jiangsu Normal University, and co-organized by the JSAI Technical Committee on Natural Language Processing and the School of Foreign Languages, Dalian University of Technology.

CLNLP 2025 provided an academic exchange platform for experts, scholars, and researchers engaged in research related to computational linguistics and natural language processing, both domestically and internationally. It sought to promote the development of research in computational linguistics and natural language processing.

The event featured keynote speeches, oral sessions, and poster presentations. The keynote speakers further explored the topics of CLNLP 2025, which was so significant and beneficial for the fields of the conference themes. We would like to express our sincere praise and gratitude to the three keynote speakers: Hwee Tou Ng, Fellow of ACL, from National University of Singapore, Singapore Yi Cai from South China University of Technology, China, and David Chiang from University of Notre Dame, USA. Oral sessions and poster sessions covered the accepted contributions, all with a central focus on Computational Linguistics and Natural Language Processing.

CLNLP 2025 received 53 submissions in response to the call for papers, with each paper being reviewed by at least two experts in the related research field. After a strict double-blind peer review, 24 full papers were accepted for publication. We thank the reviewers and program committee members for their thorough peer review of the submitted papers. We also appreciate the enthusiastic services provided by the organizing committee and volunteers who contributed to the successful organization of this conference.

Finally, we would like to express our most sincere gratitude and warmest welcome to all the participants. We hope you had a pretty good experience in Suzhou, China!

Xiao Ding
Yongquan Dong

Organization

Conference Chairs

Bing Qin	Harbin Institute of Technology, China
Xiao Ding	Harbin Institute of Technology, China
Dongyu Zhang	Dalian University of Technology, China
Bin Liu	Beijing Institute of Technology, China

Organizing Committee Chair

Xuefeng Xi	Suzhou University of Science and Technology, China

Publication Chair

Tong Xiao	Northeastern University, China

Publicity Chair

Jianxing Yu	Sun Yat-sen University, China

Session Chairs

Jinhua Cui	Huazhong University of Science and Technology, China
Xiwen Zhang	Beijing Language and Culture University, China
Bo Xu	Dalian University of Technology, China
Wei Liu	Shanghai University, China
Shengfa Miao	Yunnan University, China
Chengjie Sun	Harbin Institute of Technology, China

Local Chair

Mei Song	Jiangsu Normal University, China

Program Chairs

Yongquan Dong	Jiangsu Normal University, China
Xinying Qiu	Guangdong University of Foreign Studies, China
Huiyu Zhou	University of Leicester, UK

Program Committee

Mukesh Prasad	University of Technology Sydney, Australia
José Alfredo F. Costa	Universidade Federal do Rio Grande do Norte, Brazil
Rafael Guzmán Cabrera	University of Guanajuato, Mexico

Technical Committee

Weigang Li	University of Brasília, Brazil
Zhen Li	Shenzhen MSU-BIT University, China
Mario Kubek	Georgia State University, USA
Carlin Chun-fai Chu	Hang Seng University of Hong Kong, China
Huiru (Jane) Zheng	Ulster University, UK
Gabofetswe Malema	University of Botswana, Botswana
Peiyang Yu	Carnegie Mellon University, USA
Benyamin Ahmadnia	Tulane University of Louisiana, USA
Mu-Chun Su	National Central University, Taiwan
Francesco Zirilli	Sapienza Università di Roma, Italy
Henry Horng-Shing Lu	National Chiao Tung University, Taiwan
Ali H. Wheeb	University of Baghdad, Iraq
Swathi Ganesan	York St. John University, UK
Goh Hui Ngo	Multimedia University, Malaysia
Ghasem Mirjalily	Yazd University, Iran
Pavel Loskot	Zhejiang University-University of Illinois at Urbana Institute, China
Edwin Wang	University of Calgary Cumming School of Medicine, Canada
Apdullah Yayık	National Defense University, Turkey

Contents

The MeCab-Based Development of Lexical Complexity Analyzer for Japanese Texts in Multiple Registers and Its Application

Yong Zhong[1](✉) and Xiaomin Yang[2]

[1] College of Foreign Languages, Nanjing University of Aeronautics and Astronautics, Nanjing, China
zhongyongriyu@foxmail.com
[2] College of Foreign Languages and Literature, Fudan University, Shanghai, China

Abstract. This paper developed a software named Lexical Complexity Analyzer for Japanese Texts in Multiple Registers (LCA-JT-MR), which is built on MeCab, a widely utilized tokenization and part-of-speech tagging system for Japanese. This software offers a straightforward interface and user-friendly operation, enabling the automatic, efficient, and objective analysis of lexical complexity in both general and academic Japanese texts. It also supports analysis of native Japanese words, Chinese-origin words, and verbs. To illustrate the practical application and effectiveness of this software in Japanese L2 writing research, we employed it to study the lexical complexity of Chinese learners' Japanese doctoral dissertations on Japanese language research. The results revealed that the differences in lexical density, lexical compositionality, and lexical diversity between learners' doctoral dissertations and native speakers' journal articles were relatively small. However, lexical sophistication in the former was significantly higher than in the latter. From the application in this study, it is evident that the employment of the software significantly broadens the scope of Japanese L2 lexical complexity research and substantially enhances the efficiency and objectivity of data processing.

Keywords: MeCab · Lexical Complexity Analyzer for Japanese Texts in Multiple Registers · Chinese Learner · Doctoral Dissertations · Academic Japanese Writing

1 Introduction

Linguistic complexity, accuracy, and fluency are fundamental components of L2 proficiency [1, 2]. One aspect of linguistic complexity is lexical complexity, also known as lexical richness. This refers to the variety and complexity of vocabulary use [3, 4] and encompasses dimensions such as lexical density, lexical diversity, lexical sophistication, and lexical compositionality [4, 5]. Lexical complexity serves as an indicator of a learner's L2 expression proficiency [4, 6, 7] and has been a focal point in L2 writing research [8]. However, calculating dimensional indexes of lexical complexity manually is both challenging and subjective, and time-consuming and labor-intensive, which to

X. Ding and Y. Dong (Eds.): CLNLP 2025, CCIS 2775, pp. 1–12, 2026.
https://doi.org/10.1007/978-981-95-4788-3_1

some extent affects the progress of lexical complexity research in L2 writing. Moreover, the variation in measurement indexes and calculation methods across different studies hinders comparability, thereby impeding the advancement of lexical complexity research. To address this issue, researchers in the realm of English Education have developed some software capable of automatically calculating lexical complexity indexes for English texts, such as RANGE[1] designed by Nation and Coxhead as early as 2002, Lexical Complexity Analyzer (LCA)[2] developed by Lu [9] in 2012, and Lexical Complexity Analyzer for Academic Writing (LCA-AW)[3] released by Nasseri and Lu in 2019. These software for analyzing lexical complexity in English writing are widely utilized, yet none can process Japanese texts. To address this gap, Zhong [10] developed a software titled Lexical Richness Analyzer for Japanese Texts (LRA-JT). However, the software has several limitations: (1) it is limited to analyzing six indexes, which unfortunately includes outdated ones such as Type-Token Ratio (TTR); (2) it lacks the capability to analyze the dimension of lexical compositionality; (3) it fails to provide more detailed complexity analysis of subordinate lexical levels such as native Japanese words, Chinese-origin words, verbs, etc.; (4) it is constrained to the analysis of general Japanese texts and lacks the capability to analyze academic Japanese texts. To further advance the study of lexical complexity in L2 writing in the realm of Japanese Education, particularly focusing on academic Japanese writing, this paper aims to develop a software based on MeCab, a widely utilized tokenization and part-of-speech tagging system for Japanese. This new software will be capable of analyzing both general and academic Japanese texts, and also support analysis of native Japanese words, Chinese-origin words, and verbs. Concurrently, we will demonstrate its application methods and effectiveness through a concrete study example.

2 Overview of Software Development

2.1 Selection of Measurement Dimensions and Indexes

We extensively reference dimensions and indexes used in previous studies [5, 9–16] and software (RANGE, LCA, LCA-AW, and LRA-JT), as well as Japanese lexical inherent characteristics and limitations of existing software, to enable the software to systematically measure 27 indexes under four dimensions of lexical complexity in both general Japanese texts and academic Japanese texts on Japanese Linguistics Research (i.e., Japanese language research and Japanese education research). The specific calculation methods for the indexes of each dimension are as follows (all methods exclude inherent nouns, number words, English words, and auxiliary marks):

(1) Lexical Density Indexes: 1) Ratio of Tokens of Specific-Meaning Words (R-Tok-SMW). Calculate the ratio of tokens of specific-meaning words to the total number of tokens in the text. The specific-meaning words referred to in this context are

[1] Downloaded from https://www.wgtn.ac.nz/lals/resources/paul-nations-resources/vocabulary-analysis-programs.

[2] Downloaded from https://sites.psu.edu/xxl13/lca/.

[3] Downloaded from https://github.com/Maryam-Nasseri/LCA-AW-Lexical-Complexity-Analyzer-for-Academic-Writing.

exclusively those words whose part of speech is "noun-the ordinary noun-adverb possible", "adjective-the general", "adverb", "verb-the general", "noun-the ordinary noun-sa changing possible", "noun-the ordinary noun-adjectival verb possible", "adjectival verb-the general", "noun-the ordinary noun-the general", "exclamation-the general" or "adjectival verb-tari" in the UniDic dictionary annotation system (for more details, see [13]); 2) Ratio of Tokens of Content Words (R-Tok-CW). Calculate the ratio of tokens of content words (nouns, verbs, adjectives, adjectival verbs, and adverbs) to the total number of tokens in the text; 3) Ratio of Tokens of Independent Words (R-Tok-IW). Calculate the ratio of tokens of independent words (nouns, verbs, adjectives, adjectival verbs, adverbs, pronouns, conjunctions, exclamations, and noun-connecting words) to the total number of tokens in the text.

(2) Lexical Diversity Indexes: 1) Uber. $(\lg tokens)^2$ / $(\lg tokens - \lg types)$; 2) Uber of Native Japanese Words (Uber-NJW):3) Uber of Chinese-Origin Words (Uber-COW):4) Uber of Verbs (Uber-V) (indexes 2–4 are calculated in a similar way to index 1); 5) Standardized Type-Token Ratio (STTR). Calculate the mean of type-token ratios for every 300 words; 6) STTR of Native Japanese Words (STTR-NJW). Calculate the mean of type-token ratios for every 100 native Japanese words; 7) STTR of Chinese-Origin Words (STTR-COW). Calculate the mean of type-token ratios for every 100 Chinese-origin words; 8) STTR of Verbs (STTR-V). Calculate the mean of type-token ratios for every 50 verbs.

(3) Lexical Sophistication Indexes: 1) Ratio of Types of Low-Frequency Words (R-Typ-LFW). For daily written Japanese, calculate the ratio of types of low-frequency words (not in the top 5,000 from the short-unit words list of the Balanced Corpus of Contemporary Written Japanese (BCCWJ)[4]) to the total word types in the text. For daily spoken Japanese, calculate the ratio of types of low-frequency words (not in the top 5,000 from the short-unit words list of the Corpus of Spontaneous Japanese (CSJ)[5]) to the total word types in the text. In academic Japanese writing on Japanese language research, calculate the ratio of types of low-frequency words (neither in the BCCWJ's top 5,000 nor in the top 1,000 words from the short-unit words list of the self-built Corpus of Native Speakers' Japanese Journal Articles on Japanese Language Research[6]) to the total word types in the text. In academic Japanese writing on Japanese education research, calculate the ratio of types of low-frequency words (neither in the BCCWJ's top 5,000 nor in the top 1,000 words from the short-unit words list of the self-built Corpus of Native Speakers' Japanese Journal Articles on Japanese Education Research[7]) to the total word types in the text; 2) Ratio of Types of Low-Frequency Native Japanese Words (R-Typ-LFNJW); 3) Ratio of Types of Low-Frequency Chinese-Origin Words (R-Typ-LFCOW); 4) Ratio of Types of Low-Frequency Verbs (R-Typ-LFV); 5) Ratio of Tokens of Low-Frequency Words (R-Tok-LFW); 6) Ratio of Tokens of Low-Frequency Native Japanese Words (R-Tok-LFNJW); 7) Ratio of Tokens of Low-Frequency Chinese-Origin Words (R-Tok-LFCOW); 8) Ratio of Tokens of Low-Frequency Verbs (R-Tok-LFV) (indexes 2–8

[4] Downloaded from https://clrd.ninjal.ac.jp/bccwj/bcc-chu.html.

[5] Downloaded from https://clrd.ninjal.ac.jp/csj/chunagon.html#data.

[6] The corpus contains 200 Japanese journal articles.

[7] The corpus contains 200 Japanese journal articles.

are calculated in a similar way to index 1). Among these indexes, indexes 1–4 are type-based, while indexes 5–8 are token-based.

(4) Lexical Compositionality Indexes: 1)Average Form Length (AFL).Calculate the average number of characters for all word lemmas; 2)Average Form Length of Native Japanese Words (AFL-NJW); 3)Average Form Length of Chinese-Origin Words (AFL-COW); 4)Average Form Length of Verbs (AFL-V) (indexes 2–4 are calculated in a similar way to index 1); 5) Average Pronunciation Length (APL). Calculate the average number of kanas for all word pronunciations; 6) Average Pronunciation Length of Native Japanese Words (APL-NJW); 7) Average Pronunciation Length of Chinese-Origin Words (APL-COW); 8) Average Pronunciation Length of Verbs (APL-V) (indexes 6–8 are calculated in a similar way to index 5).

Among the above dimensions, lexical density and lexical diversity represent horizontal aspects, focusing on the breadth (i.e., quantity) of vocabulary known to learners. These indexes respectively gauge the informational content and richness of the text's word usage. Conversely, lexical sophistication and lexical compositionality are vertical aspects, emphasizing the depth (i.e., quality) of vocabulary mastery. Their corresponding indexes assess the difficulty of the vocabulary employed in the text and the intricacy of its formal structure.

2.2 MeCab-Based Software Programming as Well as Reliability and Validity Analysis

One of the most fundamental and critical tasks in calculating Japanese lexical complexity indexes is to process the text with precise tokenization and part-of-speech tagging. In this paper, we utilize MeCab 0.996[8], a widely adopted tokenization and part-of-speech tagging system for Japanese. The tokenization accuracy of MeCab ranges from 0.9730 to 0.9765 for native speakers' corpora [17], and as high as 0.9884 for learner's corpora [18]. During tokenization and part-of-speech tagging, to calculate indexes in subordinate lexical levels such as native Japanese words and Chinese-origin words, it is necessary to tag the type of each word (e.g., Native Japanese Word, Chinese-Origin Word, etc.) simultaneously. To achieve this, we have integrated the Modern Written Dictionary and Modern Spoken Dictionary in the Unidic dictionaries, developed by the National Institute for Japanese Language and Linguistics, which can automatically tag the type of each word and unify all different writing forms and word variations into their lemma forms[9]. For instance, the lemmas of "大きい(*oo kii*)" (big), "おおきい(*oo kii*)" (big), and "おっきい(*okkii*)" (big) are all "大きい(*oo kii*)" (big). This unification facilitates accurate counting of types in the text.

Subsequently, We employed Python 3.10.11 to programmatically invoke MeCab (equipped with the Unidic dictionaries) and develop a function to automatically calculate lexical complexity indexes for both general Japanese texts (including daily written and spoken forms) and academic Japanese texts on Japanese Linguistics Research (papers on Japanese language research and Japanese education research). Additionally,

[8] Downloaded from http://taku910.github.io/mecab/#download.

[9] For more information, see the official website: https://clrd.ninjal.ac.jp/unidic/.

we constructed a user-friendly graphical interface leveraging the third-party package PySimpleGUI 4.60.3. The developed software has been christened Lexical Complexity Analyzer for Japanese Texts in Multiple Registers (LCA-JT-MR), aptly capturing its primary functionalities, and made publicly available for free on the webpage: https://mp.weixin.qq.com/s/PKID_GDS5dkwiS7bg4j6KA. Regarding the operating instructions for this software, within the main interface, users are prompted to choose from among four distinct text types, each directing them to a specialized sub-interface for lexical complexity analysis. Subsequently, users must specify the directory containing the plain text documents for analysis, select the desired analytical indexes, and designate the storage location for the resulting data. Upon activating the "开始分析(*kai shi fen xi*)" (start analysis) button, the software swiftly executes all analyses, and the outcome is written into an Excel spreadsheet, labeled LCAresults.xlsx which is automatically saved at the designated storage location.

Regarding the reliability and validity of the software, its calculation of indexes is fully automated according to a well-defined method and fixed steps. This automation ensures that the results for the same text are consistent across different times and occasions, indicating high re-testing reliability. On the other hand, we employ MeCab (equipped with the Unidic dictionaries) for tokenization, part-of-speech tagging, and type tagging due to its high accuracy. Moreover, the indexes used are all reliable and valid, selected based on previous research and software. This significantly ensures the content validity of the software.

3 Application in Japanese L2 Writing Research

The software LCA-JT-MR, capable of automatically calculating lexical complexity in both general Japanese texts and academic Japanese texts pertaining to Japanese Linguistics Research, is primarily applicable to three research areas: (1) studies on the lexical complexity of learners' Japanese L2 compositions. This includes analyzing the development of lexical complexity in learners' Japanese compositions, identifying factors influencing this complexity, and assessing the impact of writing instruction on it; (2) investigations into the lexical complexity of learners' daily spoken Japanese. This involves exploring the state of development of lexical complexity in learners' daily spoken Japanese, determining influencing factors, and evaluating the impact of speaking instruction; (3) analyses related to the lexical complexity of learners' Japanese academic papers on Japanese Linguistics Research. This encompasses studying the state of development of lexical complexity in learners' bachelor's theses, master's theses, doctoral dissertations and journal articles on Japanese language research and Japanese education research, identifying factors that affect this complexity, and assessing the influence of academic Japanese writing instruction. To illustrate the specific application methods and efficacy of LCA-JT-MR in related research, this section present a study example on the lexical complexity in Chinese learners' academic Japanese writing.

3.1 Background and Purpose of the Study

The research on L2 lexical complexity originated in the 1980s [19, 20]. Subsequently, extensive research has been conducted on general English as a second language.

Presently, the research is broadening from general English to academic English [21–27] as well as other languages such as Japanese [10, 14–16, 28, 29]. Nevertheless, there is a notable scarcity of studies examining lexical complexity in academic Japanese writing. On the other hand, given the multitude of Chinese learners tasked with producing high-caliber master's and doctoral dissertations in Japanese at universities in China and Japan, exploring the lexical complexity traits of academic Japanese writing is crucial for enhancing their dissertation quality. Consequently, this study investigates the lexical complexity of Chinese learners' Japanese doctoral dissertations on Japanese language research, aiming to further L2 acquisition theory and methodology, offer tangible references and foundations for teaching academic Japanese writing, improve learners' academic Japanese vocabulary skills, and develop academic Japanese writing textbooks.

3.2 Research Design

The research questions are based on the current state of research and are as follows:

(1) How does lexical density in Chinese learners' dissertations differ from that of native speakers' articles?
(2) How does lexical diversity in Chinese learners' dissertations differ from that of native speakers' articles?
(3) How does lexical sophistication in Chinese learners' dissertations differ from that of native speakers' articles?
(4) How does lexical compositionality in Chinese learners' dissertations differ from that of native speakers' articles?

We have independently constructed a medium-sized academic Japanese thematic corpus called Academic Japanese Corpus on Japanese Linguistics based on our research needs. The corpus contains a total of 550 Japanese texts, with a capacity (i.e., total word count) of 7,562,315 words. In this study, we utilize two sub-corpora: the Sub-corpus of Chinese Learners' Japanese Doctoral Dissertations on Japanese Language Research (1,345,185 words. Hereafter referred to as the Sub-corpus of Dissertations) and the Sub-corpus of Native Speakers' Japanese Peer-reviewed Journal Articles on Japanese Language Research (1,406,534 words. Hereafter referred to as the Sub-corpus of Articles). The first is an observational corpus, while the second serves as a reference corpus, offering a comparative framework.

Finally, we used the Lexical Complexity Analyzer for Japanese Language Research Texts module of LCA-JT-MR to efficiently, objectively, and systematically measure the following 19 indexes under four dimensions of lexical complexity: (1) Lexical Density Indexes: R-Tok-SMW, R-Tok-CW, R-Tok-IW; (2) Lexical Diversity Indexes: STTR, STTR-NJW, STTR-COW, STTR-V; (3) Lexical Sophistication Indexes: R-Typ-LFW, R-Typ-LFNJW, R-Typ-LFCOW, R-Typ-LFV, R-Tok-LFW, R-Tok-LFNJW, R-Tok-LFCOW, R-Tok-LFV; (4) Lexical Compositionality Indexes: APL, APL-NJW, APL-COW, APL-V. Regarding the data analysis, we used Python to perform descriptive statistical analysis of the data for the indexes as well as the corresponding independent sample T-tests and Mann-Whitney U tests based on the results of the normal distribution and variance homogeneity test.

3.3 Findings and Discussion

Lexical Density in Chinese Learners' Doctoral Dissertations. The descriptive statistical analysis results for the lexical density indexes of texts in the Sub-corpus of Dissertations and Sub-corpus of Articles are shown in Table 1.

Table 1. The descriptive statistical analysis results for the lexical density indexes.

	R-Tok-SMW		R-Tok-CW		R-Tok-IW	
	M	*SD*	*M*	*SD*	*M*	*SD*
Sub-corpus of Dissertations	0.42	0.03	0.53	0.02	0.55	0.02
Sub-corpus of Articles	0.42	0.03	0.52	0.02	0.55	0.02

Subsequent independent samples T-tests and Mann-Whitney U tests revealed no significant differences between Chinese learners' dissertations and native speakers' articles across all lexical density indexes ($p > 0.05$). This suggests that both groups utilize specific-meaning, content, and independent words with similar intensity, resulting in minimal variation in lexical density. The results bear relevance to prior research by Zhong [10], Zhang [14], and Yang et al. [15], which indicate that lexical density in Chinese learners' compositions is initially high but gradually diminishes as proficiency increases, eventually converging with or mirroring that of native speakers' in the advanced learning stage. The progression of lexical density in learners' academic Japanese writing is probably similar to that observed in undergraduate compositions, characterized by an initial increase followed by a decrease as learners advance from novice academic writing stages, such as the bachelor's thesis, through to doctoral dissertations, eventually approximating the lexical density typical of native speakers' articles.

Lexical Diversity in Chinese Learners' Doctoral Dissertations. The descriptive statistical analysis results for the lexical diversity indexes of texts in the Sub-corpus of Dissertations and Sub-corpus of Articles are presented in Table 2.

Table 2. The descriptive statistical analysis results for the lexical diversity indexes.

	STTR		STTR-NJW		STTR-COW		STTR-V	
	M	*SD*	*M*	*SD*	*M*	*SD*	*M*	*SD*
Sub-corpus of Dissertations	0.37	0.02	0.41	0.01	0.49	0.04	0.43	0.03
Sub-corpus of Articles	0.38	0.03	0.41	0.02	0.52	0.06	0.42	0.04

Subsequent independent samples T-tests and Mann-Whitney U tests revealed no significant differences between Chinese learners' dissertations and native speakers' articles in three indexes: STTR, STTR-NJW, and STTR-V ($p > 0.05$). However, a significant difference was observed in the STTR-COW ($p < 0.05$). This suggests that the lexical diversity of learners' dissertations is generally comparable to that of native speakers' articles, but remains lower in terms of the diversity of Chinese-origin words. These findings align with Yang et al. [15] and Zhong [10], which found that the lexical diversity in Chinese learners' compositions first rises and then decreases from the beginner to the advanced stage, and finally stays at a position very close to that of native speakers' compositions. That is, the learners' awareness of lexical diversity, which they had taken great care to develop and adapt from the beginner's level, was maintained up to the dissertation writing stage. However, why did the learners' dissertations still have the problem of insufficient lexical diversity in Chinese-origin words? This may be due to the influence of negative native language transfer. In light of the high linguistic quality expected in dissertations, learners start to employ Chinese-origin words that bear both similarities and differences to their native language with excessive caution, i.e., they dare not actively and boldly use different types of Chinese-origin words that they are not sure of. In fact, negative native language transfer does cause learners to misuse Chinese-origin words at various levels such as pronunciation, morphology, part of speech, lexical meaning and collocation [30]. Consequently, teachers should motivate Chinese learners to counteract the adverse influence of native language transfer and assist them in utilizing a broader range of Chinese-origin words, which should be their assets, during the instruction of academic Japanese writing.

Lexical Sophistication in Chinese Learners' Doctoral Dissertations. The descriptive statistical analysis results for the two types of lexical sophistication indexes of texts in the Sub-corpus of Dissertations and Sub-corpus of Articles are shown in Tables 3 and 4, respectively.

Table 3. The descriptive statistical analysis results for the type-based sophistication indexes.

	R-Typ-LFW		R-Typ-LFNJW		R-Typ-LFCOW		R-Typ-LFV	
	M	*SD*	*M*	*SD*	*M*	*SD*	*M*	*SD*
Sub-corpus of Dissertations	0.27	0.04	0.22	0.06	0.30	0.04	0.23	0.07
Sub-corpus of Articles	0.18	0.04	0.12	0.04	0.21	0.05	0.13	0.05

Subsequent Mann-Whitney U tests revealed significant differences between Chinese learners' dissertations and native speakers' articles in all type-based sophistication indexes ($p < 0.05$), but not in all token-based sophistication indexes ($p > 0.05$). This indicates that learners' dissertations employ a greater variety of low-frequency words than those of native speakers' articles, yet the frequency of these words is essentially equivalent in both. In other words, learners' pronounced preference for utilizing a diverse range of low-frequency words in their dissertations results in exceptionally high lexical sophistication, whereas native speakers tend to reuse a limited variety of low-frequency words to maintain reasonable lexical sophistication. Related research on Japanese L2 composition by Zhong [10], Zhang [14], and Yang et al. [15] indicates that the use of

Table 4. The descriptive statistical analysis results for the token-based sophistication indexes.

	R-Tok-LFW		R-Tok-LFNJW		R-Tok-LFCOW		R-Tok-LFV	
	M	*SD*	*M*	*SD*	*M*	*SD*	*M*	*SD*
Sub-corpus of Dissertations	0.05	0.01	0.02	0.01	0.11	0.02	0.03	0.01
Sub-corpus of Articles	0.05	0.02	0.02	0.01	0.11	0.05	0.03	0.02

low-frequency words increases from beginner to advanced stages, reaching parity with native speakers at the advanced level. Notably, learners continue to employ a diverse range of low-frequency words beyond the advanced stage, leading to an elevated proportion of such words in their master's and doctoral dissertations. Upon observation, we found that most of the low-frequency words used in learners' doctoral dissertations were words containing Chinese characters. For instance, the low-frequency words "歌い上げる(*uta i a geru*)" (sing up), "呼び上げる(*yo bi a geru*)" (call up), "数え上げる(*kazo e a geru*)" (count up), "働きかけ(*hatara kikake*)" (work), and "喪失(*sousitu*)" (lose) used in the sentence "したがって、複合動詞「歌い上げる・呼び上げる・数え上げる」が対象に働きかけをしておらず、「-上げる」自体に含まれている対象への働きかけを喪失したと言えよう。(*sitagatte, hukugoudousi "uta i a geru, yo bi a geru, kazo e a geru" ga taisyou ni hatara kikake wo si te ora zu, "- a geru" zitai ni huku ma re te iru taisyou he no hatara kikake wo sousitu si ta to i eyo u.*)" (Thus, we can say that the compound verb "uta i a geru, yo bi a geru, kazo e a geru" does not work on the object, and that it loses the work on the object contained in "- a geru" itself.). The learners' preference for low-frequency words containing Chinese characters reflects the strong influence of native language transfer. Teachers need to remind learners not to use low-frequency words too diversely in their future teaching, so as not to cause excessive lexical sophistication.

Lexical Compositionality in Chinese Learners' Doctoral Dissertations. The descriptive statistical analysis results for the lexical compositionality indexes of texts in the Sub-corpus of Dissertations and Sub-corpus of Articles are presented in Table 5.

Table 5. The descriptive statistical analysis results for the lexical compositionality indexes.

	APL		APL-NJW		APL-COW		APL-V	
	M	*SD*	*M*	*SD*	*M*	*SD*	*M*	*SD*
Sub-corpus of Dissertations	2.21	0.07	1.66	0.04	3.23	0.15	2.59	0.06
Sub-corpus of Articles	2.19	0.08	1.65	0.05	3.20	0.14	2.57	0.09

Subsequent independent samples T-tests and Mann-Whitney U tests revealed no significant differences between Chinese learners' dissertations and native speakers' articles across all lexical compositionality indexes ($p > 0.05$). This indicates that the lexical compositionality of the former has been approximately the same as that of the latter. In other words, even when faced with words that are complex to pronounce, the learners were able to overcome their difficulties and actively memorize and use them. This may be due to the simplicity of Japanese phonology. Compared to most other languages such as Chinese and English, Japanese phonology is less varied and the combinations are very simple [31]. Therefore, for most learners, Japanese vocabulary is relatively easy to pronounce, and they possess enough confidence and motivation to acquire and use words with complex pronunciations.

Summary. In the above, we conducted statistical analyses on 19 indexes across four lexical complexity dimensions in Chinese learners' Japanese doctoral dissertations and native speakers' Japanese journal articles, yielding the following primary conclusions: (1) there is not significant difference between Chinese learner's dissertations and native speaker's articles in terms of lexical density and lexical compositionality; (2) the lexical diversity of Chinese learners' dissertations is generally comparable to that of native speakers' articles, but remains lower in terms of the diversity of Chinese-origin words; (3) the lexical sophistication of Chinese learners' dissertations is much higher than that of native speakers' articles. These findings suggest that teachers need to guide learners in understanding the complex effects of native language transfer and awareness of lexical diversity in future academic Japanese writing instruction, aiming to prevent students from overusing or underusing certain words in academic writing. From this study, it is evident that the employment of LCA-JT-MR significantly broadens the scope of Japanese L2 lexical complexity research and substantially enhances the efficiency and objectivity of data processing.

4 Conclusion

Since the advent of automated tools for calculating lexical complexity in English texts, research on lexical complexity in L2 writing within English Education has progressed rapidly. Conversely, studies on lexical complexity in Japanese L2 writing, particularly in academic Japanese contexts, have been less advanced due to factors such as the absence of specialized software for Japanese text analysis. To address this gap, this paper developed a reliable and valid lexical complexity analyzer for both general and academic Japanese texts based on MeCab, and utilized it in a study example. The study shows that this software broadens the scope of L2 lexical complexity research and enhances the efficiency and objectivity of data processing. Moreover, the employment of the standardized software in future studies could improve the comparability between different investigations. We anticipate that this software will serve as a valuable auxiliary resource, enabling the researchers within Japanese Education to achieve new breakthroughs in the study of lexical complexity in Japanese L2 writing.

Acknowledgment. This work was supported in part by the Humanities and Social Sciences Research Fund of the Ministry of Education under Grant 23YJC740095. Y. Zhong and X. Yang appreciates the constructive feedback from the anonymous reviewers, which greatly improved the quality of this manuscript.

References

1. Ellis, R., Barkhuizen, G.: Analysing Learner Language. Oxford University Press, Oxford (2005)
2. Housen, Kuiken, F.: Complexity, accuracy and fluency in second language acquisition. Appl. Linguistics **4**, 461–473 (2009)
3. Wolfe-Quintero, K., Inagaki, S., Kim, H.Y.: Second Language Development in Writing: Measure of Fluency, Accuracy, and Complexity. University of Hawaii Press, Honolulu (1998)
4. Read, J.: Assessing Vocabulary. Cambridge University Press, Cambridge (2000)
5. Bulté, B., Housen, A.: Defining and operationalizing L2 complexity. In: Housen, A., Kuiken, F., Vedder, I. (eds.), Dimensions of L2 Performance and Proficiency: Complexity Accuracy and Fluency in SLA. Amsterdam: John Benjamins (2012)
6. Wan, L.: A study of lexical richness in second language writing of Chinese English majors. Foreign Language World **1**, 40–46 (2010)
7. Zhu, H., Wang, J.: Developmental features of lexical richness in English writing: a longitudinal study based on a self-constructed corpus. Foreign Lang. World **6**, 77–86 (2013)
8. Zhu, H., Liu, Y.: A case study on the dynamic development of lexical complexity in second language writing. Shandong Foreign Lang. Teach. **42**(5), 54–64 (2021)
9. Lu, X.: The relationship of lexical richness to the quality of ESL learners' oral narratives. Mod. Lang. J. **96**(2), 190–208 (2012)
10. Zhong, Y.: Development of Lexical Richness Analyzer for Japanese Texts and its application to second language writing research. Jpn/Japan Stud. **2**(1), 19–28 (2023)
11. Ure, J.: Lexical density and register differentiation. In: Perren, G., Trim, J. (eds.) Applications of linguistics: Selected papers of the second international congress of applied linguistics, pp. 443–452. Cambridge University Press, Cambridge (1971)
12. Laufer, B., Nation, P.: Vocabulary Size and Use: Lexical richness in L2 Written Production. Appl. Linguis. **16**(3), 307–322 (1995)
13. Sano, D., Maruyama, T., Yamazaki, M., et al.: A trial of text classification on the Balanced Corpus of Contemporary Written Japanese by utilizing lexical density. Internal Report of the National Institute for Japanese Language and Linguistics, pp. 1–61 (2009)
14. Zhang, J.: A study on the development of output vocabulary breadth knowledge of Japanese language majors. Contemp. Foreign Lang. Stud. **3**, 31–35 (2015)
15. Yang, X., Zhong, Y., Zhao, Y.: An empirical study on Chinese learners' Japanese lexical richness development. Second Lang. Learn. Res. **2**, 59–72+133–134 (2021)
16. Chen, Y., You, X.: Characterizing the dynamic development of Japanese learners' lexical complexity. J. Jpn. Lang. Study Res. **4**, 72–83 (2023)
17. Kudo, T., Yamamoto, K., Matsumoto, Y.: Morphological analysis of Japanese using conditional random fields. IPSJ Res. Rep. Nat. Lang. Process. **47**, 89–96 (2004)
18. Mao, W.: A study on the reliability of Japanese automatic part-of-speech tagger. Technol. Enhanced Foreign Lang. Educ. **3**, 10–14 (2012)
19. Linnarud, M.: Lexical in composition: a performance analysis of Swedish L2 learners' written English. Malmo, LiberForlagMalmo (1986)
20. Hyltenstam, K.: Lexical characteristics of near-native second-language learners of Swedish. J. Multiling. Multicult. Dev. **1**, 67–84 (1988)
21. Gonzalez, M.: The intricate relationship between measures of vocabulary size and lexical diversity as evidenced in non-native and native speaker academic compositions (Doctoral Dissertation). College of Education and Human Performance: University of Central Florida (2013)
22. Pietilä, P.: Lexical diversity in L2 academic writing: a look at M.A. thesis conclusions. In: Pietilä, P., Doró, K., Pípalová, R. (eds.), Lexical issues in L2 writing. Newcastle upon Tyne: Cambridge Scholars Publishing, pp. 105–125 (2015)

23. Bae, J., Min, S.: Genre-based analysis of lexical complexity in L2 college students' academic writing. J. Lang. Sci. **25**(1), 289–314 (2018)
24. Ha, H.S.: Lexical richness in EFL undergraduate students' academic writing. English Teach. **74**(3), 3–28 (2019)
25. Nasseri, M., Thompson, P.: Lexical density and diversity in dissertation abstracts: revisiting English L1 vs. L2 text differences. Assessing Writing **47**, 100511 (2021)
26. Maamuujav, U., Olson, C.B., Chung, H.: Syntactic and lexical features of adolescent L2 students' academic writing. J. Second. Lang. Writ. **53**, 100822 (2021)
27. Martínez, A.C.L.: The role of syntactic and lexical complexity in undergraduate writing quality. Revista Ibérica **47**, 251–274 (2024)
28. Mao, W.: A study on Chinese Japanese learners' composition vocabulary and high-frequency words. Technol. Enhanced Foreign Lang. Educ. **4**, 9–15 (2013)
29. Mao, W.: A study on the application of data mining techniques in the characterization of learners' compositions. J. Jpn. Lang. Study Res. **2**, 72–81 (2022)
30. Zhang, H.: Analysis of negative Chinese language transfer in second language acquisition: Taking the example of Chinese-origin words in Japanese. J. Lang. Lit. Stud. (Foreign Lang. Educ. Teach.) **7**, 32–36 (2016)
31. Takamizawa, M., Hunter, Y., Ikeda, Y., et al.: The basics of Japanese language teaching. Beijing, Foreign Language Teaching and Research Press (2009)

A Study of Low-Resource Kazakh Named Entity Recognition

Aierzhati Hayinaer, Ziyang Ye, and Lin Xu(✉)

School of Computer and Mathematical Sciences, The University of Adelaide, Adelaide, SA 5000, Australia
aierzhati.hayinaer@student.adelaide.edu.au,
{ziyang.ye,lin.xu}@adelaide.edu.au

Abstract. Named-Entity Recognition (NER) identifies specific entities within a text, such as names of people, places, organizations, and institutions. While the technology can identify unique names, it faces challenges in domain-specific applications, and accurately targeting low-resource languages is even more challenging. The Kazakh language is an agglutinative and morphologically rich low-resource language. This study addresses the issue of data sparsity resulting from the language's multi-dimensional features and the challenges posed by the unclear boundaries and ambiguity in the tourism domain. In this paper, we propose a low-resource Kazakh NER model based on small samples that benefits from word and stem-level embedding and dependencies across adjacent labels. This model uses words and stems as linguistic features for word embedding, enhances semantic features, and trains word vectors with the Skip-gram model. Our model includes Convolutional Neural Networks (CNN) and Bidirectional Long Short-Term Memory (Bi-LSTM) with a Conditional Random Field (CRF). It explores the integration of Kazakh linguistic features with deep learning and attention mechanisms, validating the proposed model for two script datasets on Arabic and Cyrillic letters of Kazakh with promising results.

Keywords: Low Resources · Named Entity Recognition · Kazakh Language · Deep Learning · Natural Language Processing

1 Introduction

Named Entity Recognition (NER) represents a fundamental task within the Natural Language Processing (NLP) domain, specifically regarding identifying proper names or specific entities within textual data. The objective of NER is to facilitate the extraction of information by identifying and categorizing specific entities, such as names of people, places, organizations, dates, and times and also proper names. Its applications include information retrieval, relational extraction, and question and answer systems.

NER technology is now relatively mature, and NER can recognize entities such as proper names. However, there are instances where entities specific to a

X. Ding and Y. Dong (Eds.): CLNLP 2025, CCIS 2775, pp. 13–27, 2026.
https://doi.org/10.1007/978-981-95-4788-3_2

particular domain are challenging to recognize, and accurately recognizing entities in low-resource languages is even more difficult. Kazakh is a representative example of a low-resource language. It belongs to the Altaic language family, which is characterized by complex morphology and the use of different character scripts in the world. Furthermore, lot of researchers do research in the field of Kazakh NLP, but there are notable areas for improvement in the available research on named entity recognition in Kazakh, particularly in comparison to the extensive body of work on this topic in other languages, such as English and Chinese, which are rich in resources.

This paper presents a study of named entity recognition in the Kazakh language. The choice of this language is motivated by the fact that it exhibits adhesive features and is a Morphologically Complex Language (MCL). The latter attribute will likely give rise to data sparsity issues, which may affect the training performance of the neural network model constructed for this purpose. Secondly, when this NER study is applied to the Kazakh language in the field of tourism, it is found that the Kazakh entity names of tourist attractions exhibit several complex problems, including fuzzy boundaries, nesting of entities within each other, ambiguity, etc.

Accordingly, this study employs Kazakh words and stems as distinctive linguistic attributes for word embedding while incorporating entity labels into the neural network through a multi-attention mechanism. This approach yields a compact-sample-based low-resource Kazakh NER model, which utilizes the Skip-gram model tool of the word2vec model to train word vectors to predict the context of a known current word. This Kazakh NER model includes Convolutional Neural Networks (CNN) and Bidirectional Long Short-Term Memory (Bi-LSTM) with a Conditional Random Field (CRF). This study presents a novel approach to combining Kazakh linguistic features with neural network modeling, utilizing a deep learning technique. The proposed method is evaluated on two datasets, one based on the Arabic alphabet and the other on the Cyrillic alphabet of Kazakh. The study also demonstrates the potential of this approach in the context of Kazakh NER in Chinese tourism, which presents unique challenges compared to other languages. The findings suggest that this research can be extended to other agglutinative languages with similar characteristics.

This paper is organized as follows: Sect. 2 reviews related work, Sect. 3 presents the research problem, Sect. 4 details the model architecture, Sect. 5 discusses the experimental results, and Sect. 6 concludes with future work.

2 Related Work

Since the term "Named Entity Recognition-NER" was first introduced at the "6th Conference on Natural Language Learning" [1], research in this field has progressed rapidly. NER is a method for recognizing key information and involves processing large amounts of unstructured text. The initial approaches to NER were based on traditional lexical and rule-based methods. These relied on features drawn from a range of language corpora and necessitated the involvement of linguists with expertise in the language in question, who were responsible for annotating the linguistic rules. The advent of deep learning has prompted a shift in research on NER methods, moving away from traditional techniques towards applying deep learning and various neural network models. Bidirectional Long Short-Term Memory (Bi-LSTM) [2] initially became the preferred tool in NER due to its exceptional capacity to acquire contextual semantic information. Subsequently, Huang et al. [3] proposed the technique of Bi-LSTM-CRF, which introduced Conditional Random Fields (CRF) to the network architecture of Bi-LSTM. This addressed the limitation of the Bi-LSTM network's inability to proofread label sequences, leading to enhanced entity recognition and classification outcomes. Subsequently, the researchers incorporated a convolutional neural network (CNN) into the Bi-LSTM+CNN+CRF [4] model, thereby facilitating a more precise capture of the deep textual characteristics associated with different types.

As neural network technology has continued to evolve, Bengio et al. [5] have employed a neural network model to derive a low-dimensional dense vector representation of words. In 2013, Mikolov et al. [6] introduced the word2vec model, which maps the sparse word vectors in one-hot encoding to a low-dimensional dense vector, thereby reducing resource consumption. However, the word2vec model does not effectively utilize global statistical information. Consequently, Pennington et al. [7] proposed the Glove model, based on the word2vec model, and designed to utilize global statistical information more effectively.

The Attention Model (AM) [8], as a technique applied to deep learning, can assist neural networks in effectively capturing vector features, thereby enhancing the performance of the model. The Attention Model facilitates a deeper understanding of the data and enables the more efficient extraction of text vector features. The use of attention mechanisms and pre-trained models has become prevalent in the field of NER. However, there are still limitations to these approaches. Kazakh NER studies employed several different approaches, that included NER based on a maximum entropy model for phrase recognition [9] and NER based on a conditional random field model [10]. Recently, research based on deep learning has also been conducted. Tolegen et al. [11] proposed a deep learning model incorporating the Kazakh language's morphological features and achieved superior results, also proposed including morphological features, specifically the word roots of the Kazakh language, into the neural network models under consideration.

Akhmed-Zaki et al. [12] proposed and validated a BERT+Bi-LSTM+CRF-based approach for recognizing Kazakh entities. For solving multi-classification tasks, based on datasets for named entity recognition in the Kazakh language also using LSTM and BERT models [13]. In their research [14] explored the potential of deep learning models incorporating the morphological features of the Kazakh language. While these literature studies have contributed to the field, there are still some limitations in integrating Kazakh linguistic features with deep learning methods.

Currently, most studies on successful entity recognition are conducted on large resource corpora, such as those in the English and Chinese languages. The studies on NER are contingent upon the size and quality of the data within the corpus. Notable examples of NER data include the CoNLL2002 [1], CoNLL2003 [15], and Wikiann [16] datasets. The earliest CoNLL 2002 dataset is derived from the Spanish Shared Tasks dataset from the Spanish news agency EFE. It contains four types of entities: person names (PER), place names (LOC), organization names (ORG), and others (MISC). The CoNLL 2003 dataset contains 1,393 English and 909 German news articles. The Wikiann dataset is a cross-language dataset for NER and linking, containing approximately 1.5 million named entities in 282 languages. Tolen et al. constructed a dataset of Kazakh entity names [10], and Yeshpanov et al. constructed a practical database of Kazakh entity names, KazNERD [17], the dataset on which our study is based and our model is validated by Cyrillic in this study.

3 Description of the Research Problem

3.1 The Complex Morphological Features of Kazakh

As an agglutinative language, where Kazakh words are formed by combining root or stem forms with prefixes or suffixes, it is possible to generate hundreds or thousands of different word forms by adding these extensions. This phenomenon contributes to the challenge of data sparsity in training models.

The advent of Large Language Models, deep learning techniques, and an array of neural network models, which have the potential to address numerous challenges in natural language processing, like ChatGPT [18]. Nevertheless, this study posits that, particularly in the context of low-resource, small-sample language information processing, the model's performance can be further optimized by exploiting its unique linguistic characteristics. Accordingly, this paper begins examining the Kazakh lexical issue to characterize the language with nouns in the context of NER, and the approach is intended to enhance the semantic features of the model.

Representation of Morphological Features of Words. Kazakh words are composed of a few prefixes, roots or stems, and a large number of suffix components. These constituents are further distinguished as either morphological or inflectional suffixes. Moreover, different lexical formations adhere to specific rules of word formation [19]. The following example illustrates the order rules for inflectional affixes attached by the noun words:

word = (prefix) + stem + plural affixes + personal affixes + case affixes + predicative person. E.g. Kazakh sentences about traveling:

ٴبىز ساباقتاستارىمىزبەن بىرلىكتە جەمەنەي اۋدانىنىڭ قويتاس كورىنىس وڭىرىنە
بارىپ قايتپاقشى بولىپ وتىرمىز

Write and read this Kazakh sentence from right to left, so the sentence means "Together with our classmates, we plan to go for a preview around the Kewoitas Scenic Area in Gimnai County." The simple sentence "We are with our classmates" is translated into Kazakh as a word containing 18 Arabic letters, ساباقتاستارىمىزبەن, and his word formation cuts are shown below (Suffix formation word):

ساباق / تاس / تار / ى / مىز / بەن

It consists of the stem "ساباق". Five suffixes spliced on the back: "ى", "تار", "تاس", "مىز" and "بەن". Word "ساباقتاستارىمىزبەن" Containing five stems, the specific stems and meanings of the word segmentation are shown in Table 1, each of which has its meaning, illustrating the complex morphological features of the Kazakh language and the richness of its vocabulary.

Table 1. Examples of Kazakh Word Segmentation.

Word Slicing	Word Stem	Mean Word Stem
ساباقتاستارىمىزبەن		Together with our classmates
ساباق / تاستارىمىزبەن	ساباق	Class
ساباقتاس / تارىمىزبەن	ساباقتاس	Classmate
ساباقتاستار / ىمىزبەن	ساباقتاستار	Classmates
ساباقتاستارىم / ىزبەن	ساباقتاستارىم	My classmates
ساباقتاستارىمىز / بەن	ساباقتاستارىمىز	Our classmates

Note: "/" is the delimiter.

Ambiguity Characterization. There is a lot of ambiguity in the names of entities in Kazakh texts in the field of tourism with multiple meanings of words and unclear boundaries. E.g. Kazakh sentences:

مەن اق قاباعا ساياحاتپەن كەلدىم

The meaning is "I've come to visit the White Habba".

Where the Kazakh word "اق قابا" (White Habba) The entities express different and nested meanings depending on the entity in which it is located. Phrase "اق قابا" is the name of a scenic area, but where the word "قابا" (Habahe) is a place name, and its appearance in the name of a scenic spot has the ambiguity of a place name. Therefore, for this problem, it is necessary to consider the structural features of entities in the field of tourism, boundary problems, etc. In this paper, we study named entity recognition in the Kazakh language by using words and stems as linguistic features for word embedding. Entity labelling is also introduced into a neural network.

4 Methodology

4.1 Pre-training WordStem Vectors

The word2vec model, proposed by Mikolov et al., includes two important models: CBOW (Continuous Bag-Of-Words Model) and Skip-Gram. The CBOW and Skip-Gram models are important. The CBOW modelling tool calculates the probability of occurrence of a word based on the first N words and the following N words of a word. The Skip-Gram modelling tool predicts the probability of the previous and subsequent words based on a word. The word2vec modelling technique reduces the consumption of resources and improves the speed of training of the model.

In the Skip-Gram model [20], the central word, w_t is used to predict the surrounding words, with the objective function being:

$$\mathcal{L}_\theta = -\frac{1}{T}\sum_{t=1}^{T}\sum_{-n\leq j\leq n, j\neq 0}\log P(w_{t+j}|w_t) \tag{1}$$

where the $\mathcal{L}_\theta$ function predicts the context word vector based on the centre word w_t, if the word vectors of two words are similar, the probability of the same word as their context is similar.

Text sentences in Kazakh language are separated by space symbols between words, and Word Embedding is the process of converting sentences into vectors by mapping words to real numbers.

In this study, the text's stem information is extracted from the original dataset, and the Skip-Gram model of the word2vec modeling tool is used to train the sequences of words and stems of the Kazakh tourism text to get the embedded representations of their corresponding words and stems. The Skip-Gram model does the whole word vector embedding process. The embedded representations of words and stems are combined so that the model effectively avoids the data sparsity problem and improves its semantic performance. Then, the embedded representations of words and stems are transferred to the following network to extract further contextual features.

4.2 Model Architecture

The named entity recognition problem is a sequence labeling problem. The overall architecture of the Kazakh named entity recognition model is shown in Fig. 1, which consists of five main modules: Word Embeddings, augmented semantic feature representation layer (CNN), Bi-LSTM, multi-head attention mechanism, and CRF layer.

In our model, the semantic enhancement representation enhances the expressive ability of the model by obtaining the Kazakh language feature information

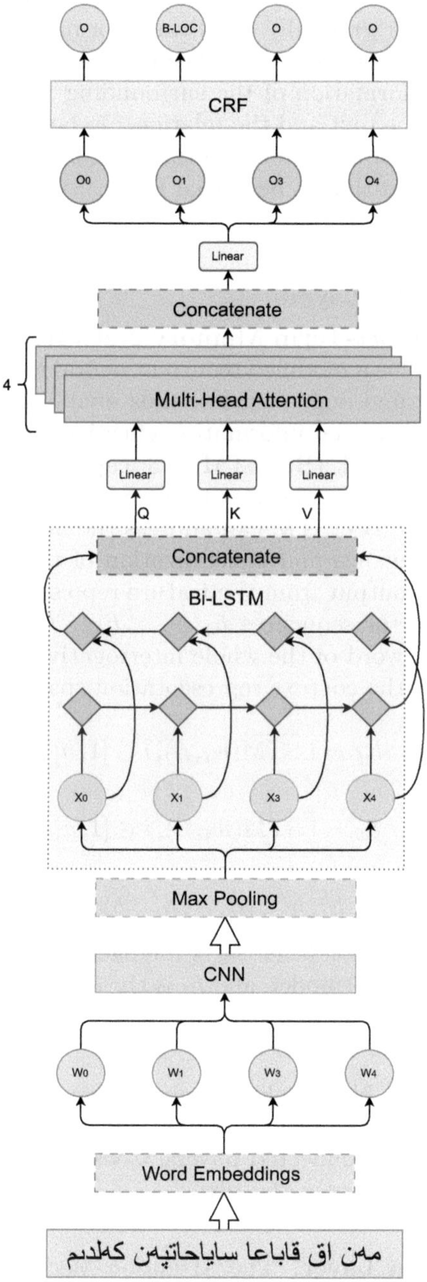

Fig. 1. Kazakh Named-Entities Recognition Model

through word embedded representation, stemmed embedded representation and so on. Then, the above vector representation is passed into the neural network. This neural network layer gradually fuses the information of neighboring nodes through multi-layer iteration so that the vector representation of each node can contain the semantic information of the surrounding nodes, capturing the contextual information in the text and the relationship between the entities; finally, the mechanism of multiple attention is introduced to pay attention to the textual semantic information that is beneficial for entity recognition, and predicts entity labels through the CRF layer.

4.3 Description of the Layers

Bidirectional Long Short-Term Memory Network. The Long Short-Term Memory (LSTM) [21,22] is a modified recurrent neural network that circumvents the necessity for long time dependencies, thus enabling the model to capture and analyze complex sequential information effectively. The Bidirectional Long Short-Term Memory Network (Bi-LSTM) [23] captures contextual information in the sequence by processing the input sequence separately in both forward and backward directions. Bi-LSTM can address the bias issue in LSTM models and enhance the performance and generalization of the model. The word vectors $w_1, w_2 \dots w_i \dots w_n$ output from the feature representation layer are used to generate the hidden vector sequences $h_1, h_2 \dots h_i \dots h_n$ through the Bi-LSTM model, and the context word of the whole interrogative S is encoded as h_i, and finally w_i is mapped to the context representation space:

$$h_f = \overrightarrow{\text{LSTM}}(w_i, \beta), i \in [1, n] \tag{2}$$

$$h_b = \overleftarrow{\text{LSTM}}(w_i, \beta), i \in [1, n] \tag{3}$$

$$h_i = \{h_1^f : h_1^b, h_2^f : h_2^b, \dots h_i^f : h_i^b \dots h_n^f : h_n^b\} \tag{4}$$

where h_f is the forward hidden layer, h_b is the backward hidden layer, β denotes the parameters of the LSTM model, and h_i is the output vector of the Bi-LSTM layer.

Convolutional Neural Networks. Convolutional Neural Networks (CNN) [24] was first proposed by LeCun et al. It consists of Convolutional Layers, Pooling Layers, and Fully Connected Layers. CNNs help to recognize entities in text by learning local features in the text.

Attention Mechanism Layer. The Attention Mechanism Layer uses multi-head attention to the space of different positions of the vector, and the attention mechanism improves the model's ability to recognize keywords. To highlight the importance of key information, we apply the attention mechanism after Bi-LSTM to selectively assign higher weights to key content. After obtaining the output of the previous layer, we train multiple attention on the current word and calculate the similarity of Q(query), K(key), and V(value) to get the weights [25].

The similarity between Query and Key is calculated using the following scaled dot product model as shown in Eq. (5):

$$\text{sim}(Q, K) = \frac{Q^T \cdot K}{\sqrt{d}} \tag{5}$$

where d is a parameter used to regulate the dot product model, its value can be determined according to the dimension of the model word vector to ensure that the final integration result is not too high, thus reducing the time and complexity of the calculation.

The correlation between the two words is then expressed by using the softmax function, calculated as shown in Eq. (6):

$$\text{Attention}(Q, K, V) = \text{softmax}\left(\frac{QK^T}{\sqrt{d_k}}\right)V \tag{6}$$

where d_k is the dimension of matrix K, where note that the scoring function is computed using dot product similarity.

Feature Decoding Layer. The feature vectors generated by the upper layer model exclusively consider the contextual information inherent to the sentence, yet they cannot account for the interdependence between tags. For this issue, we utilize the Conditional Random Field (CRF) [26] model to calculate the probability of tag sequences and identify the optimal ones.

Suppose the output sequence of the previous layer is $H = \{h_1, h_2, ..., h_n\}$, input to the CRF layer for decoding, for a given sentence sequence as $x = \{x_1, x_2, ..., x_n\}$, the random conditional probability predicts the output label sequence as $y = \{y_1, y_2, ..., y_n\}$ the score is calculated as:

$$s(H, Y) = \sum_{i=1}^{N} P_{i,y_i} + \sum_{i=1}^{N} T_{y_{i-1},y_i} \tag{7}$$

where T denotes the label transfer matrix of the CRF. The CRF uses the Viterbi algorithm to compute the optimal predicted label sequences, computed as.

$$Y^* = argmax(S(x, y)) \tag{8}$$

where Y^* is the label with maximum conditional probability.

5 Experiment

5.1 Dataset

The Kazakh language is written in three scripts-Arabic, Cyrillic, and Latin in the whole world. China employs the Arabic letter derived from the Arabic alphabet and comprises 33 letters. Kazakhstan utilizes the Cyrillic letter, which contains 42 letters. This section validates our Kazakh entity recognition model using three distinct sets.

The first dataset-Arabic is based on Haisa and Altenbek [14], plus Kazakh names and place names, which were pre-processed and cleaned to form the basis of our primary pre-trained input data. The second dataset-Cyrillic, KazNERD [17]. The data were annotated using the BIO tagging scheme [27] to identify person, place, and organization names, representing B(Begin), I(Inside) and O(Outside). The third dataset is combine of the first dataset and the Arabic translation of the second dataset. This dataset provides more trainable data for our experiments. All the datasets were divided into training, testing, and validation set. Statistics of specific information of the datasets used in the experiments are shown in Table 2.

Table 2. Statistics for Different Data Sets.

Data Set	Training	Validation	Test
Kazakh (Arabic)	5751	785	785
Kaz NERD (Cyrillic)	8108	793	847
Combine (Arabic)	13859	1578	1632

5.2 Parameter Settings

The experiments were conducted using Python with PyTorch as the deep learning framework on a Windows operating system. The hardware configuration consists of an Intel Core i9-13900HX CPU, an NVIDIA GeForce RTX 4060 GPU with 8 GB video memory, and CUDA 12.6 as the GPU acceleration library. The model training parameters are shown in Table 3.

Table 3. Model Parameter Values.

Model Parameter	Value	Model Parameter	Value
Emb Dimension	100	GGNN Dimension	200
Window Size	6	Learning Rate	0.005
Minimum Frequency	1	Optimizer	Adam
Batch Size	256	Epoch	50

5.3 Experimental Results and Analysis

This experiment evaluates the proposed method from multiple perspectives, and then gives the experimental results and analysis.

Setting of Evaluation Indicators for the Experiment. To evaluate the effectiveness of the NER model for Kazakh language entity recognition, this study adopts Precision (P), Recall (R), and F_1 value (F_1) as the evaluation indexes, and follows is the formula of each evaluation index:

$$Precision = \frac{T_p}{T_p + F_p} \tag{9}$$

$$Recall = \frac{T_p}{T_p + F_n} \tag{10}$$

$$F_1 = \frac{2PR}{P + R} \tag{11}$$

where T_P denotes the number of correctly recognized entities; F_n denotes the number of incorrectly recognized entities out of the recognized entities; F_P denotes the number of non-entities.

Baseline Model. In order to verify the validity of this model, the following baseline was chosen: For CRF [10]: very early researchers conducted CRF-based Kazakh classification studies, and this experiment uses a CRF model with only word features. For Bi-LSTM+CRF [11]: this model is a combination of CRF and deep learning model Bi-LSTM for Kazakh entity recognition.

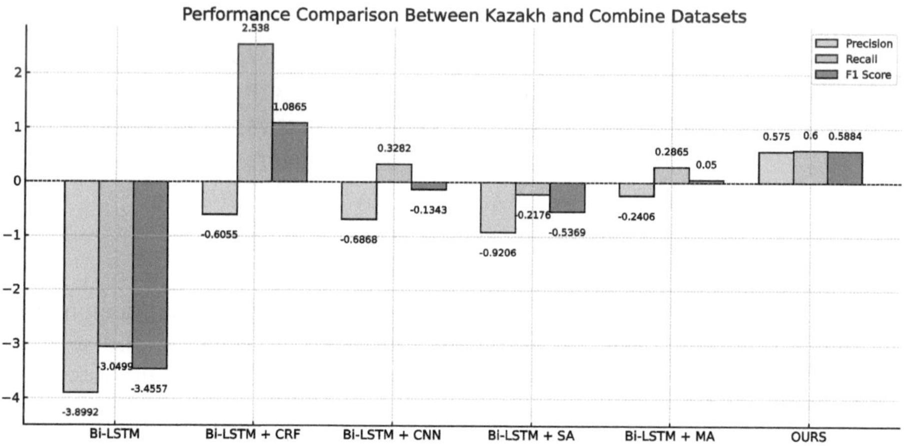

Fig. 2. Performance Comparison Between Kazakh and Combine Datasets

Results and Analysis. From Fig. 2, it can be observed that Bi-LSTM performs well on the Kazakh dataset due to its simple structure, which allows it to extract basic features effectively in low-resource scenarios.

However, as the dataset expands to the Combine dataset, the increased data complexity exposes the limitations of Bi-LSTM's modeling capabilities, leading to a significant decline in performance. Similar trends can be seen in other models as well.

Table 4. Performance Comparison of Models on Different Script Datasets.

Dataset	Model	P (%)	R (%)	F1 (%)
Kazakh	Bi-LSTM	81.4889	77.2409	79.3080
	Bi-LSTM+CRF	79.9719	72.6001	76.1079
	Bi-LSTM+CNN	81.1756	73.7444	77.2818
	Bi-LSTM+SA	82.9353	75.0794	78.8121
	Bi-LSTM+MA	82.3321	74.0623	77.9785
	OURS	78.8209	75.1300	76.9312
Kaz NERD	Bi-LSTM	77.7899	73.9854	75.8400
	Bi-LSTM+CRF	79.0055	74.4016	76.6345
	Bi-LSTM+CNN	80.8249	75.4422	78.0409
	Bi-LSTM+SA	81.9318	75.0260	78.3269
	Bi-LSTM+MA	83.2563	75.0260	78.9272
	OURS	81.3725	77.7315	79.5103
Combine	Bi-LSTM	77.5897	74.1910	75.8523
	Bi-LSTM+CRF	79.3664	75.1381	77.1944
	Bi-LSTM+CNN	80.4888	74.0726	77.1475
	Bi-LSTM+SA	82.0147	74.8618	78.2752
	Bi-LSTM+MA	82.0915	74.3488	78.0285
	OURS	79.3959	75.7300	77.5196

Note: SA refers to SelfAttention MA to MultiAttention

In contrast, our work, which integrates multiple components, demonstrates the ability to extract features stably in low-resource scenarios and adapt to complex samples through enhanced contextual modeling and feature interaction capabilities as the data increases. Its consistent performance improvement highlights the advantages of the OURS model in handling diverse and large-scale datasets, showcasing stronger generalization ability and robustness. As showing in Table 4, the OURS model achieves the highest Recall among all experiments, highlighting distinct advantages of OURS model.

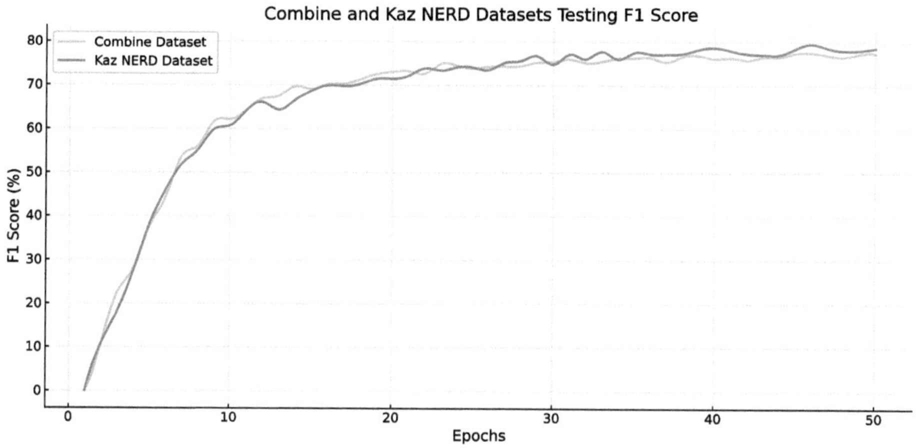

Fig. 3. Combine and Kaz NERD Datasets Testing F1 Score

Comparison Experiment. Figure 3 illustrates that the F1 scores for both the Combine and KazNERD datasets start relatively low during the early stages of training but eventually reach high values by the end of the training phase. The higher F1 score achieved on the KazNERD dataset with a smaller amount of data can likely be attributed to the Cyrillic Kazakh entity names, which often begin with uppercase letters, facilitating the identification of such entities. In contrast, the Arabic Kazakh script lacks case distinctions, and entity name words do not begin with uppercase letters, posing a greater challenge for entity name recognition. This explains the lower training F1 scores observed for the Combine dataset, which uses the Arabic script.

6 Conclusion

This study investigates named entity recognition for the low-resource and small-sample Kazakh language. It employs stemming and word embedding techniques to enhance semantic features. Additionally, entity labels, including names of people, places, and organizations, are introduced into the neural network. This network utilizes a combination of CNN and Bi-LSTM further to improve the performance of the NER model. Subsequently, the neural network technique and the attention mechanism are employed again with the multi-attention mechanism. Finally, entity labels are predicted through the CRF layer, constructing a NER model suitable for low-resource languages. This model is then validated on different datasets, yielding favorable results.

References

1. Sang, E.T.K., De Meulder, F.: Introduction to the CoNLL-2002 shared task: language independent named entity recognition. In: Proceedings 6th Conference Natural Language Learning - Vol. 20 (COLING,: Stroudsburg, PA, USA: Association for. Comput. Linguist, vol. 2002, pp. 1–4 (2002)
2. Yin, J., Luo, S., Wu, Z., Pan, L.: Chinese named entity recognition with character-level BiLSTM and soft attention model. J. Beijing Inst. Technol. **29**(1), 60–71 (2020). https://doi.org/10.15918/j.jbit1004-0579.18161
3. Huang, Z., Xu, W., Yu, K.: Bidirectional LSTM-CRF models for sequence tagging. arXiv preprint arXiv:1508.01991 (2015). https://doi.org/10.48550/arXiv.1508.01991
4. Ma, X., Hovy, E.: End-to-end sequence labeling via bi-directional LSTM-CNNs-CRF. In: Proceedings of the 54th Annual Meeting Association Computing Linguistics (Volume 1: Long Papers), pp. 1064–1074 (2016). https://doi.org/10.18653/v1/P16-1101
5. Bengio, Y., Ducharme, R., Vincent, P.: A neural probabilistic language model. Adv. Neural. Inf. Process. Syst. **13**, 1137–1155 (2000)
6. Mikolov, T., Chen, K., Corrado, G., Dean, J.: Efficient estimation of word representations in vector space. arXiv preprint arXiv:1301.3781 (2013)
7. Pennington, J., Socher, R., Manning, C.D.: Glove: global vectors for word representation. In: Proceedings 2014 Conference Empirical Methods Natural Language Process. (EMNLP), pp. 1532–1543 (2014)
8. Vaswani, A., Shazeer, N., Parmar, N., Uszkoreit, J., Jones, L., Gomez, A.N., et al.: Attention is all you need. In: Proceedings of the Advances Neural Information Processing System, vol. 30, Curran Associates, Inc., pp. 5998–6008 (2017)
9. Altenbek, G., Wang, X.L., Haisha, G.: Identification of basic phrases for Kazakh language using maximum entropy model. In: Proceedings of the COLING,: 25th International Conference Computational Linguistics: Technical Papers, vol. 2014, pp. 1007–1014 (2014)
10. Tolegen, G., Toleu, A., Zheng, X.: Named entity recognition for Kazakh using conditional random fields. In: Proceedings 4th International Conference Computer Processing of Turkic Languages, pp. 118–127 (2016)
11. Tolegen, G., Toleu, A., Mamyrbayev, O., Mussabayev, R.: Neural named entity recognition for Kazakh. In: Proceedings of the International Conference Computational Linguistics and Intelligent Text Processing, pp. 3–15. Springer Nature, Cham (2019). https://doi.org/10.1007/978-3-031-24340-0_1
12. Akhmed-Zaki, D., Mansurova, M., Barakhnin, V., Kubis, M., Chikibayeva, D., Kyrgyzbayeva, M.: Development of Kazakh named entity recognition models. In: Nguyen, N.T., Hoang, B.H., Huynh, C.P., Hwang, D., Trawiński, B., Vossen, G. (eds.) ICCCI 2020. LNCS (LNAI), vol. 12496, pp. 697–708. Springer, Cham (2020). https://doi.org/10.1007/978-3-030-63007-2_54
13. Oralbekova, D., Mamyrbayev, O., Zhumagulova, S., Zhumazhan, N.: A comparative analysis of LSTM and BERT models for named entity recognition in Kazakh language: A multi-classification approach. In: Agarwal, N., et al. (eds.): MSBC 2024, CCIS 2211, pp. 116–128. Springer Nature, Cham (2024). https://doi.org/10.1007/978-3-031-72260-8_10
14. Haisa, G., Altenbek, G.: Deep learning with word embedding improves Kazakh named-entity recognition. Information **13**, 180 (2022)

15. Sang, E.T.K., De Meulder, F.: Introduction to the CoNLL-2003 shared task: language-independent named entity recognition. In: Proceedings of the 7th Conference Natural Language Learning at HLT-NAACL 2003, pp. 142–147 (2003)
16. Pan, X., Zhang, B., May, J., et al.: Cross-lingual name tagging and linking for 282 languages. In: Proceedings of the 55th Annual Meeting Association Computing Linguistics (Volume 1: Long Papers), pp. 1946–1958 (2017)
17. Yeshpanov, R., Khassanov, Y., Varol, H.A.: KazNERD: Kazakh named entity recognition dataset. In: Proceedings of the 13th Conference Language Resources and Evaluation (LREC 2022), Marseille, France: European Language Resources Association, pp. 417–426 (2022)
18. Radford, A., Narasimhan, K., Salimans, T., Sutskever, I.: Improving language understanding by generative pre-training. OpenAI (2018). https://cdn.openai.com/research-covers/language-unsupervised/language_understanding_paper.pdf
19. Altenbek, G., Wang, X.L.: Kazakh segmentation system of inflectional affixes. In: Proceedings of the CIPS-SIGHAN Joint Conference Chinese Language Processing (2010). https://aclanthology.org/W10-4124/
20. T. Mikolov, K. Chen, G. Corrado, Dean, J.: word2vec, Google Code project (2013). https://code.google.com/p/word2vec/
21. Hochreiter, S., Schmidhuber, J.: Long short-term memory. Neural Comput. **9**(8), 1735–1780 (1997)
22. Van Houdt, G., Mosquera, C., Nápoles, G.: A review on the long short-term memory model. Artif. Intell. Rev. **53**(8), 5929–5955 (2020). https://doi.org/10.1007/s10462-020-09838-1
23. Schuster, M., Paliwal, K.K.: Bidirectional recurrent neural networks. IEEE Trans. Signal Process. **45**(11), 2673–2681 (1997)
24. LeCun, Y., Bottou, L., Bengio, Y., Haffner, P.: Gradient-based learning applied to document recognition. Proc. IEEE **86**(11), 2278–2324 (1998)
25. Devlin, J., Chang, M.-W., Lee, K., Toutanova, K.: BERT: pre-training of deep bidirectional transformers for language understanding. arXiv preprint arXiv:1810.04805 (2018)
26. Lafferty, J.D., McCallum, A., Pereira, F.C.N.: Conditional random fields: probabilistic models for segmenting and labeling sequence data. In: Proceedings of the 18th International Conference Machine Learning (ICML 2001), Williamstown, MA, USA, Jun. 28–Jul. 1, pp. 282–289 (2001)
27. Ratinov, L., Roth, D.: Design challenges and misconceptions in named entity recognition. In: Proceedings 13th Conference Computational Natural Language Learning (CoNLL-2009), Boulder, CO, USA, pp. 147–155 (2009)

The Influence of Individual Mentalizing Ability on Mandarin Sentence-Final Particle Usage

Ge Song(✉)

Nanjing University of Aeronautics and Astronautics, Nanjing, China
songge2024@nuaa.edu.cn

Abstract. Mandarin sentence-final particles (SFPs) play a critical role in interpersonal communication, conveying speakers' intentions and emotions without altering the propositional truth value. Despite their linguistic significance, existing research often relies on subjective analysis and lacks empirical evidence. Furthermore, while SFP comprehension has been linked to emotional regulation and adaptability, the relationship between SFP usage and mentalizing ability remains unexplored. This study investigates how mentalizing ability influences SFP choices across generations and genders. An oral discourse task with 80 participants revealed that women with higher empathy frequently used *-ba* in other-oriented contexts, reflecting greater sensitivity to interpersonal dynamics. In contrast, middle-aged men with alexithymic tendencies preferred *-ya*, reflecting reduced emotional engagement. The findings connect SFP usage to psychological traits like empathy and alexithymia, highlighting SFPs' role in interpersonal relationships and their cognitive underpinnings.

Keywords: Mandarin · Sentence-Final Particles · Production Experiment · Mentalizing Ability

1 Introduction

In East Asian languages, sentence-final elements, particularly those positioned at the peripheral right-hand region of the predicate, are crucial in shaping the interaction between grammatical structure and pragmatic meaning. These elements not only convey the speaker's attitude toward the proposition but also encode subtle emotional nuances that facilitate interpersonal communication. Among these elements, sentence-final particles (SFPs) are recognized as a distinctive linguistic feature within the East Asian linguistic sphere. SFPs function as both grammatical markers and pragmatic tools, signaling interpersonal modality and enhancing the communicative intent of the speaker.

In Mandarin Chinese, SFPs constitute a well-documented and extensive system, reflecting the language's rich capacity for encoding social and emotional meanings. These particles allow speakers to express their intentions, attitudes, and emotions in nuanced ways, without altering the propositional content of an utterance [1, 2]. Furthermore, they perform essential functions in managing and adjusting interpersonal relationships, highlighting their role as key facilitators of social interaction [3]. By integrating

X. Ding and Y. Dong (Eds.): CLNLP 2025, CCIS 2775, pp. 28–38, 2026.
https://doi.org/10.1007/978-981-95-4788-3_3

semantic, syntactic, and pragmatic dimensions, Mandarin SFPs illustrate the intricate interplay between linguistic structure and communicative goals. As such, their study provides valuable insights into the broader dynamics of language use in East Asian linguistic communities.

The selection of SFPs can have a profound impact on interpersonal dynamics within communication. These seemingly minor linguistic elements encode nuanced interpersonal and emotional information that extends beyond the propositional content of an utterance. For example, in response to the question, "How many cars do you have?" a reply such as "I have three" would typically be interpreted as a neutral, factual statement. However, appending an SFP, as in "I have three *-ne*," may subtly convey a boastful or self-satisfied undertone. This unintended shift in pragmatic meaning has the potential to cause discomfort to the listener, illustrating the delicate interplay between linguistic choice and social perception. Such examples underscore the importance of selecting appropriate SFPs, as their proper usage is integral to the successful construction and maintenance of interpersonal relationships between speakers and listeners.

SFPs in Mandarin do not affect the truth value of a proposition [4]. However, the choice of specific SFPs by speakers to convey their attitudes or emotions toward a proposition, while seemingly arbitrary, often follows identifiable patterns. The following are representative examples of the typical usage of three prominent SFPs in Mandarin.

(1)	你	先	走	吧。		
	2SG	first	go	SFP		
	"You should go first *-ba*."					
(2)	我	还	要	上	课	呢。
	1SG	still	need	attend	class	SFP
	" I still have a class to attend *-ne*. "					
(3)	风景		真	美		啊。
	scenery		really	beautiful		SFP
	"The scenery is really beautiful *-a*."					

Note: 1SG: first-person singular; 2SG: second-person singular; SFP: sentence-final particles.

The particle *-ba*, as demonstrated in example (1), is often used to signal the speaker's consideration of the listener's feelings or perspective. This pragmatic function aligns with its frequent use in other-oriented propositions, where it softens the tone of a suggestion or request, making the utterance appear more polite or accommodating [5, 6]. Such usage reflects the particle's role in fostering alignment between the speaker and listener, thereby promoting cooperative communication. Consequently, *-ba* is a common choice when the speaker aims to maintain harmony or establish rapport within an interaction. By contrast, *-ne*, as shown in example (2), is primarily associated with self-oriented propositions. It often highlights the speaker's subjective state or perspective and can convey an impression of assertiveness or unilateral intent [7]. This particle serves to draw attention to the speaker's stance or emotional involvement, which may occasionally be interpreted as self-focused or less collaborative. Additionally, *-a*, as illustrated in example (3), is typically regarded as an exclamatory particle that expresses a range of emotions, including admiration, excitement, or surprise [8]. Its flexible nature allows it to be used across diverse contexts, irrespective of propositional content.

Given their crucial role in interpersonal communication, the effective use of SFPs in Mandarin likely requires a nuanced understanding of social context and the emotional states of interlocutors. This suggests that the speaker's ability to interpret and respond to such interpersonal cues—commonly referred to as mentalizing or theory of mind (ToM)—may play a significant role in shaping SFPs usage. Mentalizing, defined as the ability to infer and attribute mental states such as beliefs, desires, and emotions to oneself and others [9], is integral to managing social interactions. It enables individuals to anticipate others' intentions and adjust their behavior accordingly, fostering relational harmony and effective communication. Mentalizing operates on two primary dimensions: cognitive mentalizing, which relates to understanding others' thoughts and perspectives, and affective mentalizing, which pertains to empathizing with their emotional experiences [10]. These dual capacities are essential in navigating complex social dynamics, particularly in conversations where speakers must align their linguistic choices with the needs and expectations of listeners. In linguistic interactions, mentalizing plays a particularly critical role in managing pragmatic phenomena, such as interpreting indirect speech, detecting irony, and using politeness strategies [11]. Such skills are indispensable in Mandarin Chinese, where SFPs encode subtle interpersonal meanings. SFPs often signal the speaker's stance or emotions and facilitate alignment with the listener, making them a key linguistic resource for sustaining effective social interaction [3].

Importantly, it can be inferred that individual differences in mentalizing ability may influence the selection and usage of SFPs. Speakers with stronger mentalizing skills are likely to exhibit greater sensitivity to the social nuances conveyed by SFPs, potentially enabling them to adjust their utterances in ways that maintain relational harmony and align with listeners' expectations. Conversely, individuals with reduced mentalizing capacity may encounter difficulties in selecting appropriate SFPs, which could lead to pragmatic mismatches or communication challenges. However, this relationship remains largely unexplored, and no prior research has specifically investigated how mentalizing ability shapes SFPs usage in Mandarin. Addressing this gap, the present study aims to examine the interplay between individual mentalizing ability and SFP selection by employing a discourse completion task, providing new insights into the cognitive mechanisms underlying Mandarin pragmatics.

Furthermore, If SFPs function as elements of interpersonal modality that help sustain social interactions with listeners, it is reasonable to assume that their production is influenced by the speaker's social attributes, such as gender and age. These attributes likely shape how SFPs are used to manage interpersonal dynamics, reflecting differences in communicative styles, social roles, and cultural expectations.

It is hypothesized that individuals with higher empathic ability will produce the other-oriented particle *-ba* more frequently in listener-oriented contexts, as their heightened sensitivity to interlocutors' needs enables better alignment and relational harmony in communication.

2 Methods

2.1 Participants

Eighty native Mandarin speakers participated in the experiment, including 40 younger adults (20 males; age range: 18–29, $M = 22.2$, $SD = 3.1$) and 40 middle-aged adults (20 males; age range: 51–60, $M = 55.0$, $SD = 2.4$). Prior to participation, all individuals were fully briefed on the purpose and procedures of the study, and informed consent was obtained. Upon completion of the experiment, participants were compensated for their time.

2.2 Stimuli

The discourse completion task was designed to assess SFPs usage in Mandarin across three discourse contexts: other-oriented (advice), self-oriented (declaration), and non-person-referenced (exclamation). Each scenario comprised four components: (1) Situation Description (2) Perspective Setting (3) Incomplete Utterance and (4) Comprehension Check Question.

In the other-oriented context, participants were asked to provide advice to an interlocutor named "Ming," a gender-neutral name. For example, in one scenario, the participant was placed in a shopping mall and informed that Ming could not locate an electronics store. The task involved completing the utterance "*You should ask the cashier ().*" by adding an appropriate SFP, such as *-ba*. In the self-oriented context, participants were instructed to make declarations. For instance, in a supermarket setting, the participant was prompted to complete the utterance "*I have been here many times ().*" with a suitable SFP like *-ne*. In the non-person-referenced context, participants were asked to express exclamatory remarks in response to general situations. One scenario, for instance, required participants to describe the variety of fruits in a supermarket by completing the sentence, "*The variety of fruits is so abundant ().*" with an appropriate SFP like *-a*. For each scenario, a Comprehension Check Question was included to ensure that participants fully understood the preceding discourse. This question explicitly addressed the content of the context, such as "Is Ming unable to find the electronics store?" in the other-oriented scenario.

All scenarios were set in daily conversational contexts, with no differentiation made regarding gender, social hierarchy, or relational intimacy between interlocutors. The speech acts in the task were standardized according to the specific discourse contexts: providing advice in other-oriented scenarios, making declarative statements in self-oriented scenarios, and expressing exclamatory remarks in non-person-referenced scenarios. A total of 24 scenarios were prepared, with 8 scenarios per discourse context.

2.3 Psycholinguistic Measures

To investigate individual differences in mentalizing ability and their influence on SFPs usage, this study utilized four psychometric instruments: the Autism Spectrum Quotient (AQ), the Empathy Quotient (EQ), the Interpersonal Reactivity Index (IRI), and the

Toronto Alexithymia Scale-20 (TAS-20). These measures comprehensively assess cognitive and emotional empathy, as well as alexithymic traits, offering a detailed evaluation of participants' mentalizing capacities.

The AQ [12] assesses autistic traits in adults with normal intelligence, focusing on social cognition and communication. Its five subscales —Social Skills, Attention Switching, Attention to Detail, Communication, and Imagination— provide a broad understanding of individual differences in these areas. The Chinese version of the AQ [13] ensures cultural applicability in Mandarin-speaking populations.

The IRI [14] conceptualizes empathy as a multidimensional construct that integrates both cognitive and emotional components. It includes four dimensions: Empathic Concern (EC), Personal Distress (PD), Perspective Taking (PT), and Fantasy Scale (FS). EC reflects other-oriented emotions such as sympathy and concern for others, emphasizing affective responses to others' experiences. PD captures self-oriented feelings of anxiety or unease in tense interpersonal situations, highlighting the emotional toll of empathy. PT assesses the cognitive ability to adopt another person's psychological perspective, facilitating effective social interactions and mutual understanding. FS measures the imaginative capacity to engage with fictional characters, reflecting a broader spectrum of cognitive and emotional empathy. Together, these dimensions provide a comprehensive framework for understanding individual differences in empathy. For this study, a culturally adapted Chinese version of the IRI [15] was utilized to ensure its relevance to the Mandarin-speaking participants.

The EQ [16] focuses specifically on emotional empathy, evaluating the ability to perceive, understand, and respond to others' emotions. The Chinese version of the EQ, developed by [17], was used to measure empathic tendencies in Mandarin speakers.

The TAS-20 [18] assesses alexithymia through three dimensions. Difficulty Identifying Feelings (DIF) reflects challenges in recognizing and distinguishing one's emotions and bodily sensations. Difficulty Describing Feelings (DDF) pertains to struggles in articulating emotions to others. Externally Oriented Thinking (EOT) captures a preference for focusing on external facts rather than internal emotional experiences. For this study, the Chinese adaptation of the TAS-20 [19] was utilized to assess alexithymic traits among Mandarin-speaking participants, ensuring cultural and linguistic relevance.

Together, these tools enable a detailed assessment of individual mentalizing abilities by capturing both cognitive and emotional dimensions. Their integration in this study provides the necessary foundation for analyzing how specific psychological traits, such as empathy and alexithymia, may influence SFPs usage in Mandarin.

2.4 Experimental Procedure

Participants were instructed to read the visually presented contextual scenarios on the screen and understand the information provided. Following this, an incomplete utterance with a blank space at the end was displayed. Participants were asked to imagine themselves in the described scenario and orally complete the utterance by adding an appropriate SFP.

To ensure full comprehension of the context, a comprehension check question related to the scenario was presented at the end of each trial, requiring a verbal "yes" or "no" response. Several practice trials were conducted before the main experiment to familiarize participants with the procedure. During the main experiment, all stimulus scenarios were presented in a randomized order to minimize sequence effects. The presentation of each trial component —from the situation description to the comprehension check question— was automated using Microsoft PowerPoint 2021.

2.5 Analysis

The relationship between the frequency of SFP usage, categorized by utterance orientation, and psychological ability scores was analyzed using Pearson's correlation analysis. Prior to the analysis, the usage frequency of each SFP was normalized by converting it into a ratio, calculated as the frequency divided by the total number of trials under the corresponding condition. Correlation coefficients were then computed to examine the association between usage ratios and psychological ability scores. All analyses were conducted using R version 4.2.0 (R Core Team, 2022).

Building on the correlation results, further analysis was conducted to evaluate the effects of gender and generation on specific SFPs that exhibited significant correlations with psychological ability scores. A generalized linear mixed-effects model (GLME) was applied for this purpose. The dependent variable was the use of the target SFP (coded as 1 for use and 0 for non-use), while the independent variables included standardized psychological ability scores and generation. Random effects accounted for variability across participants and contextual stimuli. The GLME analyses were performed using the lme4 [20] and lmerTest [21] packages in R.

For all statistical tests, the significance level was set at $\alpha = 0.05$.

3 Results

3.1 Accuracy

The accuracy rate for the comprehension check questions averaged 94.2% ($SD = 6.0$) for the younger group and 91.5% ($SD = 6.5$) for the middle-aged group. These findings suggest that participants maintained focus throughout the task and exhibited a strong grasp of the discourse content.

3.2 Results of the Correlation Analysis

The analysis focuses on significant correlation coefficients between the usage ratios of SFPs and various psychological indicators. For women, the usage ratio of *-ba* in other-oriented utterances showed a moderate positive correlation with the EC subscale of IRI ($r = 0.49$). In contrast, for men, the usage ratio of *-ya* in self-oriented utterances exhibited moderate positive correlations with the DDF subscale of TAS-20 ($r = 0.42$) and the overall TAS-20 score ($r = 0.43$).

3.3 Results of GLME Analysis

Based on the previous results, GLME analysis was conducted for women using the EC subscale of IRI as a factor, and for men using the overall TAS-20 score as a factor.

For women, the analysis revealed that the main effect of generation on the usage of *-ba* in other-oriented utterances was significant ($\beta = -0.746$, $p < 0.001$), with middle-aged women using *-ba* more frequently than younger women. The main effect of the IRI-EC score was also significant ($\beta = 0.298$, $p < 0.001$), indicating that individuals with higher EC scores used *-ba* more often regardless of generation. Additionally, a significant interaction effect between generation and the IRI-EC score was observed ($\beta = 0.339$, $p < 0.001$). Younger women with low EC scores used *-ba* less frequently, while middle-aged women consistently used *-ba* more frequently, regardless of their EC scores (Table 1, Fig. 1).

Table 1. The use of *-ba* in other-oriented utterances by female.

	β	95% confidence interval	z	p
(Intercept)	1.477	[1.473, 1.480]	855.400	<0.001
Generation	−0.746	[−0.749, −0.742]	−432.200	<0.001
IRI_EC	0.298	[0.295, 0.301]	172.700	<0.001
Generation*IRI_EC	0.339	[0.335, 0.342]	196.300	<0.001

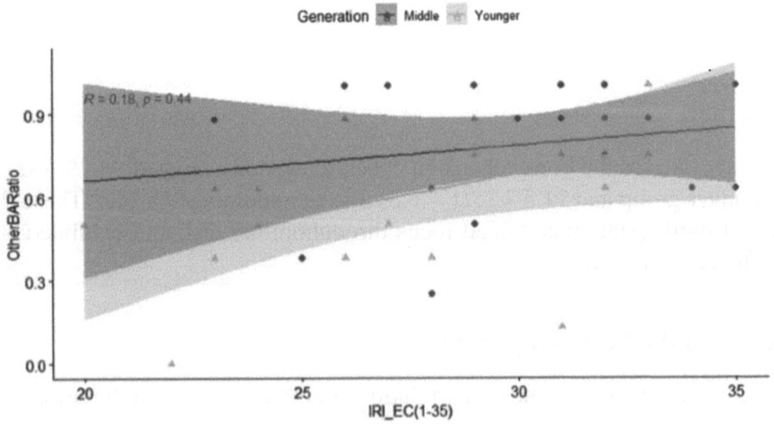

Fig. 1. Relationship between the proportion of the use of *-ba* in other-oriented propositions by female generations and EC scores of the IRI subscale.

Note: IRI_EC: Subscale "Empathic Concern (EC)" of the Interpersonal Reactivity Index (IRI); Other BA Ratio: Proportion of the use of *-ba* in other-oriented propositions.

Middle: Middle-aged group (n = 20); Younger: Younger group (n = 20).

For men, the analysis revealed that the main effect of the overall TAS-20 score on the usage of *-ya* in self-oriented utterances was significant ($\beta = 1.889$, $p < 0.001$). Men with higher TAS-20 scores used *-ya* more frequently, regardless of generation. A significant interaction effect between generation and TAS-20 scores was also found ($\beta = -1.673$, $p < 0.01$). Middle-aged men with higher TAS-20 scores used *-ya* more frequently, whereas younger men rarely used *-ya*, regardless of their TAS-20 scores (Table 2, Fig. 2).

Table 2. The use of *-ya* in self-oriented utterances by male.

	β	95% confidence interval	z	p
(Intercept)	−0.949	[−1.798, -0.099]	−2.188	0.029
Generation	−0.402	[−1.524, 0.720]	−0.701	0.483
TAS-20	1.889	[0.928, 2.850]	3.854	0.000
Generation*TAS-20	−1.673	[−2.911, -0.436]	−2.651	0.008

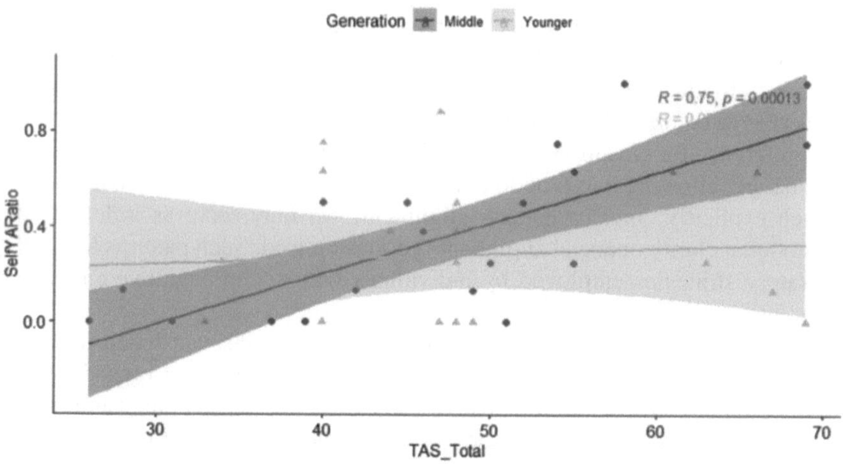

Fig. 2. Relationship between the proportion of the use of *-ya* in self-oriented propositions by male generations and total scores of the TAS-20.

Note: TAS_Total: Total score of the Toronto Alexithymia Scale-20 (TAS-20); SelfYARatio: Proportion of the use of *-ya* in self-oriented propositions.

Middle: Middle-aged group (n = 20); Younger: Younger group (n = 20).

4 Discussion

This study explored the relationship between individual psychological attributes and the usage of SFPs in Mandarin, with a specific focus on empathic ability and alexithymia. The findings reveal significant gender and generational differences in SFP usage, underscoring the intricate interplay between social cognition, psychological traits, and linguistic behavior.

The results showed that women with higher EC scores used the other-oriented particle *-ba* more frequently in listener-oriented contexts. EC, a core dimension of emotional empathy, reflects an individual's ability to experience and respond to others' emotions [22]. The particle *-ba*, often associated with politeness and listener alignment [6], serves as a linguistic tool for fostering relational harmony. It is plausible that empathic individuals are more adept at leveraging such particles to maintain cooperative communication. This finding aligns with previous research suggesting that empathic individuals are more attuned to interpersonal dynamics and exhibit greater sensitivity to social cues [23].

The stronger association between EC scores and *-ba* usage in younger women compared to middle-aged women may reflect generational differences in language use. Younger individuals often demonstrate more variability in linguistic choices due to ongoing socialization processes and less rigid adherence to societal norms [24]. Middle-aged women, on the other hand, may rely on socially "appropriate" language patterns that are consistent across varying levels of empathy, reflecting the stabilizing influence of age and societal expectations [25].

The results also indicate that men with higher alexithymic tendencies used *-ya* more frequently in self-oriented utterances. Alexithymia, characterized by difficulties in identifying and describing one's emotions, is often associated with reduced emotional awareness and impaired social cognition [18]. This finding aligns with studies suggesting that alexithymic individuals may struggle with contextually appropriate language use due to limited access to emotional information [26].

The preference for *-ya* among alexithymic individuals may stem from its neutral and versatile nature, allowing it to function in both self- and other-oriented contexts. Unlike *-ba*, which explicitly conveys listener alignment, *-ya* may serve as a default choice when emotional clarity or social alignment is compromised. Such patterns highlight the compensatory strategies employed by individuals with social-cognitive challenges in linguistic interactions.

Although this study did not account for tonal variations, it is worth considering their potential influence on SFP usage. Previous research has shown that prosodic features, such as tone and intonation, play a critical role in conveying speaker intent and emotional nuances [27]. For instance, the particle *-ya* can be pronounced with varying tones to express subtle differences in meaning, such as surprise or reproach. It is conceivable that alexithymic individuals might rely on atypical tonal patterns, further contributing to the observed individual differences in *-ya* usage.

This study focused on typically developing adults, shedding light on how individual differences in empathy and alexithymia influence pragmatic language use. However, the findings raise important questions about SFP usage in populations with atypical social cognition, such as individuals with Autism Spectrum Disorder (ASD). Research indicates that individuals with ASD often face challenges in interpreting and producing socially nuanced language due to deficits in theory of mind and emotional regulation [12]. Examining how such populations use SFPs could provide valuable insights into the intersection of language, cognition, and social interaction.

Additionally, this study highlights the need for a more nuanced understanding of generational and cultural factors in SFP usage. As linguistic practices evolve, the role of social norms and cultural expectations in shaping pragmatic language use warrants further investigation. Cross-linguistic studies comparing SFPs in Mandarin with similar particles in other East Asian languages, such as Japanese and Korean, could illuminate universal and language-specific patterns in the interplay between empathy, social cognition, and linguistic behavior.

While the experimental design effectively controlled for contextual variability, the requirement for participants to produce a SFP in every utterance may not fully reflect naturalistic language use. In real-life interactions, individuals might choose to omit SFPs depending on their personal communication style or the specific conversational context. This limitation could have influenced the observed patterns, suggesting the need for future studies to adopt more naturalistic methods, such as conversational or observational analyses, to better capture authentic SFP usage.

5 Conclusion

This study highlights the influence of individual mentalizing ability, including empathy and alexithymia, on Mandarin SFPs usage. Women with higher empathy favored the other-oriented particle *-ba*, fostering relational harmony, while men with stronger alexithymic traits preferred the self-oriented particle *-ya*, reflecting reduced emotional engagement. Generational differences in SFP selection further underscore the role of evolving social norms. These findings contribute to a deeper understanding of how cognitive and emotional traits shape pragmatic language use, paving the way for future research on naturalistic interactions and cross-linguistic comparisons.

Acknowledgment. This study was supported by "the Fundamental Research Funds for the Central Universities", NO. NR2024015.

References

1. Chao, Y.R.: A Grammar of Spoken Chinese. University of California Press, Berkeley, CA and Los Angeles, CA (1968)
2. Liu, Y., Pan, W., Gu, W.: A Comprehensive Grammar of Modern Chinese. Kurashio Publishing, Tokyo (1983)
3. Chu, C.: Relevance and the discourse functions of Mandarin utterance-final modality particles. Lang. Linguistics Compass **3**(1), 282–299 (2009)
4. Li, C.N., Thompson, S.A.: Mandarin Chinese: A Functional Reference Grammar. University of California Press, Berkeley, CA (1989)
5. Lu, W.Y.: Sentence-final particles as attitude markers in Mandarin Chinese. Ph.D. dissertation, Univ. of Illinois at Urbana-Champaign (2005)
6. Lee-Wong, S.M.: Face support - Chinese particles as mitigators: a study of ba, a/ya and ne. Pragmatics **8**(3), 387–404 (1998)
7. Wu, G.: A unified account of the discourse function of the Chinese particle 'ne'. Macrolinguistics **3**(3), 1–25 (2009)
8. Wu, R.J.: Stance in talk: a conversation analysis of Mandarin final particles. Amsterdam/Philadelphia, John Benjamins (2004)
9. Premack, D., Woodruff, G.: Does the chimpanzee have a theory of mind? Behav. Brain Sci. **1**(4), 515–526 (1978)

10. Shamay-Tsoory, S.G.: Empathic processing: its cognitive and affective dimensions and neuroanatomical basis. In: The Social Neuroscience of Empathy, Decety, J., Ickes, W. (eds). Boston Review, pp. 215–232 (2009)
11. Sperber, D., Wilson, D.: Pragmatics, modularity and mind-reading. Mind Lang. **17**(1–2), 3–23 (2002)
12. Baron-Cohen, S., Wheelwright, S., Skinner, R., Martin, J., Clubley, E.: The Autism-Spectrum Quotient (AQ): Evidence from Asperger Syndrome/High-Functioning Autism, males and females, scientists and mathematicians. J. Autism Dev. Disord. **31**, 5–17 (2001)
13. Chan, R.W.S., Liu, W.S.: Hong Kong Working Group on ASD (2008). Available at: http://docs.autismresearchcentre.com/tests/AQ_Chinese.pdf.
14. Davis, M.H.: A multidimensional approach to individual differences in empathy. JSAS Catalog Sel. Doc. Psychol. **10**, 85 (1980)
15. Siu, A.M.H., Shek, D.T.L.: Validation of the Interpersonal Reactivity Index in a Chinese context. Res. Soc. Work. Pract. **15**(2), 118–126 (2005)
16. Baron-Cohen, S., Wheelwright, S.: The empathy quotient: an investigation of adults with asperger syndrome or high functioning autism, and normal sex differences. J. Autism Dev. Disord. **34**(2), 163–175 (2004)
17. Sher, Y.: Hong Kong Working Group on ASD (2008). available at: https://www.autismresearchcentre.com/tests/empathy-quotient-eq-for-adults/.
18. Bagby, R.M., Parker, J.D., Taylor, G.J.: The twenty-item Toronto Alexithymia Scale–I. Item selection and cross-validation of the factor structure. J. Psychosom. Res. **38**(1), 23–32 (1994)
19. Yi, J.Y., Yao, S.Q., Zhu, X.Z.: Reliability and validity analysis of the Chinese version of TAS-20. Chin. J. Mental Health **17**(11), 763–767 (2003)
20. Bates, D., Maechler, M., Bolker, B., Walker, S.: Fitting linear mixed-effects models using lme4. J. Stat. Softw. **67**(1), 1–48 (2015)
21. Kuznetsova, A., Brockhof, P.B., Christensen, R.H.B.: LmerTest package: tests in linear mixed effects models. J. Stat. Softw. **82**(13), 1–26 (2017)
22. Davis, M.H.: Empathy: A Social Psychological Approach. Brown & Benchmark Publishers, Madison (1994)
23. Batson, C.D.: Self-other merging and the empathy-altruism hypothesis: reply to Neuberg et al. (1997). J. Pers. Soc. Psychol. **73**, 517–522 (1997)
24. Holmes, J.: Women, Men, and Politeness. Longman, London (1995)
25. Holmes, J., Wilson, N.: An Introduction to Sociolinguistics, 5th edn. Routledge, Abingdon, H. K. (2017)
26. Thayer, J.F., Lane, R.D.: A model of neurovisceral integration in emotion regulation and dysregulation. J. Affect. Disord. **61**, 201–216 (2000)
27. Gussenhoven, C.: Intonation and interpretation: phonetics and phonology. In: Speech Prosody pp. 47–57 (2002)

Validating Rule-Based Classification of Historical Fake News with Event Extraction: A Case Study of the Great Moon Hoax of 1835

Wanshu Zhang(✉)

University of Luxembourg, 2 Avenue de L'Université, L-4365 Belval, Luxembourg
wanshu.zhang@uni.lu

Abstract. This paper presents a novel approach for validating an established rule-based classification system of historical newspaper articles related to the "Great Moon Hoax of 1835" using event extraction techniques. The rule-based system classifies articles into five distinct categories: "Spreading," "Debunking," "Discussing," "Recalling," and "Mentioning," based on a multidimensional framework incorporating lexical features, positional weighting, sentiment analysis, and temporal markers. The computed classification demonstrates around 95% match with the manual classification. To verify these classifications, I implement a complementary event extraction methodology that identifies event structures from historical texts. The verification framework applies hierarchical classification rules similar to the original system but derives its features from extracted events and their argumentative structures rather than lexical patterns alone. Applied to the corpus of 151 newspaper articles from the Library of Congress and British Newspaper Archive (1835–1900), this approach achieves around 86% agreement rate with the rule-based model, validating the robustness of the original classification framework. Analysis of disagreement patterns identifies specific challenges in distinguishing between "Discussing" and "Recalling" categories, where event extraction provides valuable contextual information not captured by lexical features alone. This dual-methodology approach demonstrates how event extraction can be effectively applied to historical texts to verify classification results.

Keywords: Event Extraction · Text Classification · Historical Newspapers · Fake News · Cross-Validation · Natural Language Processing · Great Moon Hoax · Computational History

1 Introduction

The proliferation of misinformation, particularly in historical contexts, presents a significant challenge to accurate information retrieval and public understanding [1]. The "Great Moon Hoax" of 1835, a series of sensational articles published by the New York Sun detailing fictitious lunar discoveries, including claims of "vespertilio-homo" (bat-like humanoids) and other lunar life forms [2, 3], serves as a salient early example of such a phenomenon. As noted by Ulf J. Bjork, the hoax "stunned readers" with its fabricated

X. Ding and Y. Dong (Eds.): CLNLP 2025, CCIS 2775, pp. 39–46, 2026.
https://doi.org/10.1007/978-981-95-4788-3_4

scientific details, making it a landmark case in the history of media misinformation [4]. Effectively identifying and categorizing historical documents related to this event—distinguishing between texts that spread the hoax, those that debunked it, those recalling it retrospectively, or merely discussing its facets—is crucial for archival research and understanding media history [5].

This paper introduces a multi-faceted approach to classifying historical texts pertinent to the Great Moon Hoax of 1835. I developed a separate event extraction model, utilizing spaCy [6], to identify key entities and relational triples within the texts. The outputs of this event extraction model serve as an independent validation mechanism, allowing us to assess the accuracy and contextual relevance of the primary model's classification, thereby offering a more robust and nuanced system for analyzing historical narratives surrounding the Great Moon Hoax. This combined methodology aims to provide a more automated and reliable framework for sifting through and understanding complex historical events documented in textual archives.

2 Data Collection and Preprocessing

2.1 Data Sources and Collection Methodology

For this study, I selected the Library of Congress (LOC) and British Newspaper Archive (BNA) as primary data sources due to their rich collections of 19th-century periodicals. The newspaper articles of the Great Moon Hoax started from August 25, 1835, so I established a collection timeframe from January 1, 1835, to December 31, 1900.

The search technique maximised relevant article retrieval using a multi-keyword approach, hence reducing false positives. Table 1 presents the four keyword combinations used and their respective results across both archives. Each keyword strategy targeted different aspects of the hoax: the original headline phrasing ("Great Astronomical Discoveries"), specific identifying elements ("Sir John Herschel," "moon," and "Cape of Good Hope"), direct references to the hoax itself, and later debunking mentions.

Table 1. Keywords and search results.

Keywords	"Great Astronomical Discoveries"	"Sir John Herschel" AND "moon" AND "Cape of Good Hope"	"Great Moon Hoax"	"Sir John Herschel" AND "moon" AND "hoax"	Total
Search results in LOC	29	64	21	68	182
Chosen results	18	45	14	9	86
Search result in BNA	57	130	12	33	232
Chosen results	11	38	11	5	65

Note: Data collected on 24 January, 2025

Manual verification was required to remove irrelevant results where keywords appeared in unrelated content since the search algorithms of both archives search complete newspaper pages instead of discrete items. Further requiring human participation in the verification process were several 19th-century newspapers displaying print quality problems including ink stains, wrinkles, and degradation affecting OCR accuracy.

2.2 OCR Quality Enhancement and Method Selection

The initial OCR quality from LOC and BNA required systematic enhancement. I evaluated multiple approaches: text correction using LLMs (ChatGPT-4o, Deepseek-V3, Claude 3.5 Sonnet), direct image OCR with these LLMs, and dedicated OCR tools (ABBYY FineReader, OnlineOCR.net, Google Drive). Testing against manually corrected gold standards from five texts using Levenstein and Cosine similarity metrics revealed that LLM-based direct image OCR outperformed correction of pre-existing OCR, with ChatGPT-4o and Claude 3.5 Sonnet achieving >96% accuracy. Among traditional tools, Google Drive showed notable effectiveness.

Qualitative analysis revealed critical performance differences: Google Drive preserved formatting but struggled with complex 19th-century layouts (multiple columns, ornamental typography), while LLMs demonstrated superior context awareness. ChatGPT-4o occasionally invented words in ambiguous contexts, whereas Claude 3.5 Sonnet conservatively flagged uncertainties. Based on accuracy, conservative error handling, and larger token limits suitable for lengthy articles, Claude 3.5 Sonnet was selected as primary OCR tool, with ChatGPT-4o for secondary verification. Residual errors remained rare and verifiable through cross-checking—for instance, Claude 3.5 Sonnet misrecognized "his" as "all" in one test case, which ChatGPT-4o correctly identified.

3 Methodology

3.1 Rule-Based Classification Model

The approach to classifying 19th-century newspaper articles concerning the Great Moon Hoax of 1835 employed a multi-faceted linguistic analysis framework built upon weighted keyword detection, contextual sentiment analysis, and discourse pattern recognition. I defined five distinct classification categories to represent the various ways in which historical texts engaged with the Moon Hoax:

"Spreading" refers to texts that present the hoax claims as factual without skepticism, often contemporary with the original hoax publication. "Debunking" encompasses texts that explicitly refute the hoax claims, identifying them as false. "Mentioning" includes texts that reference the hoax briefly, without substantial engagement. "Discussing" comprises texts that analyze the hoax from an academic or investigative perspective. "Recalling" represents texts that reminisce about the hoax as a historical event, usually has all the key elements of the topic. Representative examples of texts from each category can be found in the Appendix (Table A1).

Table 2 shows the semantic framework for classification by means of established lexical categories, therefore organising the analysis. The numbers in the square brackets are the weights of the words. And the words in the parentheses need to be added in the classification for BNA dataset. An interesting finding is that the words like "amusing" "fabulous" are negative words in this case while they have positive meaning in other texts and cases.

Table 2. Keywords and weights.

Category	Terms
Related Keywords	great moon hoax [3.0], moon hoax [2.8], lunar hoax [2.8], richard adams locke [3.0], vespertilio homo [3.0], vespertilio-homo [3.0], hydro-oxygen microscope [3.0], sir john herschel [2.5], john herschel [2.3], new york sun [2.5], man bat [2.5], biped beavers [2.5], lunar forest [2.3], lunar vegetation [2.0], vegetation on the lunar surface [2.0], great moon discoveries [2.0], great astronomical discoveries [2.0], discoveries in the moon [2.0], inhabitants of the moon [2.0], man of the moon [1.8], man in the moon [1.8], cape of good hope [1.5], lunar [0.3], lunarian [1.8], telescope [0.3]
Negative Words	hoax, hoaxes, fake, false, untrue, deception, falsehood, lie, mislead, misleading, fabrication, fabricated, deceived, fooled, tricked, duped, misled, fraud, credulity, gullible, absurd, preposterous, amusing, amuse, fabulous, gullibility, humor, humour
Positive Words	ingenious, clever, remarkable, extraordinary, brilliant, entertaining, successful, interesting, impressive, celebrated, famous, popular, important, valuable, incredible, wonderful, exciting, astonishing
Recent Time Markers	lately (for BNA, add the followings: just published, to be published, published this day, just been published)
Historical Time Markers	1835, 1838, years ago, at that time, formerly, cannot recall the exact year

The feature extraction process employs a hierarchical positional weighting system (HPWS) that emphasizes terms appearing in structurally significant positions within texts. Initial processing segments each document into a title and five equal 20% character-based body segments. The first line is treated as the title when it has $\leq$14 words and $<$100 characters; otherwise, all text is treated as body. This segmentation reflects journalistic conventions of information prioritization and facilitates more nuanced relevance assessment than full-text analysis alone.

Keywords are weighted by position: 8 $\times$ in the title; 5 $\times$ in the first 20% of the text; 3 $\times$ in the second 20%; 2 $\times$ in the third 20%; 1 $\times$ in the fourth 20%; and 3 $\times$ in the final 20%.The keywords_found list is de-duplicated by position; scoring is additive across occurrences and positions. Positional scores decrease linearly with a term's character offset within each segment (1-offset/segment_length), so earlier appearances receive higher weights.

This is supplemented by targeted lexical analysis identifying predefined negative markers (n = 28), positive markers (n = 18), recent time markers (n = 1 or 5), and historical time markers (n = 6).

Documents are classified according to a hierarchical decision framework with thresholds optimized through cross-dataset validation. The classification algorithm follows a sequence of decision rules shown in Table 3. The thresholds were chosen by experience to get the best simulation to the manual classification.

Table 3. Classification Decision Framework.

Category	Classification Rules
Spreading	No negative sentiment
Debunking	Negative sentiment AND recent time markers AND no historical markers
Mentioning	Relation score <12.0
Recalling	Relation score ≥ 31.0
Discussing	All texts not classified in above categories

The methodology was implemented in Python, utilising pandas for data processing. The algorithm was initially developed and calibrated using the LOC dataset, the accuracy rate can reach 97.67% (the classification results can convince both manual annotator and Claude 3.5 Sonnet). Then applied to the BNA dataset, fine-tuning the keywords and the relation score parameters sphere can also get good performance.

For each document, the system generates comprehensive analytical metrics, including relation scores, keyword distributions, sentiment values, and lexical pattern identification. These metrics facilitate both categorical classification and enable nuanced assessment of discursive engagement with the Great Moon Hoax narrative across different historical and cultural contexts.

3.2 Validation with Event Extraction

To validate the results from the rule-based classification model and provide an alternative computational perspective, I developed a complementary approach using modern natural language processing techniques. This validation model served both to cross-verify the classifications and to resolve edge cases where the HPWS analysis produced ambiguous results.

The validation model employed the spaCy natural language processing library, leveraging its en_core_web_sm model for advanced linguistic analysis—including syntactic parsing, entity recognition, and part-of-speech tagging—to extract subject-verb-object (SVO) triples as atomic events. This approach enhanced the rule-based framework by capturing actionable relationships, enabling precise identification of hoax-related content beyond surface-level matches.

The validation model differs mainly in the calculation logic for relation scores, while using almost the same keywords as the rule-based classification model (removing “lunar”, "man of the moon", “man in the moon”, and adding “Locke”). Flagging events as "hoax-related" if keywords appeared in SVO triples or full sentences. Through dependency parsing, it analyzed syntactic relationships to detect complex discourse patterns tied to engagement levels, while entity recognition identified key figures (e.g., Richard Adams Locke) and sources (e.g., New York Sun) to contextualize hoax references. These features collectively pinpointed discourse patterns characteristic of each tier: Recalling, Discussing, and Mentioning.

For each text, it computed core metrics: total_events (all SVO triples), hoax_events (hoax-related triples), and portion (ratio of hoax to total events). Classification rules included: "Recalling" if hoax_events $\geq$ 20 or 10 $\leq$ hoax_events $\leq$19 with portion $\geq$0.133; "Discussing" if 4 $\leq$ hoax_events $\leq$ 9 with 0.26 $\leq$ portion $\leq$0.47; and "Mentioning" if hoax_events $\leq$ 3, or 4 $\leq$ hoax_events $\leq$ 9 with portion $<$ 0.26, or 10 $\leq$ hoax_events $\leq$ 19 with portion $<$ 0.133. The same hierarchical logic applied to the BNA dataset yielded 80% agreement. Recalibrating Rule 3 (4–9 hoax events) to portion thresholds of $<$ 0.11 ("Mentioning"), 0.11–0.215 ("Discussing"), and $>$ 0.215 ("Recalling") improved agreement to 92.31%, aligning with BNA-specific discourse patterns while retaining the core framework. The thresholds were chosen manually based on domain knowledge and inspection of BNA examples; no automated optimization was used.

4 Result and Analysis

4.1 Classification Model Agreement

Across methods, agreement is high: LOC-M-R 97.67%, M-V 81.40%, R-V 81.40%; BNA-M-R 90.77%, M-V 92.31%, R-V 90.77% (Table 4), indicating strong consistency between manual labels, the rule-based classifier, and the validation model.

Table 4. Agreement Rates Between Classifications.

Dataset	Manual-Rule	Manual-Validation	Rule-Validation
LOC	97.67%	81.40%	81.40%
BNA	90.77%	92.31%	90.77%

4.2 Disagreement Analysis

In the LOC dataset, the rule-based model has only two mismatches (Recalling-Discussing, Discussing-Recalling) compared to the manual classification. This shows the difficulties to reach the same result for human judgement and quantity analysis of the relation level of the Great Moon Hoax in the overall text. The validation model has more mismatches both compared to the manual labelling and rule-based model. Most mismatches are between the categories Recalling and Discussing. This pattern reflects borderline cases around the portion/threshold cutoffs, with occasional keyword coverage/weighting effects.

In the BNA dataset, besides the similar problems in LOC, there is also a mismatch between Mentioning and Spreading, which shows there are still some sentiment-related words or satire-related words denying the Great Moon Hoax which are not in the list of keywords implemented in the models, though this is often driven by the 'no negative sentiment ⇒ Spreading' precedence rule.

5 Conclusion

This pipeline labels the 19th-century newspaper articles of Great Moon Hoax of 1835 into five classifications with high cross-method agreement (LOC 97.67%/81.40%/81.40%; BNA 90.77%/92.31%/90.77%). Errors cluster at Discussing–Recalling; weighting title/lead terms and modeling satire/negation mitigate them and reveal a shift from spread to recall/debunking.

Acknowledgment. I thank Florentina Armaselu for helpful discussion and thoughtful feedback.

Appendix-Example Texts from the Data with Manual Labels.

Table A1. Example texts from the data with manual labels.

Category	Examples
Spreading	Great Astronomical Discoveries! —By the late arrivals from England, there has been received in this country a supplement to the Edinburgh Journal of Science containing intelligence of the most astounding interest from Prof. Herschel's observatory at the Cape of Good Hope[…]
Debunking	The late New York papers are filled with details of new and strange discoveries in the moon, said to have been lately made by Sir John Herschel, at the Cape of Good Hope. […]The author, whoever he may be, is no doubt enjoying the fun in the highest degree, of seeing our 'sharp ones' for once most delightfully bitten[…]
Mentioning	EDGAR A. POE - [...] It is little known that after "The Moon Hoax" came "The Balloon Hoax," written by Poe.[…]
Recalling	The New York papers announce the death, on the 16th inst., of Richard Adams Locke, at the age of 71. Mr. Locke was the author of the celebrated moon hoax […]
Discussing	Our Moon Inhabited? —But here the question is naturally suggested whether our own moon, which is but a quarter of a million of miles from us, ought not first to be examined for signs of life, or, at least, of being fitted for the support of life[…]

References

1. Allcott, H., Gentzkow, M.: Social media and fake news in the 2016 election. J. Econ. Perspect. **31**(2), 211–236 (2017). https://doi.org/10.1257/jep.31.2.211

2. Goodman, M.: The Sun and the Moon: The Remarkable True Account of Hoaxers, Showmen, Dueling Journalists, and Lunar Man-Bats in Nineteenth-Century New York. Basic Books, New York (2008)
3. Black, J.E.: In Defense of Vespertilio-homo: Finding the Truth in the 1835 Moon Hoax. In: Sachsman, D.B., Bulla, D.W. (eds.) Sensationalism: Murder, Mayhem, Mudslinging, Scandals, and Disasters in 19th-Century Reporting. Routledge, pp. 223–240 (2013). https://doi.org/10.4324/9781315129143-17
4. Bjork, U.J.: The Moon Hoax: the New York Sun Stuns Readers with Discovery of Lunar Life. In: Sloan, W.D., Stovall, J.G. (eds.) The Media in America: A History, 7th edn. Vision Press, Northport, AL, pp. 128–129 (2005)
5. Fyfe, P.: An archaeology of Victorian newspapers. Vic. Period. Rev. **49**(4), 546–577 (2016). https://doi.org/10.1353/vpr.2016.0039
6. Honnibal, M., Montani, I.: spaCy 2: Natural language understanding with Bloom embeddings, convolutional neural networks and incremental parsing (2017). https://doi.org/10.5281/zenodo.1212303

A Hybrid Framework Integrating Dynamic Segmentation and Global Semantic Enhancement for Long-Text Matching

Peng Zhang, Guosheng Hao(✉), Xia Wang, and Yi Zhu

School of Computer Science & Technology, Jiangsu Normal University, Xuzhou, China
hgskd@jsnu.edu.cn

Abstract. Semantic matching refers to the process of measuring the similarity between texts. It is fundamental for various NLP tasks. However, challenges such as contextual fragmentation and insufficient global modeling limit its applications. This paper proposes a hybrid framework that integrates BERT and LLMs. First, a dynamic segmentation strategy is designed based on LDA topic modeling and keywords extraction to partition text segments and prevent semantic fragmentation. Second, BERT is employed to extract local features, while LLMs generate cross-paragraph global semantic supplements to improve contextual coherence. Furthermore, a weighted fusion mechanism and a bidirectional matching network are introduced to comprehensively compute similarity by integrating both local and global information. Experimental results demonstrate that the proposed model significantly outperforms existing baselines. This method effectively balances fine-grained local features and global semantic associations.

Keywords: Long-text Semantic Matching · Dynamic Segmentation Strategy · Bidirectional Matching Network

1 Introduction

In the era of information explosion, text similarity computation is essential for tasks like intelligent question answering and knowledge retrieval. While existing research primarily targets short texts or general domains, long text matching remains challenging due to complex semantics, cross-paragraph dependencies, and input length limitations.

These challenges include: (1) insufficient capture of deep semantics, (2) limited effectiveness of segmentation strategies, and (3) weak global semantic modeling. Long texts often contain multi-level semantic relationships that traditional models, which rely on local context windows, struggle to capture. Fixed-length truncation can result in over 30% loss of critical context [1, 2]. BERT-based models [3], limited to 512 tokens, often segment text arbitrarily, disrupting logical coherence [4]. Dual-tower models further lack the ability to capture overall intent and thematic unity [5]. Although models like BERT and GPT [6] enhance semantic understanding through self-attention, they still face difficulties in long text processing. Attempts such as the BTSN model [2] introduce

X. Ding and Y. Dong (Eds.): CLNLP 2025, CCIS 2775, pp. 47–55, 2026.
https://doi.org/10.1007/978-981-95-4788-3_5

dynamic segmentation and topic modeling but fall short of fully integrating local and global semantics.

To address these limitations, we propose a hybrid framework that combines BERT and large language models (LLMs) for efficient long text semantic matching. Our main contributions include: (1) integrating LDA topic modeling with TF-IDF keyword extraction for natural text segmentation, (2) leveraging LLMs to generate cross-paragraph semantic extensions to complement BERT's local features, and (3) designing a weighted fusion layer and bidirectional matching network (BMN) to integrate fine-grained and global semantic features.

2 Related Work

Text similarity computation, one of the foundational tasks in NLP, has evolved into diverse technical pathways. Existing approaches can be broadly categorized into the following four groups.

2.1 Character-Based Methods

Operate directly on the surface form of texts, leveraging techniques such as edit distance [4] or Jaccard coefficient [7], longest common subsequence (LCS) [8], and N-gram [9]. These methods are computationally efficient but generally limited in handling synonymy, abbreviation, and complex semantics.

2.2 Statistical Analysis-Based Approaches

Move beyond raw text and consider term distribution patterns. The vector space model (VSM) [10] lacks semantic abstraction. To address this, topic models such as latent semantic analysis (LSA) [11], probabilistic latent semantic analysis (PLSA) [12], and latent Dirichlet allocation (LDA) [13] reveal latent thematic structures. Nevertheless, these models often struggle with deeper semantic understanding.

2.3 Knowledge-Based Methods

Utilize external semantic resources to enhance similarity detection. Tools such as WordNet [14, 15], and HowNet [16, 17] encode lexical semantics and conceptual hierarchies. Despite their semantic richness, they require human curation and struggle with scalability.

2.4 Deep Learning Methods

Have recently emerged as state-of-the-art solutions. CNNs [18] and RNNs [19] can automatically extract hierarchical features from text. With attention mechanisms [20], models like ELMo [21], Transformer [22], and the pre-trained models, say GPT, BERT, ERNIE [20] and XLNet [23], have demonstrated significant advancements in modeling polysemy and contextual dependencies. However, these models are computationally intensive and often require domain-specific fine-tuning for optimal performance.

3 the Proposed Method

A hybrid framework is proposed to enhance the semantic matching effect for long texts. By calculating text similarity through dynamic segmentation, semantic enhancement, weighted fusion, and BMN, combined with self-attention mechanisms and adaptive prompting for fine-tuning, the framework overcomes the limitations of traditional methods and effectively improves the accuracy of semantic matching.

This framework combines BERT with LLMs to enhance the effectiveness of semantic matching for long texts. The overall model architecture is illustrated in Fig. 1, which consists of four core components processed sequentially. (1) Feature extraction and text processing: Dynamic segmentation and context-aware processing enable BERT to encode long text at the segment level, ensuring local semantic integrity and coherence. (2) Semantic enrichment and generation: LLM complements the contextual semantics of BERT-extracted features, enhancing global semantic understanding and expression. (3) Similarity computation: A weighted fusion strategy combines the outputs of BERT and LLM, while a BMN computes matching scores between text segments to capture global semantic relationships. (4) Fine-tuning and learnable adaptive cueing: Adaptive cueing combined with a self-attention mechanism guides the model to focus on key contextual information, optimizing the long text matching performance. They will be detailed in the following.

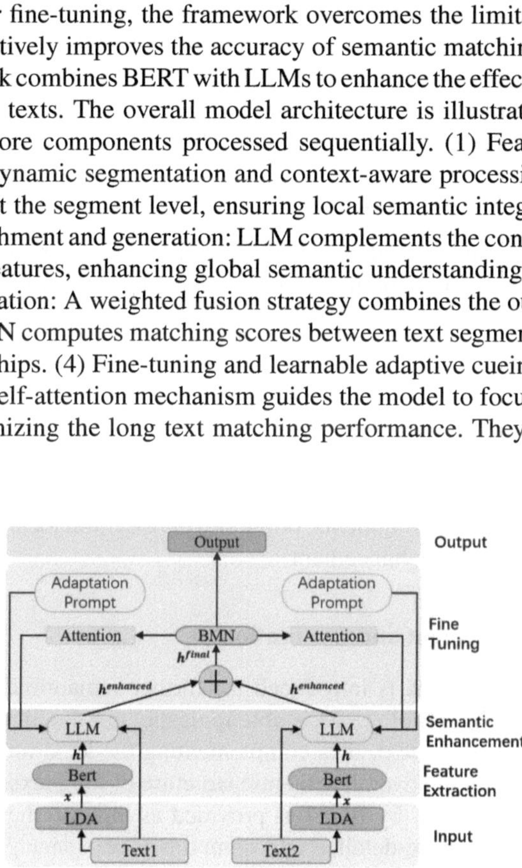

Fig. 1. Framework diagram of the Semantic Matching Model for Long Text Based on Hybrid Frame-work.

3.1 Feature Extraction and Text Processing

In the traditional BERT model, the input text is usually divided into fixed length segments. However, this static segmentation can disrupt semantic coherence, especially for long texts. To address this, we propose a dynamic segmentation and context-aware processing strategy. Specifically, this study combines topic modelling and keyword extraction techniques to identify key segments in the text, and performs dynamic segmentation based on the semantic importance of the segments.

The core of this method is to identify the keywords or topic sentences in the text using topic modelling (e.g. LDA or TF-IDF). After the segmentation, they are fed into BERT one by one. BERT is able to capture the dependency relationship between words and the contextual information in each segment. To further improve the quality of fragment representation, this paper adopts a hierarchical encoding strategy to synthesise the output information of multiple layers of BERT, especially the global contextual representation of the last layer, to enhance the semantic features of fragments at different levels.

Specifically, the topic sentences or keywords are extracted and dynamically segmented based on their semantic importance. For the ith fragment of the input text $\boldsymbol{X_i} = [\boldsymbol{x_{i1}}, \boldsymbol{x_{i2}}, \ldots, \boldsymbol{x_{in}}]$, BERT is used for encoding:

$$\boldsymbol{h_i} = \boldsymbol{BERT_{encode}}(\boldsymbol{X_i}) = BERT([\boldsymbol{x_{i1}}, \boldsymbol{x_{i2}}, \ldots, \boldsymbol{x_{in}}]) \tag{1}$$

To represent the semantics of the entire text, a hierarchical encoding strategy by averaging the output vectors h_i of all fragments applied as follows:

$$H = \frac{1}{n}\sum_{i=1}^{n} \boldsymbol{h_i} \tag{2}$$

By pooling the representations of all the fragments equally, the final unified representation $\boldsymbol{H}$ of long text is obtained.

This first stage lays the foundation by extracting meaningful semantic representations from dynamically segmented fragments, providing the essential local contextual features needed for deeper semantic enhancement.

3.2 Semantic Enhancement and Generation

In the second stage, the LLM is introduced for further semantic enhancement of the text features extracted by BERT. LLM is able to deeply get the implicit semantics and cross-text information in the text, thus complementing the local information extracted by BERT and optimizing the overall semantic structure of long texts.

Specifically, the output $\boldsymbol{h_i}$ by BERT is provided as input to the LLM. This allows each fragment to have a more detailed and comprehensive semantic representation in the generated context, improving the overall consistency and coherence of the text.

Then for each $\boldsymbol{h_i}$, the LLM generates an enhanced semantic representation $\boldsymbol{h^{enhanced}}$:

$$\boldsymbol{h_i^{enhanced}} = LLM\,(\boldsymbol{h_i}, \boldsymbol{context}) \tag{3}$$

where *context* includes preceding or adjacent fragments to improve coherence, i.e., it incorporates both the local fragment and historical segment information. This enrichment is crucial for downstream matching. Through this step, each fragment of the text is expanded into a richer semantic representation $h^{enhanced}$.

3.3 Similarity Calculation

In order to assess the similarity between texts more accurately, a combination of the outputs of BERT and LLM is proposed for integrated similarity computation.

The text fragment representations h_i and $h_i^{enhanced}$ are combined by a weighted fusion layer to obtain the final semantic representation of the text fragments as shown in Eq. (4). The weighted fusion strategy balances the contributions of BERT and LLM outputs by a learnable parameter α (α ∈ [0,1]). And it provides a differentiable and trainable integration, allowing downstream modules to adjust fusion adaptively.

$$\boldsymbol{h}_i^{\boldsymbol{final}} = \alpha \cdot \boldsymbol{h}_i + (1 - \alpha)\boldsymbol{h}_i^{\boldsymbol{enhanced}} \tag{4}$$

Then, the calculation of text similarity is performed using BMN, which obtains the global similarity between texts by calculating the match between each segment and all segments of another text:

$$sim(\boldsymbol{H}_1, \boldsymbol{H}_2) = \frac{1}{n_1 n_2} \sum_{i=1}^{n_1} \sum_{j=1}^{n_2} \textbf{sigmoid}\Big((\boldsymbol{h}_i^{\boldsymbol{final}})^T \boldsymbol{h}_j^{\boldsymbol{final}}\Big) \tag{5}$$

where n_1 and n_2 are the number of fragments in the texts $\boldsymbol{X}_1$ and $\boldsymbol{X}_2$, respectively. The averaging captures both local and global semantic relationships between texts.

This stage logically integrates the enriched representations, combining both local and enhanced global semantics to compute similarity scores between texts.

3.4 Fine-Tuning and Learnable Adaptation Cues

To further improve the effectiveness of the model, we introduces a learnable adaptive cueing and self-attention mechanism. The adaptive cueing mechanism guides the model to pay more attention to contextual relevance during the generation process by combining input cues (e.g., task-specific requirements) with historically generated responses provided as inputs to the model. The self-attention mechanism enables the model to dynamically adjust the impact of different historical information on the current generation results. The self-attention mechanism is represented as $Attention(Q,K,V) = softmax(QK^T/\sqrt{d_k})$, where Q, K, and V are the query, key, and value vectors, and d_k is the dimension of the key vector. This allows the model to focus dynamically on contextually relevant past content. Besides, an adaptation prompt is added to serves as a soft guiding signal, enabling the model to better align with task-specific semantic expectations during both training and inference.

During the fine-tuning process, the loss function $L(\theta)$ is minimized to update the parameters $\boldsymbol{\theta}$ of the model:

$$\boldsymbol{\theta}^* = argmin\boldsymbol{E}_{(\boldsymbol{X},\boldsymbol{Y})\sim \boldsymbol{D})}\big[\boldsymbol{L_{sim}}(f(X;\theta), Y) + \lambda \cdot \boldsymbol{L_{cue}}(X, Cue)\big] \tag{6}$$

where $\boldsymbol{X}$ and $\boldsymbol{Y}$ denote the input sequence and the corresponding ground truth output sampled from dataset D.

Through the combination of adaptive cueing and self-attention mechanism, the model is able to dynamically focus on important semantic units to further improve the effect of semantic matching for long texts.

4 Experimental Analysis

4.1 Data Set and Evaluation Indicators

We utilize the LCQMC dataset and a self-constructed Data Structures Base (DSB) dataset, which contains 5,000 Chinese sentence pairs split into 4,000 training, 500 validation, and 500 test samples. For DSB, six classic data augmentation techniques are applied: synonym replacement, sentence restructuring, random insertion, random deletion, homophone replacement, and sentence-level substitution to enhance text diversity and complexity.

The experiments used $F1 = (2 \times P \times R)/(P + R)$ and accuracy $Acc = correctnum/N$ as a criterion for model performance, where $P = (TP)/(TP + FP)$, $R = (FP)/(TP + FP)$, where TP, FP and FN are true positive, false positive and false negative respectively, $correct_{num}$ denotes the number of inference paths that finally reach the answer node through the test set sampled by the model proposed in this study, and N denotes the total number of samples.

4.2 Comparison Experiment

The comparison involved the original BERT, the BERT-based bipartite language model SBERT, and Transformer-DSSM [24]. The experimental results in Table 1 show that our method achieves state-of-the-art performance on DSB, and outperforms all baseline methods. On the general-purpose LCQMC, oure method achieves performance comparable to BERT but slightly lags behind Transformer-DSSM (84.5% vs. 85.1%).

Table 1. Model comparison experiment on LCQMC and DSB (%).

Model	LCQMC		DSB	
	ACC	F1	ACC	F1
BERT	84.9	86.1	86.5	87.1
SBERT	83.0	83.2	83.4	83.5
Transformer-DSSM	85.1	85.7	85.7	86.6
Ours Method	84.5	85.7	**87.0**	**87.5**

4.3 Ablation Study

In order to further validate the effectiveness of the modules in our method, ablation experiments are designed to remove the key components one by one and observe their effects on the performance. The following four versions of ablation experiments are set up: (1) w/o Dynamic Segmentation: remove dynamic segmentation and context-aware processing strategy, and directly divide text segments by fixed length. (2) w/o Semantic Enhancement: do not use LLMs to semantically complement the output of BERT, and use only the fragment representation extracted by BERT. (3) w/o BMN: use a simple vector similarity calculation method (e.g. cosine similarity) instead of BMN. (4) w/o Attention and Prompts: instead of using Self-Attention Mechanisms and Adaptive Prompts for fine-tuning, the model is directly optimized using standard fine-tuning methods. The experimental results are given in Table 2.

Table 2. Ablation Study Results (%).

Model	LCQMC		DSB	
	ACC	F1	ACC	F1
Full Model	84.5	85.7	87.0	87.5
w/o Dyn. Seg	83.6	84.0	85.9	86.4
w/o Sem. Enh	84.1	85.0	86.2	86.8
w/o BMN	83.8	84.6	86.5	86.9
w/o Att. & Prompts	84.2	85.2	86.7	87.0

The ablation study results demonstrate that each component of the hybrid framework plays a crucial and complementary role in enhancing model performance. The removal of dynamic segmentation module causes the largest performance drop, indicating its key function in preserving semantic coherence and local context in long texts. Building on this foundation, the semantic enhancement module leverages LLMs to incorporate global semantic information, significantly improving the model's overall understanding beyond BERT's fragment-level features.

5 Conclusion

The proposed hybrid framework, integrating BERT with LLMs, addresses key limitations in long-text semantic matching by introducing dynamic segmentation, semantic enhancement, weighted fusion, and BMN. Experimental results validate its advantages in capturing both local and global semantic information.

Future work could explore graph-based semantic representations to strengthen cross-domain reasoning.

Acknowledgment. The authors give their thanks for the support from National Natural Science Foundation of China (No. 62277030, 62077029), and the Society Development Foundation of Xuzhou under Grant KC23239.

References

1. Ye, Y., Minmin, Y., Jiming, L.: Research on calculation method of text similarity based on smooth inverse frequency. J. China Univ. Posts Telecommun. **27**(2), 56 (2020)

2. Luo, J., Xiong, W., Du, J., et al.: Traditional Chinese medicine text similarity calculation model based on the bidirectional temporal siamese network. Evidence-Based Complementary and Alternative Medicine (2021)
3. Devlin, J., Chang, M.W., Lee, K., et al.: Bert: pre-training of deep bidirectional transformers for language understanding. Proceedings of the 2019 conference of the North American chapter of the association for computational linguistics: human language technologies, volume 1 (long and short papers). pp. 4171–4186 (2019)
4. Liu, L., Wang, Q., Li, Y.: Improved Chinese sentence semantic similarity calculation method based on multi-feature fusion. J. Adv. Comput. Intell. Intell. Inform. **25**(4), 442–449 (2021)
5. Che, W.X., Liu, T., Qin, B., et al.: Similar sentence retrieval in chinese based on improved edit distance. High Technol. Lett. **14**(7), 15–19 (2004)
6. Floridi, L., Chiriatti, M.: GPT-3: its nature, scope, limits, and consequences. Mind. Mach. **30**, 681–694 (2020)
7. Niwattanakul, S., Singthongchai, J., Naenudorn, E., et al.: Using of Jaccard coefficient for keywords similarity. Proc. Int. Multiconference Eng. Comput. Sci. **1**(6), 380–384 (2013)
8. Xu, X., Chen, L., He, P.: Fast sequence similarity computing with LCS on LARPBS. Nanjing, China: Parallel and Distributed Processing and Applications pp. 168–175 (2005)
9. Kondrak, G.: N-gram similarity and distance. Buenos Aires, Argentina: String Processing and Information Retrieval. 12th International Conference, pp. 115–126 (2005)
10. Salton, G., Wong, A., Yang, C.S.: A vector space model for automatic indexing. Commun. ACM **18**(11), 613–620 (1975)
11. Landauer, T.K., Dumais, S.T.: A Solution to Plato's problem: the latent semantic analysis theory of acquisition, induction, and representation of knowledge. Psychol. Rev. **104**(2), 211–240 (1997)
12. Hofmann, T.: Probabilistic latent semantic analysis. Uncertainty Artif. Intell. **15**(6), 289–296 (1999)
13. Blei, D.M., Ng, A.Y., Jordan, M.I.: Latent dirichlet allocation. J. Mach. Learn. Res. **3**(1), 993–1022 (2003)
14. Miller, G.A.: WordNet: a lexical database for English. Commun. ACM **38**(11), 39–41 (1995)
15. Vij, S., Tayal, D., Jain, A.: A machine learning approach for automated evaluation of short answers using text similarity based on WordNet graphs. Wireless Pers. Commun. **111**(2), 1271–1282 (2020)
16. Hua, L., Chang-le, Z., Min, J., et al.: A hybrid approach for Chinese word similarity computing based on HowNet. International Conference on Automatic Control and Artificial Intelligence (ACAI 2012). Stevenage UK, IET, pp. 80–83 (2012)
17. Wu, K.J., Wang, J.W.: Vocabulary semantic similarity computation based on HowNet and search engine. Comput. Mod. **04**, 90–94 (2018)
18. Medsker, L.R., Jain, L.C.: Recurrent neural networks. Des. Appl. **5**, 64–67 (2001)
19. Bahdanau, D., Cho, K., Bengio, Y.: Neural machine translation by jointly learning to align and translate (2014). arXiv preprint arXiv:1409.0473
20. Yang, Z., Dai, Z., Yang, Y., et al.: Xlnet: generalized autoregressive pretraining for language understanding. San Francisco, CA, USA: Advances in Neural Information Processing Systems 32: Annual Conference on Neural Information Processing Systems 2019, pp. 5754–5764 (2019)
21. Peters, M.E., Neumann, M., Iyyer, M., et al.: Deep contextualized word representations. New Orleans, LA, USA: Proceedings of 2018 Conference of the North American Chapter of the Association for Computational Linguistics: Human Language Technologies, pp. 2227–2237 (2018)
22. Aswani, A., Shazeer, N., Parmar, N., et al. : Attention is all you need. San Francisco, CA, USA: Advances in Neural Information Processing Systems 30: Annual Conference on Neural Information Processing Systems 2017, pp. 5998–6008 (2017)

23. Zhang, Z., Han, X., Liu, Z., et al. : ERNIE: enhanced language representation with informative entities (2019). arXiv preprint arXiv:1905.07129
24. Cai, L.J., Liu, X., Liu, L., et al.: Improved short text matching model based on transformer. Comput. Syst. Appl. **30**(12), 268–272 (2021)

The Evolution of Reranking Models in Information Retrieval: From Heuristic Methods to Large Language Models

Tejul Pandit[1(✉)], Sakshi Mahendru[1], Meet Raval[2], and Dhvani Upadhyay[3]

[1] Palo Alto Networks, Santa Clara, USA
tejulpandit96@gmail.com
[2] University of Southern California, Los Angeles, USA
[3] Dhirubhai Ambani University, Gandhinagar, India

Abstract. Reranking is a critical stage in contemporary information retrieval (IR) systems, improving the relevance of the user-presented final results by honing initial candidate sets. This paper is a thorough guide to examine the changing reranker landscape and offer a clear view of the advancements made in reranking methods. We present a comprehensive survey of reranking models employed in IR, particularly within modern Retrieval Augmented Generation (RAG) pipelines, where retrieved documents notably influence output quality. We embark on a chronological journey through the historical trajectory of reranking techniques, starting with foundational approaches, before exploring the wide range of sophisticated neural network architectures such as cross-encoders, sequence-generation models like T5, and Graph Neural Networks (GNNs) utilized for structural information. Recognizing the computational cost of advancing neural rerankers, we analyze techniques for enhancing efficiency, notably knowledge distillation for creating competitive, lighter alternatives. Furthermore, we map the emerging territory of integrating Large Language Models (LLMs) in reranking, examining novel prompting strategies and fine-tuning tactics. This survey seeks to elucidate the fundamental ideas, relative effectiveness, computational features, and real-world trade-offs of various reranking strategies. The survey provides a structured synthesis of the diverse reranking paradigms, highlighting their underlying principles and comparative strengths and weaknesses.

Keywords: Rerankers · Information Retrieval (IR) · Retrieval Augmented Generation (RAG) · Learning-to-rank · Neural Rerankers · Cross-Encoders · T5 · Graph Neural Networks (GNN) · Knowledge Distillation · Large Language Models (LLM)

1 Introduction

Information retrieval (IR) systems are essential in today's digital world, with their ability to power anything from online search and recommender systems to sophisticated question-answering and knowledge management platforms. A critical component within

†Equal contribution

X. Ding and Y. Dong (Eds.): CLNLP 2025, CCIS 2775, pp. 56–67, 2026.
https://doi.org/10.1007/978-981-95-4788-3_6

these systems is the reranking stage. Reranking carefully reorders these candidates to show the user the most pertinent results after an initial, often rapid, retrieval phase that produces an extensive collection of candidate documents. This dramatically improves the overall quality and efficacy of the IR system [1]. Notably, the significant development in Large Language Models (LLMs) has subsequently driven substantial improvements and interest in Retrieval Augmented Generation (RAG) pipelines, where the precision of retrieved context, refined by reranking, is crucial for generating accurate and relevant outputs [2]. Based on [3], we represent the typical placement of the reranking component within a RAG pipeline in Fig. 1.

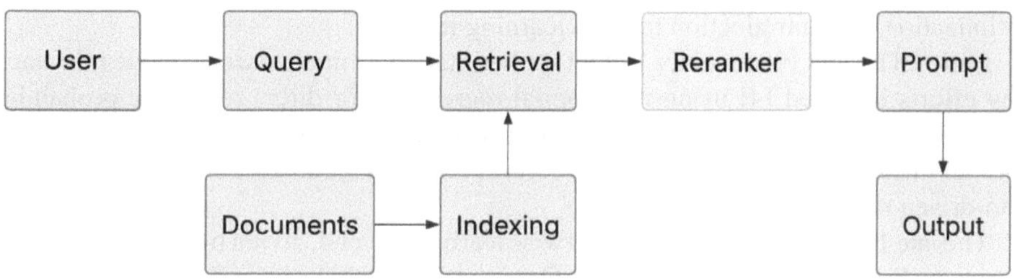

Fig. 1. RAG approach highlighting a post-retrieval step of Reranking documents.

Reranking methods have evolved significantly, from heuristic scoring and traditional learning-to-rank models to deep learning and, more recently, LLMs, enabling richer semantic understanding and inter-document relationships.

This survey provides a comprehensive exploration of the evolving field of reranking models in IR. We trace the development trajectory from classical learning-to-rank methods in Sect. 3, followed by Deep learning rerankers in Sect. 4. We also cover methods aimed at improving the efficiency of reranking models, with a particular focus on knowledge distillation techniques in Sect. 5. Finally, we examine the cutting-edge integration of LLM-based rerankers in Sect. 6. This study aims to provide scholars and practitioners with a valuable guide for navigating this ever-evolving subject by compiling significant advancements and empirical findings throughout the reranking timeline.

2 Background

Ranking approaches, which form the basis for many reranking techniques, can broadly be categorized based on their supervision strategies and how they process documents during training and scoring: pointwise, pairwise, and listwise.

Pointwise approaches consider a single document at a time within the loss function. They train a classifier or regressor to predict the relevance score of an individual document for a given query. The final ranking is then produced by sorting documents based on these predicted scores.

Pairwise approaches focus on pairs of documents. Given a pair of documents, the model aims to determine the optimal relative ordering between them, comparing this prediction against the ground truth.

Listwise approaches directly consider and optimize the ranking of an entire list of documents. These methods aim to produce the optimal ordering for the complete set of retrieved candidates.

3 Learning to Rank in Reranking Models

Learning drastically changed the reranking phase of contemporary information retrieval (IR) systems to Rank (LTR). This section of the survey charts LTR's evolutionary trajectory in reranking, focusing on methodological shifts, core problems, and model sophistication, from foundational probabilistic methods to pairwise learning, listwise optimization, and introduction to deep learning models.

Early LTR (late 1980s- early 1990s) applied statistical methods to estimate relevance. Key efforts included [4] using polynomial regression for direct relevance probability estimation, [5] with multi-stage logistic regression for composite clues, and [6] learning optimal linear combinations of expert scores, presaging meta-search. These established data-driven rankings' viability.

The late 1990s- early 2000s saw pairwise learning ascend, driven by machine learning advances. Friedman's [7] provided the Gradient Boosted Decision Tree (GBDT) foundation crucial for later LTR. Algorithms like [8] applied boosting to learn from pairwise preferences, while [9] introduced influential neural networks for pairwise ranking by minimizing cross-entropy between predicted and target pair probabilities.

Limitations of generic pairwise losses spurred refinement towards IR-specific metrics. [10] Adapted Ranking SVM by weighting misranked pairs based on IR relevance. The pivotal [11] enabled direct optimization of non-smooth IR metrics (like NDCG) by defining gradients (λ-values) based on metric changes from swaps, guiding pairwise models to optimize listwise objectives. Other works like [12] and [13] also explored pairwise regression for preferences and direct MAP optimization.

This led to explicit listwise approaches, treating entire document lists as training instances. [14] pioneered a listwise loss based on top-one probabilities.

Others like [15] and [16] (both 2007) proposed query-level losses. Boosting frameworks like [17] were adapted to optimize IR metrics directly. Probabilistic list models, such as [18] using the Plackett-Luce model, gained traction. The highly successful [19] integrated MART (GBDTs) with LambdaRank's gradients, becoming a state-of-the-art baseline. The scalability of such tree-based models was later significantly enhanced by systems like [20].

From the mid-2010s, deep learning (DL) began to dominate LTR, offering powerful representation learning and contextual modeling. Using techniques like [21] triplet loss for metric learning, neural IR models began learning potent query-document embeddings. Contextual DL models, using RNNs or Trans formers (e.g., [22–24]), excelled at capturing document interdependencies within lists. Simultaneously, DL spurred innovations in preference modeling (e.g., [25]) and end-to-end metric optimization using differentiable surrogates or black-box methods (e.g., [26, 27]). We elaborate on more sophisticated DL based rerankers in Sect. 4.

Alongside these mainstream trends, diverse strategies continued to enrich LTR. Evolutionary algorithms [28, 29] directly optimized IR metrics. Other approaches included ordinal classification [30], incorporating preference magnitudes [31], and hybrid models combining objectives or data sources [32].

4 Deep Learning Techniques for Reranking

Deep learning models have significantly advanced the reranking task by capturing intricate semantic relationships between queries and documents.

4.1 Transformer-Based Rerankers (BERT and T5)

Transformer architectures dominate recent reranking advancements, notably BERT style encoders and T5-style sequence-to-sequence models.

BERT-like Cross-Encoders Cross-encoders based on BERT [33] and its variants jointly encode query-document pairs, enabling rich token-level interactions via self-attention [34]. They output a relevance score.

Training pipelines are crucial. [35] uses sequential sparse retrieval (BM25), pointwise BERT reranking, and pairwise BERT reranking. Integrated pipelines like [36] combine retrieval, reranking, and generation using a BERT-based model trained on MS MARCO [37].

Efficiency is a key challenge. [38] offers a scalable alternative using contextualized late interaction. It encodes queries and documents independently with BERT, preserving token embeddings. Similarity is calculated via Maximum Sim ilarity (MaxSim), summing the max dot products between query and document tokens. This allows document precomputation, drastically reducing latency while maintaining accuracy. Adaptation for multilingual scenarios uses methods like Adapters or SFTMs [39] with mBERT, decoupling language and task adaptation to mitigate the "curse of multilinguality" [40].

T5-based Sequence-to-Sequence Rerankers Seq2seq models like T5 [41] offer an alternative generative approach. They frame relevance prediction as a text-to-text task, leveraging pretraining benefits.

The seminal work [42] fine-tuned T5 to generate "true" or "false" given a query-document pair, using the probability of generating "true" as the relevance score. [43] proposes directly outputting numerical scores using the T5 encoder-decoder or encoder-only architecture, supporting fine-tuning with standard ranking losses. Listwise losses often yield better performance. [44] can improve generalization by jointly training on ranking and auxiliary tasks like passage-to-query generation. [45] adapts T5 for listwise reranking using the Fusion-in-Decoder (FiD) architecture and an efficient m-ary tournament sort inference, mitigating positional biases seen in other LLM-based listwise methods[46].

4.2 Advanced Interaction and Alternative Architectures

Research also explores models that explicitly model interactions between multiple candidates or use different architectural foundations.

Methods modeling joint comparison between candidates, like [47], use a Transformer encoder to jointly encode the query and multiple candidates, capturing inter-candidate relationships efficiently within multi-stage pipelines (e.g., BE-CMC or BE-CMC-CE). [48] uses a specialized ListAttention mechanism allowing passages to attend to each other, combined with Circle Loss[49] for improved contrastive learning.

Beyond Transformers, other models are explored. [50] builds a document graph from retrieved documents, using Graph Convolutional Networks[51] to update representations based on relationships derived from Abstract Meaning Representation (AMR). [52] evaluates the Mamba architecture[53] for document reranking, showing competitive performance against Transformers but highlighting current implementation speed challenges.

5 Efficiency Techniques: Knowledge Distillation

Modern search engines and RAG systems have demonstrated considerable efficacy in question answering. However, their performance often encounters limitations when confronted with complex, knowledge-intensive tasks that demand nuanced reasoning. Such tasks, including the identification of coding/configuration errors, medical diagnosis, financial forecasting, and strategic marketing approach formulation based on case studies, necessitate more than superficial relevance matching, domain-specific knowledge.

5.1 Distillation Training Strategies for Reasoning-Aware Reranking

Based on our research across recent papers, the methodologies for distilling reasoning capabilities into smaller LMs for reranking can be broadly classified based on the nature of the supervisory signal transferred from the teacher to the student model.

We delineate two primary categories - Label Distillation & Rationale-Enhanced Distillation. [54] claims a KARD-trained 250M T5 model surpassed a fine-tuned 3B T5 model and proposes a unique distillation process to transfer the learning from LLMs to small LM using a supervised fine-tuning process. It follows a two-stage training process (training the small language model (LM) with knowledge, and training a helper "reranker"), followed by an inference process that uses both these trained components to answer new questions effectively.

In the first stage, we train the reranker via a teacher LLM that generates rationales for ground truth questions and documents, making the reranker "rationale-aware" or "reasoning-aware," bridging the gap between optimal retrieval for rationale generation and practical inference-time retrieval. In the next stage, a small LLM is trained using explicit knowledge augmentation in addition to query and rational, which is theoretically motivated to reduce the memorization burden on small LMs. [55] presents novel frameworks like RADIO (RAtio nale DIstillation) to mitigate the "preference misalignment" gap in the RAG pipeline. This gap can result in the generator receiving documents that, while generally relevant, lack the precise information needed for high-quality, reasoned responses. Recent research has begun to address this by focusing on how the reasoning process itself can inform document selection. It involves fine-tuning the reranker component, denoted as R_θ and typically instantiated as a powerful cross-encoder architecture, utilizing a contrastive learning objective.

[56] and [57] addresses the lack of explainability and transparency in neural document reranking models. It introduces a novel framework that separates and distills both direct relevance and comparative reasoning from an LLM teacher into LLaMA. Both models were evaluated across a wider range of datasets.

The seminal work [58] introduced the concept of knowledge distillation, using "soft targets" (probabilities from the teacher's softmax, often with a temperature parameter T) and a modified cross-entropy loss (or matching logits, which it shows is a special case) to transfer knowledge. It defines the basic distillation process and loss. However, this standard approach can suffer from over-calibration, where the student too rigidly imitates an imperfect teacher. [59] proposes an improved distillation process by integrating an alternative contrastive loss (LBKL) with the standard Kullback-Leibler (KL) Divergence loss [60]. This LBKL allows the student model to more conservatively and adaptively learn from the teacher, permitting deviation when the teacher's guidance might be suboptimal for certain examples. The strategy aims to balance the benefits of teacher imitation with an explicit contrastive objective, demonstrably improving re-ranking performance by making the knowledge transfer more robust to teacher errors.

5.2 Comparison & Observations

[54]'s explicit knowledge augmentation strategy might be advantageous for tasks requiring complex knowledge synthesis beyond document content. [56] is specifically optimized for generating structured, interpretable rationales and performing precise reranking of a given set of documents within a single, efficient student model. For pure document reranking with explainability, the authors found unified distillation particularly effective. [57] extends [56] distilling approach on web-scraped Q&A to specifically refine the student's ability to generate these step-by-step explanations before relevance judgment.

The development of such models is crucial for democratizing access to sophisticated reasoning capabilities, overcoming the deployment barriers of LLMs, and paving the way for more transparent and trustworthy IR systems. While not a distillation method itself, frameworks like Rank1 [61], which focus on optimizing test-time computation for reranking, stand to benefit significantly from highly efficient yet effective distilled models that can perform sophisticated reasoning within tight latency budgets.

6 LLM Based Rerankers

LLM-based rerankers are effective in listwise reranking settings where the goal is to produce an ordered document list without explicit relevance scores for individual documents [62–66]. [62] evaluates the performance of LLMs in RAG using prompting strategies and introduces RankGPT. To tackle the issue of context length limitations, it proposes a sliding window-based approach, breaking the primary prompt into smaller prompts and then merging the results of these smaller prompts. It then evaluates the model on various datasets to test the efficacy of its proposed solutions. To counter concerns that LLMs might have been trained on existing benchmark data, the paper introduces a new test set, NovelEval, with information post the knowledge cutoff date of GPT-4 [67].

Other models have also researched sliding window techniques, for example, [68] shares a SlideGar (Sliding-window-based Graph Adaptive Retrieval) algorithm to use adaptive retrieval.

[69] investigates the challenges in the recommendation system due to the disparity between the pre-training LLMs and the specific requirements of recommendation tasks. It introduces a Direct Multi-preference optimization framework and fine-tunes the model by incorporating multiple negative samples and optimizing the model to increase the probability of correct predictions and decrease incorrect predictions. [70] uses supervised fine tuning (SFT) on LLaMA [71] for recommendation systems and introduces two models, RepLLaMa and RankLLaMa. RepLLaMa encodes queries and documents into a vector representation and computes the relevance using the dot product, while RankLLaMa performs pairwise ranking of the inputs. In contrast to SFT, [72] conducts training on a large weakly supervised corpus and proposes a two-stage training framework to adapt decoder-only LLMs to text ranking progressively using Continuous Pre Training(CPT) followed by SFT. The base LLM undergoes CPT on a large-scale, diverse, weakly-supervised text-pair dataset from various sources. This stage uses the Next Token Prediction (NTP) objective to initially orient the LLM towards different aspects of relevance inherent in the text pairs. The model is fine-tuned using high-quality supervised ranking data. It proposes a new optimization strategy using a ranking loss based on the generation probability of the entire query given the document (P(q|d)), calculated via NTP, rather than relying on a last token representation.

LLMs have also been proven to be effective text rankers when used in pairwise ranking settings. [73] uses a pairwise approach where LLM is given a query and two passages to determine the relevant passage. All the comparisons made create a final score for the passage. [74] also shares a pairwise prompting approach called PRP-Graph, which leverages LLMs' output probabilities for target labels, transforming these outputs into numerical scores for enhanced text ranking.

Researchers have also used model distillations to create open-source models. [63], a LLaMa-based model is the first fully open-source LLM capable of performing high-quality listwise reranking in a zero-shot setting. It is trained in zero-shot settings using RankGPT_3.5 as a teacher model using 100K queries from the MS Marco dataset. However, [63] still lags behind the state-of-the-art RankGPT4 in effectiveness. Thus, [64] introduces RankZephyr, another open source model which bridges the gap and, in a few cases, outperforms RankGPT_4 with orders of magnitude fewer parameters. [75] studies how to construct effective GPT-free listwise rerankers based on open-source LLM models, where they used Code LLaMA-Instruct [76] for their experimental analysis.

In addition to these techniques, research has considered prompt engineering for reranking. [77] shares a novel approach to reduce human effort and unlock the potential of prompt optimization in the reranking approach by generating refined prompts through feedback and preference optimization. [78] integrates a soft prompt with a passage-specific embedding layer to form a new learnable prompt module, then concatenates with the embeddings of the raw passage to serve as new input for the LLMs.

7 Conclusion

This survey tracked the evolution of reranking algorithms from foundational Learning to Rank (LTR) methods, which established principles for optimizing result order, through the transformative impact of deep learning that enabled sophisticated pattern capture and list-wise modeling. We then examined how knowledge distillation became crucial for deploying complex models efficiently, and finally, explored the emerging role of LLMs, which offer potential for deeper semantic understanding. However, current rerankers, particularly those leveraging deep learning and LLMs, grapple with challenges such as substantial computational overhead, making real-time deployment in high-throughput systems difficult. Furthermore, issues related to bias amplification and the need for extensive, high-quality labeled data remain significant hurdles in achieving robust and fair reranking performance across diverse queries and contexts. This development demonstrates an ongoing push for more efficient and contextually sensitive result ordering, with future research probably concentrating on combining these approaches and tackling the real-world difficulties of implementing sophisticated rerankers.

References

1. What Are Rerankers and How Do They Enhance Information Retrieval? (2024). url: https://zilliz.com/learn/what-are-rerankers-enhanceinformation-retrieval
2. Rerankers and Two-Stage Retrieval. url: https://www.pinecone.io/learn/series/rag/rerankers/
3. Yunfan, G., et al.: Retrieval-augmented generation for large language models: a survey (2024). arXiv: 2312. 10997 [cs.CL]. url: https://arxiv.org/abs/2312.10997
4. Norbert, F.: Optimum polynomial retrieval functions based on the prob ability ranking principle. In: ACM Trans. Inf. Syst. 7. pp. 183– 204 3 (1989). ISSN: 1046-8188. https://doi.org/10.1145/65943.65944
5. William, S.C., Fredric, C.G., Daniel, P.D.: Probabilistic retrieval based on staged logistic regression. In: Proceedings of the 15th Annual International ACM SIGIR Conference on Research and Development in Information Retrieval. SIGIR '92. Copenhagen, Denmark: Association for Computing Machinery, pp. 198–210 (1992). ISBN: 0897915232. https://doi.org/10.1145/133160.133199
6. Brian, T.B., Garrison, W.C., Richard, K.B.: Automatic combination of multiple ranked retrieval systems. In: Proceedings of the 17th Annual International ACM SIGIR Conference on Research and Development in Information Retrieval. SIGIR '94. Dublin, Ireland: Springer-Verlag, pp. 173–181 (1994). ISBN: 038719889X
7. Jerome, H.F.: Greedy function approximation: a gradient boosting machine. In: The Annals of Statistics 29.5 pp. 1189–1232 (2001). ISSN: 00905364, 21688966. url: http://www.jstor.org/stable/2699986 (visited on 05 Nov 2025)
8. Yoav, F., et al.: An efficient boosting algorithm for combining preferences. In: J. Mach. Learn. Res. 4.null pp. 933–969 (Dec 2003). ISSN: 1532–4435
9. Chris, B., et al.: Learning to rank using gradient descent. In: Proceedings of the 22nd International Conference on Machine Learning. ICML '05. Bonn, Germany: Association for Computing Machinery, pp. 89–96 (2005). ISBN: 1595931805. https://doi.org/10.1145/1102351.1102363
10. Yunbo, C., et al.: Adapting ranking SVM to document retrieval. In: Proceedings of the 29th Annual International ACM SIGIR Conference on Research and Development in Information Retrieval. SIGIR '06. Seattle, Washington, USA: Association for Computing Machinery, pp. 186–193 (2006). ISBN: 1595933697. https://doi.org/10.1145/1148170.1148205

11. Christopher, B., Robert, R., Quoc, L.: Learning to rank with nonsmooth cost functions. In: pp. 193–200 (2006)
12. Tapio, P., et al.: Learning to rank with pairwise regularized least squares. In: SIGIR 2007 Workshop on Learning to Rank for Information Retrieval (2007)
13. Yisong, Y., et al.: A support vector method for optimizing average precision. In: Proceedings of the 30th Annual International ACM SIGIR Conference on Research and Development in Information Retrieval. SIGIR '07. Amsterdam, The Netherlands: Association for Computing Machinery, pp. 271–278 (2007). ISBN: 9781595935977. https://doi.org/10.1145/1277741.1277790
14. Zhe, C., et al.: Learning to rank: from pairwise approach to listwise approach. Tech. rep. MSR-TR-2007-40. p. 9 (2007). url: https://www.microsoft.com/en-us/research/publication/learning-to-rank-from-pairwise-approach-to-listwise-approach/
15. Tao, Q., et al.: Query-level loss functions for information retrieval. In: Information Processing & Management 44.2. Evaluating Exploratory Search Systems Digital Libraries in the Context of Users' Broader Activities, pp. 838–855 (2008). ISSN: 0306–4573. https://doi.org/10.1016/j.ipm.2007.07.016. url: https://www.sciencedirect.com/science/article/pii/S0306457307001276
16. Ming-feng, T., et al.: FRank: a ranking method with fidelity loss. Tech. rep. MSR-TR-2006-155. p. 10 (2006). url: https://www.microsoft.com/en-us/research/publication/frank-a-ranking-method-with fidelity-loss/
17. Jun, X., Hang, L.: AdaRank: a boosting algorithm for information retrieval. In: Proceedings of the 30th Annual International ACM SIGIR Conference on Research and Development in Information Retrieval. SIGIR '07. Amsterdam, The Netherlands: Association for Computing Machinery, pp. 391–398 (2007). ISBN: 9781595935977. https://doi.org/10.1145/1277741.1277809
18. Fen, X., et al.: Listwise approach to learning to rank: theory and algorithm. In: Proceedings of the 25th International Conference on Machine Learning. ICML '08. Helsinki, Finland: Association for Computing Machinery, pp. 1192–1199 (2008). ISBN: 9781605582054. https://doi.org/10.1145/1390156.1390306
19. Chris, J.C.B., et al.: Ranking, boosting, and model adaptation. Tech. rep. MSR-TR-2008-109. p. 18 (2008). url: https://www.microsoft.com/en-us/research/publication/ranking-boosting-and-modeladaptation/
20. Tianqi, C., Carlos, G.: XGBoost: a scalable tree boosting system. In: Proceedings of the 22nd ACM SIGKDD International Conference on Knowledge Discovery and Data Mining. KDD '16. ACM, pp. 785–794 (2016). https://doi.org/10.1145/2939672.2939785
21. Florian, S., Dmitry, K., James, P.: FaceNet: a unified embedding for face recognition and clustering. In: 2015 IEEE Conference on Computer Vision and Pattern Recognition (CVPR). IEEE, pp. 815–823 (2015). https://doi.org/10.1109/CVPR.2015.7298682
22. Qingyao, A., et al.: Learning a deep listwise context model for ranking refinement. In: The 41st International ACM SIGIR Conference on Research & Development in Information Retrieval. SIGIR'18. Ann Arbor, MI, USA: Association for Computing Machinery, pp. 135–144 (2018). ISBN: 9781450356572. https://doi.org/10.1145/3209978.3209985
23. Liang, P., et al.: SetRank: learning a permutation-invariant ranking model for information retrieval. In: Proceedings of the 43rd International ACM SIGIR Conference on Research and Development in Information Retrieval. SIGIR '20. Virtual Event, China: Association for Computing Machinery, pp. 499–508 (2020). ISBN: 9781450380164. url: https://doi.org/10.1145/3397271.3401104
24. Changhua, P., et al.: Personalized re-ranking for recommendation (2019). arXiv: 1904.06813 [cs.IR]. url: https://arxiv.org/abs/1904.06813

25. Marius, K., et al.: Pairwise learning to rank by neural networks revisited: reconstruction, theoretical analysis and practical performance (2019). arXiv: 1909.02768 [cs.IR]. url: https://arxiv.org/abs/1909.02768
26. Fatih, C., et al.: Deep metric learning to rank. In: 2019 IEEE/CVF Conference on Computer Vision and Pattern Recognition (CVPR). pp. 1861–1870 (2019). https://doi.org/10.1109/CVPR.2019.00196
27. Robin, S., et al.: PiRank: scalable learning to rank via differentiable sorting (2021). arXiv: 2012.06731 [cs.LG]. url: https://arxiv.org/abs/2012.06731
28. Jen-Yuan, Y., et al.: Learning to rank for information retrieval using genetic programming. In: Proceedings of ACM SIGIR 2007 Workshop on Learning to Rank for Information Retrieval (2012). 10.1109/ CyberneticsCom.2012.6381614
29. Osman, A.S.I., Dario, L.-S.: ES-Rank: evolution strategy learning to rank approach. In: Proceedings of the Symposium on Applied Computing. SAC'17. Marrakech, Morocco: Association for Computing Machinery, pp. 944–950 (2017). ISBN: 9781450344869. https://doi.org/10.1145/3019612.3019696
30. Ping, L., Chris, J.C.B., Qiang, W.: Learning to rank using classification and gradient boosting. Tech. Rep. MSR-TR-2007-74. Advances in Neural Information Processing Systems 20. (2008). url: https: //www.microsoft.com/en-us/research/publication/learning-to rank-using-classification-and-gradient-boosting/
31. Chenguang, Z., et al.: A general magnitude-preserving boosting algorithm for search ranking. In: Proceedings of the 18th ACM Conference on Information and Knowledge Management. CIKM'09. Hong Kong, China: Association for Computing Machinery, pp. 817–826 (2009). ISBN: 9781605585123. https://doi.org/10.1145/1645953.1646057
32. Sculley, D.: Combined regression and ranking. In: Proceedings of the 16th ACM SIGKDD International Conference on Knowledge Discovery and Data Mining. KDD '10. Washington, DC, USA: Association for Computing Machinery, pp. 979–988 (2010). ISBN: 9781450300551. https://doi.org/10.1145/1835804.1835928
33. Jacob, D., et al.: BERT: pre-training of deep bidirectional transformers for language understanding (2019). arXiv: 1810.04805 [cs.CL]. url: https://arxiv.org/abs/1810.04805
34. Ashish, V., et al.: Attention is all you need (2023). arXiv: 1706.03762 [cs.CL]. url: https://arxiv.org/abs/1706.03762
35. Rodrigo, N., et al.: Multi-stage document ranking with BERT (2019). arXiv: 1910.14424 [cs.IR]. url: https://arxiv.org/abs/1910.14424
36. Michael, G., et al.: Re2G: retrieve, rerank, generate (2022). arXiv: 2207.06300 [cs.CL]. url: https://arxiv.org/abs/2207.06300
37. Payal, B., et al.: MS MARCO: a human generated MAchine reading comprehension dataset (2018). arXiv: 1611.09268 [cs.CL]. url: https://arxiv.org/abs/1611.09268
38. Omar, K., Matei, Z.: ColBERT: efficient and effective passage search via contextualized late interaction over BERT (2020). arXiv: 2004.12832 [cs.IR]. url: https://arxiv.org/abs/2004.12832
39. Robert, L., Ivan, V., Goran, G.: Parameter-efficient neural reranking for cross-lingual and multilingual retrieval (2022). arXiv: 2204.02292 [cs.CL]. url: https://arxiv.org/abs/2204.02292
40. Chang, T.A., et al.: When is multilinguality a curse? Language modeling for 250 high-and low-resource languages (2023). arXiv: 2311.09205 [cs.CL]. url: https://arxiv.org/abs/2311.09205
41. Raffel, C., et al.: Exploring the limits of transfer learning with a unified text-to-text transformer (2023). arXiv: 1910.10683 [cs.LG]. url: https: //arxiv.org/abs/1910.10683
42. Nogueira, R., Jiang, Z., Lin, J.: Document ranking with a pretrained sequence-to-sequence model (2020). arXiv: 2003.06713 [cs.IR]. url: https://arxiv.org/abs/2003.06713

43. Zhuang, H., et al.: RankT5: fine-tuning T5 for text ranking with ranking losses (2022). arXiv: 2210.10634 [cs.IR]. url: https://arxiv.org/abs/2210.10634
44. Ju, J.-H., Yang, J.-H., Wang, C.-J.: Text-to-text multi view learning for passage re-ranking (2022). arXiv: 2104.14133 [cs.IR]. url: https://arxiv.org/abs/2104.14133
45. Yoon, S., et al.: ListT5: listwise reranking with fusion-in-decoder improves zero-shot retrieval (2024). arXiv: 2402.15838 [cs.IR]. url: https://arxiv.org/abs/2402.15838
46. Liu, N.F., et al.: Lost in the middle: how language models use long contexts (2023). arXiv: 2307.03172 [cs.CL]. url: https://arxiv.org/ abs/2307.03172
47. Song, J., et al.: Comparing neighbors together makes it easy: jointly comparing multiple candidates for efficient and effective retrieval (2024). arXiv: 2405.12801 [cs.CL]. url: https://arxiv.org/abs/2405.12801
48. Liu, J., et al.: ListConRanker: a contrastive text reranker with list wise encoding (2025). arXiv: 2501.07111 [cs.CL]. url: https://arxiv.org/abs/2501.07111
49. Sun, Y., et al.: Circle loss: a unified perspective of pair similarity optimization (2020). arXiv: 2002.10857 [cs.CV]. url: https://arxiv.org/abs/2002.10857
50. Dong, J., et al.: Don't forget to connect! improving RAG with graph based reranking (2024). arXiv: 2405.18414 [cs.CL]. url: https://arxiv.org/abs/2405.18414
51. Zhang, S., et al.: Graph convolutional networks: a comprehensive review. In: Computational Social Networks 6 (2019). https://doi.org/10.1186/s40649- 019–0069-y
52. Xu, Z.: RankMamba: benchmarking mamba's document ranking performance in the era of transformers (2024). arXiv: 2403.18276 [cs.IR]. url: https://arxiv.org/abs/2403.18276
53. Gu, A., Dao, T.: Mamba: linear-time sequence modeling with selective state spaces (2024). arXiv: 2312.00752 [cs.LG]. url: https: //arxiv.org/abs/2312.00752
54. Kang, M., et al.: Knowledge-augmented reasoning distillation for small language models in knowledge-intensive tasks (2023). arXiv: 2305.18395 [cs.CL]. url: https://arxiv.org/abs/2305.18395
55. Jia, P., et al.: Bridging relevance and reasoning: rationale distillation in retrieval-augmented generation (2024). arXiv: 2412.08519 [cs.CL]. url: https://arxiv.org/abs/2412.08519
56. Ji, Y., et al.: ReasoningRank: teaching student models to rank through reasoning-based knowledge distillation (2025). arXiv: 2410.05168 [cs.CL]. url: https://arxiv.org/abs/2410.05168
57. Samarinas, C., Zamani, H.: Distillation and refinement of reasoning in small language models for document re-ranking (2025). arXiv: 2504.03947 [cs.IR]. url: https://arxiv.org/abs/2504.03947
58. Hinton, G., Vinyals, O., Dean, J.: Distilling the knowledge in a neural network (2015). arXiv: 1503.02531 [stat.ML]. url: https://arxiv.org/abs/1503.02531
59. Yang, Y., et al.: Balanced knowledge distillation with contrastive learning for document re-ranking. In: Proceedings of the 2023 ACM SI GIR International Conference on Theory of Information Retrieval. ICTIR '23. Taipei, Taiwan: Association for Computing Machinery, pp. 247–255 (2023). ISBN: 9798400700736. https://doi.org/10.1145/3578337.3605120
60. Csiszar, I.: I-divergence geometry of probability distributions and minimization problems. In: The Annals of Probability 3.1. pp. 146–158 (1975). https://doi.org/10.1214/aop/1176996454
61. Weller, O., et al.: Rank1: test-time compute for reranking in information retrieval (2025). arXiv: 2502.18418 [cs.IR]. url: https://arxiv.org/abs/2502.18418
62. Sun, W., et al.: Is ChatGPT good at search? Investigating large language models as re-ranking agents (2024). arXiv: 2304.09542 [cs.CL]. url: https://arxiv.org/abs/2304.09542
63. Pradeep, R., Sharifymoghaddam, S., Lin, J.: RankVicuna: zero-shot listwise document reranking with open-source large language models (2023). arXiv: 2309.15088 [cs.IR]. url: https://arxiv.org/abs/2309.15088

64. Pradeep, R., Sharifymoghaddam, S., Lin, J.: RankZephyr: effective and robust zero-shot listwise reranking is a Breeze! (2023). arXiv: 2312.02724 [cs.IR]. url: https://arxiv.org/abs/2312.02724
65. Ma, X., et al.: Zero-shot listwise document reranking with a large language model (2023). arXiv: 2305.02156 [cs.IR]. url: https://arxiv.org/abs/2305.02156
66. Sun, S., et al.: An investigation of prompt variations for zero-shot LLM-based rankers (2025). arXiv: 2406.14117 [cs.IR]. url: https://arxiv.org/abs/2406.14117
67. OpenAI Team. GPT-4 Technical Report (2024). arXiv: 2303.08774 [cs.CL]. url: https://arxiv.org/abs/2303.08774
68. Rathee, M., MacAvaney, S., Anand, A.: Guiding retrieval using LLM-based Listwise Rankers (2025). arXiv: 2501.09186 [cs.IR]. url: https://arxiv.org/abs/2501.09186
69. Bai, Z., et al.: Finetuning large language model for personalized ranking (2024). arXiv: 2405.16127 [cs.IR]. url: https://arxiv.org/abs/2405.16127
70. Ma, X., et al.: Fine-tuning LLaMA for multi-stage text retrieval (2023). arXiv: 2310.08319 [cs.IR]. url: https://arxiv.org/abs/2310.08319
71. Touvron, H., et al.: LLaMA: open and efficient foundation language models (2023). arXiv: 2302.13971 [cs.CL]. url: https://arxiv.org/abs/2302.13971
72. Zhang, L., et al.: A two-stage adaptation of large language models for text ranking (2024). arXiv: 2311.16720 [cs.IR]. url: https://arxiv.org/abs/2311.16720
73. Huang, C.-W., Chen, Y.-N.: InstUPR: instruction-based unsupervised passage reranking with large language models (2024). arXiv: 2403.16435 [cs.CL]. url: https://arxiv.org/abs/2403.16435
74. Luo, J., et al.: PRP-Graph: pairwise ranking prompting to LLMs with graph aggregation for effective text re-ranking. In: Proceedings of the 62nd Annual Meeting of the Association for Computational Linguistics (Volume 1: Long Papers). Ed. by Lun-Wei Ku, Andre Martins, and Vivek Srikumar. Bangkok, Thailand: Association for Computational Linguistics, pp. 5766–5776 (2024). https://doi.org/10.18653/v1/2024.acl-long.313
75. Zhang, X., et al.: Rank-without-GPT: building GPT-Independent listwise rerankers on open-source large language models (2023). arXiv: 2312. 02969 [cs.CL]. url: https://arxiv.org/abs/2312.02969
76. Rozière, B., et al.: Code Llama: open foundation models for code (2024). arXiv: 2308.12950 [cs.CL]. url: https://arxiv.org/abs/2308.12950
77. Can, J., et al.: APEER: automatic prompt engineering enhances large language model reranking (2024). arXiv: 2406.14449 [cs.AI]. url: https: //arxiv.org/abs/2406.14449
78. Xuyang, W., et al.: Passage-specific prompt tuning for passage reranking in question answering with large language models (2024). arXiv: 2405.20654 [cs.CL]. url: https://arxiv.org/abs/2405.20654

A Quantitative Analysis of the Relationship Between Hakka and Gan Dialects

Yao Luo and Nankai Wu(✉)

Department of Chinese Language and Literature, Jinan University, Guangzhou, China
wnk1219583487@foxmail.com

Abstract. The relationship between Hakka and Gan dialects is a classic issue in dialect classification. Since the 1930s, many scholars have conducted detailed and in-depth discussions on this issue. Even the study of Gan dialect is largely based on the comparison of Hakka and Gan dialects. This paper examined and determined the relationship between Hakka and Gan dialects using Analytic Hierarchy Process (AHP), hierarchical clustering analysis, and Multidimensional Scaling (MDS). We conducted a quantitative analysis of 22 Hakka and Gan dialect phonetic materials. The phonetic features were weighted using AHP to obtain the average parameters. The average parameter matrix of the dialect points was then subjected to hierarchical clustering analysis and MDS analysis, yielding dendrograms and MDS distance models. The results indicate that the Gan and Hakka dialect groups are interwoven and intermingled, with no significant statistical evidence supporting the independence of the two dialect groups.

Keywords: Hakka and Gan Dialects · Analytic Hierarchy Process (AHP) · Quantitative Analysis

1 Introduction

The relationship between Hakka and Gan dialects is a classic issue in dialect classification. Since the 1930s, many scholars have conducted detailed and in-depth discussions on this issue. Even the study of Gan dialect is largely based on the comparison of Hakka and Gan dialects. Previous studies on the comparison of Hakka and Gan dialects mostly started with qualitative descriptions and feature comparisons. For example, the important criterion for distinguishing Hakka and Gan dialects is that all or part of the ancient voiced characters in Hakka dialects are classified as Yin Ping, while Gan dialects have almost none. This is a very typical feature comparison. Some scholars have also used non linguistic standards to compare and distinguish between the Hakka and Gan dialects. Whether it is qualitative description, feature comparison, or non linguistic standards, it is easy to generalize and cannot provide a comprehensive and systematic satisfactory answer to this question.

The quantitative study of language has gained popularity in international linguistic research. Since the 1970s, scholars have quantitatively compared the synchronic characteristics and diachronic evolution of Chinese and its dialects from a systematic

X. Ding and Y. Dong (Eds.): CLNLP 2025, CCIS 2775, pp. 68–79, 2026.
https://doi.org/10.1007/978-981-95-4788-3_7

perspective. This approach explores the similarities and differences among dialects, and measures the distance and degree of affinity between them. Researchers have employed several methods, including correlation coefficient statistics (Zheng Jinquan, 1973 [1]; Lu Zhiji, 1987 [2]; Zheng Jinquan, 1988 [3]), lexical statistics (Deng Xiaohua & Wang Shiyuan, 2003 [4, 5] /2007 [6]), edit distance method (Jiang Di, 2022 [7]; Zhao Zhijing, 2018 [8]), Bayesian phylogenetics (Gray & Atkinson, 2003 [9]; Greenhill, 2008 [10]; Zhang Menghan, 2019 [11]), and phonetic relationship analysis (Li Zihe, 2013 [12]; Wu Nankai, 2020 [13]). Building on prior research, this study further expands the materials and methods used in conducting a quantitative analysis of dialects. It employs the Analytic Hierarchy Process (AHP), hierarchical clustering analysis, and Multidimensional Scaling (MDS) to quantitatively analyze and classify 22 Hakka and Gan dialect phonetic materials, through a comparative analysis.

2 Overview of Hakka and Gan Dialects

The term "Gan dialect" emerged relatively late. In 1936, *Luo Changpei* [14] first discussed "Hakka and Gan dialects" in *The Lianchuan Phonological System*, suggesting that they belonged to the same linguistic family but represented different branches. In 1948, *the Academia Sinica's Institute of History and Philology* published the fifth edition of the *New Atlas of China*, which for the first time classified Gan dialect as an independent linguistic unit. Gan dialects are mainly spoken in the central and northern parts of Jiangxi Province—along the middle and lower Gan River, the Fu River basin, and the Poyang Lake region—and in eastern Hunan, southeastern Hubei, southwestern Anhui, and northwestern Fujian.

Meanwhile, Hakka dialects are widely spoken in eastern and northern Guangdong, Taiwan Province, western Fujian, and southern Jiangxi. They are also spoken in parts of western Guangdong, western Guangxi, Sichuan, Hunan, Hong Kong Special Administrative Region, Hainan, and nine other provinces and regions, spanning over 200 counties and cities. Globally, Hakka is spoken in Malaysia, Singapore, Indonesia, the Americas, Africa, and over 80 other countries and regions due to the migration of Hakka communities.

The relationship between Hakka and Gan dialects has been a central issue in dialect classification since the 1930s, drawing extensive discussions on the topic. Scholars, such as *Yuan Jiahua (1960)* [15], *Hashimoto Mantaro (1973)* [16], *Zhan Bohui (1981)* [17], *Luo Xianglin (1989)* [18], *He Da'an (1987)* [19], *Li RuLong (1992)* [20], and *Huang Xiaoping (2011)* [21], advocate classifying Hakka and Gan dialects into distinct categories. Conversely, scholars like *Li Rong (1956)* [22], *Liu Lunxin (1998)* [23], *Wang Futang (1998)* [24], *and Liu Zemin (2004)* [25] support grouping them under a single major dialect. While most scholars support their separation, it must be acknowledged that these dialects have long coexisted in Jiangxi and exhibit several phonetic similarities. To date, no single phonetic feature has been identified that can consistently and exclusively differentiate between the two.

Given the ongoing controversy surrounding the relationship between Hakka and Gan dialects, this study aims to provide a more scientific and objective explanation through quantitative analysis, thereby advancing the understanding of their relationship.

3 Materials and Methods

3.1 Sources and Objects of the Materials

We derived the data regarding the Hakka and Gan dialect from the author's field investigations. I included Hakka and Gan dialects within Jiangxi Province, and Meixian dialect in Guangdong. The sample comprises 22 dialect points in total—11 from the Gan and Hakka group each. These are as follows:

Gan dialects: Nanchang, Lushan, Yongxiu, Tonggu Gan, Fengcheng, Xinyu, Jinxian, Nanfeng, Yongxin, Suichuan Gan, and Yujiang.

Hakka dialects: Dayu, Nankang, Shangyou, Ganxian, Suichuan Hakka, Quannan, Xinfeng, Xingguo, Xunwu, and Tonggu Hakka.

This study examined phonetic features to quantitatively compare and determine the relationship between Hakka and Gan dialects. Through a qualitative and quantitative analysis of the initial consonants, vowels, and tones of the 22 dialect points, We identified 57 phonetic features, encompassing historical phonetic features and contemporary phonetic values. The phonetic features are quantified using specific proportional values. For example, for the phonetic feature "The proportional rate of phonological convergence between Middle Chinese voiced obstruents and their homorganic aspirated voiceless counterparts," I calculated the specific proportions for each dialect point. The following are the values for the Gan dialects (Table 1):

Table 1. The proportional rate of phonological convergence between Middle Chinese voiced obstruents and their homorganic aspirated voiceless counterparts.

Nanchang	Jinxian	Fengcheng	Lushan	Suichuan Gan	Tonggu Gan	Yongxin	Yongxiu	Nanfeng	Xinyu	Yujiang
93.5%	88.2%	75.8%	87.2%	74.5%	79.8%	61.6%	83.3%	79.7%	84.5%	73.7%

3.2 Quantitative Methods

Analytics Hierarchy Process (AHP). The Analytic Hierarchy Process (AHP) is a decision-making method that decomposes elements related to a decision into a hierarchical structure of objectives, criteria, and alternatives [26]. It combines qualitative and quantitative analysis to determine the relative importance of each element through pairwise comparisons. It comprises the following steps:

1. Establish a hierarchical structure model.
2. Construct a pairwise comparison matrix.
3. Conduct a single-level sorting and consistency check.
4. Perform a total-level sorting and consistency check.

Hierarchical Clustering Analysis. Clustering is an unsupervised learning process that groups objects based on their features, aiming to minimize the differences within clusters and maximize the differences between clusters. For a sample set of 22 dialect points, hierarchical clustering analysis—also known as agglomerative clustering— is used. It merges the closest clusters iteratively until all objects form a single cluster. The process involves the following steps:

1. Treat each object as a separate cluster.
2. Calculate the distances between clusters and merge the closest pair.
3. Recalculate the distances between the new cluster and the remaining clusters.
4. Repeat the process until all objects are merged into one cluster.

The Euclidean distance is commonly used in hierarchical clustering. It is defined as the square root of the sum of the squares of the differences between corresponding elements of two vectors. The formula is:

$$d_{ij} = \sqrt{,_{k=1}^{m}, \text{Ää}, \text{Ää} \left(x_{ki} - x_{kj}\right)^2} = \left[\left(x_i - x_j\right)^T\left(x_i - x_j\right)\right]^{\frac{1}{2}}, (i, j = 1, 2, \text{Ä¶}, n) \quad (1)$$

For example, in our quantitative analysis of phonetic features, I used a 22*57 information matrix, where the column vectors represent the data manifestations of each sample regarding the j-th feature.

Hierarchical clustering results in a dendrogram, which visually represents the hierarchical relationships of phonetic similarities among dialect points. However, this method has certain limitations. Hierarchical clustering can be sensitive to data variations, potentially leading to individual data points being clustered differently from traditional classifications, thereby affecting the interpretation.

Multidimensional Scaling (MDS). Multidimensional Scaling (MDS) estimates the coordinates of a set of objects in a space of a specified dimensionality based on pairwise distances between objects (He Xiaorong, 2010). It maps complex multidimensional relationships on to a lower-dimensional space—typically two-dimensional—while preserving the original relationships among objects. This method is well-suited for macro-level comparisons of Hakka and Gan dialects based on phonetic similarities.

MDS visually presents complex data relationships on a two-dimensional coordinate plane, reflecting the similarity between objects: the closer the points, the greater the similarity in properties. However, MDS results are not unique; they can be translated, rotated, or subjectively categorized within the space.

MDS is categorized into metric and non-metric MDS. Metric MDS is suitable for similarity data with actual numerical values, while non-metric MDS is appropriate for similarity data with only ordinal information. As the matrix obtained in this study represents phonetic similarity distances between dialect points—rather than actual geographical distances— non-metric MDS is used for the analysis.

4 Analysis and Results

First, we examine the results of the AHP method, which evaluates the 57 phonetic features of the 22 dialect points.

The process begins with the establishment of a hierarchical structure model. It breaks down the decision-making problem into several levels namely the objective, criterion, and alternative levels. The objective level represents the ultimate goal of the decision or the problem to be addressed, the criterion level includes key factors influencing the decision, and the alternative level lists all feasible options. In this study, the 22 dialect points and their 57 phonetic features are treated as the criterion level, with the 57 phonetic features collectively influencing the decision.

Next, a pairwise comparison matrix is constructed. Given the large size of the 57ptions. In this study, the 22 dialect points and their 57 phonetic features are treated as the criterion level, with the 5relative importance to the objective level. The resulting matrix has diagonal elements equal to 1 and other elements representing the relative importance of the factors. Features with higher average values across the 22 dialect points are assigned higher weights. For example, Feature X1, "the merger of ancient fully voiced initial consonants with corresponding aspirated initial consonants," has an average proportion exceeding 70% across all dialect points, indicating high importance and a higher weight. In contrast, Feature X2, "the reading of ancient partially voiced checked tones as yin tones," averages below 35% across all dialect points, indicating lower importance and a lower weight.

Subsequently, the single-level sorting process determines the weights of each indicator based on the constructed comparison matrix. Features with higher average values across the 22 dialect points are assigned higher weights. The weighted results are as follows (Tables 2 and 3):

Table 2. AHP results.

Feature	Eigenvector	Weight Value	Maximum Eigenvalue	CI Value
X1	3.996	7.01%	57	0.03
X2	0.571	2.00%		
X3	0.813	1.72%		
X4	0.475	0.83%		
X5	0.411	0.72%		
X6	0.195	0.34%		
X7	0.447	0.79%		
X8	2.37	4.96%		
X9	1.826	3.40%		
X10	0.678	1.19%		
X11	0.566	0.99%		
X12	0.119	0.21%		
X13	0.343	0.60%		
X14	1.456	2.56%		
Y1	0.235	0.41%		
Y2	0.42	0.74%		
Y3	0.053	0.09%		
Y4	0.555	0.97%		

(continued)

Table 2. *(continued)*

Feature	Eigenvector	Weight Value	Maximum Eigenvalue	CI Value
Y5	4.023	7.06%		
Y6	0.771	1.35%		
Y7	0.48	0.84%		
Y8	0.542	0.95%		
Y9	1.278	2.24%		
Y10	1.704	2.99%		
Y11	2.908	5.10%		
Y12	0.17	0.30%		
Y13	0.069	0.12%		
Y14	0.294	0.52%		
Y15	0.33	0.58%		
Y16	3.145	5.52%		
Y17	1.191	2.09%		
Y18	2.985	5.24%		
Y19	5.033	8.83%		
Y20	5.033	8.83%		
Y21	0.069	0.12%		
Y22	0.263	0.46%		
Y23	0.046	0.08%		
Y24	0.069	0.12%		
Y25	0.332	0.58%		
Y26	0.232	0.41%		
Y27	0.023	0.04%		
Y28	0.135	0.24%		
Y29	0.717	1.26%		
Y30	0.393	0.44%		
Y31	0.196	0.22%		
Z1	0.39	0.68%		
Z2	0.461	0.51%		
Z3	0.795	1.40%		
Z4	5.033	8.83%		
Z5	0.131	0.23%		
Z6	0.081	0.14%		
Z7	0.023	0.04%		

(continued)

Table 2. (*continued*)

Feature	Eigenvector	Weight Value	Maximum Eigenvalue	CI Value
Z8	0.046	0.08%		
Z9	0.092	0.16%		
Z10	0.172	0.30%		
Z11	0.389	0.68%		
Z12	0.389	0.68%		

Finally, a consistency check is performed. The results are as follows:

Table 3. Consistency check results.

Consistency Check Results				
Maximum Eigenvalue	CIValue	RIValue	CRValue	Consistency Check Result
57	0.03	1.712	0	Passed

The weighted comprehensive index matrix obtained from the AHP method is presented in Tables 4 and 5 for Gan and Hakka dialects, respectively:

Table 4. Comprehensive Index Matrix – Gan Dialects.

	Nanchang	Jinxian	Fengcheng	Lushan	Suichuan	Tonggu	Yongxin	Yongxiu	Nanfeng	Xinyu	Yujiang
X1	0.0656	0.0618	0.0531	0.0611	0.0523	0.0559	0.0432	0.0584	0.0559	0.0592	0.0516
X2	0.0000	0.0001	0.0002	0.0000	0.0002	0.0001	0.0008	0.0000	0.0054	0.0010	0.0002
X3	0.0000	0.0002	0.0007	0.0000	0.0010	0.0001	0.0007	0.0000	0.0014	0.0002	0.0011
X4	0.0004	0.0007	0.0006	0.0005	0.0005	0.0005	0.0007	0.0006	0.0006	0.0004	0.0005
X5	0.0001	0.0001	0.0002	0.0002	0.0004	0.0002	0.0007	0.0008	0.0001	0.0000	0.0001
X6	0.0000	0.0007	0.0000	0.0000	0.0000	0.0000	0.0000	0.0000	0.0019	0.0003	0.0000
X7	0.0018	0.0018	0.0017	0.0019	0.0001	0.0005	0.0002	0.0017	0.0007	0.0018	0.0018
X8	0.0273	0.0269	0.0274	0.0206	0.0274	0.0256	0.0268	0.0244	0.0261	0.0239	0.0217
X9	0.0175	0.0163	0.0180	0.0011	0.0195	0.0181	0.0168	0.0180	0.0000	0.0008	0.0000
X10	0.0000	0.0081	0.0000	0.0033	0.0002	0.0002	0.0028	0.0032	0.0036	0.0047	0.0086
X11	0.0005	0.0007	0.0000	0.0001	0.0012	0.0000	0.0023	0.0002	0.0035	0.0040	0.0000
X12	0.0000	0.0000	0.0000	0.0000	0.0001	0.0001	0.0000	0.0000	0.0000	0.0000	0.0000
X13	0.0015	0.0000	0.0000	0.0008	0.0008	0.0000	0.0000	0.0030	0.0015	0.0015	0.0000
X14	0.0122	0.0105	0.0092	0.0063	0.0059	0.0071	0.0059	0.0129	0.0027	0.0079	0.0115
Y1	0.0001	0.0004	0.0002	0.0001	0.0001	0.0002	0.0001	0.0002	0.0002	0.0001	0.0004
Y2	0.0005	0.0003	0.0006	0.0006	0.0007	0.0007	0.0006	0.0007	0.0004	0.0004	0.0003
Y3	0.0000	0.0000	0.0000	0.0002	0.0000	0.0000	0.0000	0.0000	0.0000	0.0000	0.0000
Y4	0.0007	0.0009	0.0010	0.0015	0.0007	0.0008	0.0004	0.0012	0.0009	0.0011	0.0006
Y5	0.0595	0.0510	0.0582	0.0601	0.0529	0.0523	0.0516	0.0542	0.0590	0.0575	0.0534
Y6	0.0014	0.0014	0.0014	0.0014	0.0014	0.0014	0.0014	0.0014	0.0054	0.0039	0.0043
Y7	0.0025	0.0004	0.0025	0.0002	0.0036	0.0003	0.0012	0.0025	0.0002	0.0022	0.0002
Y8	0.0001	0.0003	0.0000	0.0054	0.0007	0.0000	0.0001	0.0000	0.0000	0.0054	0.0000

(*continued*)

Table 4. *(continued)*

	Nanchang	Jinxian	Fengcheng	Lushan	Suichuan	Tonggu	Yongxin	Yongxiu	Nanfeng	Xinyu	Yujiang
Y9	0.0080	0.0072	0.0069	0.0062	0.0010	0.0068	0.0072	0.0073	0.0081	0.0000	0.0090
Y10	0.0029	0.0124	0.0058	0.0044	0.0146	0.0087	0.0044	0.0036	0.0100	0.0040	0.0075
Y11	0.0390	0.0361	0.0350	0.0344	0.0189	0.0281	0.0149	0.0292	0.0350	0.0381	0.0348
Y12	0.0001	0.0003	0.0001	0.0000	0.0001	0.0003	0.0000	0.0001	0.0002	0.0001	0.0001
Y13	0.0000	0.0000	0.0000	0.0000	0.0000	0.0000	0.0000	0.0000	0.0000	0.0000	0.0000
Y14	0.0001	0.0017	0.0000	0.0001	0.0000	0.0001	0.0002	0.0002	0.0034	0.0002	0.0003
Y15	0.0004	0.0008	0.0002	0.0002	0.0000	0.0003	0.0002	0.0006	0.0014	0.0008	0.0005
Y16	0.0265	0.0302	0.0453	0.0265	0.0434	0.0265	0.0255	0.0265	0.0331	0.0392	0.0337
Y17	0.0073	0.0070	0.0061	0.0095	0.0033	0.0062	0.0056	0.0065	0.0058	0.0054	0.0073
Y18	0.0373	0.0374	0.0307	0.0362	0.0295	0.0347	0.0299	0.0311	0.0372	0.0354	0.0366
Y19	0.0883	0.0883	0.0883	0.0883	0.0883	0.0883	0.0883	0.0883	0.0883	0.0883	0.0883
Y20	0.0883	0.0883	0.0883	0.0883	0.0883	0.0883	0.0883	0.0883	0.0883	0.0883	0.0883
Y21	0.0000	0.0000	0.0000	0.0000	0.0001	0.0000	0.0000	0.0000	0.0000	0.0000	0.0000
Y22	0.0005	0.0005	0.0002	0.0005	0.0005	0.0005	0.0000	0.0005	0.0000	0.0005	0.0005
Y23	0.0000	0.0000	0.0000	0.0000	0.0000	0.0000	0.0000	0.0000	0.0000	0.0001	0.0000
Y24	0.0000	0.0000	0.0002	0.0000	0.0000	0.0000	0.0000	0.0000	0.0000	0.0000	0.0000
Y25	0.0006	0.0006	0.0006	0.0006	0.0006	0.0000	0.0003	0.0006	0.0000	0.0000	0.0006
Y26	0.0000	0.0000	0.0000	0.0000	0.0000	0.0000	0.0018	0.0000	0.0000	0.0015	0.0000
Y27	0.0000	0.0000	0.0000	0.0000	0.0000	0.0000	0.0000	0.0000	0.0000	0.0000	0.0000
Y28	0.0000	0.0000	0.0000	0.0000	0.0000	0.0000	0.0002	0.0000	0.0000	0.0000	0.0000
Y29	0.0002	0.0009	0.0011	0.0043	0.0030	0.0010	0.0049	0.0007	0.0005	0.0002	0.0007
Y30	0.0020	0.0017	0.0021	0.0020	0.0010	0.0026	0.0020	0.0031	0.0018	0.0039	0.0020
Y31	0.0005	0.0009	0.0003	0.0003	0.0001	0.0006	0.0003	0.0006	0.0006	0.0006	0.0004
Z1	0.0000	0.0000	0.0000	0.0060	0.0000	0.0000	0.0000	0.0057	0.0000	0.0000	0.0000
Z2	0.0000	0.0000	0.0000	0.0000	0.0000	0.0000	0.0003	0.0000	0.0004	0.0000	0.0000
Z3	0.0000	0.0000	0.0000	0.0102	0.0000	0.0111	0.0000	0.0027	0.0000	0.0000	0.0000
Z4	0.0883	0.0883	0.0883	0.0883	0.0883	0.0883	0.0883	0.0883	0.0883	0.0883	0.0883
Z5	0.0001	0.0001	0.0002	0.0000	0.0002	0.0000	0.0002	0.0000	0.0002	0.0000	0.0000
Z6	0.0000	0.0000	0.0000	0.0000	0.0001	0.0000	0.0001	0.0000	0.0000	0.0000	0.0000
Z7	0.0000	0.0000	0.0000	0.0000	0.0000	0.0000	0.0000	0.0000	0.0000	0.0000	0.0000
Z8	0.0001	0.0000	0.0000	0.0000	0.0000	0.0000	0.0000	0.0000	0.0000	0.0000	0.0000
Z9	0.0000	0.0002	0.0000	0.0000	0.0000	0.0002	0.0000	0.0002	0.0000	0.0000	0.0000
Z10	0.0000	0.0000	0.0003	0.0000	0.0000	0.0000	0.0000	0.0000	0.0000	0.0002	0.0003
Z11	0.0000	0.0000	0.0007	0.0007	0.0007	0.0000	0.0007	0.0007	0.0000	0.0007	0.0000
Z12	0.0007	0.0007	0.0000	0.0007	0.0000	0.0007	0.0007	0.0007	0.0000	0.0000	

Table 5. Comprehensive Index Matrix – Hakka Dialects.

	Dayu	Ganzhou	Nankang	Quannan	Shangyou	Suichuan	Tonggu	Xinfeng	Xingguo	Xunwu	Meixian
X1	0.0551	0.0511	0.0544	0.0583	0.0560	0.0506	0.0577	0.0543	0.0560	0.0547	0.0582
X2	0.0015	0.0014	0.0014	0.0013	0.0000	0.0023	0.0020	0.0002	0.0018	0.0018	0.0034
X3	0.0006	0.0007	0.0008	0.0010	0.0000	0.0010	0.0008	0.0002	0.0006	0.0009	0.0011
X4	0.0011	0.0009	0.0011	0.0010	0.0013	0.0009	0.0007	0.0011	0.0009	0.0012	0.0014
X5	0.0008	0.0008	0.0010	0.0009	0.0012	0.0010	0.0008	0.0009	0.0009	0.0007	0.0010
X6	0.0000	0.0000	0.0000	0.0000	0.0000	0.0000	0.0000	0.0000	0.0000	0.0000	0.0000

(continued)

Table 5. *(continued)*

	Dayu	Ganzhou	Nankang	Quannan	Shangyou	Suichuan	Tonggu	Xinfeng	Xingguo	Xunwu	Meixian
X7	0.0000	0.0000	0.0005	0.0000	0.0001	0.0000	0.0002	0.0001	0.0005	0.0001	0.0000
X8	0.0273	0.0280	0.0267	0.0275	0.0269	0.0266	0.0251	0.0230	0.0221	0.0025	0.0000
X9	0.0177	0.0171	0.0178	0.0172	0.0187	0.0166	0.0084	0.0123	0.0021	0.0177	0.0000
X10	0.0001	0.0000	0.0001	0.0000	0.0000	0.0000	0.0000	0.0000	0.0000	0.0000	0.0000
X11	0.0025	0.0004	0.0015	0.0012	0.0021	0.0005	0.0000	0.0005	0.0006	0.0027	0.0000
X12	0.0001	0.0001	0.0001	0.0001	0.0001	0.0001	0.0001	0.0000	0.0002	0.0001	0.0000
X13	0.0000	0.0000	0.0000	0.0000	0.0000	0.0000	0.0000	0.0000	0.0000	0.0000	0.0000
X14	0.0070	0.0055	0.0054	0.0088	0.0057	0.0056	0.0058	0.0081	0.0064	0.0065	0.0059
Y1	0.0002	0.0001	0.0002	0.0002	0.0003	0.0001	0.0002	0.0002	0.0004	0.0002	0.0001
Y2	0.0007	0.0007	0.0006	0.0008	0.0006	0.0007	0.0008	0.0008	0.0007	0.0007	0.0007
Y3	0.0000	0.0000	0.0000	0.0000	0.0000	0.0000	0.0000	0.0000	0.0000	0.0000	0.0000
Y4	0.0013	0.0012	0.0012	0.0012	0.0011	0.0009	0.0011	0.0016	0.0011	0.0013	0.0017
Y5	0.0555	0.0536	0.0582	0.0569	0.0595	0.0536	0.0562	0.0582	0.0562	0.0582	0.0654
Y6	0.0014	0.0014	0.0014	0.0014	0.0014	0.0014	0.0014	0.0014	0.0015	0.0036	0.0043
Y7	0.0012	0.0000	0.0000	0.0000	0.0006	0.0000	0.0000	0.0000	0.0000	0.0000	0.0000
Y8	0.0045	0.0001	0.0015	0.0001	0.0035	0.0000	0.0000	0.0009	0.0001	0.0000	0.0000
Y9	0.0020	0.0010	0.0019	0.0082	0.0017	0.0075	0.0073	0.0048	0.0068	0.0079	0.0085
Y10	0.0109	0.0117	0.0131	0.0168	0.0139	0.0117	0.0124	0.0109	0.0153	0.0131	0.0146
Y11	0.0224	0.0166	0.0269	0.0292	0.0275	0.0183	0.0292	0.0212	0.0287	0.0378	0.0470
Y12	0.0000	0.0001	0.0002	0.0001	0.0002	0.0001	0.0001	0.0001	0.0001	0.0000	0.0000
Y13	0.0000	0.0000	0.0000	0.0000	0.0000	0.0000	0.0000	0.0001	0.0001	0.0000	0.0000
Y14	0.0000	0.0000	0.0001	0.0000	0.0000	0.0001	0.0000	0.0000	0.0001	0.0001	0.0001
Y15	0.0002	0.0002	0.0006	0.0003	0.0007	0.0002	0.0002	0.0003	0.0006	0.0000	0.0000
Y16	0.0354	0.0302	0.0244	0.0422	0.0339	0.0380	0.0432	0.0323	0.0401	0.0411	0.0411
Y17	0.0045	0.0035	0.0051	0.0022	0.0046	0.0033	0.0043	0.0013	0.0062	0.0024	0.0013
Y18	0.0215	0.0250	0.0307	0.0266	0.0352	0.0297	0.0266	0.0285	0.0349	0.0246	0.0239
Y19	0.0883	0.0883	0.0883	0.0883	0.0883	0.0883	0.0883	0.0883	0.0883	0.0883	0.0883
Y20	0.0883	0.0883	0.0883	0.0883	0.0883	0.0883	0.0883	0.0883	0.0883	0.0883	0.0883
Y21	0.0000	0.0000	0.0000	0.0000	0.0001	0.0000	0.0000	0.0001	0.0000	0.0000	0.0000
Y22	0.0005	0.0000	0.0000	0.0005	0.0000	0.0000	0.0000	0.0005	0.0000	0.0000	0.0000
Y23	0.0001	0.0000	0.0000	0.0000	0.0000	0.0000	0.0000	0.0000	0.0000	0.0000	0.0000
Y24	0.0000	0.0000	0.0000	0.0000	0.0001	0.0000	0.0000	0.0000	0.0000	0.0000	0.0000
Y25	0.0000	0.0000	0.0000	0.0006	0.0003	0.0006	0.0006	0.0003	0.0006	0.0006	0.0006
Y26	0.0000	0.0000	0.0000	0.0000	0.0009	0.0000	0.0000	0.0000	0.0000	0.0000	0.0000
Y27	0.0000	0.0000	0.0000	0.0000	0.0000	0.0000	0.0000	0.0000	0.0000	0.0000	0.0000
Y28	0.0000	0.0000	0.0000	0.0000	0.0000	0.0002	0.0000	0.0010	0.0000	0.0000	0.0000
Y29	0.0086	0.0019	0.0008	0.0005	0.0000	0.0019	0.0008	0.0065	0.0008	0.0002	0.0001
Y30	0.0006	0.0000	0.0001	0.0000	0.0007	0.0000	0.0012	0.0000	0.0000	0.0000	0.0002
Y31	0.0000	0.0000	0.0001	0.0000	0.0000	0.0000	0.0001	0.0001	0.0002	0.0000	0.0002
Z1	0.0000	0.0000	0.0000	0.0000	0.0000	0.0000	0.0000	0.0000	0.0000	0.0000	0.0000
Z2	0.0009	0.0010	0.0008	0.0010	0.0009	0.0011	0.0000	0.0010	0.0010	0.0009	0.0009
Z3	0.0000	0.0000	0.0000	0.0000	0.0000	0.0000	0.0131	0.0000	0.0113	0.0000	0.0000
Z4	0.0883	0.0883	0.0883	0.0883	0.0883	0.0883	0.0883	0.0883	0.0883	0.0883	0.0883
Z5	0.0002	0.0000	0.0000	0.0000	0.0001	0.0001	0.0000	0.0000	0.0000	0.0000	0.0000
Z6	0.0000	0.0001	0.0001	0.0000	0.0001	0.0000	0.0000	0.0000	0.0001	0.0000	0.0000
Z7	0.0000	0.0000	0.0000	0.0000	0.0000	0.0000	0.0000	0.0000	0.0000	0.0000	0.0000

(continued)

Table 5. *(continued)*

	Dayu	Ganzhou	Nankang	Quannan	Shangyou	Suichuan	Tonggu	Xinfeng	Xingguo	Xunwu	Meixian
Z8	0.0000	0.0000	0.0000	0.0001	0.0000	0.0000	0.0000	0.0000	0.0000	0.0000	0.0000
Z9	0.0000	0.0000	0.0000	0.0000	0.0000	0.0000	0.0002	0.0000	0.0000	0.0000	0.0000
Z10	0.0000	0.0003	0.0003	0.0000	0.0002	0.0002	0.0000	0.0000	0.0003	0.0003	0.0000
Z11	0.0007	0.0007	0.0007	0.0007	0.0007	0.0007	0.0007	0.0007	0.0007	0.0007	0.0007
Z12	0.0007	0.0007	0.0007	0.0007	0.0007	0.0007	0.0007	0.0007	0.0007	0.0007	0.0007

The hierarchical clustering results obtained from the weighted comprehensive index matrix using AHP are as follows:

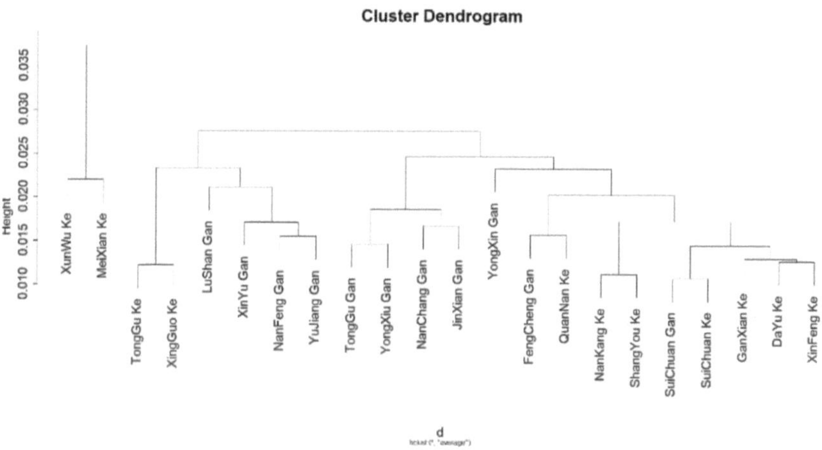

Fig. 1. Cluster results of AHP weighted analysis.

Figure 1 presents the results of the hierarchical clustering analysis based on the AHP-weighted comprehensive index matrix. The dendrogram shows that Gan and Hakka dialect groups are interwoven, with no clear statistical evidence supporting the independence of the two dialect groups. The first major branch includes Xunwu Hakka and Meixian Hakka, while the second encompasses the remaining Hakka and Gan dialects. However, the lack of clear separation—evidenced by the intermingling of dialects at multiple branching points—suggests a close relationship. For example, Gan dialects such as Lushan Gan and Fengcheng Gan are closely related to Hakka dialects such as Tonggu Hakka and Quannan Hakka. This pattern suggests a close affinity between Gan and Hakka dialects. Similar to the empirical weighting method, the AHP method can groups certain Gan dialects at lower levels. For instance, the fourth level clusters Lushan Gan, Xinyu Gan, Yujiang Gan, and Nanfeng Gan into a small group, while another branch clusters Tonggu Gan, Yongxiu Gan, Nanchang Gan, and Jinxian Gan into another small group. This further indicates that the differences between Hakka and Gan dialects are more appropriately viewed as internal variations within a larger dialect continuum.

The AHP method emphasizes the average values of features, assigning higher weights to features with higher average values. Compared to the empirical weighting method, AHP reduces human intervention and is more objective in the weighting process. The results show that the Gan dialects of Yongxin, Suichuan, and Fengcheng are always deeply intertwined with Hakka dialects, regardless of whether the weighting method emphasizes differentiation or objectivity. This suggests a close relationship between these dialects.

Therefore, the clustering results obtained through AHP analysis cannot clearly separate Hakka and Gan dialects, reflecting their close association.

The results of the MDS analysis are displayed in a two-dimensional scatter plot (Fig. 2), which allows for an intuitive visualization of the distances between the 22 dialect points:

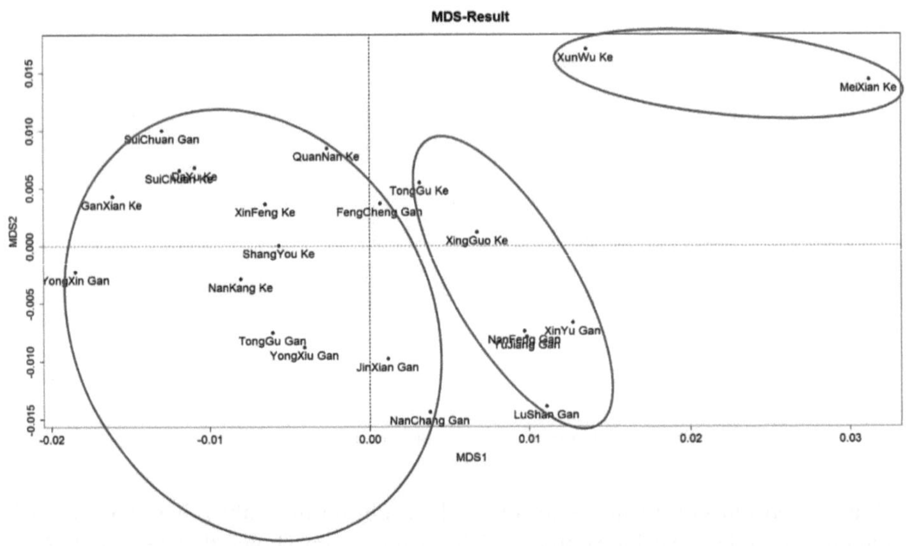

Fig. 2. MSD Multidimensional Scale Analysis Scatter Plot.

5 Conclusion

The relationship between Hakka and Gan dialects has been a longstanding issue in dialect classification since the 1930s. While most scholars their separation, more detailed surveys have shown that these dialects have long coexisted in Jiangxi and share numerous phonetic similarities. To date, no single phonetic feature has been identified that can consistently and exclusively differentiate Hakka and Gan dialects. Our quantitative analysis shows that the Gan and Hakka dialect groups are interwoven and intermingled, with no significant statistical evidence supporting their independence.

Acknowledgments. This work is supported by National Social Science Foundation (No. 16ZDA211, 17JJD740001 and 22&ZD213).

References

1. Zheng, J.: Calculation of communication degree in chinese dialects. Chinese Language 1 (1973)
2. Lu, Z.: A quantitative description of the kinship relationships among chinese dialects. Social Sciences in China 1 (1987)
3. Zheng, J.: A quantitative study on the relationship between chinese dialects and familiarity. Chinese Language 2 (1988)
4. Deng, X., Wang, S.: Mathematical classification and analysis of Tibeto Burman languages. Chinese Language 4 (2003)
5. Deng, X., Wang, S.: Quantitative study on the kinship of miao yao language family: etymological statistical analysis method. Chinese Language 3 (2003)
6. Deng, X., Wang, S.: Mathematical classification and temporal depth of Zhuang Dong languages. Chinese Language 6 (2007)
7. Jiang, D.: Automatic clustering and zoning of Chinese dialects and related computational methods. Journal of Jinan University (Philosophy and Social Sciences Edition) 3 (2022)
8. Zhao, Z.: A Quantitative Study on the Linguistic Similarity Relationships in the East Asian-Pacific Region. Shanghai: Doctoral Dissertation, Shanghai Normal University (2017)
9. Gray, R.D., Atkinson, Q.D.: Language-tree divergence times support the Anatolian theory of Indo-European origin. Nature **426**, 6965 (2003)
10. Greenhill, S.J., Blust, R., Gray, R.D.: The Austronesian Basic Vocabulary Database: From Bioinformatics to Lexomics. Evol. Bioinform. 4 (2008)
11. Zhang, M., Zheng, S., Li, J.: Reconciling the father tongue and mother tongue hypotheses in Indo-European populations. National Science Review 6 (2019)
12. Li, Z.: A Study on the Primitive Naxi Language and Its Historical Status. Doctoral Dissertation of Peking University, Beijing (2013)
13. Wu, N.: Monosyllabic tones in Chinese dialects: types, perception, and systems. Doctoral Dissertation of Peking University, Beijing (2020)
14. Luo, C.: Linchuan Phonology. Science Press, Beijing (1940/1958)
15. Yuan, J.: An Outline of Chinese Dialects (Second Edition). Wenzi Gaihe Press, Beijing (1960/1983)
16. Hashimoto, M.J.: The Hakka Dialect:a linguistic study of its phonology, syntαx and lexicon. Cambridge University Press, Cambridge (1973)
17. Zhan, B.: Modern Chinese Dialects. Hubei Education Press, Wuhan (1981)
18. Luo, X.: An Inquiry into the Origin and Development of the Hakka People. China Overseas Chinese Publishing House, Beijing (1989)
19. He, D.: On the Gan Dialect. Sinology Studies 1 (1987)
20. Li, R., Zhang, S.: A Survey Report on the Hakka and Gan Dialects. Xiamen University Press, Xiamen (1992)
21. Huang, X.: A Comparative Study of Vocabulary in Hakka and Gan Dialects - Centered on Six Points. Doctoral Dissertation of Sun Yat-sen University, Guangzhou (2011)
22. Li, R.: The Division of Chinese Dialects. Dialects 4 (1989)
23. Liu, L.: Comparative Study of Hakka and Gan Dialects. China Social Sciences Press, Beijing (1999)
24. Wang, F.: On the Division and Merger of Hakka Dialect and Gan Dialect. Dialects 1 (1998)
25. Liu, Z.: A Study on the Historical Stratification of the Hakka-Jiangxi Dialect. Doctoral Dissertation of Shanghai Normal University, Shanghai (2004)
26. He, X.: Multivariate Statistical Analysis[M]. China Renmin University Press, Beijing (2019)

LLM-Based Evaluation of Low-Resource Machine Translation: A Reference-less Dialect-Guided Approach with a Refined Sylheti-English Benchmark

Md. Atiqur Rahman[1(✉)], Sabrina Islam[1], and Mushfiqul Haque Omi[2]

[1] Islamic University of Technology, Gazipur, Bangladesh
atiqurrahman23@iut-dhaka.edu
[2] United International University, Dhaka, Bangladesh

Abstract. Evaluating machine translation (MT) for low-resource languages poses a persistent challenge, primarily due to the limited availability of high-quality reference translations. This issue is further exacerbated in languages with multiple dialects, where linguistic diversity and data scarcity hinder robust evaluation. Large Language Models (LLMs) present a promising solution through reference-free evaluation techniques; however, their effectiveness diminishes in the absence of dialect-specific context and tailored guidance. In this work, we propose a comprehensive framework that enhances LLM-based MT evaluation using a dialect-guided approach. We extend the ONUBAD dataset by incorporating Sylheti-English sentence pairs, corresponding machine-translations, and Direct Assessment (DA) scores annotated by native speakers. To address the vocabulary gap, we augment the tokenizer vocabulary with dialect-specific terms. We further introduce a regression head to enable scalar score prediction and design a Dialect-Guided (DG) prompting strategy. Our evaluation across multiple LLMs shows that the proposed pipeline consistently outperforms existing methods, achieving the highest gain of + 0.1164 in Spearman correlation, along with notable improvements in other evaluation settings. The dataset and the code are available at https://github.com/180041123-Atiq/MTEonLowResourceLanguage.

Keywords: Machine Translation Evaluation · Large Language Models (LLMs) · Low-Resource Languages · Prompt Engineering

1 Introduction

Evaluating the quality of machine-translated text traditionally relies on regression systems that depend heavily on human-generated reference translations [1]. However, producing such references is costly and difficult to scale, especially for low-resource, dialect-rich languages. These challenges are further intensified by the scarcity, inconsistency, or complete absence of annotated ground truth data [2]. As a result, the lack of scalable evaluation frameworks not only hampers the advancement of these languages in digital space but also threatens their long-term preservation, including the rich cultural and historical heritage they embody.

X. Ding and Y. Dong (Eds.): CLNLP 2025, CCIS 2775, pp. 80–88, 2026.
https://doi.org/10.1007/978-981-95-4788-3_8

With the emergence of Large Language Models (LLMs), new opportunities have surfaced for reference-less evaluation of machine translations. LLMs are capable of modeling semantic relationships and contextual meaning across languages, making them promising tools for assessing translation quality [3]. However, generating reliable quality scores such as Direct Assessment (DA) scores [4] remain a non-trivial task. These scores demand sensitivity to both grammatical accuracy and cross-lingual semantic equivalence, which LLMs may not consistently deliver without targeted guidance.

In this work, we investigate the effectiveness of LLMs for machine translation (MT) evaluation in low-resource, dialect-rich settings, where traditional methods falter due to the absence of reference translations and annotated data. We propose a reference-less evaluation framework that leverages LLMs' ability to interpret regional language variation, guided by a dialect specific prompting strategy that enables inference of DA scores without full finetuning. Our key contributions are:

- We expanded an existing dataset by adding 520 new Sylheti source sentences, their human-translated English references, machine-generated translations for the entire set of 1500 sentences, and Direct Assessment (DA) scores rated by native Sylheti speakers.
- Dialect-Guided prompting strategy to improve the reference-less MT evaluation of low-resource language.
- We enhance the model by incorporating a dialect-aware tokenizer and a lightweight regression head that leverages the rich feature representations of the pre-trained LLM to predict Direct Assessment (DA) scores.

2 Background

The WMT 2023 shared task [5] marked a significant advancement in low-resource MT evaluation by introducing new language pairs and providing diverse evaluation resources. A key challenge addressed was quality estimation (QE) without reference translations, promoting scalable evaluation methods. However, dialect-rich language varieties remained largely overlooked. In many South and East Asian countries, distinct dialects are spoken across various regions and communities. These dialects often suffer from limited linguistic resources, largely due to their lack of digital presence [6]. One core barrier to their inclusion in the digital sphere is the absence of effective MT evaluation frameworks tailored for dialect rich, low-resource languages. Without effective methods to assess translations in these dialects, there is limited incentive for the development of MT systems targeting them. This persistent gap in technological inclusion not only reinforces their digital marginalization but also poses a significant threat to the preservation of the cultural heritage and linguistic identity embedded within these dialectal varieties.

Although XLM-RoBERTa [7]-based quality estimation (QE) models dominated early submissions to the WMT shared tasks, the emergence of large language models (LLMs) signals a potential paradigm shift in the evaluation of machine translation (MT). Sindhujan et al. investigated the application of LLMs for reference-less MT evaluation in low-resource scenarios [8]. Their approach used Annotation-Guided (AG) prompting, providing LLMs with the same guidelines as human DA annotators to instruct quality scoring based on defined criteria. While this strategy yielded promising outcomes, it lacked explicit mechanisms to account for language or dialect-specific features, thereby limiting its effectiveness in linguistically diverse or dialect-rich environments.

General purpose LLMs are typically trained on corpora that underrepresented low-resource languages, resulting in tokenizers that poorly segment dialect specific terms. This affects the model's ability to interpret and evaluate translations accurately. Chalkidis et al. fine-tuned BERT for legal text with tokenizer adjustments to better capture legal terminology [9]. Dagan et al. highlights through extensive experiments that extending or replacing a tokenizer can lead to significant improvements [10]. However, in scenarios without broad multilingual training support, building a tokenizer from scratch for machine translation (MT) evaluation may compromise the model's inherent multilingual capabilities, which are equally essential for reliable evaluation across language pairs.

Moreover, LLMs tend to generate verbose outputs, making them unsuitable for scalar DA scoring. To address this, recent research has explored leveraging LLM embeddings as feature representations for downstream regression tasks [11]. These embeddings have shown promising results, often outperforming traditional feature engineering approaches in high-dimensional regression settings. Thus, embedding-based regression presents a viable and effective pathway for integrating their rich representations into structured evaluation tasks.

3 Methodology

We propose a comprehensive framework that combines an enhanced Sylheti-English dataset annotated with Direct Assessment (DA) scores, a novel dialect-guided prompting strategy, and the integration of a dialect-aware tokenizer. To better align with human evaluation, we train a lightweight regressor head that predicts translation quality scores directly from the LLM output, enabling consistent assessments without reference translations. This mapping is defined in Eq. (1) where θ represents the parameters of the frozen LLM combined with the trained linear layer, $Prompt_{DG}$ is our dialect-guided prompt defined in Eq. (3), and $\hat{y}$ denotes the predicted translation quality score.

$$f_\theta : (Prompt_{DG}) \rightarrow \hat{y} \tag{1}$$

This approach introduces minimal overhead since the regressor consists of a single linear layer while the LLM backbone remains frozen. Likewise, the extended tokenizer introduces only a few dialect-specific tokens, with negligible impact on speed or model size. The overview of our proposed pipeline is shown in Fig. 1.

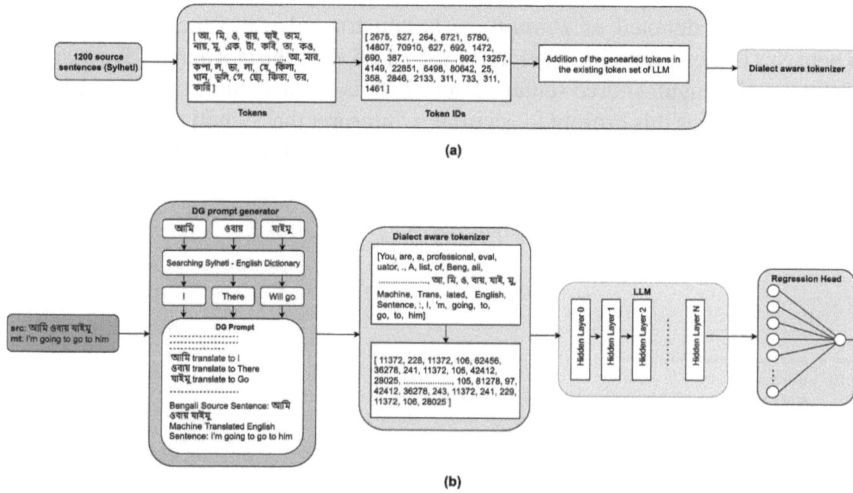

Fig. 1. Overview of the proposed pipeline. 1(a) illustrates the process of creating a dialect-aware tokenizer using dialect-specific vocabulary tailored to the target dialect and 1(b) presents the complete pipeline, integrating the extended tokenizer with dialect-guided prompting and regression-head to effectively perform the evaluation task.

3.1 Sylheti-English Benchmark

Bengali is a low-resource language in natural language processing (NLP), with dialects like Sylheti, Chittagong, and Barisal being even more underrepresented. To address this, ONUBAD [12] introduced a parallel corpus translating these dialects into Standard Bangla and English using expert translators, providing 1,540 words, 130 clauses, and 980 sentences per dialect. For our study, we focused on the Sylheti-English pair and adapted the dataset for LLM-based machine translation (MT) evaluation. We extracted the 980 Sylheti-English sentence pairs, corrected inconsistencies, and added 520 new sentence pairs, all translated by native speakers and cross-validated for accuracy, resulting in 1,500 high-quality sentence pairs. To simulate a real-world MT evaluation scenario, we generated translations using the NLLB-200 model [13], recognized for its multilingual capabilities [5]. Two native Sylheti speakers evaluated the outputs using Direct Assessment (DA) guidelines [4], scoring them based on semantic equivalence and fluency. The scores were then averaged and the resulting value was z-normalized to reduce inter-annotator variability and minimize the effect of outliers. [8].

3.2 Dialect-Guided Prompting Strategy

We propose a Dialect-Guided (DG) prompting strategy to guide LLMs in evaluation, where the dialectal context is explicitly integrated into the prompt. We define a word map G, in Eq. (2), where G represents the glossary of Sylheti terms paired with their English equivalents.

$$G = \{(w_i, t_i) | w_i \in Sylheti, t_i \in English\} \quad (2)$$

The DG prompt, denoted as $Prompt_{DG}$, is constructed using the components in Eq. 3. Where Sys is the system instruction for the LLM, G is the word map, $S_{sylheti}$ is the Sylheti-influenced Bengali source sentence, and T_{MT} is the machine-translated English sentence. The LLM uses this prompt to accurately interpret the Sylheti dialectal features and evaluate the machine translation quality. A template of the prompt is illustrated in Fig. 2.

$$Prompt_{DG} = \{Sys|G|S_{sylheti}|T_{MT}\} \tag{3}$$

```
You are a professional machine translation evaluator.
You will be given:
        - A list of Bengali words influenced by the Sylheti dialect,
          along with their English translations, to help you better understand the dialect.
        - A sentence in Bengali that includes words from the Sylheti dialect.
        - A machine-translated English sentence.

After evaluating whether the English sentence is an accurate translation of the Bengali
source, your task is to provide only a score from 0 to 100, no need for explanation. The
score may be a floating-point number.

For your reference, here is a list of Bengali words influenced by the Sylheti dialect,
along with their English translations:

আমি translate to I
ওবায় translate to There
যাইমু translate to Go

Now evaluate the following and give only the score:
Bengali Source Sentence: আমি ওবায় যাইমু
Machine Translated English Sentence: I'm going to go to him
Score:
```

Fig. 2. A template of the Dialect-Guided (DG) Prompt used in our study. The Bengali (Sylheti) words and their corresponding English translations within the prompt are specific to each input and will vary with different inputs. This example illustrates the template applied to the input sentence "আমি ওবায় যাইমু".

3.3 Dialect-Aware Tokenizer

Figure 1(a) shows how we adapted the tokenizer associated with LLM to handle Sylheti dialectal variations. We trained a tokenizer on Sylheti sentences and compared its vocabulary with the original LLM tokenizer. Unique Sylheti tokens were added to the LLM's tokenizer, improving its ability to process dialect influenced text and boosting performance in downstream tasks like translation evaluation.

3.4 Regression Head

To improve DA score prediction, we added a regression head on top of a frozen LLM. This head was fine-tuned to map the LLM's contextual outputs to human-annotated scores, mimicking expert evaluation. Freezing the LLM preserved its language understanding and minimized overfitting on our small dataset (1200 samples). The head, matching the LLM's output dimension, was trained with MSE loss to align with human scoring. This setup enabled efficient quality estimation without full model fine-tuning.

3.5 Implementation Details

We used an 80:5:15 split, resulting in 1,200 samples for the training set, 75 samples for the validation set, and 225 samples for the testing set. Byte-Level BPE tokenizer [14] was used to capture dialectal variations through sub-word tokenization. Hugging Face Transformers managed the LLMs, while PyTorch was used to implement and fine-tune a lightweight regression head for predicting DA scores. Input sequence lengths were limited to 512 tokens to balance performance and efficiency. Adam optimizer was used with a $2e^{-5}$ learning rate to avoid overfitting on the small dataset. Prompts followed Llama-style chat templates for consistency. To optimize memory and speed, we applied 4-bit quantization and FP16 precision, allowing the deployment of larger models and batch sizes on limited hardware. All experiments ran on a single NVIDIA RTX A5000 GPU (24GB VRAM) with 50GB system RAM, motivating design choices that favored efficiency and stability.

4 Results

4.1 Performance of the Proposed Pipeline

We evaluated the performance of Llama-2-7B [15], Llama-2-13B, OpenChat [16] and Gemma [17] using three different pipelines: the SOTA AG (Annotation-Guided) [8], our proposed pipeline with the DG prompting, and our pipeline with DAG (Dialect + Annotation-Guided) prompt instead of the DG prompt. To assess model performance, we computed both the Pearson correlation coefficient [18] and the Spearman rank correlation coefficient [19] between the predicted and actual Direct Assessment (DA) scores.

Table 1. Evaluation of proposed pipeline utilizing the Pearson correlation coefficient.

	AG	DG	DAG
Llama-2-7B	0.1779 ± 0.0023	**0.2443 ± 0.0015**	0.2039 ± 0.0086
Llama-2-13B	0.1765 ± 0.0008	**0.279 ± 0.0041**	0.2196 ± 0.0106
OpenChat	0.2299 ± 0.0144	**0.2826 ± 0.0091**	0.2614 ± 0.0187
Gemma	**0.3247 ± 0.0012**	0.3079 ± 0.0033	0.2945 ± 0.0035

Table 1 presents the Pearson correlation results across all models and pipelines. Notably, DG consistently outperformed AG and DAG for Llama-2-7B, Llama-2-13B and OpenChat, achieving the highest correlation scores among all evaluated settings. Similarly, Table 2 displays Spearman rank correlations, where DG again resulted in the top performance for the three models.

Table 2. Evaluation of proposed pipeline using the Spearman rank correlation coefficient.

	AG	DG	DAG
Llama-2-7B	0.1506 ± 0.0028	$\mathbf{0.2337 \pm 0.0046}$	0.1794 ± 0.0072
Llama-2-13B	0.1496 ± 0.0018	$\mathbf{0.2579 \pm 0.0064}$	0.1951 ± 0.0121
OpenChat	0.1984 ± 0.0143	$\mathbf{0.2852 \pm 0.0153}$	0.2441 ± 0.0209
Gemma	$\mathbf{0.3566 \pm 0.0021}$	0.3488 ± 0.0023	0.3322 ± 0.0014

While Gemma showed slightly better performance with AG prompting, AG consistently underperformed across all other models. DAG demonstrated improved performance over AG but did not surpass DG, confirming the effectiveness of incorporating dialect specific cues into the prompt.

The highest Pearson and Spearman correlations, 0.2826 and 0.2852, respectively, were achieved by OpenChat using our pipeline. DG led to an approximate 58% improvement in the Spearman correlation score for Llama-2-13B compared to AG which is a significant accomplishment.

4.2 Ablation Study

To assess the individual impact of each proposed component of our pipeline, specifically the dialect-aware tokenizer, the fine-tuned regression head, and the dialect-guided prompting strategy, we performed an ablation study using the OpenChat model, which demonstrated the strongest overall performance in our experiments. The results, presented in Table 3, demonstrate the incremental benefits of each component.

Table 3. Ablation Analysis of the Proposed Pipeline Using Pearson Correlation Coefficient (OpenChat Model).

Dialect-Aware Tokenizer	Regression Head	DG Prompt	Pearson Correlation Coefficient
×	×	×	-0.1446
✓	×	×	0.0336
✓	✓	×	0.2312
✓	✓	✓	**0.2734**

Without any modifications, OpenChat achieved a baseline Pearson correlation score of -0.1446, indicating poor agreement between predicted and reference DA scores. Introducing the dialect-aware tokenizer resulted in a substantial improvement, increasing the score by approximately 123% to 0.0336 which is a critical shift from negative to positive correlation, indicating initial alignment between predicted and reference scores. Incorporating the fine-tuned regression head further boosted the score to 0.2312, enabling the model to better generate scalar quality predictions. Finally, applying the dialect-guided prompting strategy raised the score to 0.2734, underscoring the value of incorporating dialect-specific cues directly into the evaluation process.

5 Discussion

The evaluation results in Table 1 underscore the effectiveness and robustness of our proposed methodology in the context of reference-less machine translation (MT) evaluation. Our pipeline mostly outperforms the baseline Annotation-Guided (AG) strategy and its combined variant (DAG), establishing the superiority of embedding dialect specific linguistic cues directly into the prompt.

A key insight from the results is that the DG strategy improves the model's performance in all LLMs but also does so more significantly than the DAG setup. DAG incorporates both dialect-aware tokenization and annotation guidelines, which can increase the complexity of the prompt and potentially overwhelm the LLM, making it harder to focus on evaluating translation quality. In contrast, DG only provides information related to the dialect through targeted prompting, simplifying the task for the LLM leading to more effective translation evaluation.

When examining model wise performance, Llama-2-13B saw the most substantial gain under the DG setup, improving from 0.1765 (AG) to 0.279 (DG). This shows that larger models capable of disambiguating dialect-specific expressions are better at leveraging the richer contextual signals offered by dialect-oriented strategies.

Similarly, OpenChat, which is pretrained on a wide range of instruction-following and evaluation tasks, showed strong performance even though it wasn't specifically trained for MT evaluation. Our pipeline improved its correlation score from 0.2299 (AG) to 0.2826 (DG) as well showing that dialect-awareness can complement instruction tuned models with general purpose evaluation capabilities.

Turning to Gemma, we observed that although it achieved the highest Pearson correlation overall (0.3247 in AG), it did not yield its best performance under our DG prompting (dropping slightly to 0.3079). Though the difference in Pearson correlation between AG and DG for Gemma is marginal, Spearman rank correlation is nearly identical to the best-performing setup. This suggests that our pipeline still preserves ranking fidelity, even if it marginally trails in raw score correlation.

We employed chat-tuned variants of Llama-2 and OpenChat in our experiments, but did not include the chat-tuned variant of Gemma. We attribute Gemma's lower performance with DG to its lack of instruction or chat tuning. Unlike Llama-2 and OpenChat, which are fine tuned for instruction-rich, multi-turn prompts, Gemma lacks native support for such interactions, making our dialect-guided prompts a better fit for chat optimized models.

6 Conclusion

In summary, our pipeline sets a strong precedent for reference-less machine translation evaluation, particularly in low-resource, dialect-rich settings. By augmenting large language models with explicit dialectal context through tokenizer extension and targeted prompting, we significantly improve alignment with human judgments. Notably, larger models, such as LLaMA-2-13B, derive the greatest benefit, while models less optimized for dialectal prompts, like Gemma, attain competitive results, underscoring the versatility of our approach in low-resource MT settings. However, our method does rely on a dialect-specific dictionary to map low-resource dialect words to high-resource language equivalents which is a manageable consideration when extending the approach to other dialects or languages.

References

1. Takahashi, K., Sudoh, K., Nakamura, S.: Automatic machine translation evaluation using a source and reference sentence with a cross-lingual language model. J. Natur. Lang. Proc. **29**(1), 3–22 (2022)
2. Haddow, B., et al.: Survey of low-resource machine translation. Computational Linguistics **48**(3), 673–732 (2022)
3. Kocmi, T., Federmann, C.: Large language models are state-of-the-art evaluators of translation quality (2023). arXiv preprint arXiv:2302.14520
4. Bentivogli, L., et al.: Machine translation human evaluation: an investigation of evaluation based on post-editing and its relation with direct assessment. Proceedings of the 15th International Workshop on Spoken Language Translation (IWSLT 2018) (2018)
5. Blain, F., et al.: Findings of the WMT 2023 Shared Task on Quality Estimation. Eight conference on machine translation. Association for Computational Linguistics (2023)
6. Moseley, C., (ed.): Atlas of the World's Languages in Danger. Unesco (2010)
7. Conneau, A., et al.: Unsupervised cross-lingual representation learning at scale. arXiv preprint arXiv:1911.02116 (2019)
8. Sindhujan, A., et al.: When LLMs Struggle: Reference-less Translation Evaluation for Low-resource Languages. arXiv preprint arXiv:2501.04473 (2025)
9. Chalkidis, I., et al.: LEGAL-BERT: The muppets straight out of law school. arXiv preprint arXiv:2010.02559 (2020)
10. Dagan, G., Synnaeve, G., Roziere, B.: Getting the most out of your tokenizer for pre-training and domain adaptation. arXiv preprint arXiv:2402.01035 (2024)
11. Tang, E., Yang, B., Song, X.: Understanding LLM Embeddings for Regression. arXiv preprint arXiv:2411.14708 (2024)
12. Sultana, N., et al.: ONUBAD: A comprehensive dataset for automated conversion of Bangla regional dialects into standard Bengali dialect. Data in Brief **58**, 111276 (2025)
13. Costa-Jussà, M.R., et al.: No language left behind: Scaling human-centered machine translation. arXiv preprint arXiv:2207.04672 (2022)
14. Wang, C., Cho, K., Gu, J.: Neural machine translation with byte-level subwords. Proceedings of the AAAI conference on artificial intelligence Vol. 34. No. 05 (2020)
15. Touvron, H., et al.: Llama 2: Open foundation and fine-tuned chat models. arXiv preprint arXiv:2307.09288 (2023)
16. Wang, G., et al.: Openchat: Advancing open-source language models with mixed-quality data. arXiv preprint arXiv:2309.11235 (2023)
17. Team, G., et al.: Gemma: Open models based on gemini research and technology. arXiv preprint arXiv:2403.08295 (2024)
18. Cohen, I., et al.: Pearson correlation coefficient. Noise reduction in speech processing, 1–4 (2009)
19. Zar, J.H.: Spearman rank correlation. Encyclopedia of biostatistics 7 (2005)

Acoustic Study of Intergenerational Differences in Nasalized Monophthongs in Eastern Guangdong Min Dialect

Diyuan Yang[1], Yuxuan Xi[2], and Lüye Qin[2(✉)]

[1] School of Electronics and Information, Guangdong Polytechnic Normal University, Guangzhou, China

[2] School of Literature and Communication, Guangdong Polytechnic Normal University, Guangzhou, China

Luyeqin001@gpnu.edu.cn

Abstract. Nasalized vowels are syllables with nasal consonant endings. When the nasal consonant ending is weakened, the vowel part takes on a nasal characteristic. Among the three major dialects of Guangdong, only the Min dialect has this characteristic. This characteristic is not easily distinguished by non-native speakers. The documentation of nasalized monophthongs in Eastern Guangdong Min has predominantly relied on transcribers' perception rather than precise data. Most research on this topic remains at the phonetic description level, lacking acoustic analysis. This study conducts an acoustic analysis of the nasalization degree of the vowel /ĩ/ across three age groups (elderly, middle-aged, young) in Eastern Guangdong Min, examining the retention of nasalized vowels /ĩ/ in actual pronunciation and discussing the necessity and feasibility of acoustic measurement for recording nasalized vowels. The findings reveal that the elderly exhibit the highest nasalization degree, with a discernible nasalization trend in non-nasalized vowels based on the data. In contrast, middle-aged and young speakers partially confuse nasalized and non-nasalized vowels. This underscores the importance of enhancing precision in describing nasalized vowels according to actual conditions during dialectal phonetic transcription.

Keywords: Eastern Guangdong · Min Dialect · Nasalized Vowels · Phonetic Experimentation

1 Introduction

Huilai Min dialect belongs to the Eastern Guangdong Min dialect group. The neighboring Shantou Min dialect has 26 nasalized finals, while the nasalization phenomenon in the finals of Huilai(惠来) County's Huicheng(惠城) District, under Jieyang(揭阳) City, remains unclear. Xu Fuqiong (2017) [1] outlined four sources of nasalized finals in Eastern Guangdong Min dialect, including the weakened forms of nasal-coded rhymes (primarily from the Middle Chinese Xian, Shan, Dang, and Geng rhyme groups). A small number of other nasal-coded rhyme groups and some non-nasal-coded rhymes with non-m-, n-, ŋ-initials are also nasalized. Currently, discussions on nasalized finals in the Eastern Guangdong Min dialect region remain limited.

X. Ding and Y. Dong (Eds.): CLNLP 2025, CCIS 2775, pp. 89–96, 2026.
https://doi.org/10.1007/978-981-95-4788-3_9

Fang Qiang and Li Aijun (2003) [2] studied nasalized vowels in Mandarin by applying FFT transformation to vowel segments to obtain spectrograms. They measured the values of P0, A1, P1, and P2 in the spectrograms, using A1-P0, A1-P1, and A1-P2 as parameters to quantify nasalized vowels, and examined the manifestations of nasalization degrees for different vowels (a, i, u) across frequency bands. Shue et al. (2011) [3] focused on the VoiceSauce speech analysis program, which can extract values such as A1, A2, and H1. Xu Yuhang and Zhang Ling (2018) [4] used this program to extract A1, H1, and H2 values for nasalized vowels in the Chaozhou dialect, employing A1-P0 to assess the degree of vowel nasalization and the influence of nasal initials on finals. Ling Feng et al. (2019) [5] provided an overview of all acoustic parameters extractable by VoiceSauce, including three fundamental frequency measurement methods, offering methodological guidance for scholars using the program.

Most academic research on nasalized vowels has focused on phonetic contrasts, yet these findings have not been systematically applied to various dialects to thoroughly examine the characteristics and evolutionary trends of nasalized vowels across different dialects. From an acoustic analysis perspective, this article annotates nasalized vowels in Praat, extracts data using VoiceSauce software, and then imports the data into SPSS software for analysis using one-way ANOVA and t-test. It explores the nasalization of vowels in Huicheng District, Huilai County, analyzes the evolution of nasalization from an intergenerational perspective, and attempts to explore the changing trends of nasalization.

2 Phonetic Experiment

2.1 Experimental Design

In the Huilai Min dialect, there are three pairs of nasalized and non-nasalized monophthongs: i-ĩ, e-ẽ, and a-ã. Since the e sound is centrally located and its position can easily change, this study focuses on the stable vowels i and a.

Additionally, because female pronunciation is more variable than male pronunciation, we selected female speakers as the subjects of our survey, with participants from the elderly, middle-aged, and young generations adhering to the requirements of the dialect survey. Speaker information: Elderly speaker (born in 1955), elementary school education, engaged in small commodity trade, has never left the local area, and only speaks Huicheng Min dialect; middle-aged speaker (born in 1983), college education, has taught at Huicheng Primary School for over 20 years, proficient in Mandarin and Cantonese; Young speaker (born in 2004), a university student, proficient in Mandarin and Huicheng. Syllables with a CV-CṼstructure, listed in Table 1, were read aloud by the speakers, with each word read three times and repeated twice.

Syllables described as "having sound but no character" were explained; if speakers could not comprehend them, those syllables were excluded from recording to avoid unnatural pronunciation. Details of the experimental characters are provided in. The experimental hypothesis was: nasalization is most pronounced in the elderly population, while confusion exists in the production of nasalized finals among middle-aged and young populations, with some nasalized words already losing nasalization in the latter groups. To ensure statistical significance in the phonetic data, this study intentionally

Table 1. Experimental word list.

	$C_1 V_1$	$C_1\tilde{V}_1$	C_1V_2	$C_1\tilde{V}_2$
	i	ĩ	a	ã
p	bì(币coin)[pi31]	biǎn(扁flat)[pĩ53]	bǎo(饱full)[pa53]	*(adsorb)[pã33]
ph		bí(鼻nose)[phĩ31]		
t	dī(低low)[ti34]	chán(缠entangle)[thĩ55]	dǎ(打bit)[ta31]	dǎn(胆gallbladder)[tã53]/dān(担pole)[tã53]
th		tiān(天sky)[thĩ33] tiān(添add)[thĩ33]	tā(他he)[tha33]	
k	jì(记remember)[ki31]	jiàn(见see)[kĩ31]	jiāo(胶glue)[ka33]	gǎn(敢dare)[kã53]
kh			jiǎo(脚foot)[kha33]	
tsh			chǎo(炒stir-fry)[tsha53]	
ts	sì(寺temple)[tsi31]/zǐ(紫purple)[tsi53]	qián(钱money)[tsĩ55]		*(take)[tsã33]

Note:"*"indicates that this meaningful syllable exists in the phonological system, but there is no corresponding Chinese character."h"Indicates that the initial consonant is aspirated.

increased the sample size by collecting speech data from three speakers. Each speaker clearly pronounced every sample word three times and formed sentences with them. During acoustic measurements, syllables with unclear or improper articulation were discarded.

2.2 Acoustic Measurements

The A1-P0 value in finals can be used to measure the degree of nasalization. A1 is the harmonic peak near the first formant, while P0 is a low-frequency harmonic value, typically the first harmonic (H1) or second harmonic (H2). For individuals with a lower pitch range, P0 corresponds to H2; for those with a higher pitch range, P0 corresponds to H1, reflecting nasal resonance. Typically, a lower A1-P0 value indicates stronger nasalization, while a higher value suggests weaker nasalization(Chen 1996) [6]. Also, The amplitude difference between the highest harmonic near F1 and the subsequent harmonic reflects the degree of nasalization (Du Tian 2020) [7]. Further, we conducted multivariate analysis of variance (MANOVA) with age and vowel type as fixed factors and nasalization status as dependent variables. Results revealed that the age-vowel type interaction significantly influenced nasalization.

VoiceSauce Data Parameter Extraction Settings. Click the "Setting" option in the main window to configure parameters, and a settings window like the one in Fig. 1 will appear. We used the default VS Straight algorithm. Since all three speakers were female, the upper limit was set to 350 Hz, and the lower limit to 150Hz. For male speakers, set the upper frequency limit at 500 Hz and the lower limit at 250 Hz. The middle section is for formant and bandwidth parameters, where we employed Praat's extraction algorithm. Before using Praat's extraction algorithm, place the Praat application in a "Praat" folder within the VS software directory. The number of extracted formants is adjustable between 4-7 for fine-tuning suboptimal results.

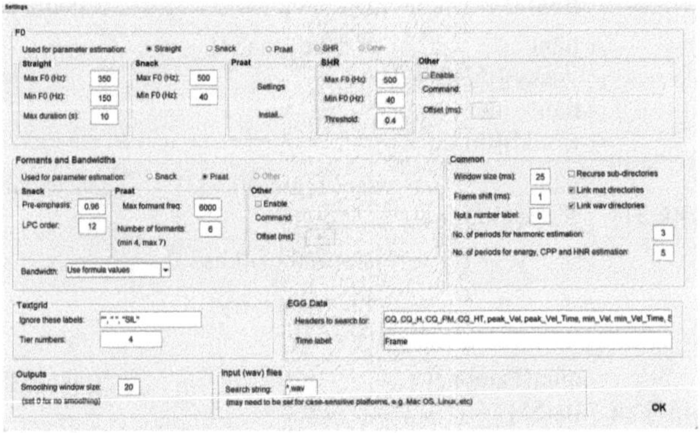

Fig. 1. VoiceSauce Parameter Settings.

Below the formant and bandwidth parameter section is the TextGrid configuration area. The first line specifies annotations to ignore, with default settings being "", " ", and "SIL", meaning segments labeled as blank, space-only, or "SIL" are skipped. Additional labels to ignore can be added in double quotes on the first line, separated by commas. The layer number indicates which row in the TextGrid contains the annotations, defaulting to the first row.

Parameter Extraction. Upon clicking "Parameter Estimation" in the main window, a new window appears. Click "Browse..." next to "Input (*.wav) directory:" and select the folder containing your WAV files. Since TextGrid files define vowel boundaries, ensure each WAV file has a corresponding TextGrid file with the identical filename in the same folder. Next, click "Parameter Selection", choose "F0 (straight)", "Formants (Snack)", "H1, H2, H3", and "A1, A2, A3", then click "OK" to exit. After measurements complete, invoke the "Output to Text" window from the main interface to export the final data. At the window's top-left, select the data to export (all parameters are selected by default; click any parameter, then choose "H1* (H1c)" and "A1* (A1c)"). When exporting, to mitigate potential "consonant-vowel transition" effects in the first third and weakening in the last third of the vowel segment, select "use sub-segments", enter "3" to divide the segment into three equal parts, extracting data from the start, midpoint, and endpoint. Click "start!" to export; the data is saved as "output.txt" in the audio file location. Import the results into Excel; the A1-P0 value is obtained by subtracting A1-H1.

T tests and One-way ANOVA. *T-test.* To measure the differences between non-nasalized vowels a 、 i and their nasalized counterparts ã 、 ĩ across three age groups (the elderly, middle-aged, and young individuals), we categorized the data of non-nasalized vowel i and nasalized vowel ĩ from young speakers into one group, and the data of non-nasalized vowel a and nasalized vowel ã from young speakers into another group. The same grouping principle was applied to middle-aged and elderly speakers, and a T-test was conducted separately for each group.The results of the T-test are presented in Fig. 2.

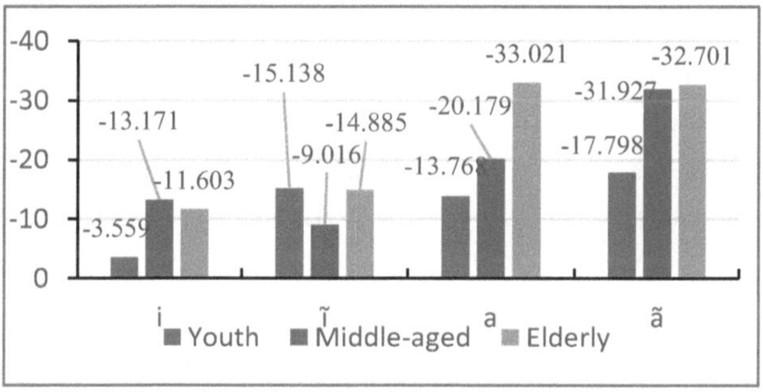

Fig. 2. Degree of nasalization Among Young, Middle-aged, and Elderly Groups.

One-way ANOVA. To examine differences in vowel nasalization degrees among the elderly, middle-aged, and young speakers, we grouped the data as follows: non-nasalized vowel i from all age groups into one category, nasalized vowel *ĩ* from all age groups into another category, and applied the same grouping principle to non-nasalized vowel a and nasalized vowel *ã*. In SPSS, import the data and navigate to *Analyze > Compare Means > One-way ANOVA*. Then place speaker type (age group) in the *Factor* box and the A1-P0 values in the *Dependent Variable* box. SPSS will automatically compute the data. The results of the T-test are presented in Table 2.

2.3 Experimental Results

As shown in Fig. 2, it is evident that the A1-P0 values for the vowel i produced by elderly speakers have significantly decreased, while the values for the vowel a have shown a slight increase. The nasalization degree of vowels in middle-aged speakers does not reach the level of the elderly, however, the vowel a still exhibits nasalization. Comparatively, vowel a in middle-aged speakers shows higher nasalization than vowel i. Among young speakers, the nasalization degree of vowel is weaker, while vowel exhibits higher nasalization. The nasalization degrees in middle-aged and young speakers are low than in the elderly, trending toward denasalization.

Table 3 shows Younger and Older speakers exhibit significant differences ($p \leq 0.05$) between oral vowel i and nasalized vowel ĩ, but not between oral vowel a and nasalized vowel ã, suggesting nasalization confusion. Middle-aged speakers show no significant difference between oral vowel i and nasalized vowel ĩ, but significant differences between oral vowel a and nasalized vowel ã. Then, four groups: older/middle-aged/younger speakers' oral vowel i, nasalized vowel ĩ, oral vowel a, and nasalized vowel ã, using A1-P0 values as the dependent variable, have performed by One-way ANOVA.

Table 2. Results of and tests (values) and mean values for nasalized vowels among the elderly, middle-aged, and youth(Significance α=0.05).

	Vowel comparison	p-value	Mean value
Youth	i vs ĩ	<0.001*	i=3.559, ĩ=-15.138
	a vs ã	0.061	a=-13.768, ã=-17.798
Middle-aged	i vs ĩ	0.084	i=-13.171, ĩ=-9.016
	a vs ã	<0.001*	a=-20.179, ã=-31.927
Elderly	i vs ĩ	0.047	i=-11.603, ĩ=-14.884
	a vs ã	0.841	a=-33.020, ã=-32.700

Table 3. The p-value obtained from multiple comparisons of variance analysis of elderly, middle-aged and young data(α=0.05).

	Comparison group	p-value	Nasalization degree comparison
i	Youth vs. Middle-aged	<0.001*	Youth<Middle-aged
	Youth vs. Elderly	<0.001*	Youth<Elderly
	Middle-aged vs. Elderly	0.741	Middle-aged<Elderly
ĩ	Youth vs. Middle-aged	0.036	Youth>Middle-aged
	Youth vs. Elderly	0.992	Youth<Elderly
	Middle-aged vs. Elderly	0.009	Middle-aged< Elderly
a	Youth vs. Middle-aged	0.012	Youth<Middle-aged
	Youth vs. Elderly	<0.001*	Youth<Elderly
	Middle-aged vs. Elderly	<0.001*	Middle-aged<Elderly
ã	Youth vs. Middle-aged	<0.001*	Youth<Middle-aged
	Youth vs. Elderly	<0.001*	Youth<Elderly
	Middle-aged vs. Elderly	0.895	Middle-aged<Elderly

Table 2 reveals that there is a marked difference between the non-nasalized vowel i and its nasalized counterpart ĩ among young speakers, whereas no significant difference is observed between the non-nasalized vowel a and its nasalized form ã. For middle-aged speakers, there is no notable difference between the non-nasalized i and nasalized ĩ, but a significant difference exists between the non-nasalized a and nasalized ã. Among elderly speakers, a significant difference is found between the non-nasalized i and nasalized ĩ, while the nasalization status of the vowel a requires clarification through an analysis of Table 3. The T-test results for the middle-aged group demonstrate a significant difference between their non-nasalized vowel a and nasalized vowel ã. And there is no significant difference in the nasalized vowel ã between the middle-aged and elderly groups. This show that the vowel a in the elderly group does exhibit the trend of nasalization.

To investigate the perception of nasalized vowels in the Huilai dialect region and non-dialect regions, this study selected two groups of participants for a perception experiment. Due to word count limitations, the test results are summarized as follows: participants from the Huilai dialect region served as the experimental group, while participants from the non-Huilai dialect region served as the control group. Participants were aged between 25 and 50, with four participants in each group and an equal number of males and females. The results of the perception experiment showed that in the listening and identification experiment using natural speech samples, the non-dialect group could not distinguish between nasalized and non-nasalized sounds, while the dialect group could partially distinguish between nasalized sounds. In the confirmation experiment using synthetic samples, the dialect group participants perceived a boundary between the two tones, but it was not obvious. The control group participants could not distinguish between nasalized and non-nasalized sounds. This proves that the measurement of Min nasalization is indeed necessary. Notably, within the dialect group, there was a significant difference in the accuracy rates of distinguishing between nasalized and non-nasalized i and a. The accuracy rate for distinguishing i was higher. Moreover, there were no significant differences in nasal sound discrimination accuracy among listeners from different regions of Huilai. Gender and age also influenced nasal sound accuracy rates, with females performing better than males and younger adults outperforming older adults. Therefore, even for researchers who are male elderly men native to Min dialects, experimental methods prove particularly crucial—particularly in studies of nasalized a vowels.

The results of the multivariate analysis of variance in this study indicate that age and vowel type have a significant impact on nasalization. Nasalized vowels are only found in Min dialects in the Lingnan region, and they serve as a marker of dialect identity (William Labov 2007) [8]. They can also be regarded as a marker of local belonging and affection. Elderly people have deep feelings for their hometown, so they use this phonetic feature as ã marker of identity. As a result, even in some vowels without nasalization, such as ĩ and ã, nasalization may spread. This spread does not affect the Huicheng phonological system. Phonetics (Peter Ladfoged 2022) [9] shows that the nasalization of ĩ is easy to acquire but also easy to lose. The nasalization of ã is difficult to acquire, but once formed, it is relatively stable. This study confirms the above conclusions: nasalization of the vowel ã has already formed in middle-aged individuals, with ã clear boundary between nasalized and non-nasalized forms. Nasalization of the vowel ĩ has weakened in middle-aged individuals. Nasalization of the vowel ĩ has already formed in young individuals, but nasalization of the vowel ã is still in the process of formation. Similarly, the weakening or incomplete development of these nasal sounds does not affect the phonological of Hui cheng dialect.

3 Conclusion

In previous dialect literature, the recording of speech materials from speakers with nasalized and non-nasalized pronunciations relied solely on the personal judgment of researchers, leading to varying records across different materials. We compared the vocal data of the elderly, middle-aged, and young groups through one-way analysis of variance and post hoc multiple tests, and concluded that the nasalized vowel ã only showed significant differences between the young and middle-aged groups, while there was no significant difference between the middle-aged and elderly groups. The characteristics of nasalized vowel ã may be less affected by age; There are significant differences in the nasalized vowel ĩ between young and middle-aged, middle-aged and elderly, while there is no significant difference between young and elderly. This suggests that nasalization features may be less influenced by age. It indicates a generational shift in nasalized vowels: nasalized finals ĩ,ã and non-nasalized finals a,i are not passed down through generations but coexist simultaneously. Within individuals of different generations, these two types of finals show a tendency to merge. In short, we cannot simplistically state that in spoken words such as "jì(记remember)[ki31] and jiàn(见see)[kĩ31]" or "dǎ(打bit) [ta31] and dǎn (胆gallbladder)[tã53]," their finals are [i]-[ĩ] or [a]-[ã]. Based on the results of acoustic analysis, we believe that these two vowels exhibit similar pronunciation characteristics in middle-aged or young people. However, as people age, nasal and non nasal sounds may not differ significantly in pronunciation due to aging vocal function.

Acknowledgements. This study is supported by the General Project of China National Philosophy and Social Sciences (Grant No.24BYY059).

References

1. Xu, F.: The diffusion phenomenon of nasalized vowels in eastern min dialects. J. Guangxi Nor. Univ. (Philosophy and Social Sciences Edition) **53**(5), 94-100 (2017)
2. Fang, Q., Li, A.: Study on mandarin nasalized vowels: Proceedings of the 6th National Conference on Modern Phonetics, vol. 1, Tian Jin, pp. 52–56 (2003)
3. Shue, Y., Patricia, K., Chad, V., Kristine, Y.: Voice Sauce: A Program for Voice Analysis, Proceedings of the ICPhS XVII, Hong Kong, pp. 1846–1849 (2011)
4. Yuhang, Xu., Zhang, L.: Nasal initials in chaozhou dialect: rules, evolution, and stratification: studies of the Chinese. Language **387**(6), 705–708 (2018)
5. Lin, F., Shi, M., Yuan, D., Shen, R.: Issues in Phonation Studies and the Use of VoiceSauce. Dialect (4), 385–397 (2019)
6. Chen, M.Y.: Acoustic Correlates of Nasality in Speech. Ph.D. thesis, pp. 45–47. Massachusetts Institute of Technology, Cambridge (1996)
7. Du, T.: Experimental study of vowel nasalization based on two analytical methods——Take Dongkou dialect as an example: Master of Art in Linguistics and Applied Linguistics in the Graduate school, pp. 1–2. Hunan University (2020)
8. Labov, W.: Principles of linguistic change: Social Factors, 1st edn. Peking University Press, BeiJing (2007)
9. Peter, L., Sandra, F.D.: Vowels and Consonants, 3rd edn. Wiley Blackwell Press, New Jersey (2012)

Quantitative Analysis of Word Length and Frequency in Hmong Language

Qian Luo(✉)

Jinan University, Guangzhou, China
lqluo0915@163.com

Abstract. This study presents the first quantitative characterization of lexical properties in Hmong, an understudied Sino-Tibetan language, through analysis of a purpose-built corpus. Employing word-length distribution modeling, Zipfian analysis, and statistical validation, we demonstrate three key findings: Hmong exhibits characteristically short word lengths, where tonal features influence length measurement but not frequency distribution; Word-length distribution follows a bimodal pattern, with an inverse correlation between length and usage frequency; Word-frequency distributions conform to a Right-Truncated Modified Zipf-Alekseev model, exhibiting three distinct regimes—slow decay (high-frequency words), near-Zipfian decay (mid-frequency words), and accelerated decay (low-frequency words). These results reveal fundamental self-organization principles governing the Hmong lexical system, providing new insights into the typological diversity of Sino-Tibetan languages.

Keywords: Hmong Language · Word Length · Word Frequency · Zipf's Law

1 Introduction

The Miao are one of the largest ethnic minorities in China. The Miao language belongs to the Hmong–Mien language family. Chinese Miao people are primarily divided into three dialect groups: Eastern (Western Hunan), Central (Eastern Guizhou), and Western (Sichuan, Guizhou, and Yunnan). The Western dialect has the largest number of speakers and the widest geographic distribution.

Traditional Miao lexical research has followed two main approaches: single-point descriptions of core vocabulary and loanwords (Shi 2003 [1]; Xiong 2005 [2]); and specialised subsets, such as kinship terms and classifiers (Wang & Wang 1983 [3]; Ji 2013 [4]). However, current quantitative research is often limited to small wordlists of 1,000–2,000 items for lexical composition analysis (Minett & Wang 2003 [5]), cognate comparison (Serva & Petroni 2008 [6]), or morpheme productivity studies (Krott 1996 [7]).

Word length and frequency analysis offers crucial morphological insights, typically measured in syllables (Mendenhall 1887, 1901 [8, 9]), graphemes (Chen & Liu 2016 [10]), or phonemes (Popescu et al. 2013 [11]), revealing distinct distribution patterns. As a transboundary language, Hmong provides a valuable opportunity for lexicometric

X. Ding and Y. Dong (Eds.): CLNLP 2025, CCIS 2775, pp. 97–108, 2026.
https://doi.org/10.1007/978-981-95-4788-3_10

research, facilitating intralinguistic analysis and cross-national comparisons of Miao dialects.

2 Materials and Methods

The Miao language has a long history, but it lacked a widely used written script for a long time. Materials are fragmented across different dialects and are mostly transcribed using the International Phonetic Alphabet (IPA), resulting in inconsistent datasets. However, through fieldwork and text processing, we have developed a corpus of 35,698 validated sentences containing 254,051 lexical items. This enables analysis of word length and frequency.

2.1 Corpus Design and Sources

This study focuses on Dananshan Hmong Village in China's Guizhou Province, which is considered the standard reference for the Sichuan-Guizhou-Yunnan Hmong dialect. As the ancestral homeland of Hmong communities across the globe, the dialect spoken in Dananshan holds particular significance for cross-cultural research.

The Hmong sentence corpus was systematically constructed through four key phases: initial fieldwork documented natural language patterns and established a communicative scenario framework; this framework guided the development of a comprehensive "Hmong Language Communication Function Outline"; native speakers then performed text transcription based on this framework; subsequent computational organisation took place in Excel, alongside manual linguistic annotation, including word segmentation and part-of-speech tagging.

China's modern Hmong orthography, which was developed in the 1950s using a Latin-based alphabet similar to that used for Lao Hmong, features a left-to-right writing system comprising 56 consonants, 29 vowels, and eight tonal markers. Spaces are used to separate syllables, and tone markers must be attached strictly. Syllabic segmentation follows consonant-vowel combinations (e.g., "k/h/m" plus vowels), while vowel clusters are treated as single units (e.g., "uad"). This system distinguishes between monosyllabic and polysyllabic words systematically.

2.2 Parameter Definitions

Word Length and Word Length Distribution. Word length can be quantified in three ways: orthographically (by counting letters), syllabically (by counting syllables), or phonetically (by counting phonemes). Our study uses the orthographic method to analyse minimum and maximum lengths, as well as central tendencies, ensuring methodological consistency with corpus linguistics standards.

Word length frequencies typically investigate the frequency of words of different lengths in syllables [12]. The distribution of word lengths within a corpus reveals fundamental patterns in a language's morphological structure, lexical formation processes, and historical development.

Word Frequency and Word Frequency Distribution. A word frequency analysis measures the occurrence of terms in a corpus using two metrics: absolute frequency (raw counts) and relative frequency (the proportional occurrence, expressed as a decimal or percentage).

The relative frequency is calculated as follows:

$$h_i = \frac{f_i}{N} \quad (1)$$

where fi = absolute frequency and N = total number of words.

The average word frequency across a corpus is:

$$\overline{f} = \frac{N}{S_w} \quad (2)$$

where S_w is the number of unique words.

The distribution of word frequencies reveals a universal linguistic pattern: a small core vocabulary accounts for the majority of textual occurrences, while most words appear rarely. This fundamental imbalance is formalised by Zipf's law ($F \times r = C$).

Word Length and Word Frequency. The relationship between word length and frequency examines how frequently words appear in relation to their syllable count. In *The Psycho-Biology of Language* (1935: 38), George K. Zipf states the following: "In view of the evidence of the stream of speech we may say that the length of a word tends to bear an inverse relationship to its relative frequency." Köhler's hypothesis, which has exerted a significant influence on the field, posits that words of a shorter length are used more frequently than those of a longer length. The aforementioned relationship can be expressed in mathematical terms as follows:

$$L = a \times F^{-b} \quad (3)$$

where L is word length, F is word frequency, and a and b are constants.

2.3 Methods

This quantitative linguistic study uses descriptive statistical analysis (Excel/SPSS) to examine central tendency and dispersion measures, alongside Altmann-Fitter modelling, to identify mathematical patterns in Hmong language data.

3 Results

3.1 Word Length and Word Length Distribution

The Hmong sentence corpus contained a small number of untranslated loanwords (e.g., "WIFI", "BRT") that did not conform to native morphological patterns. These low-frequency items (0.07% of the total number of tokens) were excluded, resulting in the analysis of 253,878 tokens. Word lengths were measured and processed using SPSS (see Table 1).

Table 1. Statistics on average word length in the Hmong sentence corpus.

	M	Me	Mo	SD	R	Min	Max
(+Tone)	4.96	4	4	2.313	24	2	26
(-Tone)	3.67	3	3	1.868	20	1	21

Quantitative analysis reveals that tonal marks have a significant impact on Hmong word length measurements (see Table 1): the mean length increases from 3.67 to 4.96 characters when tonal marks are included, with corresponding shifts in the modal and median values (both from 3 to 4 characters). The tonal marks dataset exhibits greater variability (higher standard deviation), reflecting length fluctuations induced by tonal marks. This primarily operates at the syllable level, given that Hmong's lexicon is dominated by monosyllabic and disyllabic forms (97% combined frequency; see Table 2), with tonal marks consistently adding one character per marked syllable.

Table 2. Distribution of word length in the Hmong sentence corpus (N = 253,878).

Word Type	Count (n)	Percentage (%)
Monosyllabic	185982	73.26
Disyllabic	62906	24.78
Trisyllabic	4062	1.60
Tetrasyllabic	893	0.35
Pentasyllabic	30	0.01
Hexasyllabic	5	0.00

Pentasyllabic and hexasyllabic words are extremely rare in the Hmong language and consist exclusively of loanwords, so we have excluded them from further analysis. Instead, our study focuses on words ranging from one to four syllables, for which we calculate the average word length. The results are presented in Table 3.

The Menzerath–Altmann law was discovered in phonology by A. Gregoire in 1899. It was later described by Paul Menzerath and fully formulated for the entire language system as follows: "The longer a language construct, the shorter its constituents." This was later formalised mathematically by Gabriel Altmann (1980) as $y = ax^{-b}$. However, our analysis of Hmong corpus data (see Table 3 and Fig. 1) reveals distributional patterns that diverge from this established principle.

Figure 1 shows that there are significant deviations from the Menzerath-Altmann law in Hmong syllable length distributions. These deviations are due to high-frequency function words favouring short syllables disproportionately, and communicative complexity driving the adoption of polysyllabic loanwords. Unlike alphabetic languages such as English and Spanish or pre-attached tonal systems such as Vietnamese and

Table 3. Average length of words with different syllables in the Hmong sentence corpus.

	M	Me	Mo	SD	R	Min	Max
M(+ Tone)	3.77	4	4	0.86124	5	2	7
M(-Tone)	2.77	3	3	0.86121	5	1	6
D(+ Tone)	3.93	4	4	0.645	4	3	7
D(-Tone)	2.93	3	3	0.645	4	2	6
Tr(+ Tone)	3.94	4	4	0.56004	3.33	2.67	6
Tr(-Tone)	2.94	3	3	0.55998	3.33	1.67	5
Te(+ Tone)	4.01	4	3.75	0.58788	3.5	2.75	6.25
Te(-Tone)	3.01	3	2.75	0.58788	3.5	1.75	5.25

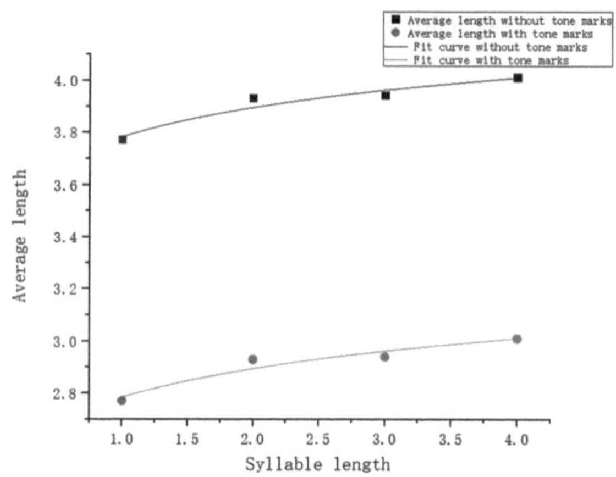

Fig. 1. Function fitting of the average syllable length in Hmong.

Pinyin, Hmong's post-attached tonal notation (adding one to two characters per syllable) uniquely impacts length measurements. While this system creates predictable per-syllable lengthening, it also generates complex variation patterns in mixed word samples (see Table 1), demonstrating the substantial influence of tonal marks on phonological length metrics.

Although tone affects word length measurement, its impact on overall word distribution patterns is negligible. As demonstrated in our analysis of word length distribution (Fig. 2), we have accounted for tonal marks to ensure comprehensive results.

The Hmong language exhibits a distinctive bimodal word length pattern (see Fig. 2), which contrasts with the right-skewed distributions typical of Chinese [13], English, and Spanish [12]. Although it shares the Sino-Tibetan tendency of Chinese for monosyllabism (dominance of 2–3 characters), the historical contact situations of Hmong have generated a secondary polysyllabic cluster through loanwords and compounds, creating

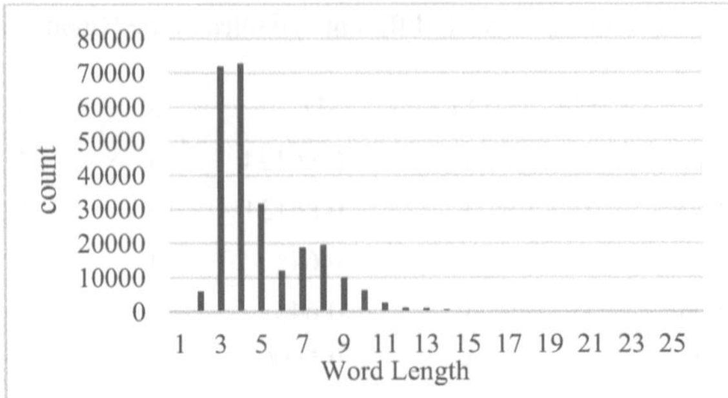

Fig. 2. Distribution characteristics of word lengths in the Hmong sentence corpus.

distributional similarity with Arabic and Farsi [14]. This dual clustering reflects the language's unique morphological development at the intersection of native monosyllabic tendencies and borrowed polysyllabic structures.

3.2 Word Frequency Distribution Pattern

The average word frequency indicates how frequently a word appears in a given corpus. A higher average frequency suggests that certain words are used more frequently, whereas a lower average indicates a more even distribution of word usage. This metric is calculated by dividing the total number of instances of a word by the number of unique words (types):

$$\overline{F} = \frac{253878}{7401} \approx 34.3032 \quad (4)$$

In the formula above, the total number of words in the sentence bank is 253,878 and the number of different words is 7,401.

The average word frequency indicates how frequently words typically appear in a given language. As shown in Table 4, the Hmong lexicon exhibits distinct patterns of word frequency distribution, revealing systematic variations in lexical usage.

Table 4. Hmong language word frequency distribution (partial).

Word	Frequency	Word Frequency	Word	Frequency	Word Frequency
god	10076	1.36	ib	3972	0.54
lek	8958	1.21	nad	3858	0.52
gaox	8403	1.14	hend	3709	0.50
leuf	6354	0.86	zhit	3438	0.46
nil	4844	0.65	yaos	3402	0.46
mol	4248	0.57	dol	3199	0.43

Table 4 identifies *god* ("I"), *gaox* ("you"), *nil* ("he/she"), and grammatical markers *lek* ("of/the") and *leuf* (past tense) as exceptionally high-frequency items, reflecting their fundamental roles in deixis and syntactic structuring. Our frequency analysis reveals that the top 1,000 words (90% coverage) comprise 865 native terms (300–800 occurrences) and 135 loanwords (e.g., *taof* "set", *bid saif* "competition"), demonstrating Hmong's lexical stratification between native core vocabulary and borrowed modern terminology.

Quantitative analysis reveals an inverse correlation between word length and frequency in Hmong (Tables 5, Fig. 3). These findings align with Köhler's (1986) power law ($L = a \times F^{-b}$) and the communicative efficiency principle: shorter, more frequent words minimize articulatory effort while maintaining semantic precision [15]. The fitted curves demonstrate this robust negative correlation, confirming the cross-linguistic validity of length–frequency optimization in Hmong's phonological system.

Table 5. Frequency-length relationship in Hmong (total corpus size: N).

Word Length	Avg. Frequency	Word Length	Avg. Frequency	Word Length	Avg. Frequency
2	420.86	11	6.10	20	2.38
3	202.19	12	3.62	21	1
4	117.57	13	4.43	22	1
5	60.917	14	3.39	23	1
6	23.737	15	2.25	24	2.5
7	20.15	16	2.46	25	1
8	16.11	17	2.12	26	1
9	9.11	18	1.94		
10	8.84	19	2.56		

$a = 712.59$, $b = 2.052$, $R^2 = 0.9698$

Our analysis reveals a strong inverse correlation between word length and frequency in Hmong ($y = 712.59x^{-2.052}$, $R^2 = 0.9698$). These findings empirically validate Köhler's power law and the psycholinguistic principle of articulatory economy within the Hmong phonological system.

Verification of Zipf's Law. Zipf's law has become the dominant model for written texts. However, it has not been widely validated in spoken registers, particularly for less studied languages such as Hmong. This study addresses this issue by conducting a quantitative analysis of spoken frequency distribution in Hmong (see Table 6) and testing Zipf's inverse power-law hypothesis.

Table 6 shows that of the 30 most common words in the Hmong language database, only one—*ib nzhik* ("a little")—is not monosyllabic. This suggests a preference for concise and efficient word forms. These 30 words account for almost 30% of the entire

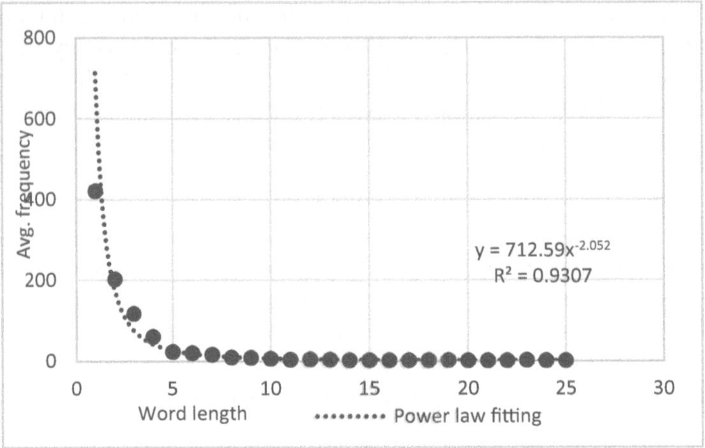

Fig. 3. Fitting the relationship between word frequency and word length.

Table 6. The top 30 most frequent words in the Hmong sentence corpus (N = total word count).

Rank	Word	Frequency	(%)	Rank	Word	Frequency	(%)
1	god	10076	0.0397	16	yat	2718	0.0107
2	lek	8958	0.0353	17	rongt	2659	0.0105
3	gaox	8403	0.0331	18	bib	2417	0.0095
4	leuf	6354	0.0250	19	muab	2220	0.0087
5	nil	4844	0.0191	20	ib nzhik	2178	0.0086
6	mol	4248	0.0167	21	uat	2085	0.0082
7	ib	3972	0.0156	22	douf	1683	0.0066
8	nad	3858	0.0152	23	duax	1658	0.0065
9	hend	3709	0.0146	24	doub	1633	0.0064
10	zhit	3438	0.0135	25	sangd	1552	0.0061
11	yaos	3402	0.0134	26	naox	1549	0.0061
12	dol	3199	0.0126	27	nenb	1535	0.0060
13	muax	3114	0.0123	28	dout	1434	0.0056
14	lob	3112	0.0123	29	haik	1421	0.0056
15	nyaob	2731	0.0108	30	nuaf	1403	0.0055

database, further reinforcing the idea that a small subset of highly frequent words dominates everyday language use.

In order to test Zipf's law more rigorously, we fitted a power-law model ($y = ax^b$) to the rank-frequency distribution of all the words in the database. As shown in Fig. 4.

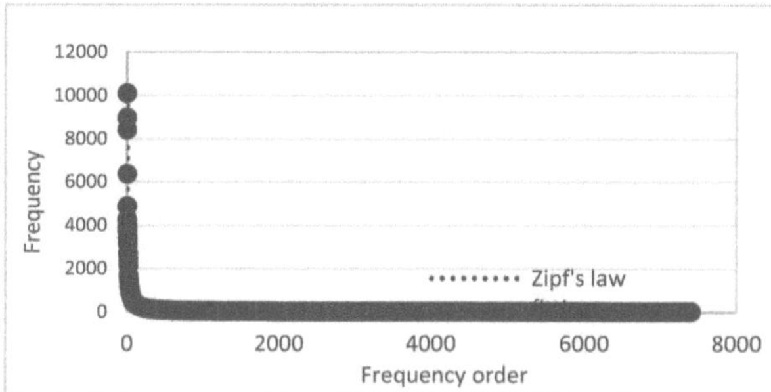

Fig. 4. Zipf's law fitting of word frequency order and frequency in the Hmong sentence corpus.

Our quantitative analysis reveals Hmong's adherence to Zipf's law, with Fig. 4 demonstrating an excellent power-law fit ($y = 737183x^{-1.539}$, $R^2 = 0.9747$) between word rank and frequency. The linearized log-log plot (Fig. 5) further confirms this relationship through its characteristic straight-line pattern, providing robust empirical evidence that Hmong's spoken lexicon follows the same fundamental distributional principles observed in written languages.

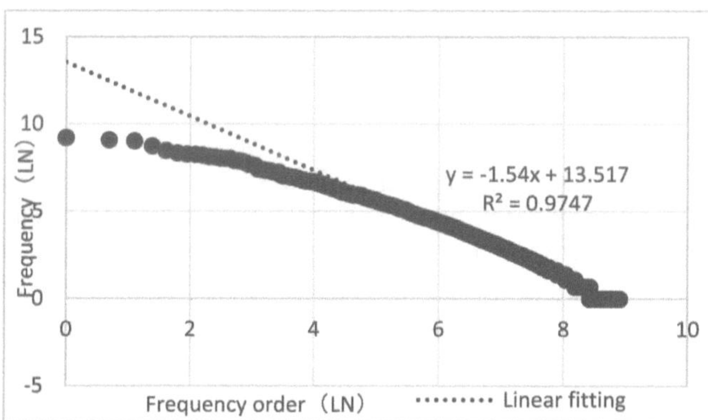

Fig. 5. Linear fitting of word frequency and order in the Hmong sentence corpus.

Figure 5 confirms that Zipf's law governs Hmong lexical frequency, exhibiting the characteristic power-law relationship ($y = -1.54x + 13.517, R^2 = 0.9747, p < 0.01$). The steeper-than-expected slope (-1.54 versus the theoretical value of -1) reveals an exceptional degree of frequency concentration in the core of the Hmong vocabulary. This enhanced lexical efficiency is best modelled by a right-truncated modified Zipf–Alekseev distribution (see Fig. 6), which suggests that there are unique optimisation mechanisms in the spoken register of Hmong that intensify the typical frequency–rank relationship observed cross-linguistically.

Zipf's Law provides a theoretical framework, but empirical data shows deviations in language distribution [16]. The classical formulation overestimates low-frequency words in shorter corpora. Our enhanced model achieves superior accuracy for constrained

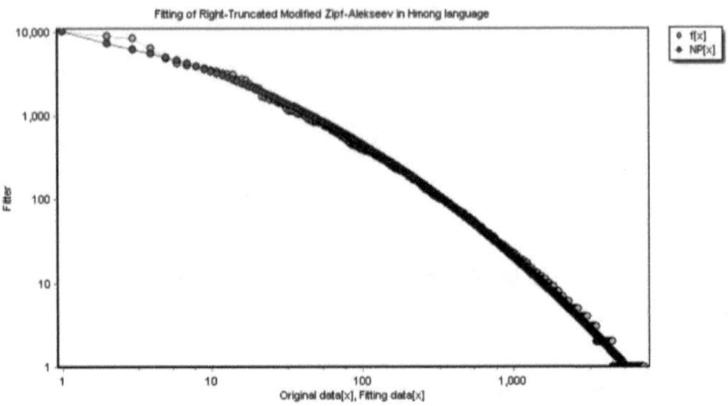

Fig. 6. Right-truncated modified Zipf-Alekseev fitting in the Hmong sentence corpus.

datasets ($R^2 = 0.9820$) through novel truncation and correction parameters. Key parameters reveal $C = 0.0117$ (minimal prediction-observation deviation); $a = 0.1662$ (slower high-frequency decay, indicating core vocabulary concentration in Hmong); and $b = 0.1019$ (elevated medium-frequency occurrence, likely reflecting loanword prevalence).

This extension of Zipf's law, which incorporates Alekseev's correction and right truncation, is particularly effective for finite texts and endangered language corpora such as Hmong.

4 Discussion

The bimodal distribution of word length in Hmong shows a significant correlation with patterns of lexical frequency, revealing how the language navigates three competing demands: communicative economy, semantic precision and contact-induced change. We combined these bimodal length and frequency distributions to create Table 7.

Table 7. The bimodal distribution of words and their frequency.

Peak area	Word length	Vocabulary quantity	Word frequency ratio
Peak area 1	2–5	1492	71.6%
Peak area 2	6–10	4412	26%
Tail peak area	> 11	1497	2.4%

Table 7 shows that Hmong has a bimodal word length distribution, with clear peaks for short words (two to five characters) and long words (six to ten characters). Despite comprising only 1,492 lexical items, short words account for 71.6% of usage frequency, highlighting their pivotal role in core linguistic expression. While longer words (6–10 characters) comprise the majority of the vocabulary (4,412 words), they are used less frequently. Words exceeding 11 characters are the least frequent (2.4%), reflecting specialised domain vocabulary. This distribution exemplifies the principle of language economy: short words dominate communication, medium-length words contribute to lexical richness and long words primarily serve specialised functions.

Zipfian analysis (Fig. 5) reveals further frequency-dependent patterns. The fitted curve exhibits three distinct segments: high-frequency bending, mid-frequency linearity and low-frequency dispersion [17]. The segmented analytical approach adopted in this study (see Table 8) enables the capture of these distinct attenuation mechanisms, thereby providing a precise characterisation of the unique lexical distribution of the Hmong language.

Table 8. Fitting analysis of different frequency bands

Frequency band	Rank	Slope(α)	Fitting equation	R^2
High-frequency	$r \leq 100$	-0.8391	y = -0.8391x + 9.9926	0.972
Mid-frequency	$100 < r \leq 1000$	-1.3109	y = -1.3109x + 12.213	0.9976
Low-frequency	$r > 1000$	-1.7552	y = -1.7552x + 15.286	0.9637

Research confirms that Zipf's law exhibits a tripartite structural pattern in most languages [16]. Our power-law analysis also reveals three distinct regimes:

(1) the high-frequency range (|α|=0.8391); Gradual decay suggests the uniform usage of core vocabulary, including assimilated Chinese loans (e.g., "*hend*", "*douf*"), which are characterised by phonological simplicity and high utility.
(2) Mid-frequency range (|α|=1.3109, $R^2 = 0.9976$): Near-Zipfian behaviour reflects modern concepts, with loanwords (e.g., "*jib chang*") and neologisms showing polysyllabic tendencies. Post-loanword removal reveals accelerated decay ($y = -0.8303x + 8.6824$, $R^2 = 0.9022$), indicating a preference for borrowing over derivation.
(3) Low-frequency range (|α|=1.7552): Rapid decay reflects specialised terms and the decline of traditional vocabulary.

This shift in distribution demonstrates how language contact and modernisation are reshaping the lexical architecture of the Hmong language, affecting frequency patterns and distributions of word length.

5 Conclusion

Combined analysis of word length and frequency distribution provides fundamental insights into language as a self-organising system. Word length is a diagnostic feature of linguistic typology; the bimodal distribution observed in the Hmong language reflects its characteristics as an isolating language, its unique lexical structures and the impact of lexical borrowing.

Although word frequency patterns generally adhere to Zipf's Law, systematic deviations can reveal a language's core architectural components, which comprise both native vocabulary and assimilated loanwords. When communicating, speakers strategically select lexical resources to strike the right balance between linguistic efficiency and semantic clarity, adapting dynamically to contextual requirements.

Due to research conditions and time constraints, the current corpus is limited to the Miao dialects of Hmong and is small. At the same time, the absence of comparable spoken corpora and transcribed texts for other Miao dialects has prevented cross-dialect comparative analysis.

References

1. Shi, D.: Semantic variations of Chinese loanwords and native words in Miao language. Ethnic Languages **5**, 43–52 (2003)
2. Xiong, Y.: Chinese loanwords in foreign Hmong. In: Abstract of the 38th International Sino-Tibetan Conference (2005)
3. Wang, F., Wang, D.: Adverbs in Guizhou Weining Miao language. Linguistic Studies 2 (1983)
4. Ji, F.: A Study on Noun Quantifiers in Qiandong Miao Language. Guizhou Ethnic Studies **4**, 211–215 (2013)
5. Minett, J.W., Wang, W.S.Y.: On detecting borrowing: distance-based and character-based approaches. Diachronica **20**(2), 289–330 (2003)
6. Serva, M., Petroni, F.: Indo-European languages tree by Levenshtein distance. Europhys. Lett. **81**(6), 68005 (2008)
7. Krott, A.: Some remarks on the relation between word length and morpheme length. J. Quantit. Linguist. **3**(1), 29–37 (1996)
8. Mendenhall, T.C.: The characteristic curves of composition. Science **214s**, 237–246 (1887)
9. Mendenhall, T.C.: A mechanical solution of a literary problem. The Popular Science Monthly, 97–105 (1901)
10. Chen, H., Liu, H.: How to measure word length in spoken and written Chinese. J. Quantitat. Linguis. **23**(1), 5–29 (2016)
11. Popescu, I.-I., et al.: Word length: Aspects and languages. Iss. Quantit. Linguist. **3**, 224–281 (2013)
12. Smith, R.D.: Distinct word length frequencies: distributions and symbol entropies. arxiv preprint arXiv:1207.2334 (2012)
13. Chen, H., Liu, H.: A diachronic study of Chinese word length distribution. Glottometrics **29**, 81–94 (2014)
14. Rothschild, L.: The distribution of English dictionary word lengths. J. Statist. Plann. Infer. **14**(2–3), 311–322 (1986)
15. Jackendoff, R., Pinker, S.: The nature of the language faculty and its implications for evolution of language (Reply to Fitch, Hauser, and Chomsky). Cognition **97**(2), 211–225 (2005)
16. Yu, S., Xu, C., Liu, H.: Zipf's law in 50 languages: its structural pattern, linguistic interpretation, and cognitive motivation. arXiv preprint arXiv:1807.01855 (2018)
17. Moreno-Sánchez, I., Font-Clos, F., Corral, Á.: Large-scale analysis of Zipf's law in English texts. PLoS ONE **11**(1), e0147073 (2016)

An Evaluation Framework for Speech Translation Systems: Addressing Acoustic Factors and Error Propagation

Zixuan Wang[1] and Xiaojun Zhang[1,2](✉)

[1] School of Humanities and Social Sciences, Xi'an Jiaotong-Liverpool University, Suzhou, China
Xiaojun.Zhang01@xjtlu.edu.cn

[2] Anhui Provincial Key Laboratory of Multimodal Cognitive Computation, Anhui University, Anhui, China

Abstract. As speech translation systems become increasingly integrated into real-world applications, there is a growing need for comprehensive evaluation frameworks that reflect both linguistic accuracy and functional performance. Existing evaluation methods often overlook acoustic difficulties and error propagation which significantly affect system input and output. This study proposes a unified evaluation framework tailored for both cascading and end-to-end speech translation systems. It considers acoustic difficulties factors and error propagation and allows for reward mechanisms in cases where translation stages correct upstream errors. A case study evaluating a cascading system using varied-accent English speeches demonstrates that the proposed framework effectively captures system performance across diverse conditions. While the framework is only on system level and dependent on subjective human ratings, it provides a solid foundation for future development of objective, fine-grained evaluation standards.

Keywords: Speech Translation System · Translation Evaluation

1 Introduction

Speech translation is the task of automatically translating a spoken signal in one language into text or speech in another language. Over time, speech translation systems have evolved through two main models: the cascaded and the end-to-end speech translation system.

In the early stages of development, speech translation systems were primarily implemented using a cascaded approach [1], where ASR (Automatic Speech Recognition) and MT (Machine Translation) were treated as sequential components in a pipeline. It can deliver reasonable performance and high adaptability across different languages and domains. However, this approach also presents several challenges. For example, it requires consistent training and maintenance for both the ASR and MT modules. Moreover, it is prone to error propagation, where mistakes from the ASR stage negatively affect the MT output [2].

X. Ding and Y. Dong (Eds.): CLNLP 2025, CCIS 2775, pp. 109–129, 2026.
https://doi.org/10.1007/978-981-95-4788-3_11

To overcome the limitations of cascaded models, Bérard et al. [3] and Weiss et al. [4] introduced the first end-to-end speech translation system. Unlike traditional systems that treat transcription and translation as separate stages, this approach integrates both processes into a single framework. Researchers have shown that end-to-end models yield promising results when compared to cascaded models.

Nonetheless, end-to-end models are not without challenges. Key obstacles include data scarcity, modeling complexity, and practical deployment issues. First, annotating speech data is labor-intensive, making labeled training data limited [5]. Furthermore, end-to-end systems must perform both cross-modal and cross-lingual mapping simultaneously, which increases the modeling burden. In practical applications, issues such as real-time processing, long-form audio segmentation, gender bias, named entity translation, and handling of code-switching speech further complicate the performance [6]. Moreover, since end-to-end models function more like black boxes, they complicate the ability to diagnose errors or optimize individual components within the system [7]. In fact, recent evaluations have shown that in 6 out of 8 instances, cascaded systems outperformed end-to-end systems [8].

Accurate recognition of spoken word pronunciation is essential for the effectiveness of speech translation systems. However, the speech recognition process is often susceptible to acoustic challenges which can significantly degrade overall system performance. For systems trained primarily on standard language, the presence of non-native speakers can introduce accented pronunciations that deviate from the training data, often resulting in decreased speech recognition accuracy.

However, even when a speaker uses standard language, other factors can still affect performance. For instance, background noise—originating from equipment, traffic, HVAC systems, surrounding conversations, or echoes—can significantly degrade speech recognition accuracy [9]. On the one hand, background noise can impair the system's ability to accurately recognize spoken words. On the other hand, such noisy environments often cause speakers to increase their vocal effort—a phenomenon known as the Lombard effect [10]. The Lombard effect is where speakers increase their vocal intensity in response to loud background noise, accompanied by several vocal adjustments aimed at improving speech intelligibility. Under the Lombard effect, vowel durations typically increase, while the durations of unvoiced stops and fricatives decrease. Additionally, speakers often exhibit an increase in pitch and a shift in the first formant frequency [11]. And even for native speakers, challenges such as similar-sounding words and word segmentation errors can hinder recognition accuracy [12]. Speaker variability further complicates the process—factors such as accent, dialect, speech rate, and individual vocal characteristics all contribute to recognition difficulty [9]. In specialized domains, out-of-vocabulary (OOV) words present another obstacle, as the system may lack the necessary lexical coverage to accurately process these terms [13].

Although speech translation technology has advanced significantly, the development of reliable and comprehensive evaluation methods has not kept pace. Most existing research focuses on output quality using automated metrics or human judgments, often overlooking the impact of acoustic challenges and error propagation. As more and more speech translation systems are deployed commercially, there is an urgent need for a holistic evaluation framework that assesses both linguistic accuracy and practical performance. Such a framework is essential for effectively identifying and selecting the most suitable systems for real-world applications.

This research addresses the question: How can a unified evaluation framework be designed to effectively assess speech translation systems, while accounting for acoustic difficulties and error propagation across different system models? In this paper, Sect. 2 reviews existing evaluation methods for speech translation systems. Section 3 introduces our proposed evaluation framework tailored for cascading models, while Sect. 4 presents its adaptation for end-to-end architectures. Section 5 offers a case study demonstrating the application of the framework to a cascading system using varied-accent English speech. Section 6 concludes the study, and Sect. 7 discusses its limitations and potential directions for future work.

2 Related Work

The evaluation of speech translation systems has been the subject of extensive research, with various methodologies proposed to assess their effectiveness. In the early stages, researchers conducted Accuracy-Based Evaluations (ABE) [14] on systems such as JANUS, which consisted of a speech recognizer, a machine translation module, and a speech synthesis module [15]. In their approach, the researchers segmented spoken utterances into semantically meaningful units known as Semantic Dialogue Units (SDUs). Each SDU was scored individually for the source and target utterances, and the scores were then compared to evaluate translation accuracy. Building upon the ABE approach, researchers later introduced Task-Based Evaluation (TBE), which focuses on goal completion, assessing whether the system successfully achieves specific communicative objectives [16]. In this framework, outputs are annotated with tags indicating task success or failure.

In recent years, researchers have explored new approaches to evaluating speech translation systems. For instance, Fantinuoli and Prandi [17] evaluated the quality of a real-time speech translation engine by comparing its output to that of professional simultaneous interpreters. To conduct this comparison, they adopted a framework originally developed for the assessment of human interpreters and applied it to manually evaluate both human and machine performance. Chen et al. [18] proposed a text-free evaluation metric specifically for end-to-end speech translation (BLASER). Their method utilizes LASER encoders to embed speech segments directly into vector representations, allowing for the computation of quality scores without relying on intermediate text transcriptions. To ensure evaluation reliability, they developed training and testing datasets containing over 40,000 human annotations. Javorský et al. [19] evaluated speech translation systems using a continuous rating approach combined with factual questionnaires administered to judges with varying levels of source language proficiency. In this setup, human evaluators continuously indicated their level of satisfaction by pressing buttons in real time.

While these studies offer valuable insights, they typically require a substantial amount of manual labor for annotation, which limits their scalability and practicality in broader applications. Besides, they do not account for acoustic conditions and error propagation, both of which significantly affect system input and output. To address this gap, our study proposes an evaluation framework that integrates both acoustic factors and error propagation, thereby offering a more comprehensive and realistic assessment of speech translation systems.

3 Evaluation for Cascaded Model

This section outlines the evaluation methodology used to assess the performance of cascaded speech translation systems. The evaluation includes calculating the Raw Quality Scores for both ASR and MT, their corresponding Adjusted Quality Scores, the Synthesis Score, and the Final System Score.

3.1 Raw Quality Score (RQS)

Traditionally, the evaluation of ASR output has relied on the Word Error Rate (WER) metric Levenshtein [20], which assesses recognition accuracy by quantifying the number of substitutions, insertions, and deletions at the word level. Despite its widespread adoption, WER has faced criticism for its limited scope. Specifically, it evaluates performance at the lexical level without accounting for contextual meaning, syntactic structure, or communicative intent [21, 22]. In response to these limitations, several alternative metrics have been proposed. These include Character Error Rate (CER), which is more suitable for languages with non-space-separated scripts; Match Error Rate (MER), which attempts to balance recognition accuracy with meaningful matches; and Word Information Lost (WIL), which estimates the information loss in a recognition hypothesis [23].

For Machine Translation, it has traditionally been evaluated using automated metrics such as BLEU [24], TER [25], and METEOR [26]. These metrics primarily focus on word or phrase level comparisons and assess surface-level similarity between system output and reference translations. However, they fall short in capturing broader contextual nuances, semantic fidelity, and pragmatic appropriateness. As such, reliance on automated metrics alone is often inadequate for comprehensively evaluating translation quality. To address these limitations, the Multidimensional Quality Metrics (MQM) framework [27] has been proposed as a more robust and context-sensitive approach. MQM provides a fine-grained, hierarchical taxonomy of error types, enabling evaluators to assess translation quality across multiple linguistic and functional dimensions. Although the framework requires substantial manual annotation effort, it offers a more reliable and nuanced assessment of MT output.

Building on the MQM framework and addressing the limitations of WER, this study proposes the use of MQM to evaluate both ASR and MT outputs. In this approach, ASR output is treated similarly to monolingual translation text, enabling its evaluation based on criteria such as accuracy and fluency, dimensions commonly used in translation quality assessment.

Calculation Procedure. The Raw Quality Score (RQS) provides an initial quality assessment for both ASR and MT outputs without any adjustments. MQM principles have been modified here to suit the unique characteristics of speech translation systems, which involve both ASR and MT stages. The calculation of RQS consists of the following steps.

Step 1 Error Identification and Severity Assignment.

In this step, evaluators identify errors in the ASR and MT outputs according to MQM framework. Then, evaluators assign each error with an appropriate severity level (e.g., neutral, minor, major and critical) based on MQM guidelines (Table 1).

Table 1. Severity Level and Definition [27].

Severity	Penalty (SPM)	Definition
Critical	25	The Severity Level of an error that renders the entire content unfit for purpose or poses the risk for serious physical, financial, or reputational harm. In many systems, a single Critical Error would automatically trigger a Fail Rating
Major	5	The Severity Level of an error that seriously affects the understandability, reliability, or usability of the content for its intended purpose or hinders the proper use of the product or service due to a significant loss or change in meaning or because the error appears in a highly visible or important part of the content
Minor	1	The Severity Level of an error that does not seriously impede the usability, understandability, or reliability of the content for its intended purpose, but has a limited impact on, for example, accuracy, stylistic quality, consistency, fluency, clarity, or general appeal of the content
Neutral	0	The Severity Level of an error that differs from a quality evaluator's preferential translation or that is flagged for the translator's attention but is an acceptable translation

Step 2 Severity Penalty Multiplier and Error Type Weight Assignment.

The Severity Penalty Multiplier (SPM) serves as a mechanism for quantifying the impact of errors based on their severity in the evaluation of translation or system output. In accordance with the MQM framework, commonly adopted penalty values are 1 for Minor errors, 5 for Major errors, and 25 for Critical errors (Table 1). These values are not arbitrarily assigned; rather, they are designed to ensure that more severe errors exert a proportionally greater influence on the overall penalty score. For example, a Critical error carries 25 times the penalty of a Minor error, reflecting its potential to substantially compromise usability, intelligibility, or compliance with legal or professional standards [27].

Beyond severity, not all error types are equally consequential in every context. The Error Type Weight (ETW) allows evaluators to adjust the significance of different error categories based on domain-specific priorities. According to MQM, by default, all error types may have an ETW of 1, meaning they contribute equally to the penalty if their severity levels match. However, depending on the application, certain errors may warrant stricter penalties [27].

Step 3 Raw Quality Score Calculation.

The initial step in computing the Raw Quality Score (RQS) involves calculating the Absolute Penalty Total (APT), which represents the cumulative penalty assigned across all identified errors in the evaluated text.

$$APT = \sum_{i,j} Error\ Count_{ij} \times SPW_j \times ETW_i \quad (1)$$

where:

i: Index for Error Types.

j: Index for Severity Level.

To normalize for differences in text length, the Per-Word Penalty Total (PWPT) is then derived by dividing the APT by the Evaluation Word Count (EWC) which is defined as the number of words in the source text, rather than the system output.

$$PWPT = \frac{APT}{EWC} \quad (2)$$

The RQS is finally calculated for ASR and MT separately. In subsequent sections, this raw score will be refined to produce Adjusted Quality Scores for both ASR and MT. These adjustments aim to provide a more accurate and equitable evaluation by incorporating external and internal factors that influence system performance.

$$RQS = 100 - (\mathrm{PWPT} \times 100) \quad (3)$$

3.2 Adjusted Quality Score (AQS) for ASR

In real-world applications, speech translation systems are often exposed to a variety of acoustic challenges. Evaluating ASR performance solely based on recognition accuracy, without accounting for acoustic conditions, presents an incomplete and potentially misleading picture of system capability. To address this limitation, this study proposes the Acoustic Difficulty Value (ADV), a composite, normalized metric designed to quantify the acoustic complexity of the input environment. The ADS consolidates acoustic factors that are known to impact ASR performance. By incorporating the ADV into the evaluation process, we adjust the RQS for ASR, which compensates for adverse conditions and provides a more equitable measure of system performance.

To take into consideration of all the acoustic difficulty factors, we adopted Multi-Attribute Utility Theory (MAUT), which is a well-established decision-making framework commonly employed in multi-criteria decision-making (MCDM) to support complex evaluations involving multiple, independently measured factors. A central tenet of MAUT is that decision-makers evaluate each attribute individually and then assign weights to reflect the relative importance of each attribute in the overall decision-making process [28]. The standard MAUT procedure, as outlined by Von Winterfeldt and Edwards [29], includes the following steps:

- Defining a set of alternatives and identifying value-relevant attributes.
- Evaluating each alternative with respect to each attribute.
- Assigning weights to the attributes based on their perceived importance.
- Aggregating the weighted attribute scores to produce an overall utility score for each alternative.

Conducting sensitivity analyses and deriving recommendations.

Drawing inspiration from this framework, the ADV proposed in this study is calculated using the principles of MAUT. In this approach, acoustic factors are treated analogously to decision-making criteria in multi-criteria evaluation. By adopting MAUT as the underlying mathematical foundation, this study systematically incorporates multiple acoustic variables, each independently assessed, into a single score. The ADV will serve as a critical component in the computation of the AQS for ASR, enabling the evaluation to account for environmental and speaker-related challenges that may impact system performance.

Calculation Procedure. To compute the AQS for ASR, the process begins with the ADV calculation, following a procedure adapted from MAUT. This process involves several steps.

Step 1 Selection of Acoustic Factors.

We provide a list of possible acoustic factors to consider; however, additional, or customized factors can be incorporated as needed (Table 2). This framework is designed to offer a flexible evaluation approach, allowing for adaptability based on specific conditions.

Step 2 Rating Acoustic Conditions.

A Likert scale evaluation is used to assess acoustic factors, relying on human judgment due to the difficulty of precisely measuring each factor. Since acoustic conditions can be subjective, human raters evaluate the environment based on predefined criteria. To ensure fair and reliable assessments, multiple raters can independently score the factors, and inter-rater agreement can be measured to validate consistency. We provide the criteria for the 1–5 scale (Table 3).

Step 3 Computation of Acoustic Difficulty Value.

The ADV (Acoustic Difficulty Value) is designed to provide a normalized score for all acoustic factors. Through min-max normalization, each acoustic factor is transformed into a standardized scale ranging from 0 to 1. In this study, although the scale is set to range from 1 to 5, a customized scale can be applied in this formula if needed. A rating of 1 in the evaluation criteria indicates no issues, so its normalized value is set to 0. As the focus of the analysis is on identifying factors that negatively impact performance, only those factors with ratings above 1 are considered in the normalization process. Therefore, N refers to the number of factors with an average rating greater than 1.

$$ADV = \frac{1}{N}\sum_{i=1}^{n}\left(\frac{R_i - R_{Min}}{R_{Max} - R_{Min}}\right) \tag{4}$$

where:

R_i: : The average rating (if multiple raters) value to be normalized.

R_{Min}: Minimum possible rating value in the scale.

Table 2. Acoustic Factors and Definition.

Category	Explanation	Rating
Background Noise	Is there any non-speech noise (e.g., traffic, typing, chatter) interfering with the clarity of the speech?	Scale: 1–5 (1 = no background noise, 5 = very noisy)
Reverberation	Does the speech sound echoey or “roomy” due to sound reflecting off surfaces?	Scale: 1–5 (1 = no noticeable reverb, 5 = heavy reverb)
Echo	Is there a distinct, delayed repetition of the speaker’s voice?	Scale: 1–5 (1 = no echo, 5 = strong echo)
Crosstalk	Is there overlapping speech from other speakers that interferes with the main speaker?	Scale: 1–5 (1 = no crosstalk, 5 = constant crosstalk)
Distance to Microphone	Does the distance of the speaker from the mic affect volume or clarity?	Scale: 1–5 (1 = ideal distance, 5 = too far/unclear)
Microphone Quality	Is the audio crisp and clear, or distorted/compressed due to poor mic quality?	Scale: 1–5 (1 = high quality, 5 = poor quality)
Accent/Dialect	Does the speaker use an unfamiliar accent or dialect that affects intelligibility?	Scale: 1–5 (1 = very clear, 5 = very difficult to understand)
Speaking Rate	Is the speech too fast or too slow, affecting comprehension?	Scale: 1–5 (1 = natural pace, 5 = extremely fast/slow)
Vocal Effort	Does the speaker sound too quiet, too loud, or strained?	Scale: 1–5 (1 = consistent and natural, 5 = poor vocal effort)
Lombard Effect	Does the speaker raise their voice due to background noise (speaking louder unnaturally)?	Scale: 1–5 (1 = unaffected, 5 = strong Lombard effect)
Speech Disfluency	Are there many hesitations, fillers, or corrections (e.g., “uh,” “um,” restarts)?	Scale: 1–5 (1 = fluent speech, 5 = very disfluent)
Out-of-Vocabulary (OOV) Words	Are there many rare, made-up, or unexpected words not commonly found in a typical vocabulary?	Scale: 1–5 (1 = no OOV words, 5 = many OOV words)
Low resource language	Is the language spoken underrepresented in training data or speech tools?	Scale: 1–5 (1 = widely supported, 5 = extremely low-resource)

Table 3. Scale Criteria.

Score	Criteria
1	No Impact: No perceptible issues. Audio is clear and fully intelligible
2	Minor Impact: Slight imperfections (e.g., faint noise, trivial distortion) that do not impede understanding. Issues are noticeable but easily ignored
3	Moderate Impact: Clear but non-critical flaws (e.g., intermittent noise, mild muffling). Requires occasional listener effort but remains mostly intelligible
4	Major Impact: Frequent disruptions (e.g., loud background noise, significant distortion). Intelligibility is challenged, requiring substantial listener effort to comprehend
5	Severe Impact: Unintelligible or chaotic (e.g., overwhelming noise, severe clipping). Communication fails entirely or requires repeated corrections

R_{Max}: Maximum possible rating value in the scale.
N: : The number of factors (above rating of 1).
Step 4 Calculation of AQS for ASR.

The AQS aims to compensate the ASR Raw Quality Score by accounting for acoustic difficulties. A lower ASR score under severe acoustic conditions will result in a higher compensation, while a higher ASR score under less challenging acoustic conditions will result in smaller compensation. Even in cases where the ASR score is higher, severe acoustic conditions will still lead to some compensation. However, the maximum adjusted score will not exceed a score of 100.

$$AQS_{ASR} = RQS_{ASR} + (100 - RQS_{ASR}) \times ADV \tag{5}$$

3.3 Adjusted Quality Score (AQS) for MT

ASR errors inevitably affect MT results in a cascading model. If MT errors are identified, it would be unfair to penalize MT alone without considering the propagated errors from ASR. Furthermore, our experiments have shown that in some cases, MT is able to correct ASR errors. While some of these corrections may be minor, they demonstrate the system's robustness and should be rewarded. In our study, we adjust the MT Score to account for error propagation and to reward instances where MT successfully corrects ASR errors.

Calculation Procedure. The first component of the AQS involves compensating propagation errors from the ASR stage. When calculating the Raw Quality Score, evaluators should have already identified errors in the MT output. In this subsequent step, evaluators are required to further classify each error based on its origin, for exmaple, whether it arises from the MT component itself or is the result of error propagation from the ASR stage. Once all propagated errors are identified, a separate Raw Quality Score should be calculated exclusively for these propagation-induced errors (calculate again the RQS with only progagration errors). The propagation compensation factor is calculated by dividing the RQS_{MT} by the RQS_{Prop}. Since RQS_{MT} is typically equal to or lower than

RQS_{Prop}, the resulting ratio reflects the extent to which MT performance is affected by propagated errors. A value closer to 1 indicates that most errors stem from earlier stages, suggesting that the MT component itself performs well and the system's actual performance is better than the raw score implies.

It is important to note that in some cases if evaluators assign multiple errors with a Critical severity level, the resulting RQS may be reduced to zero. This outcome can significantly impact the calculation of the AQS. Therefore, evaluators must exercise caution when assigning the Critical severity level. This level should be reserved for errors that severely compromise the usability or comprehensibility of the entire output. In cases where the impact is substantial but does not render the material unusable, a Major severity level should be assigned instead.

The second component of the AQS involves rewarding the machine translation system for correcting errors originating from the ASR stage. Evaluators should identify instances where the MT component successfully rectifies ASR-generated errors and classify these corrections according to their severity level—minor, major, or critical. Corresponding reward weights are assigned as follows: 0.2 for minor corrections, 1 for major corrections, and 5 for critical corrections. If no corrections are identified, the reward score will be zero.

It is important to note that, in some cases, the cumulative reward may result in an Adjusted MT Score exceeding the maximum threshold of 100. In such instances, a capping mechanism should be implemented to ensure the score remains within an acceptable range. The specific cap value can be defined by the evaluators, depending on the evaluation context and objectives.

$$AQS_{MT} = \underbrace{\frac{RQS_{MT}}{RQS_{Prop}}}_{PropagationCompensation} \times 100 + \underbrace{\sum_{k \in Severity} (w_k \times n_k)}_{Reward} \tag{6}$$

$$w_k = \begin{cases} 0.2 & if\ k = Minor \\ 1 & if\ k = Major \\ 5 & if\ k = Critical \end{cases}$$

where:

RQS_{MT}: Raw Quality Score of MT.
RQS_{prop}: Raw Quality Score of MT by ASR error propogation.
k: Severity Level.
w_k: Reward per correction for k.
n_k: Number of corrections for k.

3.4 Synthesis Score

In the cascaded model pipeline, the final stage involves speech-to-text synthesis. While the Raw Quality Score primarily focuses on assessing the accuracy and fluency of the content itself, the Synthesis Score is designed to evaluate the quality of the final text output as a product. We provide a flexible set of evaluation criteria for speech-to-text modes (Table 4). Evaluators may select any combination of criteria from the provided list or introduce customized criteria to suit the specific evaluation goals. The evaluation process is designed to be user-centered and can be conducted by end users, professional translators, or technical evaluators. As the evaluation focuses solely on the final output as product, there is no strict requirement for evaluators to be bilingual professionals.

Table 4. Criteria and Ranking for Speech-to-text Mode.

Criteria	Explanation	Rating
Paragraph Segmentation	Does the text split into logical paragraphs/sentences based on speech pauses or topic shifts?	Scale: 1–5 (1 = no segmentation, 5 = natural breaks)
Punctuation Accuracy	Are punctuation marks (commas, periods) and capitalization used correctly to enhance readability?	Scale: 1–5 (1 = missing/chaotic, 5 = flawless)
Line Breaks and Wrapping	Does text wrap neatly without awkward mid-word splits or excessively long lines?	Scale: 1–5 (1 = jarring breaks, 5 = smooth wrapping)
Scrolling Smoothness	Does text scroll smoothly, and stay visible long enough to be read (without lingering)?	Scale: 1–5 (1 = too brief, 5 = fluid and well-timed)
Latency	Does the output delay heavily when compared to input speech?	Scale: 1–5 (1 = heavy delay, 5 = no delay)

Calculation Procedure. The goal of this calculation is to convert human rating scores into a standardized 0–100 scale. The first step involves normalizing subjective human ratings using a simple linear transformation, where each increment on the original scale corresponds to a fixed increase of 25 points on a 0–100 scale. This method preserves the proportional meaning of responses while offering sufficient granularity.

$$S_{norm} = (R - 1) \times 25 \tag{7}$$

where:

R: Subjective rating ($1 \leq R \leq 5$).

S_{norm}: Normalized score ($0 \leq S_{norm} \leq 100$).

Once the scores are normalized, the overall performance score is calculated by averaging the normalized scores across n selected criteria, as shown in the following formula:

$$S_{syn} = \frac{1}{n}\sum_{i=1}^{n} S_{norm,i} \tag{9}$$

3.5 Final System Score (FSS)

The FSS represents the overall evaluation of the system by integrating the component scores from ASR, MT, and synthesis. The score is calculated using the following formula, where α, β, and γ are customizable weights that determine the relative importance of each component. Evaluators may adjust these weights according to the specific goals or priorities of their evaluation.

$$FSS_{System} = AQS_{ASR} \times \alpha + AQS_{MT} \times \beta + S_{syn} \times \gamma \quad (10)$$

where:

$$\alpha + \beta + \gamma = 1$$

4 Adapted Evaluation for End-to-End Model

This section presents the adapted evaluation methodology for end-to-end speech translation systems, based on the framework introduced in Sect. 3.

4.1 Raw Quality Score (RQS)

The Raw Quality Score remains the initial step in evaluating end-to-end speech translation models and is calculated using the MQM-based methodology described in Sect. 3.1. Unlike cascaded systems, end-to-end models do not include distinct ASR and MT stages; thus, only a single RQS is computed for the final output. End-to-end systems can be further categorized into speech-to-text and speech-to-speech modes. For speech-to-text models, the output text is directly evaluated. For speech-to-speech models, the output speech is first transcribed into text before undergoing quality assessment.

4.2 Adjusted Quality Score (AQS)

Although end-to-end models do not explicitly separate ASR and MT stages, adjustments to the Raw Quality Score are still necessary. As discussed in Sect. 3.2, acoustic conditions significantly impact system performance. This influence persists even in integrated models, where acoustic challenges may affect early encoding stages and propagate through the entire pipeline. Therefore, the RQS for end-to-end systems is still adjusted based on the Acoustic Difficulty Value of the given speech with the same formula.

4.3 Synthesis Score

For end-to-end models, the evaluation and calculation of both speech-to-text and speech-to-speech mode will be the same as in Sect. 3.4. However, for speech-to-speech mode, we will provide a list of criteria for speech-to-speech mode (Table 5).

Table 5. Criteria and Ranking for Speech-to-speech Mode.

Criteria	Explanation	Rating
Intelligibility	How clearly are words understood?	Scale: 1–5 (1 = unintelligible, 5 = very intelligible)
Pronunciation Accuracy	Are words pronounced correctly?	Scale: 1–5 (1 = many errors, 5 = flawless)
Voice Naturalness	Does the voice sound human-like (vs. robotic/mechanical)?	Scale: 1–5 (1 = unnatural, 5 = indistinguishable from human)
Prosody and Intonation	Does the voice modulate pitch, rhythm, and stress naturally (e.g., questions rise in pitch)?	Scale: 1–5 (1 = monotone, 5 = expressive)
Speaking Rate	Does the speech pacing match the context (e.g., no unnaturally slow/fast delivery)?	Scale: 1–5 (1 = pacing mismatched, 5 = perfect pacing)
Emotional Expressivity	Does the tone convey intended emotions (e.g., excitement, sadness)?	Scale: 1–5 (1 = emotionless, 5 = highly expressive)
Latency	Does the output synthesis delay heavily compared to input speech?	Scale: 1–5 (1 = heavy delay, 5 = no delay)
Audio Quality	Are there background noise?	Scale: 1–5 (1 = unusable, 5 = pristine)
Speaker Similarity	How closely does the output voice match the target speaker's voice?	Scale: 1–5 (1 = no resemblance, 5 = identical)
Lip-Sync Accuracy	Does synthesized speech match lip movements in video input?	Scale: 1–5 (1 = mismatch, 5 = perfect sync)

4.4 Final System Score (FSS)

Although end-to-end models do not have separate ASR and MT stages, the FSS can be calculated in a similar manner to the adjusted scoring method outlined in Sect. 3.5, incorporating both content quality and external influencing factors such as acoustic difficulty and synthesis performance.

$$FSS_{System} = AQS \times \alpha + S_{syn} \times \beta \tag{11}$$

where:

$$\alpha + \beta = 1$$

5 Case Study

We apply this evaluation framework to assess the performance of an interpreting system called iFLYREC, a Multilingual Simultaneous Interpreting System that follows a typical cascading model architecture. The test speeches are sourced from the International

Dialects of English Archive[1] (IDEA) which provides a wide range of English accents, varying audio qualities, and diverse speaker demographics. For the evaluation, we used several recordings of the same speech, "Comma Gets a Cure[2]", spoken by different individuals.

We evaluated four speeches, information of which can be found in Table 6. In calculating the Raw Quality Scores, we focus exclusively on the dimensions of Accuracy and Fluency, assigning an equal weight of 1 to each. Error severity penalties are applied in accordance with the MQM framework, with point values of 1 for Minor, 5 for Major, and 25 for Critical errors. The total number of identified errors, along with those attributed to error propagation, are summarized in Table 7.

Table 6. List of speeches.

No	Speaker Information	Speech Source
1	Chinese, Male, 1997	https://www.dialectsarchive.com/england-112
2	Spanish, Female, 1973	https://www.dialectsarchive.com/washington-5
3	British, Male, 1969	https://www.dialectsarchive.com/beijing-2
4	American, Female, 1997	https://www.dialectsarchive.com/spain-4

Table 7. Speech Error Summary.

Speech No. 1 (Chinese)					
Total ASR Error					
Critical	Major	Minor	Neutral	RQS (ETW 1 for A/F)	AQS (ADV = 0.69)
0	21	16	5	67.3	89.9
Total MT Error					
Critical	Major	Minor	Neutral	RQS (ETW 1 for A/F)	AQS
0	24	13	0	64.1	96.4 + 0.2
Total Propagation Error					
Critical	Major	Minor	Neutral	RQS (ETW 1 for A/F)	
0	23	9	0	66.5	
Total Error Correction					
Critical	Major	Minor	Neutral	Rewards	
0	0	1	0	0.2	

We found that in most cases, errors arose due to error propagation. However, there were also instances where the system successfully corrected minor errors. For example,

[1] https://www.dialectsarchive.com

[2] https://www.dialectsarchive.com/comma-gets-A-cure.

the original text 'The letter implied that the animal…' was transcribed by ASR as 'The letter employed that the animal…', which constitutes an error. Despite this, the translation stage correctly interpreted the intended meaning, producing 'The letter writes that the animal…'. In such cases, we assign a reward to reflect the system's robustness and ability to recover from upstream errors.

Component scores were calculated for each speech, as summarized in the Table 8. Two of the speeches have severe acoustic difficulties, with ADV of 0.69 and 0.75—spoken by Chinese and Spanish speakers. For each speech, two raters provided acoustic evaluations, and Table 9. It presents detailed rating results along with inter-rater agreement, assessed using Percent Agreement and Cohen's Kappa [30], as well as correlation measures based on Cronbach's Alpha [31] and the Pearson Correlation Coefficient [32]. The remaining two speeches, delivered by British and American speakers, were considered standard and acoustically clear. As a result, the ADV is marked as N/A, and RQS for ASR was not calculated.

Table 8. Scores of Speeches.

Accent	RQS ASR	RQS MT	AQS ASR	AQS MT	ADV
Chinese	67.3	64.1	89.9	96.4 + 0.2	0.69
Spanish	64.1	64.5	91.0	97.1	0.75
Average	**65.7**	**64.3**	**90.5**	**96.9**	
British	94.9	93.2	94.9	97.7 + 0.2	N/A
American	93.5	94.6	93.5	99.2	N/A
Average	**94.2**	**93.9**	**94.2**	**98.6**	

Table 9. Inner Rater Agreement of Acoustic Difficulties.

Speech No. 1 (Chinese)			
Criteria	Rater 1	Rater 2	Agreement
Background Noise	1	1	0
Reverberation	1	1	0
Echo	1	1	0
Crosstalk	1	1	0
Distance to Microphone	1	1	0
Microphone Quality	1	1	0
Accent /Dialect	3	2	1
Speaking Rate	1	1	0
Vocal Effort	1	1	0
Lombard Effect	1	1	0

(*continued*)

Table 9. (*continued*)

Speech No. 1 (Chinese)			
Criteria	Rater 1	Rater 2	Agreement
Speech Disfluency	5	5	0
OOV Words	1	1	0
Low resource language	1	1	0
Percentage Agreement	**Cohen's kappa**	**CronBach's Alpha**	**Pearson (R)**
92.3%	0.723	0.986	0.974
Speech No. 2 (Spanish)			
Criteria	Rater 1	Rater 2	Agreement
Background Noise	1	1	0
Reverberation	1	1	0
Echo	1	1	0
Crosstalk	1	1	0
Distance to Microphone	1	1	0
Microphone Quality	1	1	0
Accent /Dialect	4	5	1
Speaking Rate	1	1	0
Vocal Effort	1	1	0
Lombard Effect	1	1	0
Speech Disfluency	3	4	−1
OOV Words	1	1	0
Low resource language	1	1	0
Percentage Agreement	**Cohen's kappa**	**CronBach's Alpha**	**Pearson (R)**
84.62%	0.447	0.973	0.998
Speech No. 3 (British)			
Criteria	Rater 1	Rater 2	Agreement
Background Noise	1	1	0
Reverberation	1	1	0
Echo	1	1	0
Crosstalk	1	1	0
Distance to Microphone	1	1	0
Microphone Quality	1	1	0
Accent /Dialect	1	1	0
Speaking Rate	1	1	0

(*continued*)

Table 9. (*continued*)

Speech No. 3 (British)			
Criteria	Rater 1	Rater 2	Agreement
Vocal Effort	1	1	0
Lombard Effect	1	1	0
Speech Disfluency	1	1	0
OOV Words	1	1	0
Low resource language	1	1	0
Percentage Agreement	**Cohen's kappa**	**CronBach's Alpha**	**Pearson (R)**
100%	n/a	n/a	n/a
Speech No. 4 (American)			
Criteria	Rater 1	Rater 2	Agreement
Background Noise	1	1	0
Reverberation	1	1	0
Echo	1	1	0
Crosstalk	1	1	0
Distance to Microphone	1	1	0
Microphone Quality	1	1	0
Accent /Dialect	1	1	0
Speaking Rate	1	1	0
Vocal Effort	1	1	0
Lombard Effect	1	1	0
Speech Disfluency	1	1	0
OOV Words	1	1	0
Low resource language	1	1	0
Percentage Agreement	**Cohen's kappa**	**CronBach's Alpha**	**Pearson (R)**
100%	n/a	n/a	n/a

Results indicate that the system performs notably better in acoustically clear conditions, as evidenced by higher ASR and MT scores (above 90 points) for the British and American speakers. In contrast, under severe acoustic challenges, the ASR and MT scores for Chinese and Spanish speeches dropped to approximately 65 points. However, after applying the acoustic difficulty values, the adjusted ASR scores for the Chinese and Spanish accent speeches rose significantly, averaging 90.5, which falls in the same score range of the British and American average. Similarly, the adjusted MT scores for the same speeches averaged around 97, again showing small deviation from the scores of the acoustically clear speeches.

We invited two raters rate on their experience in viewing the translation of the speech spoken by Chinese speaker (the inter-rater agreement can be found in Table 10).

Table 10. Inter-rater Agreement of Synthesis.

Speech No. 1 (Chinese)			
Criteria	Rater 1	Rater 2	Agreement
Paragraph Segmentation	5	5	0
Punctuation Accuracy	2	3	−1
Line Breaks and Wrapping	1	1	0
Scrolling Smoothness	4	4	0
Latency	3	4	−1
Percentage Agreement	**Cohen's kappa**	**CronBach's Alpha**	**Pearson (R)**
60%	0.500	0.968	0.938

As a result, the synthesis score was 55. Then, we calcualte final adjusted system score for this system (using the score of Chinese speech as an example). We set α and β as 0.4, which means we view both ASR and MT stage as same important and we set γ as 0.2. The final system score was 85.6.

$$FSS_{System} = (89.9 + 96.6) \times 0.4 + 55 \times 0.2 = 85.6 \tag{12}$$

In general, we believe that our evaluation framework more accurately reflects the true capabilities of the system, with only small deviation.

6 Conclusion

This study presents a comprehensive evaluation framework designed to assess both cascaded and end-to-end speech translation systems in a more holistic and realistic manner. The proposed framework integrates multiple metrics—including the Raw Quality Score, Adjusted Quality Score, Synthesis Score, and Final System Score—and explicitly accounts for key challenges such as acoustic difficulty and error propagation across system components. By incorporating the MQM-based error annotation scheme along with novel constructs such as the Acoustic Difficulty Value and propagation compensation mechanisms, the framework offers a more nuanced and accurate reflection of system performance.

Through a case study involving the iFLYREC cascading system and diverse English speech samples from the International Dialects of English Archive, we demonstrated the framework's effectiveness in capturing performance variances under real-world conditions. Crucially, our findings reveal that adjusting for acoustic difficulty and error propagation significantly narrows the perceived performance gap introduced by non-native accents and complex audio inputs.

This research contributes an important step toward standardized, scalable, and context-aware evaluation of speech translation technologies. By emphasizing both external input variability and internal system dynamics, the framework lays the groundwork for more equitable benchmarking, targeted system improvement, and more reliable deployment in multilingual, accent-diverse environments.

7 Limitation

While the proposed evaluation framework provides a more comprehensive approach to assessing speech translation systems, several limitations remain. First, it is currently designed for system-level evaluation rather than fine-grained, sentence-level analysis. This restricts its ability to capture localized errors and nuanced performance differences. Future work should explore sentence-level extensions to improve diagnostic accuracy and granularity.

Second, a significant challenge arises when the Raw Quality Score—whether for ASR or MT—drops to zero due to the assignment of multiple critical severity errors by human annotators. In such cases, the Adjusted Quality Score also defaults to zero, potentially failing to reflect the system's underlying capabilities. This limitation suggests that the framework may be less reliable in scenarios where extreme human scoring skews the overall results.

Third, the current evaluation was conducted on a relatively small dataset using a single cascading speech interpretation system. As such, the findings may not fully generalize across different datasets, languages, or system architectures. To enhance the framework's robustness and applicability, future studies should incorporate more diverse speech samples and evaluate a broader range of speech translation systems, including end-to-end models.

Finally, the framework currently depends heavily on human ratings, which introduces subjectivity and variability. Although guided by established criteria such as MQM, these ratings could benefit from increased objectivity. One potential direction is to define quantifiable standards—for example, mapping background noise levels (e.g., Signal-to-Noise Ratio) to specific rating scales. Additionally, automating key aspects of the evaluation process—such as MQM annotation, rating, and scoring—through the use of neural machine learning models could greatly improve scalability, consistency, and efficiency.

Acknowledgements. This paper is supported by the Open Project of Anhui Provincial Key Laboratory of Multimodal Cognitive Computation, Anhui University (No. MMC202414) and XJTLU Research Development Funding (No. RDF-22-01-053).

References

1. Stentiford, F.W.M., Steer, M.G.: Machine translation of speech. Br. Telecom. Technol. J. **6**(2), 116–122 (1988)
2. Bentivogli, L., Cettolo, M., Gaido, M., Karakanta, A., Martinelli, A., Negri, M., Turchi, M. Cascade versus Direct Speech Translation: Do the Differences Still Make a Difference? (2021). https://doi.org/10.48550/arxiv.2106.01045
3. Bérard, A., Pietquin, O., Servan, C., Besacier, L.: Listen and translate: A proof of concept for end-to-end speech-to-text translation. In: Proceedings of the NIPS Workshop on End-to-End Learning for Speech and Audio Processing. Barcelona, Spain (2016)
4. Weiss, R.J., Chorowski, J., Jaitly, N., Wu, Y., Chen, Z.: Sequence-to-sequence models can directly translate foreign speech. In: Proceedings of the Conference of the International Speech Communication Association (INTERSPEECH), pp. 2625–2629. Stockholm, Sweden (2017)

5. Pino, J., Xu, Q., Ma, X., Dousti, M.J., Tang, Y.: Self-training for end-to-end speech translation (2020). https://doi.org/10.48550/arxiv.2006.02490
6. Xu, C. et al.: Recent advances in direct speech-to-text translation (2023).https://doi.org/10.48550/arxiv.2306.11646
7. Chen, X., Zhang, S., Bai, Q., Chen, K., Nakamura, S.: LLaST: Improved end-to-end speech translation system leveraged by large language models (2024). https://doi.org/10.48550/arxiv.2407.15415
8. Anastasopoulos, A. et al.: Findings of the IWSLT 2022 Evaluation Campaign. In: Proceedings of the 19th International Conference on Spoken Language Translation (IWSLT 2022), pp. 98–157. Association for Computational Linguistics, Dublin, Ireland (2022)
9. Charan, G., et al.: Unveiling the challenges of speech recognition in noisy environments: A comprehensive review of issues and solutions. In: Challenges in Information, Communication and Computing Technology, vol. 2, 1st edn., pp. 407–412. CRC Press (2025). https://doi.org/10.1201/9781003559092-70
10. Lombard, É.: Le signe de l'élévation de la voix. Annals Maladiers Oreille, Larynx, Nez, Pharynx **37**, 101–119 (1911)
11. Hansen, J.H.L.: Analysis and compensation of stressed and noisy speech with application to robust automatic recognition. Signal Process. **17**(3), 282 (1989). https://doi.org/10.1016/0165-1684(89)90010-8
12. Duta, N., Schwartz, R., Makhoul, J.: Analysis of the errors produced by the 2004 BBN speech recognition system in the DARPA EARS evaluations. IEEE Trans. Audio Speech Lang. Process. **14**, 1745–1753 (2006). https://doi.org/10.1109/TASL.2006.878268
13. Errattahi, R., El Hannani, A., Salmam, F., Ouahmane, H.: Incorporating label dependency for ASR error detection via RNN. Procedia Comput. Sci. **148**, 266–272 (2019). https://doi.org/10.1016/j.procs.2019.01.069
14. Gates, D., et al.: End-to-end evaluation in JANUS: a speech-to-speech translation system. In: Wahlster, W. (ed.) Dialogue Processing in Spoken Language Systems, pp. 195–206. Springer, Berlin Heidelberg (1997). https://doi.org/10.1007/3-540-63175-5_47
15. Waibel, A.: Interactive translation of conversational speech. Computer **19**(7), 41–48 (1996)
16. Levin, L. et al.: Lessons learned from a task-based evaluation of speech-to-speech machine translation. In: Proceedings of the Second International Conference on Language Resources and Evaluation (LREC'00). European Language Resources Association (ELRA), Athens, Greece (2000)
17. Fantinuoli, C., Prandi, B.: Towards the evaluation of automatic simultaneous speech translation from a communicative perspective. In: Proceedings of the 18th International Conference on Spoken Language Translation (IWSLT 2021), pp. 245–254. Association for Computational Linguistics, Bangkok, Thailand (2021)
18. Chen, M. et al.: BLASER: A Text-Free Speech-to-Speech Translation Evaluation Metric. In: Proceedings of the 61st Annual Meeting of the Association for Computational Linguistics (Volume 1: Long Papers), pp. 9064–9079. Association for Computational Linguistics, Toronto, Canada (2023)
19. Javorský, D., Macháček, D., Bojar, O.: Continuous Rating as Reliable Human Evaluation of Simultaneous Speech Translation. In: Proceedings of the Seventh Conference on Machine Translation (WMT), pp. 154–164. Association for Computational Linguistics, Abu Dhabi, United Arab Emirates (2022)
20. Levenshtein, V.I.: Binary codes capable of correcting deletions, insertions, and reversals. Soviet Phys. Doklady **10**, 707–710 (1966)
21. He, X., Deng, L., Acero, A.: Why word error rate is not a good metric for speech recognizer training for the speech translation task? In: 2011 IEEE International Conference on Acoustics, Speech and Signal Processing (ICASSP), pp. 5632–5635. IEEE (2011). https://doi.org/10.1109/ICASSP.2011.5947637

22. Sasindran, Z., Yelchuri, H., Prabhakar, T.V., Rao, S.: H_eval: A new hybrid evaluation metric for automatic speech recognition tasks. https://doi.org/10.48550/arxiv.2211.01722 (2022)
23. Morris, A., Maier, V., Green, P.: From WER and RIL to MER and WIL: Improved evaluation measures for connected speech recognition. In: Proceedings of Interspeech 2004, pp. 1–4. https://doi.org/10.21437/Interspeech.2004-668
24. Papineni, K., Roukos, S., Ward, T., Zhu, W.-J.: Bleu: a Method for Automatic Evaluation of Machine Translation. In: Proceedings of the 40th Annual Meeting of the Association for Computational Linguistics, pp. 311–318. Association for Computational Linguistics, Philadelphia, Pennsylvania, USA (2002)
25. Snover, M., Dorr, B., Schwartz, R., Micciulla, L., Makhoul, J.: A Study of Translation Edit Rate with Targeted Human Annotation. In: Proceedings of the 7th Conference of the Association for Machine Translation in the Americas: Technical Papers, pp. 223–231. Association for Machine Translation in the Americas, Cambridge, Massachusetts, USA (2006)
26. Banerjee, S., Lavie, A.: METEOR: An Automatic Metric for MT Evaluation with Improved Correlation with Human Judgments. In: Proceedings of the ACL Workshop on Intrinsic and Extrinsic Evaluation Measures for Machine Translation and/or Summarization, pp. 65–72. Association for Computational Linguistics, Ann Arbor, Michigan (2005)
27. Lommel, A., Uszkoreit, H., Burchardt, A.: Multidimensional quality metrics (MQM): a framework for declaring and describing translation quality metrics. Tradumàtica **12**, 455–463 (2014). https://doi.org/10.5565/rev/tradumatica.77
28. Jansen, S.J.T., Coolen, H.C.C.H., Goetgeluk, R.W.: The multi-attribute utility method. In: The Measurement and Analysis of Housing Preference and Choice, pp. 101–125. Springer, Netherlands (2011). https://doi.org/10.1007/978-90-481-8894-9_5
29. von Winterfeldt, D., Edwards, W.: Decision Analysis and Behavioral Research. Cambridge University Press, Cambridge (1986)
30. McHugh, M.L.: Interrater reliability: the kappa statistic. Biochemia Medica **22**(3), 276–282 (2012). https://doi.org/10.11613/BM.2012.031
31. Taber, K.S.: The use of Cronbach's alpha when developing and reporting research instruments in science education. Res. Sci. Educ. **48**(6), 1273–1296 (2018). https://doi.org/10.1007/s11165-016-9602-2
32. Pearson, K.: Mathematical contributions to the theory of evolution. III. Regression, heredity, and panmixia. Philos. Trans. R. Soc. Lond. Ser. A **373**, 253–318 (1896)

GeoRAG: A Geographic Retrieval Augmented Generation Framework Based on Urban Spatio-Temporal Knowledge Graph

Tao Chen[1,2], Shengfa Miao[1,2](✉), Shuangfeng Cai[1,2], Houcheng Liu[3], Yongkang Mu[1,2], Kaiming Yu[1,2], Hualong Deng[1,2], Xin Jin[1,2], Qian Jiang[1,2], Hua Jiang[1,2], Puming Wang[1,2], Dinan Ma[4], and Ahmed Zahir[1,2]

[1] School of Software, Yunnan University, Kunming 650000, China
miaoshengfa@hotmail.com
[2] Engineering Research Center of Cyberspace, Kunming 650000, China
[3] Yunnan Information Technology Security Evaluation Center, Kunming 650000, China
[4] Yunnan Key Laboratory of Media Convergence, Kunming, China

Abstract. This paper focuses on addressing the challenges of enabling Large Language Models (LLMs) to perform urban spatial reasoning. Existing methods have a main limitation: Retrieval Augmented Frameworks (RAG) lack effective spatial knowledge injection and fail to adequately address spatial semantics, it leads to insufficient knowledge perception of urban spatial scenarios in LLMs. To overcome this issue, we propose a novel geographic retrieval-augmented generation framework (GeoRAG). The approach avoids significant computational overhead and prevents sacrificing generalizability. GeoRAG uses OpenStreetMap data to automatically build a spatio-temporal knowledge graph (STKG). STKG organizes and stores urban spatio-temporal knowledge. GeoRAG incorporates both hierarchical and proximity based spatial features, it introduces a dual retrieval mechanism, the mechanism combines placename matching and coordinate based querying. The retrieved results need to serve as supplementary knowledge for LLMs. To inject contextual spatial knowledge into large models, a spatial prompt template was designed. Our template enabled seamless integration of the knowledge retrieved with LLMs. The experimental results on the CityGPT benchmark show that GeoRAG significantly improves the spatial reasoning performance of Qwen2.5-32B. It achieves relative accuracy gains of 11.89%, 13.25%, and 7.49% on Beijing, London, and New York datasets respectively. This demonstrates the effectiveness of plug-and-play geographic augmentation for LLMs.

Keywords: GeoRAG Framework · Urban Spatio-Temporal Knowledge Graph · Large Language Models

1 Introduction

Large Language Models (LLMs) have demonstrated strong general reasoning capabilities across various natural language processing (NLP) tasks, but LLMs' ability to accurately perceive and reason about urban geospatial information remains limited. In

X. Ding and Y. Dong (Eds.): CLNLP 2025, CCIS 2775, pp. 130–140, 2026.
https://doi.org/10.1007/978-981-95-4788-3_12

recent years, LLMs have also shown promising potential in urban spatial cognition tasks, including answering geographical questions, navigation, and spatial relationship inference. Despite LLMs' general reasoning ability, LLMs still struggle with accurate interpreting and reasoning over urban geospatial information. When models are applied to tasks requiring fine-grained spatial awareness, such as topology-based reasoning and multi-entity proximity analysis, the effect is more pronounced.

Existing efforts to enhance the spatial reasoning ability of LLMs mainly fall into two categories, supervised fine-tuning (SFT) and Retrieval Augmented methods. SFT approaches rely on spatially annotated datasets and task-specific instruction tuning to encode geographic knowledge directly into model parameters, such as CityGPT [1], BB-GeoGPT [2]. Although effective in domain-specific scenarios, these methods are associated with a high cost. Training large models typically requires substantial computational resources. Finetuning a model with 70 billion parameters requires eight A100 GPUs. Fine-tuning may also degrade general performance across unrelated tasks [1].

Retrieval Augmented Generation (RAG) [3] methods aim to avoid fine-tuning by injecting external knowledge into LLMs at inference time. Methods like UrbanKGent [4] and SpatialRAG [5] construct or utilize geographic knowledge graph and spatial databases [6] to provide relevant context for spatial reasoning. However, both UrbanKGent and SpatialRAG fail to integrate the surrounding entity information of geographical entities. As a result, the models lack the ability to perceive the surrounding information of geographical entities.

To address these issues, we propose GeoRAG which is a lightweight and plug-and-play geographic RAG framework that enhances LLMs' urban spatial reasoning abilities without requiring parameter updates. GeoRAG utilizes a 3D spatio-temporal knowledge graph automatically constructed from OpenStreetMap data, modeling spatial hierarchy, geometry, and temporal periodicity. A dual-retrieval mechanism, which combines placename matching and coordinate-based spatial querying, enables dynamic information injection into LLMs. In addition, a spatial prompt template is used to translate structured knowledge triples into natural-language prompts, ensuring compatibility with LLMs. Our key innovations include:

- Spatio-temporal knowledge graph, a 3D semantic structure, integrates temporal cycles, spatial geometry, and administrative hierarchies.
- GeoRAG, a fine-tuning-free framework, enables the injection of spatio-temporal knowledge from a knowledge graph into LLMs, addressing the challenge of insufficient perception of geographical surrounding information in LLMs.
- GeoRAG improves the performance of Qwen2.5-32B on the CityGPT benchmark by 5.4%-11.89%, outperforming large-parameter models like LLaMA3.1-405B [7].

2 Methodology

2.1 Overview

To overcome the challenges of insufficient spatial perception in current LLMs, we propose GeoRAG, a lightweight, RAG tailored for urban spatial reasoning. Unlike traditional supervised fine-tuning approaches, GeoRAG eliminates the need for fine-tuning model parameters, instead, it injects structured geographic context into LLMs during inference, enabling plug-and-play spatial enhancement.

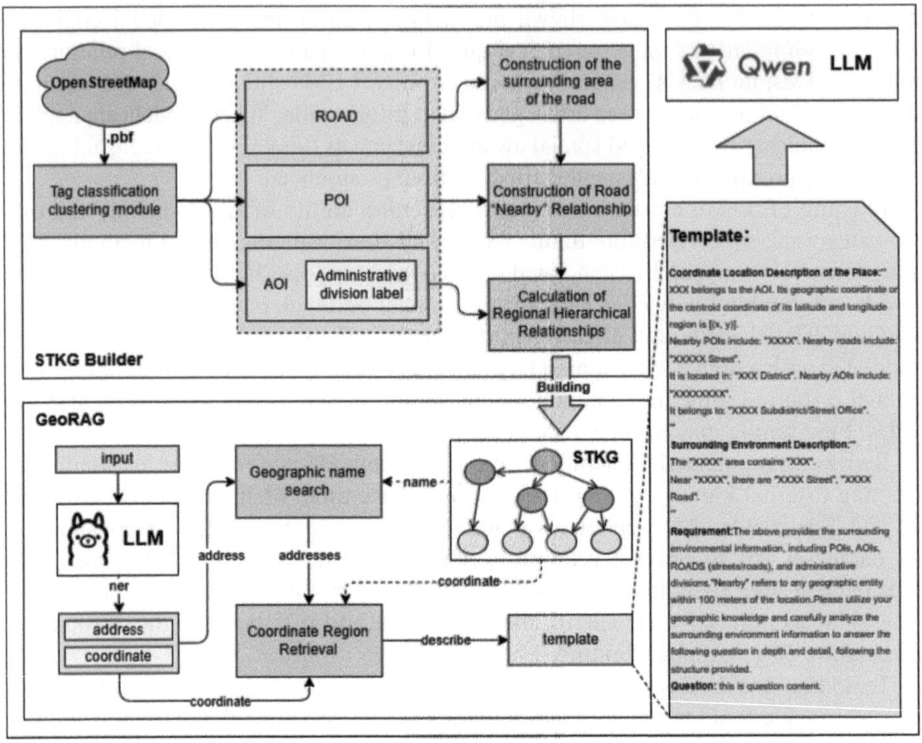

Fig. 1. Architecture of GeoRAG: a geo-knowledge-enhanced RAG with dual-layer retrieval, combining entity names and geospatial positions for contextualized spatial descriptions.

GeoRAG consists of three core modules:

- **Spatio-Temporal Knowledge Graph (STKG) Construction:** A structured geographic knowledge graph is automatically constructed from open-source OpenStreetMap (OSM) data. This graph encodes seven core entity types, namely "Province", "City", "District", "Street", "Road", "AOI" (Areas of Interest), and "POI" (Point of Interest), as well as three foundational spatial relationships, namely "Contain", "Belong To", and "Nearby". By integrating vertical administrative hierarchies, horizontal geometric relationships and temporal attributes, the resulting knowledge graph captures both macro-level and micro-level urban spatial semantics.
- **Dual-Layer Geographic Retrieval:** To retrieve relevant knowledge subgraphs, a dual-retrieval mechanism that leverages both textual and spatial cues is adopted. Specifically,

  – **Name-based retrieval:** Match extracted geographic entities from user queries to graph nodes.
  – **Coordinate-based retrieval:** Query nearby entities using Haversine-distance proximity [8] ranking within a specified radius.

- **Spatial Prompt Generation and Integration:** Retrieved triples are translated into natural language prompts using a spatial template schema (e.g., "Tsinghua University is near Wudaokou and belongs to Haidian District"). These prompts are then concatenated with the user query and input into the LLMs, injecting external knowledge at the context level without fine-tuning [3].

In the GeoRAG framework, urban spatial knowledge is structured into a knowledge graph, as illustrated in Fig. 1. This approach maintains the model's generalization ability. The designed dual-retrieval mechanism and spatio-temporal template enable the injection of contextual knowledge, thereby enhancing the models' perception of geographical scene knowledge.

Subsequently, this paper will elaborate on the schema of the STKG and the design of each module within the GeoRAG.

2.2 Knowledge Graph Design Methodology

To provide a structured and extensible foundation for spatial reasoning, GeoRAG constructs a 3D urban spatio-temporal knowledge graph that encodes geographic entities, spatial relations, and temporal dimensions. This knowledge graph serves as an external, interpretable, and updatable memory that complements LLMs during inference [9].

This modeling schema allows fine-grained representation of both point-based and region-based urban features, aligning with semantic-driven geographic modeling frameworks such as GeoKG [4] and S-GMKG [10].

In relationship modeling, we use GIS-based spatial analysis algorithms to compute intersections between areal features. We also encode nested administrative hierarchies. These steps help us build a 3D spatio-temporal geographic knowledge system. This system integrates temporal periodicity, horizontal spatial geometry, and vertical hierarchical dependencies [11]. This structure provides an extensible and standardized external knowledge source for LLMs.

As illustrated in Fig. 2, the proposed schema defines seven core entity types for urban spatio-temporal reasoning Province, City, District, Street, Road, AOI, and POI and models their interactions through three foundational relationships:

- "Nearby": calculated using the Haversine [8] distance to quantify spatial closeness between entities.
- "Contain": representing hierarchical inclusions such as administrative boundaries or spatial functional zones.
- "Belong To": indicating administrative or spatial subordination among entities.

We construct a 3D spatio-temporal knowledge graph:

$$G = (V, E), \tag{1}$$

where:

- V = {vi} is the set of geographic entities (e.g., Province, City, District, Street, Road, AOI, POI).
- E = {(h, r, t)} is the set of directed edges, each representing a spatial relation r ∈ {contains, belongTo, nearby} between head entity h and tail entity t.

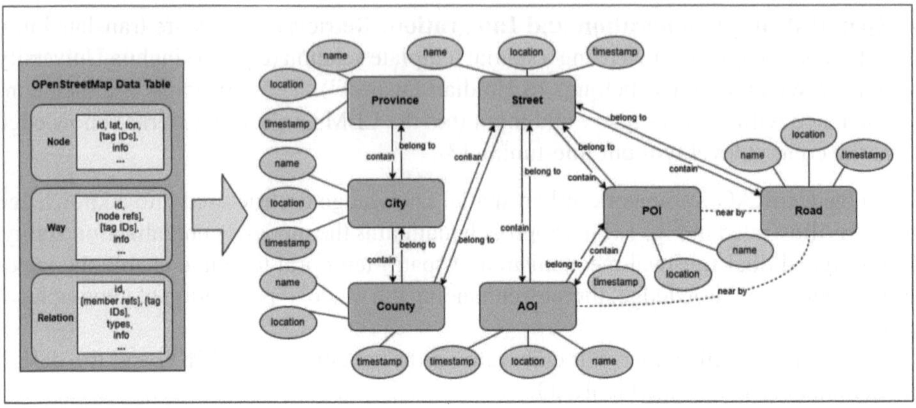

Fig. 2. Schema for transforming OpenStreetMap data into a 3D spatio-temporal knowledge graph, defining seven entity types (Province, City, District, Street, Road, AOI, POI) and three spatial relations (Nearby, Contain, Belong To).

As illustrated in Fig. 3. During the construction of the knowledge graph, a composite modeling strategy is designed, integrating vertical hierarchical expansion and horizontal spatial flattening in a seamless manner. The vertical hierarchy strictly follows the national administrative zoning standard, which is Province-City-District-Street. This adherence establishes a clear tree-like structure between administrative entities. In contrast, the horizontal component uses coordinate-based spatial computations to determine topological relationships between areal and point entities, such as AOI-POI and Street-POI, thus forming multilevel nested structures (s (large AOI and small AOI, AOI-POI and Street-AOI/POI). This composite strategy draws on recent advances in multiscale graph structuring [4, 10].

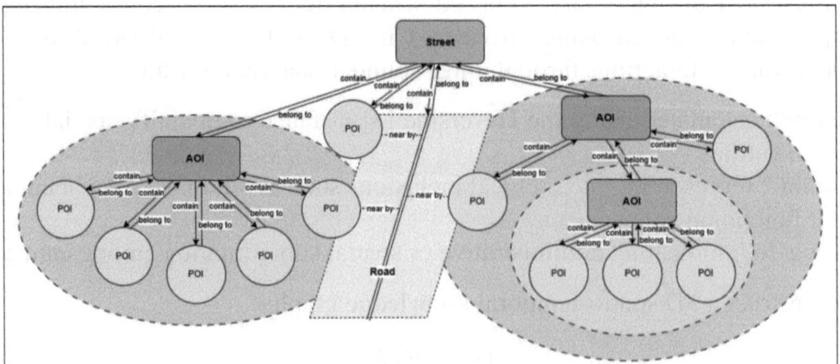

Fig. 3. Spatial relationships in the urban knowledge graph are modeled via GIS analyses [12] and rule-based hierarchies, combining vertical containment (zoning) and horizontal proximity (Haversine).

To model proximity between roads and POIs, the framework constructs buffer rectangles around road centerlines and computes spatial intersections using point-in-polygon algorithms. This technique, proven effective and scalable in spatial encoding systems such as TorchSpatial [13], enables efficient modeling of spatial adjacency. The final knowledge graph supports flexible hierarchical expression, features a clear and logical structure, and is highly compatible with LLMs interfaces [2, 4, 10].

2.3 A Geo-Knowledge Enhanced Retrieval Augmented Generation Framework

To alleviate the limitations of instruction-tuned LLMs in urban geospatial tasks [1, 5], including high computational cost, general knowledge degradation, generalization across cities, and semantic hallucination [14]. This study proposes GeoRAG, a context-enhanced framework that integrates structured geographic knowledge graph with RAG. GeoRAG provides a more robust spatial reasoning approach for LLMs by embedding geographical knowledge into the context without fine-tuning the weights of large models. This is consistent with the latest trend of enhancing LLMs based on open-ended prompts [15–18].

GeoRAG consists of three core modules: Named Entity Recognition (NER) [19], Dual-Layer Retrieval, and Enhanced Generative Prompting, as illustrated in Fig. 1. These modules work together to inject rich geospatial knowledge into LLMs without the need for fine-tuning.

NER: LLMs such as LLaMA3-70B [7] are employed in a "model-as-tool" paradigm to extract both location names and their geocoordinates from user inputs. Given an input text T, we perform **NER** to obtain:

$$\{(e_i, c_i)\} = NER(T), \tag{2}$$

where:

- T is the input text query.
- ei denotes the i-th extracted geographic entity name.
- ci = (φ_i, λ_i) denotes the corresponding latitude (φ_i) and longitude (λ_i).

Dual-Layer Retrieval Mechanism: Building on the NER results, a two-step retrieval strategy is applied to expand spatial context coverage and mitigate the limitations of static-range Graph-RAG approaches [3, 5]:

(a) **Name-based Retrieval:** Match the extracted entity names against the knowledge graph G = (V, E) to fetch topological subgraphs:

$$S_{name} = \{(h, r, t) \in \varepsilon | h \in \{e_i\} \vee t \in \{e_i\}\}, \tag{3}$$

where S_{name} is the set of triples whose head or tail entity matches any extracted entity name e_i.

(b) **Coordinate-based Retrieval:** Query spatial neighborhoods around each ci within a predefined radius r (e.g., 0.5 km) using the Haversine distance for proximity ranking:

$$d((\Phi_1, \lambda_1), (\Phi_2, \lambda_2)) = 2R * \arcsin(\sqrt{sin^2\frac{\Phi_2 - \Phi_1}{2} + cos\Phi_1 cos\Phi_2 sin^2\frac{\lambda_2 - \lambda_1}{2}}), \quad (4)$$

where:

These two sets are then unified to form the overall retrieval subgraph:

$$S = S_{name} \cup S_{coord}, \quad (6)$$

where the symbol " ∪" represents the union operation, which is used to concatenate the contextual content from both ends of the text, and the "S" denotes the overall retrieval subgraph combining both name-based and coordinate-based results.

Enhanced Generative Prompting: Structured knowledge graph triples (h, r, t) ∈ S are transformed into natural language prompts, effectively bridging the gap between RDF-style data and text-based LLMs inputs [7]. Each triple is mapped as:

$$\phi_{prompt}(h, r, t) = \text{"}h \; is \; r \; t\text{"}, \quad (7)$$

which transforms each triple (h, r, t) ∈ S into a natural language snippet. For example, "Wudaokou is adjacent to Qinghua East Road and near 3 shopping centers".

$$P = \{\phi_{prompt}(h, r, t) | (h, r, t) \in S\}, \quad (8)$$

where P is the concatenation of all prompt snippets forming the contextual knowledge input. Finally, the original user query T and the constructed prompt P are jointly input into the LLMs:

$$response = LLMs([T; P]), \quad (9)$$

where [T; P] denotes the combined sequence of the original query T and the spatial prompt context P fed into the LLMs.

In summary, the GeoRAG pipeline integrates Named Entity Recognition (NER) through LLMs as a tool, dual-layer retrieval, and enhanced generative prompting. This pipeline enhances LLMs by adding interpretable geospatial context. The method significantly enhances urban spatial cognition without the need for parameter-level fine-tuning.

3 Experiments

3.1 Datasets

Experiments are conducted on the CityImage task from the CityGPT [1] benchmark suite. This suite is designed to evaluate the geospatial perception capabilities of LLMs. The dataset encompasses five major types of spatial entities: District, Boundary, Road, Landmark, and Node. Each entity type is associated with a set of diverse spatial questions. The CityImage dataset comprises curated samples from three representative global cities: Beijing, London, and New York. This composition enables the cross-city evaluation of spatial generalization [20].

Baselines: The performance of GeoRAG-enhanced models is compared against a wide range of competitive baselines, including:

- Lightweight models: ChatGLM3-6B [21], Qwen2.5-7B [22], LLaMA3-8B [7].
- Mid-size models: Gemma2-9B [23], Mistral-Small-24B [24], Gemma2-27B [23], Qwen2.5-32B [22].
- Large-scale models: Qwen2.5-72B [22], LLaMA3.1-70B [7], LLaMA3.1-405B [7].
- Closed-source baselines: GPT-3.5 [11], GPT-4o mini [11].

A GeoRAG-enhanced variant of Qwen2.5-32B is also included. This variant serves as the main implementation target for evaluation.

Evaluation Metric: The accuracy of the answers is used as the primary evaluation metric. For each question, the model-generated answer is compared with the ground-truth label. The accuracy is reported separately for each city.

3.2 Experimental Results and Analysis

In Table 1, compared to the base Qwen2.5–32B model, the GeoRAG-enhanced variant achieves accuracy improvements of +11.89%, +13.25%, and +7.49% on the Beijing, London, and New York datasets, respectively. Notably, GeoRAG outperforms all evaluated LLMs on the Beijing dataset and ranks second in the other two cities, despite using fewer parameters than most large-scale models. These results confirm the efficacy of GeoRAG in injecting high-quality geographic knowledge without compromising model generalization. The improvements are achieved without any parameter tuning, highlighting the effectiveness of structured knowledge integration through Retrieval Augmented prompts. Moreover, GeoRAG consistently enhances performance across cities, demonstrating strong cross-city transferability—a critical property in practical urban applications.

Table 1. Model accuracy comparison across cities. The best-performing model is highlighted in bold, and the second-best is underlined. All results are reproduced from Feng et al. (2024)* [1], except for GeoRAG-Qwen2.5-32B, which is obtained from our own experiments.

Model Name	Beijing	London	New York
ChatGLM3–6B	0.300	0.269	0.315
Qwen2.5–7B	0.325	0.303	0.311
LLama3–8B	0.286	0.312	0.331
Gemma2–9B	0.097	0.168	0.168
Mistral-Small–24B	0.288	0.315	0.332
Gemma2–27B	0.326	0.363	0.346
Qwen2.5–32B	0.400	0.360	0.383
LLama3.1–70B	0.357	0.372	0.412

(continued)

Table 1. *(continued)*

Model Name	Beijing	London	New York
Qwen2.5–72B	0.408	0.345	**0.417**
LLama3.1–405B	0.417	**0.451**	0.400
GPT-3.5	0.269	0.297	0.354
GPT-4o mini	0.319	0.386	0.369
GeoRAG-Qwen2.5–32B	**0.454**	0.415	0.414
Vs. Qwen2.5–32B	**+11.89%**	**+13.25%**	**+7.49%**

4 Conclusion

In our study, we propose a framework called Geographic Retrieval-Augmented Generation (GeoRAG), which is a lightweight and tuning-free framework. GeoRAG enhances the urban spatial reasoning capabilities of LLMs. This is achieved by integrating structured geographic knowledge through a RAG strategy. Unlike traditional fine-tuning approaches, it avoids the risk of degrading generalization, GeoRAG injects contextual spatial knowledge into LLMs at inference time using a structured 3D spatio-temporal knowledge graph and a dual-layer geographic retrieval mechanism.

Through extensive evaluations on the CityGPT benchmark across three representative cities (Beijing, London, and New York), GeoRAG consistently improves the performance of Qwen2.5–32B and outperforms several larger-scale models, achieving relative accuracy gains of up to 13.25% without any parameter tuning. These results demonstrate the effectiveness of structured geographic augmentation for spatial reasoning tasks and highlight the framework's scalability, transferability, and plug-and-play nature.

Despite these promising results, several limitations remain. First, the knowledge graph is currently static and may lack timely updates in rapidly evolving urban environments. Second, the framework primarily focuses on spatial relationships and does not yet incorporate multimodal signals such as imagery or sensor data. Third, reasoning over complex spatial topologies remains a challenging direction for future improvement.

To address these challenges, we identify three future research directions:

- **Dynamic knowledge updating:** Incorporating real-time spatial data streams (e.g., urban APIs, IoT sensors) to maintain the freshness of geographic knowledge [10, 17],
- **Advanced spatial retrieval:** Leveraging embedding-based retrieval and hierarchical graph attention to enhance context precision and scalability [3, 6, 9].
- **Multimodal geographic grounding:** Integrating visual and remote sensing data with structured knowledge to support richer spatial understanding and decision-making [2, 11, 13, 18].

We believe that GeoRAG offers a promising step toward scalable and interpretable geographic reasoning in LLMs and can serve as a foundation for future work in urban intelligence, spatial computing, and geospatial human–AI interaction.

Acknowledgment. This work is supported by the National Key Research Development Program of China under Grant No.2024YFC3014300, and the Yunnan Province Major Science and the Technology Project under Grant No.202302AD080006, and the Tsinghua University Initiative Scientific Research Program under Grant No. 2024Z04W01001, and the Research Foundation of the Department of Nat-ural Resources of Hunan Province under Grant No.HBZ20240123, and the Tianjin Flood Controland Emergency Command Platform Construction Project under Grant No.JZ120205A0042024, and the open project of Yunnan Key Laboratory of Media Convergence No.220245204.

References

1. Feng, J., Du, Y., Liu, T., Guo, S., Lin, Y., Li, Y.: Citygpt: Empowering urban spatial cognition of large language models (2024). arXiv preprint arXiv:2406.13948
2. Zhang, Y., et al.: Bb-geogpt: a framework for learning a large language model for geographic information science. Inf. Process. Manag. **61**(5), 103808 (2024)
3. Arslan, M., Ghanem, H., Munawar, S., Cruz, C.: A survey on rag with LLMS. Procedia Comput. Sci. **246**, 3781–3790 (2024)
4. Ning, Y., Liu, H.: Urbankgent: A unified large language model agent framework for urban knowledge graph construction (2024). arXiv preprint arXiv:2402.06861
5. Yu, D., Bao, R., Mai, G., Zhao, L.: Spatial-rag: Spatial retrieval augmented generation for real-world spatial reasoning questions (2025). arXiv preprint arXiv:2502.18470
6. Peng, Z., Kuai, X., Ke, S., Dong, X., Guo, R.: Enhancing geodatabases operability: advanced human-computer interaction through rag and multi-agent systems. Big Earth Data, 1–26 (2025)
7. Grattafiori, A., Dubey, A., Jauhri, A., Pandey, A., Kadian, A., Al-Dahle, A., Letman, A., Mathur, A., Schelten, A., Vaughan, A., et al.: The llama 3 herd of models (2024). arXiv preprint arXiv:2407.21783
8. Robusto, C.C.: The cosine-haversine formula. Am. Math. Mon. **64**(1), 38–40 (1957)
9. Xu, L., et al.: Evaluating large language models on geospatial tasks: a multiple geospatial task benchmarking study. Int. J. Digit. Earth **18**(1), 2480268 (2025)
10. Liang, J., Hou, S., Zhao, A., Xu, Q., Xiang, L., Li, R., Wu, H.: Design and application of a semantic-driven geospatial modeling knowledge graph based on large language models. Geosp. Inf. Sci. 1–20 (2025)
11. Liang, J., Zhao, A., Hou, S., Jin, F., Wu, H.: A gpt-enhanced framework on knowledge extraction and reuse for geographic analysis models in google earth engine. Int. J. Digit. Earth **17**(1), 2398063 (2024)
12. Quattrochi, D.A., Goodchild, M.F.: Scale in Remote Sensing and GIS. CRC Press (1997)
13. Wu, N., Cao, Q., Wang, Z., Liu, Z., Qi, Y., Zhang, J., Ni, J., Yao, X., Ma, H., Mu, L., et al.: Torchspatial: A location encoding framework and benchmark for spatial representation learning (2024). arXiv preprint arXiv:2406.15658
14. Han, H., Wang, Y., Shomer, H., Guo, K., Ding, J., Lei, Y., Halappanavar, M., Rossi, R.A., Mukherjee, S., Tang, X., et al.: Retrieval-augmented generation with graphs (graphrag) (2024). arXiv preprint arXiv:2501.00309
15. Huang, C., Chen, S., Li, Z., Qu, J., Xiao, Y., Liu, J., Chen, Z.: Geoagent: To empower llms using geospatial tools for address standardization. In: Findings of the Association for Computational Linguistics ACL 2024, pp. 6048–6063 (2024)
16. Cheng, J., Wang, J., Zhang, Y., Ji, J., Zhu, Y., Zhang, Z., Zhao, X.: Poi-enhancer: An llm-based semantic enhancement framework for poi representation learning. In: Proceedings of the AAAI conference on artificial intelligence, vol. 39, pp. 11509–11517 (2025)

17. Nie, T., et al.: Joint estimation and prediction of city-wide delivery demand: A large language model empowered graph-based learning approach. Transp. Res. Part E Logist. Transp. Rev. **197**, 104075 (2025)
18. Shi, M., Janowicz, K., Verstegen, J., Currier, K., Wiedemann, N., Mai, G., Majic, I., Liu, Z., Zhu, R.: Geography for ai sustainability and sustainability for geoai. Cartogr. Geogr. Inf. Sci. 1–19 (2025)
19. Liu, P., Guo, Y., Wang, F., Li, G.: Chinese named entity recognition: the state of the art. Neurocomputing **473**, 37–53 (2022)
20. Yang, A., Fu, C., Jia, Q., Dong, W., Ma, M., Chen, H., Yang, F., Wu, H.: Evaluating and enhancing spatial cognition abilities of large language models. Int. J. Geograph. Inf. Sci. 1–36 (2025)
21. GLM, T., Zeng, A., Xu, B., Wang, B., Zhang, C., Yin, D., Zhang, D., Rojas, D., Feng, G., Zhao, H., et al.: Chatglm: A family of large language models from glm-130b to glm-4 all tools (2024). arXiv preprint arXiv:2406.12793
22. Yang, A., Li, A., Yang, B., Zhang, B., Hui, B., Zheng, B., Yu, B., Gao, C., Huang, C., Lv, C., et al.: Qwen3 technical report (2025). arXiv preprint arXiv:2505.09388
23. Team, G., Riviere, M., Pathak, S., Sessa, P.G., Hardin, C., Bhupatiraju, S., Hussenot, L., Mesnard, T., Shahriari, B., Ram´e, A., et al.: Gemma 2: Improving open language models at a practical size (2024). arXiv preprint arXiv:2408.00118
24. Jiang, F.: Identifying and mitigating vulnerabilities in llm-integrated applications. Master's thesis, University of Washington (2024)

EGMP: Enhanced Generative Multimodal Prompt for Few-Shot Multimodal Aspect-Based Sentiment Analysis

Shuangfeng Cai[1,2], Shengfa Miao[1,2](✉), Tao Chen[1,2], Houcheng Liu[3], Dinan Ma[4], Yongkang Mu[1,2], Xin Jin[1,2], Qian Jiang[1,2], Hua Jiang[1,2], Puming Wang[1,2], Hualong Deng[1,2], and Ahmed Zahir[1,2]

[1] School of Software, Yunnan University, Kunming 650000, China
miaoshengfa@hotmail.com
[2] Engineering Research Center of Cyberspace, Kunming 650000, China
[3] Yunnan Information Technology Security Evaluation Center, Kunming, China
[4] Yunnan Key Laboratory of Media Convergence, Yunnan Daily Press Group, Kunming 650228, China

Abstract. Multimodal Aspect-Based Sentiment Analysis (MABSA) aims to jointly identify aspect terms and their corresponding sentiment polarity from text-image pairs. Recent studies have applied prompt-based learning to MABSA tasks, which leverage the existing knowledge of pre-trained language models to fine-tuning with only a small number of samples, thereby significantly reducing the demand for data. However, these existing studies still exhibit notable deficiencies. They fail to fully explore the features of each modality and have only established a coarse-grained alignment between the textual and visual modalities, lacking a fine-grained cross-modal interaction. To address the aforementioned limitations, this paper proposes a novel Enhanced Generative Multimodal Prompt (EGMP) model. Specifically, we first employ GPT-4 combined with Chain-of-Thought (CoT) reasoning to generate image descriptions for visual semantic enhancement. Furthermore, to tackle the challenges of imprecise cross-modal alignment between image regions and textual aspects, a Syntax-aware Aspect-guided Fine-grained Alignment Module is introduced, which simultaneously filters semantically relevant information for each specific aspect from both textual tokens and visual patches, ultimately achieving aspect-region-opinion alignment. Finally, based on the semantically aligned representations, we construct enhanced multimodal embeddings with prompt for different tasks. Extensive experiments conducted on two benchmark datasets demonstrate that the proposed method outperforms the strong baseline model in two MABSA-related tasks.

Keywords: Multimodal Aspect-Based Sentiment Analysis · Enhanced Generative Multimodal Prompt · Fine-grained Alignment

X. Ding and Y. Dong (Eds.): CLNLP 2025, CCIS 2775, pp. 141–153, 2026.
https://doi.org/10.1007/978-981-95-4788-3_13

1 Introduction

In recent years, Multimodal Aspect-Based Sentiment Analysis (MABSA), as a fine-grained sentiment analysis task, has garnered significant attention [1, 2]. MABSA consists of three key subtasks: Multimodal Aspect Term Extraction (MATE), Multimodal Aspect-oriented Sentiment Classification (MASC), and Joint Multimodal Aspect-Sentiment Analysis (JMASA). Given a text-image pair, MATE [3, 4] aims to extract all aspect terms present in the text. MASC [5, 6] centers on determining the sentiment polarity of a specified aspect. Meanwhile, JMASA [7, 8] targets the end-to-end extraction of both aspect terms and their corresponding sentiments.

In the field of MABSA, most existing studies rely on complete training datasets to train models, while some research [9, 10] further improves performance by incorporating additional data. However, the process of gathering and annotating large-scale multimodal data for MABSA is both time-consuming and labor-intensive [11]. To tackle this challenge, PVLM [12] and UP-MPF [13] attempted to adapt prompt-based learning methods for MASC tasks. These approaches reformulated MASC as a Masked Language Modeling (MLM) task using three pre-defined sentiment categories. However, the uncertainty in both the quantity and content of aspect terms per sample makes MLM ineffective for addressing practical challenges in JMASA and MATE tasks; GMP [14] introduced a generative multimodal prompt framework designed for few-shot MABSA scenarios encompassing JMASA, MASC, and MATE tasks. Nevertheless, this approach fails to fully leverage both visual and syntactic structure information, failing to achieve sufficient fine-grained alignment between textual and visual modalities, ultimately resulting in suboptimal cross-modal information fusion.

To overcome these limitations, an innovative enhanced generative multimodal prompt model is introduced. Specifically, our model first employs Large Language Models (LLMs) combined with Chain-of-Thought (CoT) reasoning to generate contextualized, emotionally rich image descriptions, maximize the utilization of visual information and effectively bridging the cross-modal representational gap. Subsequently, to accurately aggregate sentiment information and achieve fine-grained alignment between image regions and textual aspects, a Syntax-aware Aspect-guided Fine-grained Alignment Module is introduced. The proposed module initially builds a syntax-aware graph convolutional network by leveraging dependency probability matrices, which can explicitly model the alignment between aspect terms and their corresponding opinion expressions, and effectively reduce the impact of parsing errors on model performance. Then, an aspect-guided cross-modal attention mechanism jointly selects semantically relevant features from text tokens and visual patches, thereby aligning aspects with image regions. Finally, based on the semantically aligned representations, we construct enhanced multimodal embeddings with prompt for different tasks and feed them into a BART model based on a multimodal encoder-decoder architecture to generate the final triplet sequence. In summary, we main contributions can be summarized as follows:

- We proposed a novel enhanced generative multimodal prompt model for the Multimodal Aspect-Based Sentiment Analysis. This model employs GPT-4 combined with Chain-of-Thought (CoT) reasoning to generate image descriptions for enhanced visual semantics, while utilizing the syntactic structure of given sentences to improve aspect-related semantic feature extraction.

- We design a syntax-aware aspect-guided fine-grained alignment mechanism to achieve fine-grained semantic alignment of aspect-region-opinion.
- Through extensive experimentation on our constructed few-shot dataset, the experimental results indicate that the proposed model significantly outperforms existing competitive baselines, particularly in JMASA and MASC tasks, with the empirical evidence clearly validating its effectiveness.

2 Methodology

2.1 Overview

Task Definition. Given a tweet comprising an image V and a sentence $T = (w_1, w_2, \ldots, w_n)$ composed of n words, our objective is to generate a sequence Y in a few-shot multimodal setting, which comprehensively identifies all relevant aspects and precisely annotates their corresponding sentiment polarities. In MABSA, the output is formally defined as: $Y = [(a_1^s, a_1^e, s_1), \ldots, (a_i^s, a_i^e, s_i), \ldots, (a_k^s, a_k^e, s_k)]$, where a_i^s and a_i^e denote the start and end position indices of the i-th aspect in the sentence, s_i represents the aspect's sentiment polarity, with possible labels {negative, neutral, positive}, and k is the total aspects count in the tweet.

Model Preview. Figure 1 outlines our model architecture, which is built on a BART-based encoder-decoder framework [15].

2.2 Multimodal Encoder

In this section, a multimodal encoder designed to obtain multimodal representations. Capitalizing on BART's exceptional performance in text representation learning, we employ the pre-trained BART model to generate textual embeddings. First, we incorporate the large language model GPT-4 with chain-of-thought reasoning to generate image captions, denoted as C. These semantically rich captions serve as auxiliary prompts for BART, effectively bridging the modality gap by providing linguistically encoded visual information. Subsequently, the BART [16] model creates text embeddings for the original text input as well as the image captions, denoted as E_T and E_C.

$$C = GPT - 4V(I). \tag{1}$$

For visual modality processing, we employ the NF-ResNet architecture [17] to extract image feature representations. These visual features are then linearly projected into a shared embedding space aligned with the text modality:

$$V = Reshape(W_v ResNet(I) + b_v) = [v^1, \ldots, v^j, \ldots, v^{l_v}], v^j \in \mathbb{R}^{d_t}, \tag{2}$$

where V is denoted as the reshaped image representation, projection matrix $W_v \in \mathbb{R}^{d_v \times d_{nt}}$,$nt = l_v \times d_t$, with l_v representing the count of visual slots retained in the original image representation. The multimodal embedding E_M can be obtained. Then, we input E_M into the BART Encoder. This process generates the multimodal representation$H$, integrating visual and textual elements for further processing.

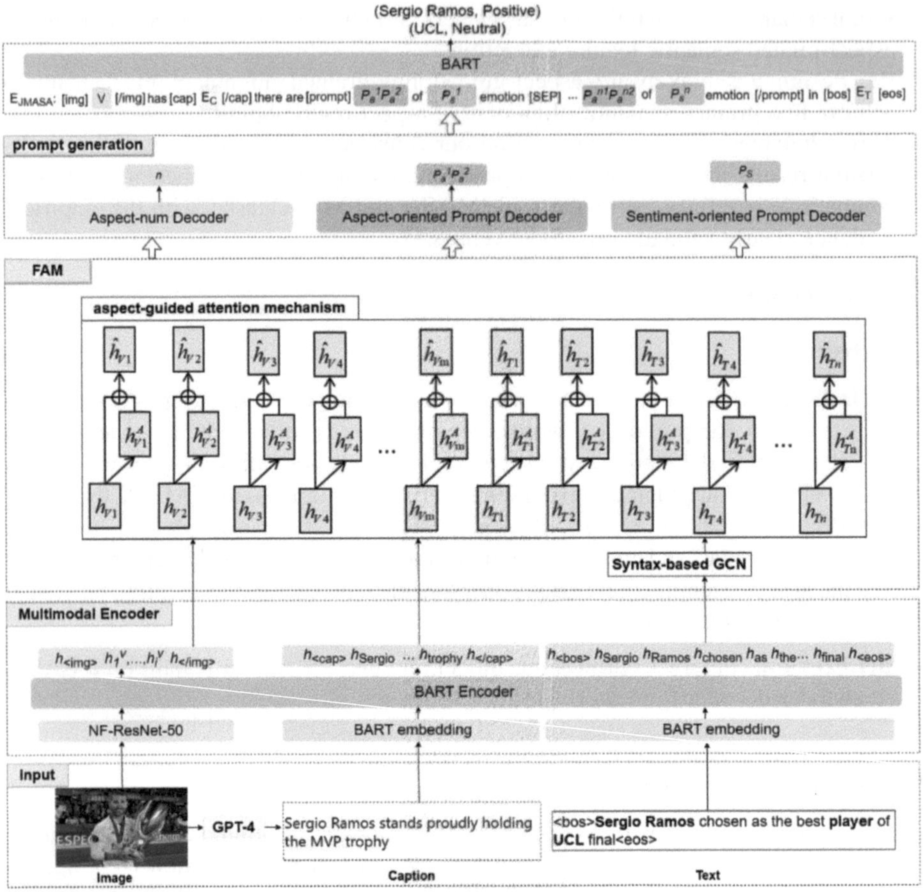

Fig. 1. The overview of our proposed Enhanced Generative Multimodal Prompt. The architecture primarily consists of three modules: the multimodal encoder, the syntax-aware aspect-guided fine-grained alignment module (FAM), and the prompt generation module. The input includes tweet image-text pairs and their corresponding image captions.

2.3 Syntax-Aware Aspect-Guided Fine-Grained Alignment Module (FAM)

In this section, we constructed a Textual Graph Convolutional Network, which constructs structured connections between words by parsing syntactic dependency trees to achieve accurate aspect-opinion alignment. Subsequently, we use the aspect-guided attention mechanism to capture and align information related to specific aspects in text and images according to the syntactically enhanced multimodal representation, while effectively filtering out the interference of irrelevant information.

Syntax-based GCN. We take the hidden features output by the BART model as the initial node representations of the text graph. In the process of constructing the text graph, we utilize the advanced LAL-Parser dependency analysis model [18] and take its output dependency arc probability matrix as the adjacency matrix $A^t \in \mathbb{R}^{n \times n}$. For each node in the text graph, we update its hidden representation through the following formula:

$$h_i^{(k)} = \sigma\left(\sum_{h_j \in \mathcal{N}_i} A_{ij}^t W_t^{(k)} h_j^{(k-1)} + b^{(k)}\right), \tag{3}$$

we define the hidden representation of node i at the k-th layer as $h_i^{(k)}$; $\mathcal{N}_i$ stands for the collection of neighboring nodes connected to node i; A_{ij}^t is an element of the adjacency matrix, reflecting the dependency probability between nodes i and j. As the number of graph convolutional layers increases, each node progressively aggregates information from its neighboring nodes, thereby learning richer contextual semantic representations. After k layers of graph convolution operations, we ultimately obtain the graph-based text representation $(H^{syn})^T$.

Considering that the prevalent informal expressions (e.g., colloquial phrases and omitted structures) and complex sentence structures in online reviews are often insensitive to syntactic dependencies, this model has achieved adaptive handling of syntactic dependency sensitivity through a dynamic fusion mechanism. Specifically, this mechanism dynamically integrates atomic-level textual features with syntax-aware textual features. Now, the final multimodal representation is denoted as $\tilde{H}$.

Aspect-guided Attention Mechanism. We employ the spaCy NLP toolkit to perform syntactic parsing (https://spacy.io/) and extract nouns or noun phrases as candidate aspects. Within the syntactically augmented hidden representations $\tilde{H}$ we concurrently construct a candidate aspect representation set $H^{CA} = \{h_1^{CA}, \ldots, h_i^{CA}, \ldots, h_k^{CA}\}$, where k denotes the number of detected noun phrases in the current sentence. To explicitly model semantic relationships between candidate aspects and hidden states $\tilde{H}$, we propose a novel Candidate Aspect-guided Attention Mechanism. The attention distribution α_t of the t-th hidden state across k candidate aspects is computed through the following equation:

$$Z_t = \tanh\Big(\big(W_{CA} H^{CA} + b_{CA}\big) \oplus \big(W_H \tilde{h}_t + b_H\big)\Big), \tag{4}$$

$$\alpha_t = softmax(W_\alpha Z_t + b_\alpha), \tag{5}$$

here $Z_t \in \mathbb{R}^{2d \times k}$ denotes the comprehensive feature. The matrices $W_{CA} \in \mathbb{R}^{d \times d}$, $W_H \in \mathbb{R}^{d \times d}$, $W_\alpha \in \mathbb{R}^{1 \times 2d}$. The attention distribution α_t is a k-dimensional vector, where each element $\alpha_{t,i}$ quantifies the attention weight assigned by the t-th hidden feature to the i-th candidate aspect. Subsequently, the attention distribution α_t is utilized to compute a weighted sum of candidate aspect features H^{CA}, generating aspect-aware hidden features h_t^A:

$$h_t^A = \sum_i^k \alpha_{t,i} h_i^{CA}. \tag{6}$$

Given that not all visual blocks contribute to prediction, a learnable gating mechanism is introduced to refine feature representation. This mechanism produces a fusion coefficient g_t that dynamically balances the contributions between the hidden feature $\tilde{h}_t$ and the aspect-aware feature h_t^A:

$$g_t = sigmoid(W_g\left[\tilde{h}_t; h_t^A\right] + b_g), \tag{7}$$

$$\widehat{h}_t = g_t\tilde{h}_t + h_t^A(1 - g_t), \tag{8}$$

where $\widehat{h}_t \in \widehat{H}$ is the output of the alignment module guided by aspects. To optimize multimodal alignment and suppress noise interference, we designed a specific pre-training strategy in the FAM, which is based on the task of image-text correlation detection from the TRC dataset [19].

2.4 Prompt Generation Module

Aspect Count Predictor (ACP). In JMASA and MATE tasks, where the number of aspects is typically unknown, accurately determining the aspect count for each instance is crucial. To address this challenge, we formulate aspect count prediction as a dedicated subtask, implemented through an Aspect-Count BART Decoding Component for precise prediction:

$$h_n^{acp} = BART_D^{acp}(\widehat{H}; E_{bos}), \tag{9}$$

$$n_{pred} = softmax\big(MLP\big(h_n^{acp}\big)\big). \tag{10}$$

Finally, we employ cross-entropy loss to optimize this subtask:

$$\mathcal{L}_{subtask} = -\sum\nolimits_{j=1}^{K} n_{true}^j \log(n_{pred}^j). \tag{11}$$

Aspect Prompt Generation (APG). This module is designed to generate differentiated prompt for distinct aspects by leveraging multimodal contextual information. Each aspect prompt is configured with two aspect slots, setting the instance-level prompt length to $2\,n_p$, where n_p represents the predicted aspect count. For generating the k-th aspect, the aspect prompt decoder computes the current hidden state:

$$h_{l_a}^{apg} = BART_D^{apg}(\widehat{H}; (h_{<(l_a-1)}^{apg})), \tag{12}$$

here let $l_a = 2$. The aspect-oriented prompt for the k-th aspect is obtained by processing the decoder's output through a Multi-Layer Perceptron (MLP):

$$P_a^k = MLP^k([h_1^{apg}, h_2^{apg}]), \tag{13}$$

here $P_a^k \in \mathbb{R}^{2\times d}$, the generative aspect prompts collectively represented as $AP = [P_a^1, \ldots, P_a^{n_p}] \in \mathbb{R}^{2n_p\times d}$.

Sentiment Prompt Generation (SPG). Similar to the Aspect Prompt Generation, the Sentiment Prompt Generation module utilizes multimodal contextual information to generate sentiment-oriented prompts for each aspect via a dedicated sentiment prompt decoder. Each generated sentiment prompt is allocated a single sentiment slot, thus setting the instance-level prompt length to n_p:

$$P_s = h_1^{spg} = BART_D^{spg}(\widehat{H}; E_{bos}). \tag{14}$$

Given the limited sentiment categories and their shared label space, the sentiment prompt P_s is replicated n_p times to construct the sentiment prompt $SP = [P_s^1, \ldots, P_s^{n_p}] \in \mathbb{R}^{n_p \times d}$.

2.5 Constructing Multimodal Prompts and Generate Predictive Results

To accommodate diverse task requirements across JMASA, MASC, and MATE, we construct adaptive multimodal prompts based on the predicted aspect counts, image caption, aspect prompts, and sentiment prompts. Taking JMASA as a representative case, we formulate a comprehensive multimodal prompt embedding E_{JMASA}, which is then fed into a BART-based encoder-decoder architecture for triplet sequence generation. The predictive output P_t at step t is derived through the text embedding E_T, sentiment label set embedding E_S and the hidden representation h_t^J, where E_S has a fixed length $l_s = 3$ corresponding to the three sentiment categories (positive, negative, neutral):

$$P_t = predict([E_T; E_S]h_t^J), \tag{15}$$

here $P_t \in \mathbb{R}^{l_t + l_s}$. To boosting the model's effectiveness in sequence generation tasks, we optimize the framework using a cross-entropy loss function:

$$\mathcal{L}_{generate} = -\sum\nolimits_{j=1}^{K} O^j \log(P^j). \tag{16}$$

2.6 Multitask Training

The overall loss $\mathcal{L}$ is formulated as a weighted combination of the main task loss $\mathcal{L}_{generate}$ (for JMASA, MASC and MATE objectives) and the auxiliary aspect count prediction loss $\mathcal{L}_{subtask}$, expressed as:

$$\mathcal{L} = \mathcal{L}_{generate} + \lambda \mathcal{L}_{subtask}. \tag{17}$$

3 Experiments

3.1 Experimental Settings

Datasets. Based on the sentiment category distributions in Twitter 2015 and Twitter 2017 [6], we constructed two few-shot multimodal datasets for experimental evaluation. The specific statistical details regarding these datasets are laid out in Table 1.

Implementation Details. Our framework employs BART-Base containing 140 million parameters as the primary language model and implement NF-ResNet-50 as the visual encoder. Hyperparameters GCN layers and l_v are 2 and 4 respectively, hyperparameter λ, for the JMASA task, the optimal λ is 0.1 for both datasets, while for the MATE task, the optimal λ are 0.05 for Twitter-15 and 0.1 for Twitter-17. Across all tasks, we maintain consistent training configurations including: 70 training epochs, a batch size of 4, and a hidden dimension of 768. For optimization, we set task-specific learning rates at 6.5e-5 for MATE and JMASA tasks, and 7.5e-5 for MASC. The complete system is implemented in PyTorch.

Evaluation Metrics. We evaluate model performance using task-specific metrics: for JMASA, we measure Precision (P), Recall (R), and Micro-F1 score (F1); for MASC, we assess Accuracy (Acc) and Micro-F1 score (F1); while for MATE, we report the Micro-F1 score (F1) as the primary evaluation metric.

Table 1. Statics of Twitter 2015 and Twitter 2017 datasets. Pos: Positive, Neu: Neutral, Neg: Negative, MS: Multi sentiments.

Datasets	Twitter-15					Twitter-17				
	POS	NEU	NEG	MS	All	POS	NEU	NEG	MS	All
Train	32/526	64/1084	16/214	26/277	138/2101	32/534	32/328	16/150	52/734	132/1746
Vaild	32/162	64/375	16/71	26/119	138/727	32/177	32/109	16/49	52/242	132/577
Test	167	335	68	104	674	178	107	39	263	587

3.2 Baselines

To achieve a comprehensive comparative analysis, we conducted an in-depth evaluation of the model under different tasks using various methods. **For the text-based ABSA methods**, we compare with: BART [16], D-GCN [20]. **For the JMASA and MATE tasks**, we conduct comparative evaluations with several state-of-the-art approaches: AOM [7], JML [9], CMMT [21], VLP [10], GMP [14], Entity-Aware Exemplar Retriever [22], DEQA [23]. **For the MASC task**, we evaluate against several representative approaches: KEF [24], FITE [25], IAFN [26], AMIFN [27], PAALI [28]. Furthermore, we extend and empirically assess multiple architectures originally developed for few-shot textual classification scenarios. These include: LM-SC [3], GFSC [29]. In recent years, multiple models tailored for few-shot multimodal sentiment classification have emerged, Representative approaches comprise: UP-MPF [13], FMCF [30], VERO [31].

3.3 Experimental Results and Analysis

In this section, we demonstrate the outstanding performance of our model compared to baseline models on two datasets across three tasks.

Performance on JMASA. The JMASA results are presented in Table 2. First, our model outperforms all text-based baselines, demonstrating that integrating and detecting rich visual and textual information significantly enhances performance. Second, our model surpasses all multimodal methods across every metric. Notably, it achieves improvements of 2.44% and 2.51% in F1-score on Twitter-15 and Twitter-17 compared to the second-best performing model. This validates the effectiveness of learning aspect-relevant visual regions and textual words, as well as leveraging pre-trained language models to generate multimodal prompts based on contextual cues.

Table 2. Comparative performance evaluation of various approaches for JMASA across two Twitter datasets. The best results get bold formatting, while underlines are used to denote the second-best results.

Modality	Model	Twitter-15			Twitter-17		
		P	R	F1	P	R	F1
Text	BART [16]	47.03	41.90	44.28	48.59	44.97	46.70
	D-GCN [20]	42.02	40.07	40.95	45.66	45.81	44.89
Text-Image	JML [9]	48.51	41.59	44.77	50.13	48.65	49.38
	CMMT [21]	29.85	36.23	32.65	39.64	47.83	43.34
	VLP [10]	46.56	49.08	47.77	51.32	52.22	51.76
	GMP [14]	51.67	47.19	49.33	<u>54.28</u>	53.31	<u>53.79</u>
	AoM [7]	49.06	42.82	45.73	47.56	40.15	41.51
	DEQA [23]	<u>51.80</u>	<u>52.75</u>	<u>52.27</u>	49.32	50.16	49.74
	Retriever [22]	42.33	49.61	45.66	51.38	<u>54.06</u>	52.69
	Ours	**55.14**	**54.29**	**54.71**	**57.64**	**55.02**	**56.30**

Performance on MASC. Table 3 summarizes the model performance on the MASC task under few-shot learning conditions, reporting both accuracy (Acc) and F1-score metrics. Notably, our model achieves state-of-the-art performance on both Twitter-15 and Twitter-17 datasets. In terms of accuracy, it surpasses the second-best results by 2.23% and 3.08% respectively, while demonstrating F1-score improvements of 1.70% and 1.99%. These results robustly demonstrate our model's capability to accurately detect aspect-relevant sentiment information from both visual and textual data, even in the presence of noise interference.

Table 3. Comparative performance evaluation of various approaches for MASC across two Twitter datasets.

Modality	Model	Twitter-15		Twitter-17	
		Acc	F1	Acc	F1
Text	BART [16]	65.57	57.21	64.12	61.71
	LM-SC [3]	65.47	58.02	57.51	55.97
	GFSC [29]	60.75	29.30	61.72	40.91
Text-Image	KEF [24]	55.81	43.54	46.50	29.61
	VLP [10]	59.34	44.56	60.24	56.09
	GMP [14]	67.06	60.31	66.20	64.20
	AMIFN [27]	61.97	40.80	52.46	41.89
	IAFN [26]	68.06	61.60	52.60	43.93
	FMCF [30]	66.89	<u>64.06</u>	62.76	62.57
	PAALI [28]	69.43	64.01	65.56	<u>64.31</u>
	VERO [31]	<u>70.28</u>	-	<u>69.38</u>	-
	Ours	**72.51**	**65.76**	**72.46**	**66.30**

Performance on MATE. The results for MATE are presented in Table 4. Among all models evaluated, VLP demonstrates superior performance on the MATE task, outperforming our model by 0.49% and 2.12% in F1-score on the Twitter-15 and Twitter-17 datasets respectively. This performance gap may be attributed to two main factors. First, our model exhibits a tendency to incorrectly classify certain noun phrases as aspects. Second, VLP's advantage likely stems from its utilization of supplementary data from the MVSA-Multiple Dataset and its incorporation of multiple pre-training tasks, both of which contribute to its enhanced performance.

Table 4. Results of different methods for MATE on the two Twitter datasets.

Modality	Model	Twitter-15 (F1)	Twitter-17 (F1)
Text	BART [16]	66.67	70.12
Text-Image	JML-MATE [9]	71.95	<u>82.14</u>
	VLP-MATE [10]	**77.61**	**83.35**
	GMP [14]	73.65	79.95
	Retriever [22]	69.37	78.61
	Ours	<u>77.12</u>	81.23

3.4 Ablation Experiments

To systematically investigate the effectiveness of each component in our proposed method, we conducted comprehensive ablation studies. As clearly demonstrated in Table 5, the complete model achieves optimal performance across all tasks.

Table 5. The ablation study results for the JMASA and MATE subtasks (F1-score) and MASC task (Accuracy). "w/o" denotes "without".

Model	JMASA		MASC		MATE	
	Twitter-15	Twitter-17	Twitter-15	Twitter-17	Twitter-15	Twitter-17
w/o Caption	53.24	55.38	70.59	70.07	76.23	78.82
w/o TextGCN	53.93	55.46	71.45	71.42	75.76	80.65
w/o FAM	51.73	54.80	65.48	68.55	73.45	77.61
w/o Prompt	50.67	53.02	67.51	66.67	73.52	77.64
Our	54.71	56.30	72.51	72.46	77.12	81.23

4 Conclusion

To address the challenge of few-shot multimodal aspect-based sentiment analysis, this paper proposes an enhanced generative multimodal prompt model. For precise capture of aspect-specific prompts in few-shot scenarios, we design an aspect-guided fine-grained alignment module that simultaneously filters semantically relevant information from both text tokens and visual patches. Furthermore, to properly align aspect terms with their corresponding sentiment words, we incorporate syntactic knowledge to establish linguistic relationships between words and aspect terms in sentences. Finally, relying on the semantically aligned representations, we construct task-specific multimodal prompts. The experimental data from two public datasets validates that our proposed model works effectively.

Acknowledgments. This work receives support from multiple funding sources, including the National Key Research and Development Program of China (Grant No. 2024YFC3014300), the Major Science and Technology Project of Yunnan Province (Grant No. 202302AD080006), Tsinghua University's Initiative Scientific Research Program (Grant No. 2024Z04W01001), the Research Foundation of the Department of Natural Resources of Hunan Province (Grant No. HBZ20240123), the Tianjin Flood Control and Emergency Command Platform Construction Project (Grant No. JZ120205A0042024), and the open project of Yunnan Key Laboratory of Media Convergence (Grant No. 220245204).

References

1. Hua, Y.C., Denny, P., Wicker, J., Taskova, K.: A systematic review of aspect-based sentiment analysis: domains, methods, and trends. Artif. Intell. Rev. **57**(11), 296 (2024)

2. Zhao, H., Yang, M., Bai, X., Liu, H.: A survey on multimodal aspect-based sentiment analysis. IEEE Access **12**, 12039–12052 (2024)
3. Jian, Y., Gao, C., Vosoughi, S.: Contrastive Learning for Prompt-based Few-shot Language Learners. In: Proceedings of the 2022 Conference of the North American Chapter of the Association for Computational Linguistics: Human Language Technologies, pp. 5577–5587. Association for Computational Linguistics, Seattle, United States (2022)
4. Lu, F., Yang, X., Li, Q., Sun, Q., Jiang, K., Ji, C., Li, J.: Few-shot multimodal named entity recognition based on multimodal causal intervention graph. In: Proceedings of the 2024 Joint International Conference on Computational Linguistics, Language Resources and Evaluation (LREC-COLING 2024), pp. 7208–7219 (2024)
5. Wang, S., Cai, G., Lv, G.: Aspect-level multimodal sentiment analysis based on co-attention fusion. Int. J. Data Sci. Anal., 1–14 (2024)
6. Yu, J., Jiang, J.: Adapting Bert for Target-Oriented Multimodal Sentiment Classification. IJCAI (2019)
7. Zhou, R., Guo, W., Liu, X., Yu, S., Zhang, Y., Yuan, X.: AoM: Detecting aspect-oriented information for multimodal aspect-based sentiment analysis. In: Findings of the Association for Computational Linguistics: ACL 2023, pp. 8184–8196. Association for Computational Linguistics, Toronto, Canada (2023)
8. Zhu, L., Sun, H., Gao, Q., Yi, T., He, L.: Joint multimodal aspect sentiment analysis with aspect enhancement and syntactic adaptive learning. In: Proceedings of the Thirty-Third International Joint Conference on Artificial Intelligence (2024)
9. Ju, X., Zhang, D., Xiao, R., Li, J., Li, S., Zhang, M., Zhou, G.: Joint multi-modal aspect-sentiment analysis with auxiliary cross-modal relation detection. In: Proceedings of the 2021 Conference on Empirical Methods in Natural Language Processing, pp. 4395–4405 (2021)
10. Ling, Y., Yu, J., Xia, R.: Vision-Language Pre-Training for Multimodal Aspect-Based Sentiment Analysis. In: Proceedings of the 60th Annual Meeting of the Association for Computational Linguistics (Volume 1: Long Papers). pp. 2149–2159. Association for Computational Linguistics, Dublin, Ireland (2022)
11. Zhou, J., Zhao, J., Huang, J.X., Hu, Q.V., He, L.: Masad: a large-scale dataset for multimodal aspect-based sentiment analysis. Neurocomputing **455**, 47–58 (2021)
12. Yu, Y., Zhang, D.: Few-shot multi-modal sentiment analysis with prompt-based vision-aware language modeling. In: 2022 IEEE International Conference on Multimedia and Expo (ICME), pp. 1–6. IEEE (2022)
13. Yu, Y., Zhang, D., Li, S.: Unified multi-modal pre-training for few-shot sentiment analysis with prompt-based learning. In: Proceedings of the 30th ACM International Conference on Multimedia, pp. 189–198 (2022)
14. Yang, X., Feng, S., Wang, D., Sun, Q., Wu, W., Zhang, Y., Hong, P., Poria, S.: Few-shot joint multimodal aspect-sentiment analysis based on generative multimodal prompt. In: Rogers, A., Boyd-Graber, J., Okazaki, N. (eds.) Findings of the Association for Computational Linguistics: ACL 2023, pp. 11575–11589. Association for Computational Linguistics, Toronto, Canada (2023)
15. Lewis, M., Liu, Y., Goyal, N., Ghazvininejad, M., Mohamed, A., Levy, O., Stoyanov, V., Zettlemoyer, L.: BART: denoising sequence-to-sequence pre-training for natural language generation, translation, and comprehension. In: Jurafsky, D., Chai, J., Schluter, N., Tetreault, J. (eds.) Proceedings of the 58th Annual Meeting of the Association for Computational Linguistics, pp. 7871–7880. Association for Computational Linguistics (2020)
16. Yan, H., Dai, J., Ji, T., Qiu, X., Zhang, Z.: A Unified Generative Framework for Aspect-based Sentiment Analysis. In: Proceedings of the 59th Annual Meeting of the Association for Computational Linguistics and the 11th International Joint Conference on Natural Language Processing (Volume 1: Long Papers), pp. 2416–2429. Association for Computational Linguistics (2021)

17. Brock, A., De, S., Smith, S.L.: Characterizing signal propagation to close the performance gap in unnormalized ResNets (Oct 2020)
18. Mrini, K., Dernoncourt, F., Tran, Q.H., Bui, T., Chang, W., Nakashole, N.: Rethinking Self-Attention: Towards Interpretability in Neural Parsing. In: Findings of the Association for Computational Linguistics: EMNLP 2020, pp. 731–742. Association for Computational Linguistics (2020)
19. Vempala, A., Preoţiuc-Pietro, D.: Categorizing and inferring the relationship between the text and image of twitter posts. In: Proceedings of the 57th Annual Meeting of the Association for Computational Linguistics, pp. 2830–2840 (2019)
20. Chen, G., Tian, Y., Song, Y.: Joint aspect extraction and sentiment analysis with directional graph convolutional networks. In: Proceedings of the 28th International Conference on Computational Linguistics, pp. 272–279 (2020)
21. Yang, L., Na, J.C., Yu, J.: Cross-modal multitask transformer for end-to-end multimodal aspect-based sentiment analysis. Inf. Process. Manag. **59**(5), 103038 (2022)
22. Yang, L., Wang, Z., Li, Z., Na, J.C., Yu, J.: An empirical study of multimodal entity-based sentiment analysis with chatgpt: improving in-context learning via entity-aware contrastive learning. Inf. Process. Manag. **61**(4), 103724 (2024)
23. Han, Z., Hu, M., Bai, Y., Wang, X., Luo, B.: Deqa: Descriptions enhanced question-answering framework for multimodal aspect-based sentiment analysis. In: Proceedings of the AAAI Conference on Artificial Intelligence, vol. 39, pp. 23987–23995 (2025)
24. Zhao, F., Wu, Z., Long, S., Dai, X., Huang, S., Chen, J.: Learning from adjective-noun pairs: A knowledge-enhanced framework for target-oriented multimodal sentiment classification. In: Proceedings of the 29th International Conference on Computational Linguistics, pp. 6784–6794 (2022)
25. Yang, H., Zhao, Y., Qin, B.: Face-sensitive image-to-emotional-text cross-modal translation for multimodal aspect-based sentiment analysis. In: Proceedings of the 2022 Conference on Empirical Methods in Natural Language Processing, pp. 3324–3335 (2022)
26. Zhang, P., Fu, M., Zhao, R., Zhang, H., Luo, C.: Pure: Personality-coupled multi-task learning framework for aspect-based multimodal sentiment analysis. IEEE Trans. Knowl. Data Eng. (2024)
27. Yang, J., Xu, M., Xiao, Y., Du, X.: Amifn: aspect-guided multi-view interactions and fusion network for multimodal aspect-based sentiment analysis. Neurocomputing **573**, 127222 (2024)
28. Ding, M., Zou, C., Lin, H.: Local feature alignment prompt-tuning for few-shot multimodal aspect sentiment analysis. In: ICASSP 2025–2025 IEEE International Conference on Acoustics, Speech and Signal Processing (ICASSP), pp. 1–5. IEEE (2025)
29. Hosseini-Asl, E., Liu, W., Xiong, C.: A generative language model for few-shot aspect-based sentiment analysis (2022)
30. Du, Y., Xie, R., Zhang, B., Yin, Z.: Fmcf: few-shot multimodal aspect-based sentiment analysis framework based on contrastive finetuning. Appl. Intell. **54**(24), 12629–12643 (2024)
31. Sun, K., Wu, H., Shi, B., Mensah, S., Liu, P., Dong, B.: Vero: Verification and zero-shot feedback acquisition for few-shot multimodal aspect-level sentiment classification. In: Proceedings of the AAAI Conference on Artificial Intelligence, vol. 39, pp. 25210–25218 (2025)

Do Large Language Models Grasp Implicit Inference?

Shiqi Zhu(✉) and Xingcheng Li

School of Humanities, Shanghai Jiao Tong University, Shanghai, China
2103819442zsq@sjtu.edu.cn

Abstract. Understanding implicit inferences in human communication is essential for Large Language Models (LLMs). However, existing evaluation benchmarks are predominantly English-centric and rarely systematically assess the semantic–pragmatic interface. To address these gaps, we introduce EPIc, the first Chinese dataset aimed at entailment, presupposition and scalar implicature across affirmative, negative and conditional contexts. The dataset includes 480 items derived from both natural corpora and semi-automated generation. We evaluate six LLMs using a multiple-choice task. Our results reveal a significant performance disparity, suggesting that while most models achieve near-human accuracy on presupposition, they struggle profoundly with entailment and scalar implicature, especially in negative and conditional contexts. This highlights a critical failure in reasoning about sentence monotonicity and activating scalar alternatives. Our work not only provides the first systematic evaluation of these phenomena in Chinese but also exposes fundamental limitations in the semantic–pragmatic capabilities of current LLMs, offering a valuable resource for future research. Code and dataset are available at https://github.com/6050ZSQ/EPIc.

Keywords: LLMs · Implicit Inference · Semantic–Pragmatic Interface

1 Introduction

Human communication extends beyond literal meaning and is enriched by diverse implicit inferences. Understanding these inferences is crucial for LLMs to achieve human-level communication competence.

Although recent work has evaluated LLM on phenomena like discourse connectives [1], conversational implicature [2–5] and scalar implicature [6, 7], these efforts still have two key limitations: they are predominantly English-centric and often neglect the complex inferences arising at the semantic–pragmatic interface.

From a linguistic perspective, entailment[1], presupposition and implicature (notably scalar implicature) are three distinct types of inference. Entailment operates at the semantic level and is reversed in downward-entailing contexts (e.g., negation, the antecedent of

[1] The terms *entailment*, *presupposition* and *implicature* are used in their technical linguistic sense. Specifically, *entailment* refers to a strict logical relationship in which the truth of one proposition guarantees the truth of another. This definition is narrower than that used in Natural Language Inference (NLI).

X. Ding and Y. Dong (Eds.): CLNLP 2025, CCIS 2775, pp. 154–161, 2026.
https://doi.org/10.1007/978-981-95-4788-3_14

conditionals). Presuppositions are primarily pragmatic and remain constant under such contexts. Scalar implicatures lie at the semantic–pragmatic interface and are typically canceled in downward-entailing contexts (See Fig. 1).

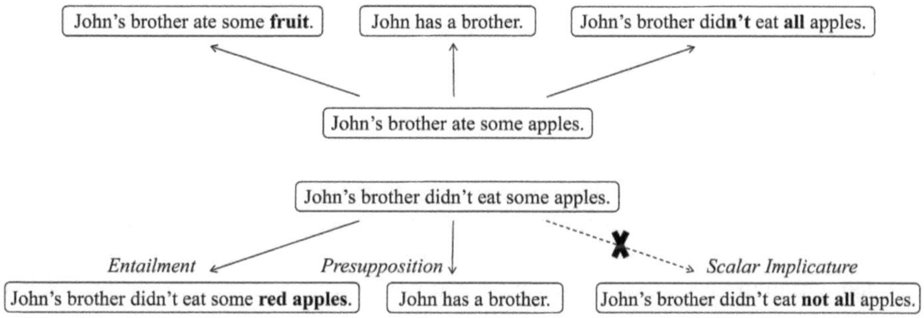

Fig. 1. Inference patterns of entailment, presupposition and scalar implicature across different monotonicity contexts. (Solid/dashed arrows denote valid/invalid inferences).

To bridge these gaps, we introduce EPIc, the first Chinese benchmark designed to evaluate entailment, presupposition and scalar implicature across affirmative, negative and conditional sentences. The dataset comprises 480 contexts, combining linguist-adapted natural examples with semi-automatically generated ones. Each context includes four inference options. We further evaluate six LLMs on EPIc, analyzing their accuracy and explanation quality.

Our main contributions are as follows:

(1) We provide EPIc, the first Chinese evaluation dataset targeting entailment, presupposition and scalar implicature with rigorous linguistic controls.
(2) We present the first work evaluating LLMs' inference understanding abilities across pragmatics and semantics in Chinese.
(3) We show that LLMs struggle with scalar implicatures and downward-entailing contexts, revealing critical limitations in their semantic–pragmatic reasoning.

2 Related Work

Early evaluation of reasoning in LLMs primarily relied on the NLI task, where models classify the relationship between a premise and a hypothesis as entailment, contradiction or neutral. Foundational datasets like SNLI [8], MNLI [9] and ANLI [10] have provided a robust foundation for assessing models' semantic understanding. Recognizing that human communication extends beyond literal meaning, recent research has increasingly focused on pragmatic reasoning. A growing body of work, in both English and Chinese, examines how well LLMs understand conversational implicatures [2–5] and figurative language [11, 12]. For presupposition, landmark datasets such as IMPPRES [7] offer a dedicated benchmark for evaluating models' understanding of presupposition triggers and their projection in English. Regarding scalar implicature, many studies have adopted methodologies from psycholinguistics to develop evaluation materials [6, 7]. However, systematic resources for evaluating presupposition and scalar implicature in Chinese remain scarce.

To address the aforementioned gaps: the scarcity of Chinese benchmarks and the neglect of the semantic–pragmatic interface, we introduce EPIc—the first Chinese benchmark offering a systematic assessment of LLMs' understanding of entailment, presupposition and scalar implicature.

3 Dataset Construction

3.1 Corpus: EPIc

The EPIc dataset comprises 480 items spanning three inference types: entailment, presupposition and scalar implicature. Since these inferences differ in their linguistic properties and are sensitive to sentence monotonicity (See Fig. 1), each inference type is embedded within three sentence structures: affirmative, negative and conditional. Across all items, the average context length is 67.48 characters, including punctuation marks. Each context is followed by four inference options, with an average length of 13.42 characters per option (See Table 1).

Table 1. Number of Questions and Average Character Length.

Inference type	Context type	# Questions	Avg. Context length	Avg. Option length
Entailment	Affirmative	60	52.52	13.31
	Negative	60	58.17	13.69
	Conditional	60	65.16	20.25
Presupposition	Affirmative	60	54.33	10.76
	Negative	60	57.92	11.18
	Conditional	60	73.57	12.48
Scalar implicature	Affirmative	60	76.62	10.65
	Negative	20	132.45	8.96
	Conditional	40	86.08	18.13

3.2 Data Sources

The contexts in the EPIc dataset were collected from two primary sources to ensure both linguistic authenticity and logical rigor.

First, a subset of contexts was carefully selected and adapted by linguists from established Chinese corpora, namely the Center for Chinese Linguistics PKU Corpus (CCL) and the BLCU Corpus Center (BCC). This selection was guided by searches for specific trigger expressions, such as possessive constructions for presupposition, hypernyms for entailment and scalar terms for scalar implicatures. These contexts span various genres, including novels, newspapers and online language, thereby ensuring linguistic naturalness and reflecting the stylistic diversity of different registers.

Additionally, we semi-automatically generated contexts by prompting LLMs with predefined inference-triggering terms (e.g., presupposition triggers, scalar terms). All generated sentences then underwent a rigorous manual screening to ensure their linguistic validity and quality, thus guaranteeing the credibility of the dataset.

Table 2. Examples entry in dataset EPIc.

Type	Context	Choices	
Entailment	他这样说时，低头一看自己的碟子里，正是**没有苹果**。自己也觉这种虚谦，虚谦得没有道理。史科莲这时也就很为难。这个苹果，一定要给祖母，岂不是不给祖母面子，若是吃了，越发显得没礼。 English Translation As he spoke, he looked down at his own plate—there were indeed **no apples**. He, too, realized that such modesty was utterly unreasonable. At that moment, Shi Kelian felt genuinely awkward. The apple must be given to Grandmother; otherwise, it would be disrespectful. But if he ate it himself, it would seem even more impolite.	Valid entailment	碟子里没有红苹果。 There was no red apple on the plate.
		Invalid entailment	碟子里没有水果。 There was no fruit on the plate.
		Contradiction	史科莲一点也不为难。 Shi Kelian was not troubled at all.
		Contradiction	他没有低头看自己的碟子。 He didn't look down at his own plate.
Presupposition	我决定去看望两个朋友的时候，正和母亲一起整理新家的厨房，我的父亲在**他的书房**里一声一声地叫我，要我去帮他整理那一大堆发黄的书籍。 English Translation When I decided to visit two friends, I was helping my mother organize the kitchen in our new home. Meanwhile, my father was calling me from **his study**, again and again, asking me to help sort through a large pile of yellowed books.	Valid presupposition	父亲有书房。 Father had a study.
		Invalid presupposition	父亲的书房朝南。 Father's study faced south.
		Contradiction	我和母亲在整理书房。 My mother and I were tidying up the study.
		Contradiction	书籍没有发黄。 The books had not yellowed.

3.3 Annotation Procedure

Writing Four Inferences. For each context, we constructed four inference options: two related inferences and two contradictory options that conflict with the context. The criteria for valid and invalid related inferences depend on the inference type and sentence monotonicity (See Table 2).

For entailment, the direction of valid inference is determined by monotonicity. In affirmative contexts, valid inferences proceed from a hyponym to a hypernym (e.g., *red apple* → *apple*), while invalid ones proceed from a hypernym to a hyponym. In contrast, in negative and conditional contexts, the valid inference direction is reversed: correct inferences move from a hypernym to a hyponym (e.g., *fruit* → *apple*) while upward inferences become invalid.

For presupposition, the valid inference is the presupposed content, regardless of whether the sentence is affirmative, negative or conditional. Invalid inferences reflect overgeneration, attributing more information than is pragmatically warranted.

For scalar implicatures, the correct inference in affirmative contexts reflects the scalar enrichment (e.g., *some* → *not all*), while the literal meaning is incorrect. In contrast, scalar implicatures are typically canceled in negative and conditional contexts, and the literal meaning is considered correct.

Verification. We recruited one linguistics graduate student and one non-linguistics graduate student to complete a multiple-choice task. In this task, they were asked to select the inferences that matched the given context from four options with no time limit. After completion, we reviewed the incorrect answers and their underlying reasoning to refine the dataset, thereby enhancing annotation accuracy and ensuring the dataset's reliability. We included a non-linguistics graduate student because individuals with a linguistics background are often familiar with the underlying theoretical motivations and tend to rely on formal analysis, which may cause them to overlook factors rooted in natural language intuition.

4 Experiment: Evaluation on LLMs

4.1 Experiment Setup and Evaluation

We evaluated the performance of six LLMs: DeepSeek-r1, DeepSeek-v3, GPT-4o-mini, OpenAI o1-mini, Gemini 2.5 Pro and Gemini 2.5 Flash. All models were accessed via official APIs using zero-shot prompts and were tested on the complete EPIc dataset.

Each question presented the model with a context and four options. The prompt was framed as follows: "You are now a native Chinese speaker. Given the following premise, please choose from the four options the one(s) you believe to be consistent with the premise. Multiple selections or no selection are allowed. Premise: Context. Options. Please respond in the format: Reason:, Answer:"[2].

This instruction explicitly permitted multiple selections or no selection, acknowledging the ambiguity inherent in certain inference types. This open-ended setting was intended to better simulate real human pragmatic judgment and to avoid forcing artificial binary choices. Besides, by requiring an explicit explanation (i.e., "Reason: …"),

[2] The original Chinese prompt is as follows: 你现在是一个中文母语者。对于以下已知情况，在给出的四个选项中，选择你认为符合已知情况的选项，允许多选或不选。已知：Context。Options。回答格式为Reason: ,Answer: 。

we were able to conduct a qualitative analysis of the models' interpretive processes in addition to quantitative accuracy metrics. All questions were evaluated independently to prevent any carryover effects or contextual priming across examples.

Model performance was quantified using accuracy, defined as the proportion of questions in which the model selected the correct inference. To provide a human benchmark, we recruited five native Chinese speakers. Each participant completed a randomly selected subset of 48 questions. Their average scores serve as an approximate estimate of human-level performance.

4.2 Results and Discussion

Figure 2 illustrates overall accuracy. All models performed well on presupposition, reaching human-comparable levels. However, entailment and scalar implicature proved more challenging, with greater performance variation ($X_e^2 = 178.473, p_e < .001; X_{si}^2 = 61.529, p_{si} < .001$). This suggests a persistent gap between LLMs and humans in comprehending implicit inferences.

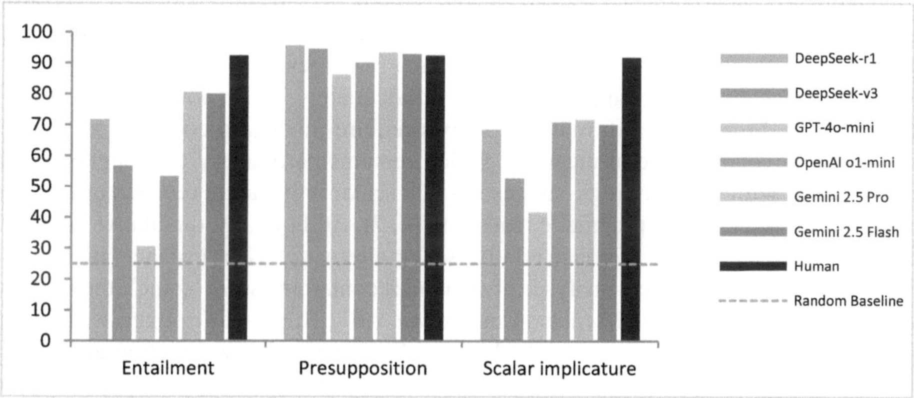

Fig. 2. Accuracy of LLMs across inference types in the multiple-choice task.

Table 3 provides a finer-grained breakdown. For entailment, models such as DeepSeek-r1, Gemini 2.5 Pro and Gemini 2.5 Flash perform strongly on affirmative sentences, with accuracy approaching ceiling levels. This suggests that these models can identify hierarchical relations between hyponyms and hypernyms. However, accuracy drops significantly across all models when the premise involves negative or conditional contexts. This contrast is especially pronounced in models like OpenAI o1-mini, whose accuracy in negative and conditional conditions decreases by approximately 50% compared to the affirmative condition. This pattern indicates that models face substantial difficulty reasoning in downward-entailing environments. Qualitative analysis of model-generated explanations shows that while models often correctly identify lexical hierarchies, they fail to apply the appropriate inference direction under negation or conditional operators. For example, the analysis by DeepSeek-r1 correctly identifies *rust* as a type of corn disease and *crop disease* as its superordinate concept. However, the model fails to establish a clear inferential direction in its final output, concluding that both the hyponym and hypernym are equally valid.

Table 3. Accuracy of LLMs on the EPIc (A = affirmative, N = negative, C = conditional).

	Entailment			Presupposition			Implicature		
	A	N	C	A	N	C	A	N	C
DeepSeek-r1	.97	.50	.68	.95	1.00	.92	.52	.65	.95
DeepSeek-v3	.77	.47	.47	.93	1.00	.90	.38	.90	.55
GPT-4o-mini	.50	.25	.17	.82	.87	.90	.32	.75	.40
OpenAI o1-mini	.88	.33	.39	.92	.92	.87	.63	.85	.75
Gemini 2.5 Pro	.97	.72	.73	.95	.92	.93	.55	.75	.95
Gemini 2.5 Flash	.97	.67	.77	.97	.90	.92	.50	.80	.95
Human	1.00	.90	.87	1.00	.97	.80	.80	1.00	.95

Scalar implicature posed the greatest difficulty. Unlike entailment, models primarily struggled with scalar implicature in affirmative sentences. This difficulty arises because scalar implicatures are typically canceled in negative and conditional contexts, allowing models to interpret such sentences literally. As a result, even models that lack scalar reasoning mechanisms can appear to perform adequately under downward-entailing environments. In contrast, affirmative contexts require models to compute pragmatic enrichment beyond the literal meaning, which remains particularly challenging. This pattern aligns with prior findings, suggesting that scalar implicature remains one of the most difficult inference of pragmatic reasoning [6, 7]. Additionally, qualitative analysis reveals that models rarely reference relative scalar alternatives. For instance, in the reasoning provided for incorrect analyses of sentences containing *yìxiē* 'some', the models failed to mention the related scalar term *suǒyǒu* 'all'. This finding suggests that the primary computational difficulty for LLMs may lie in activating scalar alternatives.

Overall, the Gemini models exhibited the most robust and balanced performance across all inference types and contexts, followed by DeepSeek-r1. Nonetheless, the poor performance of most models on entailment and scalar implicature tasks highlights the limitations of current LLMs in comprehending natural language inference.

5 Conclusion

In this paper, we present EPIc, the first Chinese dataset aimed at entailment, presupposition and scalar implicature across affirmative, negative and conditional contexts. In the experiment, we evaluated six LLMs, revealing that while most models exhibit near-human accuracy in presupposition recognition, their performance on entailment and scalar implicature remains suboptimal. Our qualitative analysis further suggests that LLMs struggle with sentence monotonicity and fail to appropriately activate scalar alternatives. Future research may explore free-text generation tasks to better capture the inference understanding abilities of LLMs.

References

1. Pandia, L., Cong, Y., Ettinger, A.: Pragmatic competence of pre-trained language models through the lens of discourse connectives. In: Bisazza, A., Abend, O. (eds.) Proceedings of the 25th Conference on Computational Natural Language Learning, pp. 367–379. Association for Computational Linguistics, Online (2021)
2. Hu, J., Floyd, S., Jouravlev, O., Fedorenko, E., Gibson, E.: A fine-grained comparison of pragmatic language understanding in humans and language models. In: Rogers, A., Boyd-Graber, J., Okazaki, N. (eds.) Proceedings of the 61st Annual Meeting of the Association for Computational Linguistics, pp. 4194–4213. Association for Computational Linguistics, Toronto, Canada (2023)
3. Reddy, S., Chen, D., Manning, C.D.: CoQA: A conversational question answering challenge. Trans. Assoc. Comput. Linguist. **7**, 249–266 (2019)
4. Yue, S., Song, S., Cheng, X., Hu, H.: Do large language models understand conversational implicature: a case study with a Chinese sitcom. In: Sun, M., Liang, J., Han, X., Liu, Z., He, Y. (eds.) Proceedings of the 23rd Chinese National Conference on Computational Linguistics, pp. 1270–1285. Chinese Information Processing Society of China, Taiyuan, China (2024)
5. Zheng, Z., Qiu, S., Fan, L., Zhu, Y., Zhu, S.: GRICE: a grammar-based dataset for recovering implicature and conversational reasoning. In: Zong, C., Xia, F., Li, W., Navigli, R. (eds.) Findings of the Association for Computational Linguistics: ACL-IJCNLP 2021, pp. 2074–2085. Association for Computational Linguistics, Online (2021)
6. Hu, J., Levy, R., Degen, J., Schuster, S.: Expectations over unspoken alternatives predict pragmatic inferences. Trans. Assoc. Comput. Linguist. **11**, 885–901 (2023)
7. Jeretic, P., Warstadt, A., Bhooshan, S., Williams, A.: Are natural language inference models IMPPRESsive? Learning IMPlicature and PRESupposition. In: Jurafsky, D., Chai, J., Schluter, N., Tetreault, J. (eds.) Proceedings of the 58th Annual Meeting of the Association for Computational Linguistics, pp. 8690–8705. Association for Computational Linguistics, Online (2020)
8. Bowman, S.R., Angeli, G., Potts, C., Manning, C.D.: A large annotated corpus for learning natural language inference. In: Márquez, L., Callison-Burch, C., Su, J. (eds.) Proceedings of the 2015 Conference on Empirical Methods in Natural Language Processing, pp. 632–642. Association for Computational Linguistics, Lisbon, Portugal (2015)
9. Williams, A., Nangia, N., Bowman, S.: A broad-coverage challenge corpus for sentence understanding through inference. In: Walker, M., Ji, H., Stent, A. (eds.) Proceedings of the 2018 Conference of the North American Chapter of the Association for Computational Linguistics: Human Language Technologies, pp. 1112–1122. Association for Computational Linguistics, New Orleans, Louisiana (2018)
10. Nie, Y., Williams, A., Dinan, E., Bansal, M., Weston, J., Kiela, D.: Adversarial NLI: a new benchmark for natural language understanding. In: Jurafsky, D., Chai, J., Schluter, N., Tetreault, J. (eds.) Proceedings of the 58th Annual Meeting of the Association for Computational Linguistics, pp. 4885–4901. Association for Computational Linguistics, Online (2020)
11. Wachowiak, L., Gromann, D.: Does GPT-3 grasp metaphors? Identifying metaphor mappings with generative language models. In: Rogers, A., Boyd-Graber, J., Okazaki, N. (eds.) Proceedings of the 61st Annual Meeting of the Association for Computational Linguistics, pp. 1018–1032. Association for Computational Linguistics, Toronto, Canada (2023)
12. Hessel, J., Marasovic, A., Hwang, J.D., Lee, L., Da, J., Zellers, R., Mankoff, R., Choi, Y.: Do Androids laugh at electric sheep? Humor "understanding" benchmarks from The New Yorker caption contest. In: Rogers, A., Boyd-Graber, J., Okazaki, N. (eds.) Proceedings of the 61st Annual Meeting of the Association for Computational Linguistics, pp. 688–714. Association for Computational Linguistics, Toronto, Canada (2023)

Chinese Lexical Analysis via Era-Aware Large Language Models

Siyuan Xue(✉)

Linguistic Institution, Chinese Academy of Social Science, Beijing, China
Xuesy@Cass.org.com

Abstract. The core tasks of Chinese lexical analysis are word segmentation and part-of-speech tagging. Existing tools are usually trained on corpora from a single period, resulting in high error rates when applied to texts from other historical stages. This study introduces an era-aware training method that explicitly incorporates temporal features. Large language models are fine-tuned on corpora representing four historical periods of Chinese: Ancient, Middle, Early Modern, and Modern. Experimental results show that the inclusion of temporal information substantially improves lexical analysis performance in all four eras. Among the evaluated models, Qwen-2-7B achieved the best overall results, with F1 scores of 97.58% (word segmentation) and 95.38% (POS) in Ancient Chinese, and 99.34% (word segmentation) in Modern Chinese. These findings demonstrate that temporal features are essential for enhancing both the accuracy and robustness of lexical analysis across different historical stages of Chinese.

Keywords: Chinese Lexical Processing · Large Language Model · Instruction Tuning

1 Introduction

Chinese lexical analysis is a fundamental task in natural language processing, encompassing word segmentation and part-of-speech (POS) tagging, which are essential for various linguistic applications. Word segmentation involves dividing continuous Chinese character strings into words based on predefined linguistic rules [1]. At the same time, POS tagging uses computational methods to automatically determine the grammatical category and syntactic role of each word in a sentence. Recently, many advanced lexical analysis tools have emerged, significantly improving historical texts' digitization and retrieval capabilities and providing strong support for large-scale linguistic research. However, these tools still face considerable challenges in practical applications, as a fixed word segmentation tool often proves limited when dealing with large-scale corpora spanning multiple historical periods. According to the previous test, many Chinese lexical tools are developed based on the modern Chinese standard, which restricts their ability to generalize across different historical periods. To address this problem, researchers have begun to gradually distinguish between different historical periods of corpora and develop lexical analysis tools tailored to the linguistic characteristics of

X. Ding and Y. Dong (Eds.): CLNLP 2025, CCIS 2775, pp. 162–175, 2026.
https://doi.org/10.1007/978-981-95-4788-3_15

each specific period. However, these tools lack of standardized systems creates significant interoperability issues, limiting their applicability in broader linguistic analysis tasks.

Recently, large language models outperformed traditional baseline models, demonstrating their strong ability to understand linguistic variations. Therefore, we aim to leverage the power of LLMs to develop a unified approach for lexical analysis across different historical periods. To this end, we introduce an instruction-tuning strategy that guides the model with task-specific prompts, enabling it to understand better and adapt to the linguistic features of various historical stages, thereby enhancing the accuracy and adaptability of lexical analysis.

The contributions of this study are as follows:

(1) This study reconstructs four lexical analysis datasets from Academia Sinica corpus resources across four historical periods of Chinese. Each dataset is annotated with dictionary-defined word classes, and providing a fundamental resource for lexical analysis within each period.
(2) This study proposes a joint learning method that incorporates era-specific information based on an LLM fine-tuning strategy. It explicitly integrates period features into word segmentation and part-of-speech tagging tasks.
(3) Comparative experiments show that without incorporating era information, model performance drops significantly on texts from different historical periods, highlighting the critical role of temporal features in improving lexical analysis accuracy.

2 Related Work

Chinese Lexical Analysis. The historical development of Chinese lexical analysis technology has evolved from early rule-based methods to statistical learning approaches and subsequently shifted towards data-driven machine learning techniques. Traditional rule-based methods rely on manually designed grammatical rules for lexical analysis; however, such methods lack flexibility and entail high maintenance costs. Later, researchers applied statistical learning methods, such as the Reverse Maximum Matching Algorithm [2], N-gram models [3], and the Hidden Markov Model [4] for Lexical analysis. Among these, sequence labeling models such as Conditional Random Fields (CRF) achieved state-of-the-art performance in Lexical analysis at the time [5].

With advanced deep learning technology, lexical analysis has gradually incorporated CNNs, RNNs, LSTMs, and Transformer-based pre-trained models [6]. These methods eliminate the need for complex feature engineering, enabling automatic extraction of deep semantic features and improving the accuracy of lexical analysis. Meanwhile, developing pre-trained language models has expanded Chinese POS analysis from modern to classical Chinese. For example, the BiLSTM-CRF model is applied for automatic lexical analysis of the ancient Chinese language [7, 8]. This paper proposes a joint approach to sentence segmentation and lexical analysis using a BiLSTM-CRF model. Experiments show that the joint model improves F1 scores for sentence segmentation, word segmentation, and part-of-speech tagging. Pre-trained model optimization was utilized for automatic word segmentation of historical texts and automatic punctuation in ancient Chinese [9]. Additionally, radical-enhanced models were introduced to improve ancient word segmentation and POS tagging [10].

Chinese Lexical Analysis with LLMs. The rise of large language models has revolutionized NLP research paradigms, and it has also provided new perspectives for lexical analysis research. CamemBERT is one of the earliest monolingual large language models applied to the part-of-speech tagging task, demonstrating strong performance in both semantic and syntactic analysis [11]. With growing interest in multilingual capabilities, Lai et al. evaluated ChatGPT across seven tasks in 37 languages, covering a spectrum from high-resource to low-resource languages [12]. Liang et al. constructed the XGLUE-POS, which includes 17 languages and is available through Huggingface Datasets. Based on this dataset, this paper evaluated ChatGPT's performance using both English task prompts and language-specific prompts, achieving part-of-speech tagging accuracy scores of 88.5% and 89.6%, respectively [13].

For the Chinese lexical analysis task, Wei et al. presented an innovative benchmark (AC-EVAL) designed to assess the advanced knowledge and reasoning capabilities of LLMs within the context of ancient Chinese [14, 15]. To enhance the lexical analysis ability of LLMs, Wang et al. introduced the first Chinese classical text analysis tool based on LLMs called 'Xunzi' which initially enabled classical text lexical analysis, relation extraction, and named entity recognition [16, 17]. Li et al. developed the 'AI Taiyan 2.0', designed explicitly for ancient Chinese punctuation, idiom recognition, word meaning interpretation, and classical-to-modern Chinese translation [18]. These studies have significantly advanced Chinese lexical analysis; however, they have not yet addressed the challenges posed by texts from different historical periods.

3 Methodology

Task Definition. This task is regarded as a sequence labeling problem, where the model determines both the optimal word sequence and the corresponding POS tag sequence jointly. Given an input text of Chinese characters: $X = \{x_1, x_2, \ldots, x_i\}$, the goal is to find an optimal sequence of words and their corresponding POS tag: $W = \{(w_1, t_1), (w_2, t_2), \ldots, (w_n, t_n)\}$. w_n refers to the output sequence of words the model is expected to produce after processing the input text. t_n refers to the part-of-speech (POS) tags corresponding to each word in the sequence.

Era-Integrated Chinese Lexical Analysis Model. Previous research has shown that joint training of related linguistic tasks facilitates more robust and accurate lexical analysis [18]. Inspired by this opinion, we propose a unified model that integrates era classification, word segmentation, and POS tagging into a joint learning framework for cross-period lexical analysis. Firstly, we construct the training data required for our experiments. Each word in a sentence is associated with a historical label, a word segmentation label, and a POS label. Then, we fine-tune the pre-trained large language model in an end-to-end way with a unified multi-task loss, enabling it to capture era-specific linguistic patterns while jointly learning lexical analysis tasks. The detailed information is illustrated below.

Data Construction. To facilitate lexical analysis across different historical stages of Chinese, we construct an experimental dataset by systematically reconstructing data based on the Academia Sinica Balanced Corpus [19]. This corpus encompasses multiple historical stages of the Chinese language, including Ancient Chinese (from the Pre-Qin), Middle Chinese (from the Eastern Han), Early Modern Chinese (from the Tang Dynasties), and Modern Chinese (from the Republican era to the present). In terms of textual diversity, the corpus includes literary works, journalistic writings, scientific, legal texts, and daily dialogues. Importantly, this corpus adopts a unified annotation scheme for word segmentation and part-of-speech tagging, providing a robust foundation for model evaluation across historical periods. Based on this corpus, we can extract representative samples from distinct historical periods and reprocess them to ensure consistency in segmentation, part-of-speech tagging, and temporal labeling. Through this reconstruction process, the dataset is aligned with the objectives of the experiment.

The primary aim of constructing an era-based corpus is to assess the generalization capabilities of models trained on mixed-era corpora when applied to texts from different historical periods. Firstly, this study selects proportionally balanced texts from four historical periods to construct a cross-era evaluation corpus. During the data pre-processing stage, punctuation marks such as '。', ';', '!' and '?' are used as sentence delimiters, with the text between two such marks treated as a complete sentence; other punctuation marks are disregarded. Subsequently, this study adopts the 12 basic part-of-speech (POS) categories defined in the Modern Chinese Dictionary as the unified annotation scheme. These categories include: noun (N), verb (V), adjective (A), adverb (D), numeral (M), quantifier (Q), pronoun (R), preposition (P), conjunction (C), auxiliary word (T), interjection (I), and onomatopoeia (O). The Modern Chinese Dictionary was compiled by linguistic experts based on years of systematic research. The twelve POS categories used in the dictionary are the result of extensive studies on the structure and historical evolution of the Chinese language, and they are widely recognized and adopted in both ancient and modern Chinese linguistic research. To ensure comparability across different historical stages, this POS annotation schema is applied uniformly throughout the dataset. The statistics of the annotated dataset are illustrated in Table 2.

Data Annotation. In this section, we annotate each sentence with era classification, word segmentation, and part-of-speech (POS) information as follows:

Era classification determines whether a given sentence belongs to one of the four historical periods: Ancient (S), Middle (Z), Early Modern (J), or Modern (X), such as the sentence of *'Supervision should be strengthened'* (应加大监管力度), the era class of this sentence is Modern, labeled as 'X', which is Modern Chinese. For example,'(X)加大监管力度'。

For word segmentation, we adopt the BMES tagging scheme, which classifies each character in a word as: B (Begin) → The first character of a multi-character word, M (Middle) → A middle character in a multi-character word, E (End) → The last character of a multi-character word, S (Single) → A single-character word. The example of word segmentation annotation: '加(B)大(E)监(B)管(E)力(B)度(E)'。

Moreover, since the corpora from different historical periods exhibit variations in lexical categorization, to ensure synchronized analysis across the four eras, we standardize POS tagging by aligning it with the classification system of authoritative dictionaries. Moreover, for POS tagging, each word is assigned an appropriate part-of-speech label based on its actual meaning. The tagging scheme includes Punctuation (PU), Onomatopoeia (O), Interjection (I), Auxiliary word (T), Conjunction (C), Preposition (P), Adverb (D), Pronoun (R), Quantifier (Q), Numeral (M), Adjective (A), Verb (V), and Noun (N). The example of word segmentation annotation:

'加(V)大(V)监(V)管(V)力(N)度(N)'.

Therefore, the integrated format for word segmentation and POS tagging follows the B-N structure, where BMES tags are combined with POS labels (e.g., B-N, M-N, E-N, S-V). The example of word segmentation and Pos tag annotation:

'加(B-V)大(E-V)监(B-V)管(E-V)力(B-N)度(E-N)'.

To accurately represent the era information of sentences, a multi-level annotation approach is adopted to label temporal information, word segmentation, and part-of-speech information in a refined approach. The example of era detection, word segmentation, and POS tagging annotation:

'加(X-B-V)大(X-E-V)监(X-B-V)管(X-E-V)力(X-B-N)度(X-E-N)'.

The original annotation data is converted into JSON format for training, including system instructions, input, and output. An example of a Chinese lexical prompt template is illustrated in Table 1.

Table 1. Chinese lexical prompt template.

*{**Instruction:** Please perform three-dimensional diachronic annotation on the input text according to the [Period] - [Word Segmentation] - [Part of Speech] hierarchy* ***Era-Detection**: Determine the time period of the input text, choosing only one from the following four periods: S (Ancient Chinese: Pre-Qin to Han Dynasties), Z (Middle Chinese: Wei-Jin to Song-Yuan Dynasties), J (Early Modern Chinese: Ming-Qing Dynasties), X (Modern Chinese: 1919-Nowadays)* ***Word Segmentation**: Segment the input text and ensure it follows the BMES format.'B' indicates the beginning of a word, 'M' indicates the middle of a word, 'E' indicates the end of a word, and 'S' indicates a single word* ***Part-of-Speech Tagging**: Accurately assign part-of-speech tags based on the actual meaning of each word. The part-of-speech tags include: N (Noun), V (Verb), A (Adjective), M (Numeral), Q (Quantifier), R (Pronoun), D (Adverb), P (Preposition), C (Conjunction), T (Auxiliary word), I (Interjection), O (Onomatopoeia), PU (Punctuation)* *When outputting, each word's part-of-speech tag will be presented in the following format: (Era-word - POS tag)* ***Input:** Input Text* ***Output:** The lexical analysis prediction of Input Text}*

After completing the data format conversion, the data is divided into corresponding training and test sets, with 20% of the training data allocated for validation to fine-tune the model.

Instruction Tuning of Lexical Analysis. To obtain the lexical analysis model, we apply supervised fine-tuning for lexical analysis tasks in each era in the second step, which includes era detection, word segmentation, and part-of-speech tagging. In supervised fine-tuning (SFT), the cross-entropy loss function is commonly used for classification tasks. The formula is as follows:

$$L_{SFT} = -\frac{1}{B}\sum_{i=1}^{B} \log P_i(y_i|x_i) \quad (1)$$

where B denotes the batch size, y_i denotes the prediction of lexical analysis, and x_i represents the system instruction and input text.

4 Experiment and Results

4.1 Data Statistics

The data set contains lexical analysis data across four historical periods: Ancient, Medieval, Early Modern, and Modern. It consolidates text data previously divided into training and test sets for each period. During the fine-tuning process, we allocated 20% of the training set as the validation set to evaluate the model's performance during training and prevent over-fitting.

Table 2. Overall statistics of the data set.

Period	Training			Test		
	Characters	Words	Sentences	Characters	Words	Sentences
Ancient	772204	490723	42500	132427	84264	7500
Medieval	331898	217229	42500	331898	38669	7500
Early Modern	973712	662473	42500	170712	116513	7500
Modern	1722640	900686	42500	300619	157859	7500

4.2 Experiment Setup

In this study, we employ traditional sequence labeling frameworks and instruction-tuned large language models in this task, allowing a comprehensive comparison of their performance in both structured annotation and semantic understanding. The models used are as follows:

(1) CKIP-transformers [20]: This is a pre-trained sequence labeling toolkit developed by the Academia Sinica CKIP team. It represents a strong baseline among transformer-based models for word segmentation and POS tagging applications.
(2) BERT-BiLSTM-CRF [21]: This classic sequence labeling architecture combines contextual embeddings from BERT with a Bi-LSTM encoder and a CRF decoding layer. This model has consistently performed strongly on Chinese lexical analysis tasks, particularly in structured linguistic scenarios.
(3) XLM-RoBERTa (base) [22]:This model is trained on large-scale general corpora from 100 languages, aiming to enhance the model's representation capability in multilingual settings.
(4) Llama3-8B-Chinese-Chat [23]: Built upon the Llama large language model, this version has been trained with an expanded Chinese vocabulary, significantly enhancing its ability to understand Chinese semantics.
(5) Qwen-2 [24]: Qwen-2 inherits the advantages of the Qwen model and is optimized using a larger and more diverse dataset. The Qwen2-7B-Instruct model is selected for training.
(6) GLM-4-9B [25]: This general-purpose Chinese-English dialogue model was developed by the KEG Lab at Tsinghua University. It is capable of Chinese semantic understanding and can handle both generation and comprehension tasks in Chinese.

4.3 Evaluation Metrics

The metrics utilized to evaluate the performance of Chinese lexical analysis are listed below:

$$\text{Precision} = \frac{\text{True Positive (TP)}}{\text{True Positive (TP)} + \text{False Positive (FP)}} \tag{2}$$

$$\text{Recall} = \frac{\text{True Positive (TP)}}{\text{True Positive (TP)} + \text{False Negative (FN)}} \tag{3}$$

$$\text{F}_1 = \frac{2 \times \text{Precision} \times \text{Recall}}{\text{Precision} + \text{Recall}} \tag{4}$$

The calculation method for word segmentation and part-of-speech (POS) tagging is based on words rather than individual characters. To assess the accuracy of a character's POS tagging, it is essential first to verify the correctness of the word segmentation. In other words, the evaluation is conducted based on accurately segmented words.

4.4 Experiment Parameters

During the training process, the LoRA (Low-Rank Adaptation) fine-tuning strategy is employed [26], freeing part of the model's parameters, significantly reducing the number of trainable parameters. This approach helps minimize computational resource consumption and memory overhead. The experiments are primarily conducted on an A-800 80GB NVIDIA GPU, using Python version 3.10.6 and CUDA version 12.4. Additionally, the DeepSpeed framework is leveraged to accelerate the training process. Detailed model training parameters for the three large language models are provided in Table 3.

Table 3. The selection of parameter value.

Parameter	Value	Parameter	Value
learning rate	5e-5	fp16	True
num_train_epoch	4	max_length	2046
per_device_train_batch_size	16	Lora Rank	8
save_steps	1000	Lora Alpha	16
Inference top-k	0.9	Temperature	0.1

5 Chinese Lexical Analysis Results

5.1 Main Results

This paper proposes an annotation strategy that incorporates temporal information and fine-tunes the model based on this strategy to improve lexical analysis across different historical periods. As shown in Table 4, Qwen-2-7B and GLM4-9B models trained with temporal information outperform traditional pre-trained language models such as CKIP-Transformers, BERT-BiLSTM-CRF and XLM-RoBERTa across all periods and tasks. Qwen-2-7B achieves the highest F1 scores, reaching 97.58% for word segmentation and 95.38% for POS tagging in Ancient Chinese, and both in Modern Chinese. Experimental results show that the proposed method outperforms traditional pre-trained language models in Chinese lexical analysis tasks. This indicates that including temporal information can improve the model's generalization ability across different periods.

Table 4. The F1 results of word segmentation and POS tagging with different models.

Models	Ancient		Medieval		Early Modern		Modern	
	WS	POS	WS	POS	WS	POS	WS	POS
CKIP-Transformers	80.71	25.59	75.25	74.34	78.60	80.80	64.68	65.53
BERT-BiLSTM-CRF	92.46	89.83	86.96	82.46	87.11	85.48	93.24	92.09

(continued)

Table 4. (*continued*)

Models	Ancient		Medieval		Early Modern		Modern	
	WS	POS	WS	POS	WS	POS	WS	POS
XLM-RoBERTa	87.58	75.00	84.82	82.53	85.93	82.57	94.56	92.87
Llama3.1-8B	96.32	91.92	94.66	92.51	97.04	91.74	98.32	**94.11**
GLM4-9B	97.57	88.39	**95.30**	**93.64**	94.40	**92.12**	97.75	93.76
Qwen-2-7B	**97.58**	**95.38**	95.17	93.47	**97.42**	92.01	**99.34**	91.67

5.2 The Evaluation of Era Information

Table 5. The word segmentation results of different LLMs with instruction tuning strategies.

Models	Strategy	Ancient	Medieval	Early Modern	Modern
Llama3.1-8B	Joint learning	96.32	94.66	97.04	98.32
	Joint learning *w/o era*	96.67	93.87	97.15	98.38
GLM4-9B	Joint learning	97.57	**95.30**	94.40	97.75
	Joint learning *w/o era*	95.69	94.30	91.86	95.49
Qwen-2-7B	Joint learning	**97.58**	95.17	**97.42**	**99.34**
	Joint learning *w/o era*	97.19	94.71	96.59	99.18

Table 6. The POS tagging results of different LLMs with instruction tuning strategies.

Models	Strategy	Ancient	Medieval	Early Modern	Modern
Llama3.1-8B	Joint learning	91.92	92.51	91.74	**94.11**
	Joint learning *w/o era*	91.81	92.09	91.03	92.55
GLM4-9B	Joint learning	88.39	**93.64**	**92.12**	93.76
	Joint learning *w/o era*	88.19	91.41	88.67	92.10
Qwen-2-7B	Joint learning	**95.38**	93.47	92.01	91.67
	Joint learning *w/o era*	87.14	92.33	88.87	88.73

The proposed method shows effective improvements in word segmentation and part-of-speech tagging. We conduct a fine-grained evaluation comparing models with and without era information to assess how temporal features influence model performance. Based on Tables 5 and 6, we found that:

(1) When era information is removed, the results show a slight decline. In the word segmentation results, Qwen2's performance decreased by 0.39% in the ancient period,

0.46% in the Middle period, 0.83% in the early modern period, and 0.16% in the modern period. In the POS tagging results, Qwen2-7B's performance decreased by 8.24% in the ancient period, 1.14% in the Middle Chinese period, 3.14% in the early modern period, and 2.94% in the modern period.

(2) Notably, the performance gap between the joint learning and the joint learning without era information is relatively small in Modern Chinese. For example, with the LLaMA3.1-8B model, the F1 score in Modern Chinese drops by only 1.56%. Similar trends are observed in other models, such as GLM4-9B (a reduction of 1.66%) and Qwen-2-7B (a reduction of 2.94%). This phenomenon illustrates that modern Chinese exhibits less vocabulary variation than ancient or early modern Chinese. Moreover, it is more extensively represented in training corpora, enabling large language models to generalize well even without explicit temporal labels.

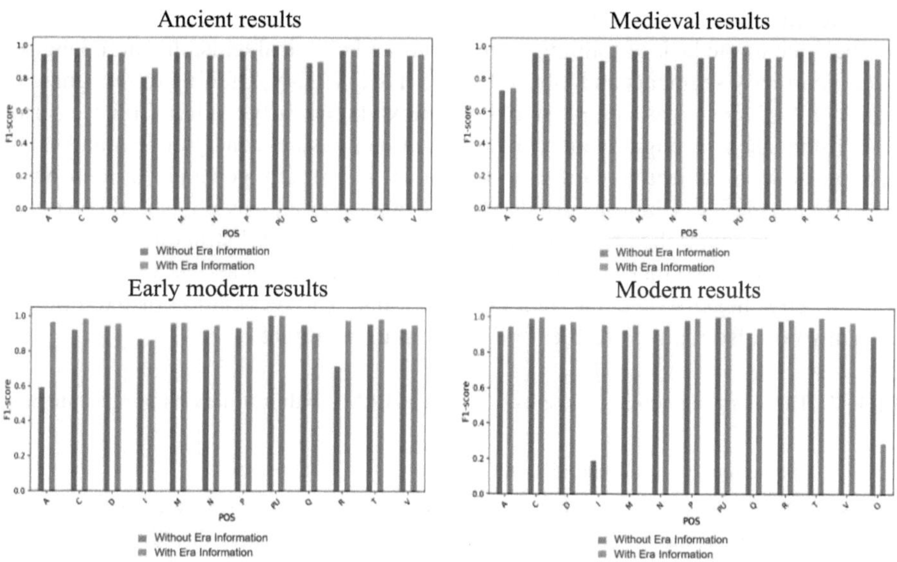

Fig. 1. The POS tagging results of different LLMs with instruction tuning strategies.

Taking the Qwen2-7B model as an example, we observe the changes in its performance across different parts of speech after incorporating temporal features. The results show that the integrated model, which incorporates era labels, word segmentation, and part-of-speech tagging, performs better predicting most tags than the model without era information. According to Fig. 1, the instruction-tuned model performs well in predicting nouns, verbs, numerals, classifiers, adverbs, prepositions, conjunctions, particles, and punctuation marks, with F1 scores for POS tagging exceeding 85%. However, there is still room for improvement in distinguishing certain part-of-speech tags, such as interjections in the ancient period, adjectives in the Middle period, pronouns and interjections in the early modern Chinese period, and interjections and onomatopoeia in the modern Chinese period.

5.3 Error Analysis

Proper nouns in ancient Chinese are relatively sparse in the model, making it difficult to capture the relevant features accurately. This is the main reason for the poor performance in part-of-speech tagging. Table 7 shows some word segmentation and POS tagging mistakes of each period. For example, '商履' as a personal name should be segmented as a complete unit. The model misclassified the part-of-speech and word boundary of '代兴' (took over and revived), where '代' and '兴' should be treated as two independent verbs, meaning 'to replace' and 'to revive', respectively. Instead, the large language model incorrectly labeled '代' as an adverb (D). This reflects the model's tendency to follow modern Chinese grammatical conventions, leading it to interpret '代' as an abstract adverb such as 'in turn' or 'subsequently', rather than correctly identifying its Classical Chinese usage as a verb meaning 'to succeed' or 'to take over.' Errors in word segmentation further lead to inaccuracies in part-of-speech tagging. In middle Chinese, '七宝' (Seven Treasures) is a typical Buddhist term referring to seven precious materials. However, due to the lack of training on religious and classical texts, the large language model incorrectly segments and labels it as '七(B-N)宝(E-N)', failing to recognize the function of '七' (seven) as a numeral in this context. In the early modern Chinese period, '閎閬' (immense and magnificent) conveys a sense of vastness and grandeur and should be annotated as an adjective. However, the model incorrectly generates a noun phrase instead. In the modern Chinese period, '推特' (Twitter) as a loanword, should be treated as a single noun rather than being split into a '推(S-V)特(S-A)' structure.

The errors indicate that the accuracy of word segmentation and part-of-speech tagging still relies heavily on contextual understanding. The recognition of fixed phrases and loanwords also requires further optimization in the future.

Table 7. The word segmentation results of different LLMs with instruction tuning strategies.

	Sentence	Ground Truth	Predict
Ancient period	乃有商履代興(Thus came the donning of ceremonial shoes, replacing the old to rise anew.)	乃(S-D)有(S-V)商**(B-N)**履**(E-N)**代**(S-V)**興(S-V)	乃(S-D)有(S-V)商**(S-N)**履**(S-N)**代**(S-D)**興(S-V)
Medieval period	七寶所成(Composed of the Seven Treasures)	七**(S-M)**寶**(S-N)**所(S-T)成(S-V)	七**(B-N)**寶**(E-N)**所(S-T)成(S-V)

(continued)

Table 7. (*continued*)

	Sentence	Ground Truth	Predict
Early modern period	身長七尺,額有肉珠,閎闊天生(He stood seven chi tall,with a fleshy protuberance (like a pearl) on his forehead,born with an imposing and majestic presence.)	身(S-N)長(S-V)七(S-M)尺(S-Q), (S-PU)額(S-N)有(S-V)肉**(B-N)**珠**(E-N)**,(S-PU)閎**(B-A)**闊**(E-A)**天(B-V)生(E-V)...	身(S-N)長(S-V)七(S-M)尺(S-Q),(S-PU)額(S-N)有(S-V)肉**(S-N)**珠**(S-N)**,(S-PU)閎**(B-N)**闊**(E-N)**天(B-V)生(E-V)...
Modern period	由410条推特组成的电影。(A film composed of 410 tweets)	由(S-P)4(B-M)1(M-M)0(E-M)条(S-Q)推**(B-N)**特**(E-N)**组(B-V)成(E-V)的(S-T)电(B-N)影(E-N)。	由(S-P)4(B-M)1(M-M)0(E-M)条(S-Q)推**(S-V)**特**(S-A)**组(B-V)成(E-V)的(S-T)电(B-N)影(E-N)

6 Conclusion

Chinese exhibits unique morphological characteristics at different historical stages, yet existing mainstream lexical analysis tools still have significant limitations in processing cross-period texts. This study systematically evaluates the performance of open-source lexical analysis tools and proposes a Chinese lexical training strategy that integrates era classification, word segmentation, and part-of-speech tagging. Experimental results show that the linguistic analysis model trained on large language models outperforms traditional pre-trained models and demonstrates strong generalization across historical periods. To improve performance, models require more annotated data and refined training strategies to better capture these linguistic variations. Future research may focus on developing lexical analysis models capable of handling mixed-period texts.

Acknowledgments. This work is supported and acknowledged by the project of the National Language Commission (WT145-59), the Youth Start-up Program of the Chinese Academy of Social Sciences (2024QQJH15) and the Key Laboratory of Linguistics, Chinese Academy of Social Sciences (2024SYZH001).

References

1. Guo, X.: Construction and Application of Chinese Corpora. Shanghai Foreign Language Education Press, Shanghai (2011)

2. Qiu, H., Xing, N.: Research on ancient chinese word segmentation based on Chinese information processing. Microcomputer Inf. **24**, 100–102 (2008)
3. Duan, L., Han, F., Song, J.H.: A comparative analysis of methods for automatically acquiring ancient Chinese characters and words. J. Chin. In. Proc. 34–42 (2012)
4. Qian, Z.Y., Zhou, Z., Dong, G.P., et al.: Research on automatic word segmentation and annotation of Chu Ci based on HMM. In: Library and Information Work, pp. 105–110 (2014)
5. Wang, X.Y., Li, B.: Automatic word segmentation of middle Chinese based on CRFs and dictionary information. In: Data Analysis and Knowledge Discovery, pp. 62–70 (2017)
6. Yu, J.S., Wei, Y., Zhang, W.: Research and application of ancient Chinese sentence segmentation based on BERT. J. Chin. Inf. Process. 57–63 (2019)
7. Cheng, N., Li, B., Ge, S.H., et al.: Integrated research on ancient Chinese automatic sentence segmentation and lexical analysis based on BiLSTM-CRF. J. Chin. Inf. Process. 1–9 (2020)
8. Liu, C., Wang, D.B., Hu, H.T., et al.: Research on automatic word segmentation of classics for digital humanities: using SikuBERT pretrained model as an example. Libr. Forum 44–54 (2022)
9. Tang, X.M., Su, Q., Wang, J., et al.: Research on automatic sentence and punctuation segmentation of classical chinese based on pretrained language models. J. Chin. Inf. Process. 159–168 (2023)
10. Chang, B.L., Yuan, Y.G., Li, B., et al.: Integrated analysis of automatic word segmentation and part-of-speech tagging for ancient chinese with radicals information. Data Anal. Knowl. Discov. 102–113 (2024)
11. Martin, L., Muller, B., Suárez, P.J.O., et al.: CamemBERT: a tasty French language model (2019). arXiv preprint arXiv:1911.03894
12. Lai, V.D., Ngo, N.T., Veyseh, A.P.B., et al.: ChatGPT beyond English: towards a comprehensive evaluation of large language models in multilingual learning (2023). arXiv preprint arXiv:2304.05613
13. Liang, Y., Duan, N., Gong, Y., et al.: XGLUE: a new benchmark dataset for cross-lingual pre-training, understanding and generation (2020). arXiv preprint arXiv:2004.01401
14. Zhang, S., Dong, L., Li, X., et al.: Instruction tuning for large language models: a survey (2023). arXiv preprint arXiv:2308.10792
15. Wei, Y., Xu, Y., Wei, X., et al.: AC-EVAL: evaluating ancient chinese language understanding in large language models (2024). arXiv preprint arXiv:2403.06574
16. Li, Z., Hu, T.F., Wang, L.J.: Research on the construction and application of large language models for ancient Chinese. Lang. Strategy Res. 22–33 (2024)
17. Wang, P.: XunziALLM. https://github.com/Xunzi-LLM-of-Chinese-classics (01 April 2024)
18. Li, S., Hu, R., Wang, L.: Construction and application of large language models for classical Chinese. Lang. Strategy Res. **9**(5) 22–33 (2024)
19. Ju, H., Ke, C., Li, Z., Hui, X.: Introduction to the Academia Sinica balanced corpus (1995). http://www.sinica.edu.tw/ftms-bin/kiwi.sh
20. CKIP Lab: CKIP-transformers. https://ckip-transformers.readthedocs.io/en/stable/ (25 Jan 2025)
21. Huang, Z., Xu, W., Yu, K.: Bidirectional LSTM-CRF models for sequence tagging (2015). arXiv preprint arXiv:1508.01991
22. Conneau, A., Khandelwal, K., Goyal, N., et al.: Unsupervised cross-lingual representation learning at scale (2019). arXiv preprint arXiv:1911.02116
23. Wang, S.Z., Zheng, Y.W.: Llama3–8B-Chinese-Chat (revision 6622a23). https://huggingface.co/shenzhi-wang/Llama3-8B-Chinese-Chat (01 April 2024)
24. Yang, A., Yang, S., Hui, Y., et al.: Qwen2 technical report (2024). arXiv preprint arXiv:2407.10671

25. Zeng, A.H., Xu, B., Wang, B.W., et al.: ChatGLM: a family of large language models from GLM-130B to GLM-4 All tools (2024). arXiv preprint arXiv:2406.12793
26. Hu, E.J., Shen, Y., Wallis, P., et al.: LoRA: low-rank adaptation of large language models (2021). arXiv preprint arXiv:2106.09685

FBMG: A Syncretic Chinese Named Entity Recognition Framework for Investment in Enterprises

Mei Song[1,2,3], Mengdi Zhang[3](✉), Zhun Li[3], Keyi Zhang[3], and Jing Guo[4]

[1] Key Laboratory of Jiangsu Intelligent Educational Technology, Jiangsu Normal University, Xuzhou 221116, China

[2] Management Science and Engineering Research Centre, Jiangsu Normal University, Xuzhou 221116, China

[3] School of Computer Science and Technology, Jiangsu Normal University, Xuzhou 221116, China

2020230571@jsnu.edu.cn

[4] The Credit Reference Center, the People's Bank of China, Shanghai 201201, China

Abstract. With the expansion of financial markets and the surge in financial text data, accurately recognizing professional entities associated with corporate investment has become crucial for financial analysis and decision-making. However, existing named entity recognition (NER) methods still struggle with accuracy, especially when identifying complex and specialized entities related to enterprise investment. To solve this problem, we propose a novel model, FBMG (FinBERT-BiLSTM-MA-Global Pointer), for Chinese named entity recognition in the field of financial investment. Firstly, the pre-trained financial language model FinBERT was used to generate dynamic semantic vectors based on the context to obtain semantic information of corporate investment corpus. Secondly, the BiLSTM-Global Pointer model architecture is used to capture long-range textual information, nested and non-nested named entities are considered from a global perspective, and a multi-head attention mechanism is incorporated on this basis for information weight assignment to fully exploit the semantic features of the text. Furthermore, considering the characteristics of different entities, the model achieved the best F1 score of 84.69% using rule-based and lexicon data enhancement, compared with other models. The experimental results show that the proposed method effectively improve the identification of corporate investment named entities, which can be a reference for similar financial entity recognition.

Keywords: Investment · Pre-trained Model · Multi-head Attention Mechanism · Global Pointer · Data Augmentation

1 Introduction

Named entity recognition (NER) plays a fundamental role in natural language processing (NLP), supporting downstream tasks such as text mining, relation extraction, and the construction of domain-specific knowledge graphs [1]. In the context of enterprise investment, NER is especially crucial for constructing investment relationship

X. Ding and Y. Dong (Eds.): CLNLP 2025, CCIS 2775, pp. 176–183, 2026.
https://doi.org/10.1007/978-981-95-4788-3_16

graphs [2], identifying potential investment risks [3], and promoting intelligent financial applications [4].

At the moment, NER for enterprise investment mostly faces the following challenges [5]: Firstly, financial terms are difficult to identify, e.g. "天使轮(angel round)", "pre-A 轮(pre-A round)", "A+ 轮(A+ round)". Secondly, the text contains multi-level nested named entities. Most financier entities begin with province or city names and end with terms such as "公司 (company)" or "集团 (group)", while most investor entities end with "资本 (capital)" or "机构 (organization)". This structure makes it difficult to accurately determine entity boundaries. Thirdly, investor and investee have inconsistent expressions. The same investor or investee may appear as a Chinese abbreviation, English abbreviation, or entity with longer length, resulting in certain identification difficulties.

To address these challenges in NER of enterprise investment, the main contributions of this work are summarized as follows:

- A novel model, FBMG (FinBERT-BiLSTM-MA-Global Pointer), is proposed by paying more attention to the complex semantic of investment phrases.
- Global Pointer and multi-head attention (MA) mechanism is introduced to effectively distinguish the entity boundaries, and also the targeted data augmentation to express the inconsistent expressions problem.
- Experimental results demonstrate that the proposed method outperforms state-of-the-art NER methods on the investment corpus.

The rest of this paper is organized as follows: In Sect. 2, the related work of NER is described. In Sect. 3, the FBMG model is introduced. The experimental results and analysis are shown in Sect. 4. Finally, we summarize this paper and provide some directions for future work in Sect. 5.

2 Related Work

With the development of deep learning, artificial intelligence has made notable strides in NER tasks in recent years. A BiLSTM-CRF model architecture was proposed by Liu et al. [6] with the incorporation of Chinese five-stroke augmented features to improve the results. Ding et al. [7] proposed a BiLSTM-CRF deep learning model for recognizing three entity types, achieving an F1 score of 90.85%. With the emergence of pre-trained models, Wang et al. [8] proposed a BERT based method for entity recognition, showing improvements over traditional methods. Liu et al. [9] suggested a semi-supervised technique for entity recognition in financial texts that uses BERT and Bootstrapping. Zhang et al. [10] suggested a BERT-BiLSTM-CRF model application for named entity recognition, which outperformed other baseline models. Liu et al. [11] proposed FinBERT, a BERT-based model for financial text, which can be applied to a variety of financial domain tasks, such as reading comprehension in the financial domain [12] and constructing knowledge graphs in the securities domain [13], but has not to be well applied to the task of recognizing named corporate investment entities. Su et al. [14] proposed the Global Pointer model, which uses rotational position encoding and global normalization to handle nested and non-nested entities, effectively solving the complexity and diversity issues in entity recognition, but it has not been applied to financial entity recognition with multi-level nested named entities.

To address the complexity of the NER problem for enterprise investment as well as the inadequacies of previous techniques, this research presents a new FBMG framework that incorporates the MA mechanism. First, the more specialized financial pre-trained language model FinBERT is utilized to extract the text's semantic content. Then, we investigate the application of the BiLSTM-Global Pointer model architecture to capture contextual information and global normalization to decode nested and non-nested named entities. On this basis, we incorporate a MA mechanism to assign weights to information based on word similarity, thereby enhancing the model's feature extraction capability. In addition, we apply rule-based and dictionary-based data enhancement techniques to further improve the recognition of entities in the enterprise investment domain. This approach effectively addresses the lack of research on named entity recognition in the financial field.

3 FBMG Model

In this paper, a unique model architecture of FinBERT-BiLSTM-MA-Global Pointer (FBMG) is presented for corporate investment NER, as illustrated in Fig. 1.

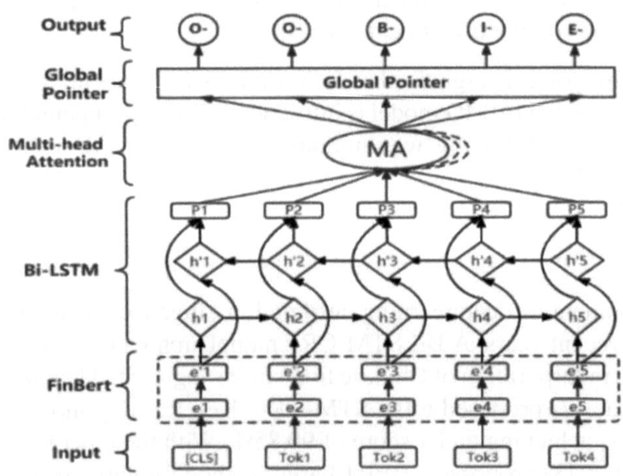

Fig. 1. Model architecture of FBMG.

First, the financial pre-trained language model FinBERT processes the input text, where the sum of word vectors, sentence vectors, and position vectors is used as input. Leveraging the financial domain knowledge embedded in FinBERT, the model captures rich semantic representations of corporate investment texts. Subsequently, the resulting embeddings are passed into a BiLSTM network. The forward LSTM captures future semantic information, while the backward LSTM captures past context. After that, to understand the dependency relationships among words, assess their contributions, and extract structural information, a MA mechanism is introduced. Finally, in order to enhance the recognition of both nested and non-nested named entities, the output from the attention module is fed into the Global Pointer model, which applies global normalization to corporate investment texts.

3.1 FinBERT (Financial Pretraining Language Model)

FinBERT is constructed upon the BERT [15] pre-training model, using both public and financial corpora for training. Unlike BERT, FinBERT includes additional pre-training tasks to capture specialized linguistic knowledge in the financial domain, enabling it to handle named entities in corporate investment texts. FinBERT uses multi-task learning for continuous updates to support various downstream tasks.

The pre-training tasks include sentence Q & A relation recognition, sentence disruption and reconstruction, capitalization prediction, and span prediction. Figure 2 shows the schematic diagram of FinBERT's pre-training architecture.

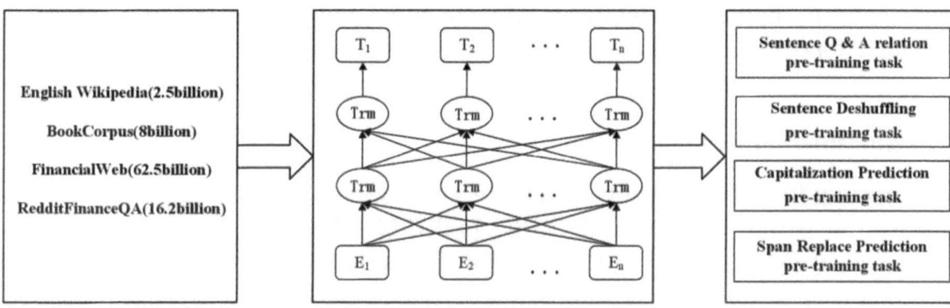

Fig. 2. FinBERT pre-training architecture.

3.2 Global Pointer Model

The investment corpus in this study contains many nested named entities, making the Global Pointer model more effective than CRF. The model uses global information and relative position encoding to account for entity start and end positions, improving recognition. Rotational position coding is introduced to enhance sensitivity to entity locations, improving contextual semantic understanding.

4 Experiment

4.1 Dataset

The dataset used in this study was constructed by crawling 3,359 investment-related entries from both domestic and international sources over the past three years using web crawler technology. After collection, data unrelated to investment events, duplicates, special symbols, and other irrelevant information were removed during data preprocessing. Upon analyzing the enterprise investment texts, five important entity categories were identified: investee, investor, investment round, investment time, and investment amount. The dataset was then labeled according to the BMOES scheme, where B represents the beginning of an entity, M and E indicate the interior and end of an entity, S denotes a single-character entity, and O represents non-entity tokens. Finally, the preprocessed and labeled data were divided into training, validation, and test sets in an 8:1:1 ratio, with each subset containing samples from all five entity categories.

4.2 Assessment Indicators

In order to evaluate the effectiveness of the model in recognition various types of entities, the precision, recall and summed mean values F_1 were chosen as the evaluation metrics for this experiment.

Experimental Environment and Parameter Settings. The experimental environment was based on Python 3.8 and the deep learning framework Pytorch version 1.7.1. The pre-training model BERT uses the common BERT-base version with a maximum sequence length of 512. The optimizer uses Adam, the number of iterations is 100, the training sample batch is 16, the learning rate is set to 1e-5, the number of attention heads set to 8,and the Dropout layer is set to 0.5.

4.3 Experimental Results and Analyses

Experimental Results and Analysis of Different Models. The FBMG model was compared with the BERT-BiLSTM-CRF (BBC), FinBERT-BiLSTM-CRF (FBC), FinBERT-Global Pointer (FG), and FinBERT-BiLSTM-Global Pointer (FBG) models using the self-constructed corpus to evaluate its entity recognition performance on corporate investment data. The results are shown in Table 1.

Table 1. Experimental results of different models (%).

Model	P	R	F_1
BBC	80.21	78.54	79.37
FBC	80.45	80.31	80.38
FG	82.44	79.78	81.09
FBG	83.07	80.42	81.72
FBMG	**84.54**	**82.39**	**83.45**

Compared to BBC, FBC achieves a 1.01% higher F1 score, as FinBERT more effectively handles financial-specific entities than BERT, which is pre-trained on general corpora and thus struggles with financial semantics. FBG further outperforms FBC by 1.34%, since CRF has difficulty with specialized and nested terms, while the Global Pointer model, with rotational position encoding, better recognizes both nested and non-nested entities and captures long-distance context. FBMG achieves an additional 1.73% improvement over FBG. Compare to use BiLSTM only, which may miss key information in long sequences, the MA mechanism of FBMG improves semantic representation by leveraging word similarity rather than strict sequence order, thereby enhancing both efficiency and global semantic understanding.

Classified Entity Identification Results and Improvement.

Examination of the Fundamental Problems. Table 2 shows the entity recognition results with the proposed model. The entities "Time" and "Round" are accurately recognized by the model, with F1 values of 92.29% and 93.47%, respectively. While the recognition performance for "Investee," "Investor," and "Money" is comparatively lower, primarily due to the presence of unregistered words and the complexity of entity structures. For example, the "Investor" and "Investee" categories often involve English terms and acronyms, and "Money" is particularly challenging due to the combination of numerical and Chinese characters with varying currency units.

Table 2. Identification results of various entities (%).

Entity Symbol	P	R	F_1
Time	93.26	91.34	92.29
Investee	77.21	72.03	74.53
Investor	83.15	81.12	82.12
Round	93.07	93.89	93.47
Money	87.19	86.01	86.59

Method of Targeted Data Augmentation. In this paper, we construct lexicons of financing companies and investment institutions to perform random entity replacement. Specifically, we build Investee and Investor entity libraries by extracting relevant entities from duplicated training samples. Entity slots in each sentence are then marked with "&F&" and "&I&" flags after extraction. Finally, random entities from the self-constructed dictionaries are substituted into these slots, and the resulting samples are merged with the original training data to generate an augmented dataset.

Experimental Results and Analysis Using Targeted Data Augmentation. The experimental results after data augmentation are shown in Tables 3 and 4. Following augmentation based on rules and dictionaries, each model's recognition performance improves. The FBG model shows the most significant improvement, with a 1.47% increase in F1 value. However, the growth rate of the model's accuracy decreases due to the increased number of entities in the training set, making it harder to identify word boundaries without word vector embeddings. The best performing model, FBMG, achieved an F1 value of 84.69%, 1.24% higher than before.

After data augmentation, recognition performance improves for all entity types. "Investee" and "Investor" entities show the greatest improvement, with F1 values increasing by 2.06% and 1.52%, respectively. And "Money" also show slight improvements. These results highlight the effectiveness of the rules and dictionary-based data augmentation technique in improving model performance for entity recognition.

Table 3. Experimental results after data augmentation.

Model	P	R	F_1
FG	82.01	81.14	81.57(+0.48)
FBG	84.29	82.13	83.19(+1.47)
FBMG	**85.86**	**83.55**	**84.69**(+1.24)

Table 4. Identification results of various entities after data augmentation (%).

Entity Symbol	P	R	F_1
Time	93.56	91.68	92.61(+0.32)
Investee	79.13	74.21	76.59(+2.06)
Investor	84.86	82.47	83.64(+1.52)
Round	93.52	94.03	93.77(+0.30)
Money	87.85	86.44	87.13(+0.54)

5 Conclusion

To the best of our knowledge, this is the first attempt to apply the FinBERT-BiLSTM-MA-Global Pointer (FBMG) framework to the task of named entity recognition in the financial domain. In this paper, we propose a novel model architecture that incorporates Global Pointer and MA mechanism for recognizing entities in corporate investment texts. The model in this paper achieves optimal results when compared to the four different frameworks, according to the experimental results on the self-constructed corporate investment corpus. It also suggests a targeted data enhancement method to further improve the recognition effect, with a final F1 value of 84.69%. The research of this paper promotes the progress of the research of NER technology of investment, and provides an important support for investment risk assessment and enterprise investment relation extraction.

In future work, we will focus on improving corpus quality and enhancing the computational efficiency and deploy ability of the FBMG model. We also plan to investigate model compression techniques, such as knowledge distillation and quantization, to facilitate deployment in resource-constrained settings. Finally, we intend to apply our model to the construction of corporate investment knowledge graphs in real-world financial field.

Acknowledgements. This work was supported by the National Natural Science Foundation of China (71503108, 62077029).

References

1. Hu, Z., Hou, W., Liu, X.: Deep learning for named entity recognition: a survey. Neural Comput. Appl. **36**(16), 8995–9022 (2024)
2. Zhang, Z.J., Ni, Z.N., Liu, Z.H., Xia, S.D.: Predicting dynamic relationship for financial knowledge graph, (in Chinese). Data Anal. Knowl. Discov. **7**(9), 39–50 (2023)
3. Gao, H.Y., Fang, J.C., M.L.: The power of FinTech in risk management: Evidence from China's banking institutions, (in Chinese). Syst. Eng.-Theor. Pract. **42**(12), 3201–3215 (2022)
4. Gong, W.H.: Improving the efficiency and ability of intelligent financial service with powerful standard, (in Chinese). China Finance **19**, 71–72 (2022)
5. Zhang, J.Y., He, G.H., Dai, Z., Liu, Y.D.: Named entity recognition of enterprise annual report integrated with bert, (in Chinese). J. Shanghai Jiaotong Univ. (Chin. Ed.) **5**(2), 117–123 (2021)
6. Liu, Y.H., et al.: Utilizing glyph feature and iterative learning for named entity recognition in finance text, (in Chinese). J. Chin. Inf. Proc. **34**(11), 74–83 (2020)
7. Ding, S.C., Fang, Z., Wang, N.: Business Domain named entity recognition based on bi-lstm-crf, (in Chinese). J. Mod. Inf. **3**, 103–110 (2020)
8. Wang, Q., Hai, E.H.: A bert-based namedentity recognition in chinese electronic medical record. In: Proc. 2020 9th International Conference on Computing and Pattern Recognition (2020)
9. Liu, Y., Li, X., Shi, J.: Named entity recognition using a semi-supervised model based on bert and bootstrapping. In: Proc. China Conference on Knowledge Graph and Semantic Computtin (2020)
10. Zhang, W., Jiang, S., Zhao, S.: A bert-bilstm-crf model for chinese electronic medical records named entity recognition. In: Proc. 2019 12th International Conference on Intelligent Computation Technology and Automation (2019)
11. Liu, Z., Liu, C., Lin, W., Zhao, J.: Pretrainingfinancial language model with multi-task learning for financial text mining, (in Chinese). J. Comput. Res. Dev. **58**(8), 1761–1772 (2021)
12. Zhang, Y., Zhang, H.: FinBERT-MRC: financial named entity recognition using BERT under the machine reading comprehension paradigm (2022). arXiv preprint arXiv: 2205.15485
13. Ren, Q.Y., Liu, J.R.: Knowledge graph construction framework in the securities domain based on finbert-crf named entity recognition model. Hans J. Data Min. **11**(3), 135–149 (2021)
14. Su, J.L., Ahmed, M., Pan, S.F.: Global pointer: novel efficent span-based apporach fornamed entity recognition (2022). arXiv preprint arXiv:2208.03054
15. Devlin, J., Chang, M.W., Lee, K.: BERT: pre-training of deep bidirectional transformers for language understanding (2018). arXiv preprint arXiv:1810.04805

Cross-Domain Transfer and Few-Shot Learning for Personal Identifiable Information Recognition

Junhong Ye, Xu Yuan, and Xinying Qiu(✉)

Department of Computer Science, School of Information Science and Technology, Guangdong University of Foreign Studies, Guangzhou, China
xy.qiu@foxmail.com

Abstract. Accurate recognition of personally identifiable information (PII) is central to automated text anonymization. This paper investigates the effectiveness of cross-domain model transfer, multi-domain data fusion, and sample-efficient learning for PII recognition. Using annotated corpora from healthcare (I2B2), legal (TAB), and biography (Wikipedia), we evaluate models across four dimensions: in-domain performance, cross-domain transferability, fusion, and few-shot learning. Results show legal-domain data transfers well to biographical texts, while medical domains resist incoming transfer. Fusion benefits are domain-specific, and high-quality recognition is achievable with only 10% of training data in low-specialization domains.

Keywords: Personally Identifiable Information (PII) · Named Entity Recognition (NER) · Cross-Domain Transfer · Multi-Domain Fusion · Few-Shot Learning

1 Introduction

Privacy protection has become a cornerstone of modern data governance, with regulations like the European Union's General Data Protection Regulation (GDPR) [4] establishing strict requirements for handling personally identifiable information (PII). As organizations increasingly rely on text-based data for research, analytics, and machine learning, the need for effective text anonymization has grown correspondingly urgent. Traditional manual anonymization approaches are costly, inefficient, and prone to human error [2], driving the development of automated PII recognition systems using Natural Language Processing (NLP) techniques [3,9,13].

However, three critical gaps remain unaddressed. First, the cross-domain transferability of PII recognition models remains largely uncharacterized [10]. Second, organizations often possess data from multiple domains, yet the potential benefits or drawbacks of combining heterogeneous training data for PII recognition remain unclear. Third, many practical deployment scenarios involve limited training data, but minimum data requirements for effective privacy protection have not been systematically evaluated.

X. Ding and Y. Dong (Eds.): CLNLP 2025, CCIS 2775, pp. 184–194, 2026.
https://doi.org/10.1007/978-981-95-4788-3_17

To address these gaps, this paper conducts a comprehensive empirical study across healthcare (I2B2), legal (TAB), and biographical (Wikipedia) domains. Our systematic evaluation across 231 experimental configurations yields the following contributions:

- **Cross-Domain Transfer Characterization**: We systematically analyze transfer performance across six domain pairs, revealing domain complexity hierarchies and identifying which domains serve as effective transfer sources.
- **Multi-domain Fusion Analysis**: We demonstrate that fusion benefits vary dramatically by target domain, providing domain-specific strategies for optimal performance.
- **Sample Efficiency Validation**: We establish that effective PII recognition is achievable with significantly reduced training data, revealing non-monotonic relationships between data size and performance.

These findings challenge conventional assumptions about data requirements. We provide our codes at https://github.com/George-SGY/multi-domain-pii-recognition.

2 Related Research

Text anonymization research has evolved from rule-based approaches to sophisticated neural models, with most work focusing on domain-specific solutions rather than cross-domain applications that motivate our investigation.

Domain-Specific PII Recognition: The medical domain has served as the primary testbed for automated PII recognition, benefiting from well-established datasets like I2B2 [14] and achieving remarkable performance with transformer-based approaches such as SciBERT [15] and BioBERT [1] reaching F1 scores exceeding 0.98 [7]. Legal domain research has been more limited, with Pilán et al. [12] introducing the Text Anonymization Benchmark (TAB) for GDPR-compliant legal document anonymization. Other domains have seen sporadic development, including email communication datasets [6, 8] and dialogue corpora [5, 11].

Cross-Domain and Multi-domain Approaches: Despite the proliferation of domain-specific datasets and models, systematic cross-domain evaluation remains scarce. Papadopoulou et al. [10] made a notable contribution with a Wikipedia-based biography corpus and distant supervision methods, but their work primarily focused on reducing annotation requirements rather than systematic transfer analysis. The broader NLP literature has extensively studied domain adaptation for tasks such as sentiment analysis and named entity recognition [2], establishing transfer learning as effective for leveraging knowledge across domains. However, these insights have not been systematically applied to PII recognition, where domain-specific privacy requirements and entity distributions may pose unique challenges.

3 Methodology

This section presents our comprehensive experimental framework for investigating cross-domain PII recognition. We systematically evaluate model performance across multiple domains, training paradigms, and data availability scenarios to address the four key research questions outlined in the introduction. Overall research framework is presented in Fig. 1.

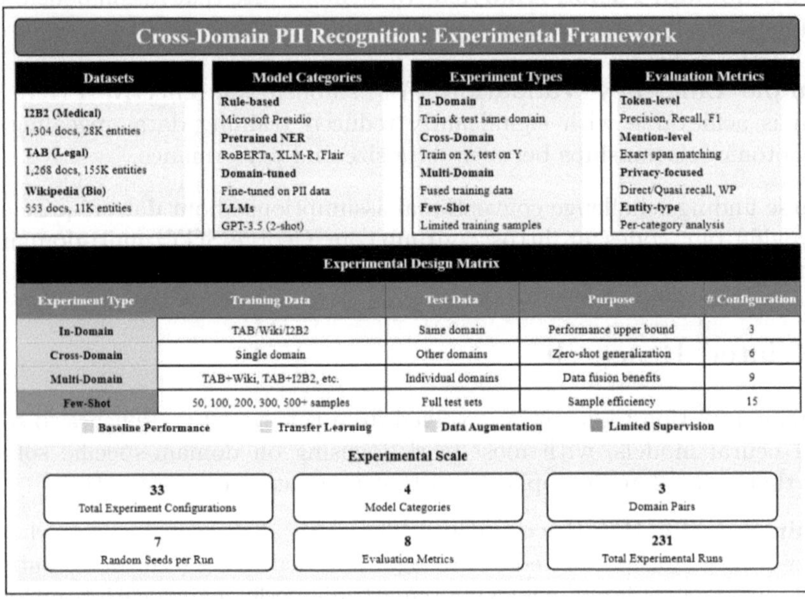

Fig. 1. Research Framework.

3.1 Datasets and Data Preparation

We selected three publicly available, human-annotated datasets representing distinct domains with varying structural characteristics and annotation schemes:

- **I2B2 (Medical Domain)**: 1,304 clinical narratives with 28,867 entity mentions across 23 fine-grained medical entity types. Contains 790 training and 514 test documents (average: 925 tokens).
- **TAB (Legal Domain)**: 1,268 legal documents with 155,006 entity mentions across 8 semantic types (PERSON, DATETIME, ORG, LOC, DEM, MISC, CODE, QUANTITY). Contains 1,014 training, 127 validation, and 127 test documents (average: 1,442 tokens).
- **Wikipedia (Biographical Domain)**: 553 Wikipedia biography entries with 10,714 entity mentions across 7 semantic types. Contains 453 training and 100 test documents (average: 96 tokens).

All datasets distinguish between direct identifiers (entities that uniquely identify individuals) and quasi-identifiers (contextual attributes that can reveal identity when combined). Text tokenization was performed using SpaCy with consistent handling across domains, and entity spans were converted to BIO tagging format.

3.2 Model Architectures

We benchmark four distinct model categories, each representing different approaches to PII recognition:

- **Rule-based Systems**: Microsoft Presidio applying regex patterns and heuristic-based entity detection
- **Pretrained NER Models**: RoBERTa-large, XLM-RoBERTa, and Flair NER models pretrained on OntoNotes 5.0, applied zero-shot without domain-specific fine-tuning
- **Domain-Tuned NER Models**: The same transformer architectures (RoBERTa, Longformer, Flair) fine-tuned on domain-specific PII data. Longformer handles longer documents with its extended attention mechanism (4096 vs. 512 tokens).
- **Large Language Models (LLMs)**: GPT-3.5-turbo evaluated under 2-shot in-context learning.

Based on preliminary experiments, we selected Longformer as our primary model for cross-domain experiments due to its consistent performance and ability to handle varying document lengths.

3.3 Experimental Design and Evaluation

We conduct four complementary experiments:

- **In-Domain Evaluation**: Models trained and tested within the same domain, establishing performance upper bounds and domain-specific baselines.
- **Cross-Domain Transfer**: Models trained on one domain's training set and evaluated on other domains' test sets, assessing zero-shot generalization capabilities across the 3 by 3 domain matrix.
- **Multi-Domain Fusion**: Models trained on merged corpora from multiple domains (e.g., TAB+Wikipedia, TAB+I2B2, all three domains) and evaluated on individual domain test sets, investigating whether diverse training data improves domain-specific performance.
- **Few-Shot Learning**: Systematic reduction of training data volume (50, 100, 200, 300, 500+ samples) to evaluate model robustness under limited supervision and validate practical deployment scenarios.

We use token-level evaluation metrics of precision, recall, and F1. All experiments are conducted across seven independent runs with different random seeds. We report median scores for robust performance estimates.

4 Results and Analysis

This section presents our experimental findings across four dimensions: in-domain performance, cross-domain transferability, multi-domain data fusion, and few-shot learning feasibility.

4.1 Baseline Performance Analysis

Table 1 presents consolidated results across all model categories and domains. Domain-tuned transformer models (Longformer, RoBERTa, Flair) consistently outperform other approaches, achieving F1 scores of 0.83–0.97. Longformer demonstrates the most balanced performance with high recall while maintaining reasonable precision. Rule-based approaches (Presidio) show the weakest performance (F1: 0.57–0.65). Pretrained NER models suffer from low and highly varied precisions (0.32–0.799). GPT-3.5-turbo demonstrates moderate performance (F1: 0.63–0.868) with superior precision compared to pretrained NER models. NER Fine-Tuned models perform second best overall after Domain-Tuned models.

Among domain-tuned models, Longformer achieves the best performances on all three evaluation metrics for medical domain (I2B2) and legal domain (TAB) and best recall for biographical domain (Wikipedia). Based on these results, we select Longformer for subsequent cross-domain experiments.

4.2 Cross-Domain Transfer Analysis

Table 2 summarizes transfer performance across all domain pairs.

Table 1. Cross-Domain Model Performance Summary. Results show F1/Recall/Precision for token-level evaluation across three domains. Best results per category are in **bold**.

Model Category	Model	TAB *F1/Rec/Prec*	Wikipedia *F1/Rec/Prec*	I2B2 *F1/Rec/Prec*	Average F1	Rank
Rule-based	Presidio	0.649/0.744/0.576	0.642/0.558/0.757	0.573/0.779/0.453	0.621	10
Pretrained NER	RoBERTa	0.563/0.886/0.413	0.833/0.870/0.799	0.466/0.838/0.323	0.621	10
	XLM-RoBERTa	0.574/0.906/0.420	0.821/0.846/0.798	0.512/0.723/0.396	0.636	9
	Flair	0.560/0.913/0.404	0.824/0.866/0.785	0.439/0.633/0.336	0.608	11
	Flair-fast	0.562/0.910/0.407	0.817/0.858/0.780	0.416/0.589/0.321	0.598	12
Domain-Tuned (PII only)	Longformer	**0.859/0.937/0.793**	0.828/**0.986**/0.713	**0.972/0.994/0.950**	**0.886**	**1**
	RoBERTa	0.857/0.934/0.791	0.834/0.982/0.723	0.959/0.937/0.982	0.883	2
	Flair	0.873/0.857/**0.889**	**0.884/0.875/0.893**	0.941/0.904/**0.982**	0.866	5
NER+ Fine-Tuned	RoBERTa	0.826/0.943/0.756	0.841/0.980/0.737	0.962/0.987/0.939	0.876	4
	XLM-RoBERTa	0.852/0.947/0.784	0.824/0.978/0.712	0.965/0.989/0.945	0.880	3
	Flair	0.869/0.856/0.882	0.877/0.866/0.888	0.948/0.913/0.985	0.865	6
	Flair-fast	0.865/0.833/0.899	0.874/0.861/0.888	0.941/0.901/0.985	0.860	7
LLM	GPT-3.5-turbo	0.738/0.728/0.748	0.868/0.907/0.833	0.630/0.765/0.535	0.745	8

Results averaged across 7 random seeds.
Domain-tuned models consistently outperform other categories, with Longformer achieving the best overall performance.

TAB → Other Domains: Legal domain training demonstrates excellent transferability to biographical content (Wikipedia F1=0.847, +2.3% improvement) while showing severe degradation for medical domains (I2B2 F1=0.264, -72.8% drop).

I2B2 → Other Domains: Medical training shows surprisingly effective transfer, maintaining baseline performance on Wikipedia (F1=0.828, 0% change) and achieving reasonable performance on TAB (F1=0.738, -14.1% drop).

Wikipedia → Other Domains: Biographical training exhibits variable performance, achieving moderate results on TAB (F1=0.421, -51% drop) but failing dramatically on medical data (I2B2 F1=0.187, -80.8% drop).

Key Insights: (1) Transfer target hierarchy: I2B2 is most difficult to transfer into, while Wikipedia is most receptive; (2) TAB provides the most effective transfer supervision for biographical domains; (3) Medical domains resist incoming transfer but provide surprisingly effective outgoing transfer.

Table 2. Cross-Domain Transfer Performance using Longformer (Token F1 scores). Diagonal entries show in-domain baselines. Best cross-domain transfers per target are in **bold**.

Train \ Test	TAB	Wikipedia	I2B2
TAB	0.859	**0.847**	0.264
Wikipedia	**0.421**	0.828	0.187
I2B2	0.738	0.828	0.972
Performance Change	**-32.5%**	**+1.15%**	**-76.8%**

Transfer Direction	F1	Recall	Precision	vs Baseline
Successful Transfers (F1 > 0.7):				
TAB → Wikipedia	0.847	0.926	0.781	+2.3%
I2B2 → Wikipedia	0.828	0.803	0.825	0%
I2B2 → TAB	0.738	0.840	0.658	-14.1%
Challenging Transfers (F1 < 0.5):				
Wikipedia → TAB	0.421	0.991	0.267	-51%
TAB → I2B2	0.264	0.990	0.152	-72.8%
Wikipedia → I2B2	0.187	0.999	0.103	-80.8%

Results averaged across 7 random seeds using Longformer architecture.
Gray cells show in-domain baselines. Performance drops show average degradation when transferring into each target domain.

4.3 Multi-domain Fusion Effects

Table 3 presents fusion results across all domain combinations.

TAB Domain benefits from multi-domain fusion, with the three-domain fusion (TWI) achieving the highest recall (0.952, +1.6% over baseline) despite a modest decrease in F1 (-0.7%). This indicates that fusion enhances privacy protection by reducing the likelihood of missed PII, even if overall balance slightly declines.

Wikipedia Domain shows nuanced responses. Adding I2B2 data (WI) raises precision (+3.1%) with negligible recall change, while combining all three domains (TWI) yields the best overall F1 (+2.5%). This suggests that the optimal strategy depends on whether precision or overall balance is prioritized, though TWI offers the strongest aggregate performance.

I2B2 Domain fusion consistently harms performance across all metrics, with F1 decreasing by 0.2âĂŞ0.5% and no recall improvements compared to baseline. This reinforces the medical domain's high specialization and indicates that domain-specific training is the only reliable strategy.

Strategy Implications: Legal documents benefit from fusion due to improved recall, biographical texts gain most from full-domain fusion, while medical records remain best served by single-domain training only.

4.4 Few-Shot Learning Feasibility

Table 4 shows performance across varying training set sizes. **TAB Domain** exhibits a non-monotonic pattern, with peak performance observed at 300 samples (−0.8% F1 vs. full data). Even with only 50 samples, the model retains 97% of full-data performance (−2.9% F1), indicating strong robustness under limited supervision.

Wikipedia Domain demonstrates particularly low sensitivity to training size. Using 200 samples (44% of the full set) yields the best F1 (+2.1%), while reductions to 50 or 100 samples still maintain performance within 2% of the full baseline. This suggests that additional training data may introduce noise or complexity rather than improving recognition quality.

I2B2 Domain shows a monotonic relationship with data volume. With 50 samples, F1 drops by 6.6%, and performance improves steadily as data increases, requiring nearly the full dataset to reach peak accuracy (F1 = 0.972). This reflects the domain's high complexity and greater dependence on large-scale supervision.

Overall, these results confirm that effective PII recognition is feasible with substantially reduced data in less specialized domains (TAB, Wikipedia), while medical records (I2B2) demand larger datasets to achieve comparable performance.

Table 3. Multi-Domain Data Fusion Effects on Target Domain Performance. Results show F1/Recall/Precision for token-level evaluation using Longformer. Best fusion results per domain are in **bold**.

Target	Training Data	F1	Recall	Precision	vs Baseline F1
TAB	TAB only (baseline)	0.859	0.937	0.793	—
	TAB + Wiki (TW)	0.841	0.946	0.757	-2.1%
	TAB + I2B2 (TI)	0.841	0.945	0.757	-2.1%
	TAB + Wiki + I2B2 (TWI)	**0.853**	**0.952**	**0.772**	**-0.7%**
Wiki	Wiki only (baseline)	0.828	0.986	0.713	—
	Wiki + TAB (TW)	0.820	**0.989**	0.700	-1.0%
	Wiki + I2B2 (WI)	0.842	0.985	0.735	+1.7%
	Wiki + TAB + I2B2 (TWI)	**0.849**	0.973	**0.753**	**+2.5%**
I2B2	I2B2 only (baseline)	0.972	0.994	0.950	—
	I2B2 + TAB (TI)	0.968	**0.994**	0.944	-0.4%
	I2B2 + Wiki (WI)	**0.970**	0.993	**0.948**	**-0.2%**
	I2B2 + TAB + Wiki (TWI)	0.967	0.991	0.944	-0.5%

Domain Characteristics	Best Strategy	F1 Effect	Recall Effect	Recommendation
TAB (Legal)	All domains (TWI)	-0.7%	+1.6%	Fusion beneficial
Wiki (Biographical)	All domains (TWI)	+2.5%	-1.3%	Fusion beneficial
I2B2 (Medical)	Domain-specific	-0.2% to -0.5%	-0.3%	Avoid fusion

Fusion combinations: TW (TAB+Wikipedia), TI (TAB+I2B2), WI (Wikipedia+I2B2), TWI (all three domains).
Results averaged across 7 random seeds. Positive percentages indicate improvement over single-domain baseline.

4.5 Summary of Key Findings

Our comprehensive evaluation yields several critical insights:

1. **Model Selection**: Domain-tuned transformers, particularly Longformer, provide optimal privacy-utility balance;
2. **Cross-Domain Transfer**: Effectiveness varies dramatically by domain pair, with TAB→Wikipedia achieving excellent results (+2.3%) while transfers into medical domains remain challenging (73–81% drops);
3. **Data Fusion Strategy**: Fusion effects are domain-specific. Legal documents benefit from all-domain fusion (TWI), which improves recall even with a small F1 trade-off. Biographical texts achieve the strongest overall performance with TWI (+2.5% F1), while medical records consistently require domain-specific training due to performance degradation under fusion.
4. **Sample Efficiency**: PII recognition is surprisingly robust to data limitations. Acceptable performance is achieved with substantially reduced data in less specialized domains (TAB and Wikipedia), whereas I2B2 demands nearly full training data due to its higher complexity.

Table 4. Few-Shot Learning Performance using Longformer. Results show F1/Recall/Precision for token-level evaluation across varying training set sizes. Best performance per domain is in **bold**.

Domain	Training Size	F1	Recall	Precision	vs Full Data	Samples/Entity
TAB	50 samples	0.834	0.940	0.770	-2.9%	0.03
	300 samples	**0.852**	**0.947**	0.774	**-0.8%**	0.19
	550 samples	0.849	0.945	0.776	-1.2%	0.35
	800 samples	0.848	0.934	0.775	-1.3%	0.52
	1014 samples (full)	0.859	0.937	**0.793**	—	0.65
Wiki	50 samples	0.815	0.975	0.702	-1.6%	0.47
	100 samples	0.819	0.979	0.704	-1.1%	0.93
	200 samples	**0.845**	0.972	**0.754**	**+2.1%**	1.87
	300 samples	0.836	0.982	0.728	+1.0%	2.80
	453 samples (full)	0.828	**0.986**	0.713	—	4.23
I2B2	50 samples	0.908	0.982	0.844	-6.6%	0.17
	100 samples	0.939	0.983	0.898	-3.4%	0.35
	300 samples	0.966	0.991	0.942	-0.6%	1.04
	500 samples	0.962	0.994	0.932	-1.0%	1.73
	790 samples (full)	**0.972**	**0.994**	**0.950**	—	2.74

Domain	Optimal Size	Performance Pattern	Data Sensitivity
TAB	30% (300 samples)	Non-monotonic	Low
Wikipedia	44% (200 samples)	Peak at mid-scale	Very Low
I2B2	100% (790 samples)	Monotonic increase	High

Results averaged across 7 random seeds. Samples/Entity shows training examples per entity type for context.
Optimal size represents training data volume that achieves best performance for each domain.

5 Conclusions

This paper presents the first large-scale empirical study of cross-domain PII recognition, evaluating model transferability, data fusion strategies, and sample efficiency across healthcare, legal, and biographical texts. Domain-tuned transformers, particularly Longformer, consistently outperform rule-based and general NER models. Cross-domain transfer is highly asymmetric: legal-domain models transfer well to biographical data, but all models perform poorly on medical text. Multi-domain fusion offers gains for legal and biographical domains when all domains are combined, but consistently harms performance on medical data.

Effective PII recognition is also achievable with as little as 10% of training data in non-specialized domains.

These findings suggest legal-domain models may be repurposed for biographical texts with minimal loss, while medical applications require domain-specific training. While results are strong across many settings, future work should address limitations in extending evaluation to conversational and social media data, improve fusion strategies, and explore synthetic data for privacy-preserving few-shot learning.

References

1. Alfalahi, A., Brissman, S., Dalianis, H.: Pseudonymisation of personal names and other PHIs in an annotated clinical Swedish corpus. In: Proceedings of the Third Workshop on Building and Evaluating Resources for Biomedical Text Mining (BioTxtM 2012), pp. 49–54 (2012)
2. Bier, E., Chow, R., Golle, P., King, T.H., Staddon, J.: The rules of redaction: identify, protect, review (and repeat). IEEE Secur. Privacy **7**(6), 46–53 (2009)
3. Dernoncourt, F., Lee, J.Y., Uzuner, O., Szolovits, P.: De-identification of patient notes with recurrent neural networks. J. Am. Med. Inform. Assoc. **24**(3), 596–606 (2017)
4. GDPR. General Data Protection Regulation. European Union Regulation 2016/679 (2016)
5. Jensen, K. N., Zhang, M., Plank, B.: De-identification of privacy-related entities in job postings. arXiv preprint arXiv:2105.11223 (2021)
6. Keila, P.S., Skillicorn, D.B.: Structure in the Enron email dataset. Comput. Math. Organ. Theory **11**, 183–199 (2005)
7. Marimon, M., et al.: Automatic de-identification of medical texts in Spanish: the MEDDOCAN Track, Corpus, Guidelines, Methods and Evaluation of Results. In: IberLEF@SEPLN, pp. 618–638 (2019)
8. Medlock, B.: An Introduction to NLP-based textual Anonymisation. In: Proceedings of LREC, pp. 1051–1056 (2006)
9. Meystre, S.M., Friedlin, F.J., South, B.R., Shen, S., Samore, M.H.: Automatic de-identification of textual documents in the electronic health record: a review of recent research. BMC Med. Res. Methodol. **10**, 70 (2010)
10. Papadopoulou, A., Lison, P., Øvrelid, L., & Pilán, I.: Bootstrapping text anonymization models with distant supervision. arXiv preprint arXiv:2205.06895 (2022)
11. Patel, N., Accorsi, P., Inkpen, D., Lopez, C., Roche, M.: Approaches of anonymisation of an SMS corpus. In: Gelbukh, A. (ed.) CICLing 2013. LNCS, vol. 7816, pp. 77–88. Springer, Heidelberg (2013). https://doi.org/10.1007/978-3-642-37247-6_7
12. Pilán, I.: The text anonymization benchmark (TAB): a dedicated corpus and evaluation framework for text anonymization. Comput. Linguist. **48**(4), 1053–1101 (2022)

13. Sánchez, D., Batet, M.: C-sanitized: a privacy model for document redaction and sanitization. J. Am. Soc. Inf. Sci. **67**(1), 148–163 (2016)
14. Stubbs, A., Uzuner, Ö.: Annotating longitudinal clinical narratives for de-identification: the 2014 i2b2/UTHealth corpus. J. Biomed. Inform. **58**, S20–S29 (2015)
15. Velupillai, S., Dalianis, H., Hassel, M., Nilsson, G.H.: Developing a standard for de-identifying electronic patient records written in Swedish: precision, recall and F-measure in a manual and computerized annotation trial. Int. J. Med. Informatics **78**(12), e19–e26 (2009)

M3FERE: Multi-Level Multimodal Fusion for Event Relation Extraction

Bo Qing, Qing He, and Wei Liu(✉)

School of Computer Engineering and Science, Shanghai University, Shanghai, China
liuw@shu.edu.cn

Abstract. Multimodal event relation extraction aims to identify logical relationships (e.g., causality, enables, reaction) between video-text event pairs, which is critical for video understanding applications. Existing methods suffer from shallow feature fusion and inadequate cross-modal interaction, limiting their performance in complex scenarios. To address these challenges, we propose M3FERE(Multi-level Multimodal Fusion for Event Relation Extraction), a novel framework featuring three key innovations: (1) Hierarchical video representation integrating global spatio-temporal features (via SlowFast) with local object-centric features through Graph Convolutional Network (GCN)-based fusion; (2) Text-guided cross-modal screening that filters irrelevant visual noise using attention mechanisms; (3) Temporal-aware event-pair modeling to capture chronological dependencies. Comprehensive evaluations on the VidSitu benchmark demonstrate that M3FERE achieves 36.07% Macro-Acc@1, outperforming established baselines such as OME (+0.48%) and SlowFast (+1.92%). Ablation studies validate the consistent improvements from global-local fusion (+0.22% accuracy) and cross-modal screening (+0.28% accuracy). This work provides a principled approach for video-text understanding, with practical applications in news analysis and social media mining.

Keywords: Multimodal Fusion · Event Relation Extraction · Graph Convolutional Networks · Cross-modal Attention · Video Understanding

1 Introduction

With the rapid advancement of internet technologies, data has evolved into an unprecedented multimodal paradigm encompassing text, images, audio, and video formats. These multimodal resources embed rich complementary semantic information, which plays a pivotal role in deciphering the profound implications of human language and contextual dependencies. As a critical cross-disciplinary research focus bridging natural language processing and computer vision, multimodal event relation extraction aims to precisely identify inter-entity relationships from heterogeneous data sources. This capability unlocks transformative potential across diverse domains—including intelligent Q&A systems, sentiment analysis, recommendation engines, and video content understanding—where integrated multimodal insights significantly enhance decision-making robustness and semantic granularity.

X. Ding and Y. Dong (Eds.): CLNLP 2025, CCIS 2775, pp. 195–206, 2026.
https://doi.org/10.1007/978-981-95-4788-3_18

Current mainstream approaches for multimodal event relation extraction typically leverage cross-modal attention and hierarchical fusion to align heterogeneous textual, visual, and temporal features. These methods have demonstrated efficacy in domains requiring contextual reasoning, including disaster response analytics, autonomous driving systems, and social media event monitoring.

In the context of Video Situation Recognition (VSR), the core objective of multimodal event relation extraction is to identify logical relationships—such as causal, enabling, reactive, or non-relevant—between event pairs described by video and text. For instance, in news video scenarios, a clip showing "vehicle collision" must be analyzed alongside the textual description "slippery road conditions" to determine whether a causal relationship exists. Similarly, for social media videos, when the video depicts a "crowd cheering" while the text mentions "team victory," their logical connection requires explicit verification. Such cross-modal alignment is crucial for accurately comprehending video content and enabling intelligent applications like video retrieval and recommendation systems.

However, current multimodal event relation extraction faces significant challenges. Existing methods exhibit notable limitations when handling this task. Taking the VidSitu [1] approach as an example, it merely concatenates video and textual features—a superficial fusion strategy that fails to explore fine-grained interactions across modalities, thereby overlooking critical semantic correlations and struggling to identify event relations in complex scenarios. Although the OME [2] model incorporates object features to enrich feature representation, it lacks effective integration of global and local features during fusion, preventing full utilization of complementary information from hierarchical features. Concurrently, the absence of a cross-modal filtering mechanism introduces noise during feature fusion, exacerbating the semantic gap and severely compromising the model's accuracy in relation judgment. Consequently, constructing an efficient multi-level feature fusion framework to organically integrate hierarchical features, alongside developing effective cross-modal filtering strategies to eliminate noise interference and bridge semantic discrepancies, emerges as a critical challenge. Addressing this is essential for advancing multimodal event relation extraction technologies and their practical applications.

To address these challenges, we propose M3FERE, a novel framework built upon three synergistic innovations:

1. A hierarchical video encoder integrating SlowFast-derived [3] global spatiotemporal features with Graph Convolutional Network (GCN)-aggregated local object features. This module models object relationships through dual-perspective aggregation:

$$\mathrm{A_{ij}} = \lambda \cdot \underbrace{\cos(\mathrm{v_i}, \mathrm{v_j})}_{\text{visual}} + (1 - \lambda) \cdot \underbrace{\|\mathrm{b_i} - \mathrm{b_j}\|_2}_{\text{geometric}} \tag{1}$$

2. A text-guided semantic filtering mechanism that dynamically weights relevant visual regions using multi-head attention:

$$\mathrm{head}_k = \mathrm{Softmax}\left(\frac{\left(F_t W_k^Q\right)\left(F_g W_k^K\right)^\top}{\sqrt{d_k}}\right) F_g W_k^V \tag{2}$$

where text features query video features to suppress background noise.

3. Temporal event modeling that chronologically organizes event-pair features $\left[F_{\text{prior}}; F_{\text{subsequent}}\right]$ to preserve causal chains.

This work delivers three key contributions:

- A hierarchical GCN fusion architecture that bridges global scene context and local object features, resolving feature misalignment in video event modeling. Our graph-structured fusion integrates SlowFast features with object-centric GCN aggregation, addressing the limitations of isolated representations in prior work (Table 1).
- A text-guided cross-modal filtering mechanism that dynamically suppresses irrelevant visual regions via multi-head attentio. Ablation studies confirm its effectiveness, boosting OME + Text baseline accuracy by 0.48%.
- Empirical advances on the VidSitu benchmark. Our approach achieves 36.07% Macro-Acc@1, outperforming the best video-only baseline (OME) by 0.29%

2 Related Work

2.1 Video Feature Extraction

Early approaches relied on hand-crafted features like HOG3D [4] and SIFT-3D [5], which suffered from limited representational capacity. With the rise of deep learning, two-stream networks [6] and 3D-CNNs [7] became dominant. The I3D model [8] extended 2D convolutions temporally through inflation, yet struggled with long-range dependencies. SlowFast innovated with dual-path architecture: its slow path captures spatial semantics while the fast path models motion dynamics, significantly advancing spatiotemporal representation. However, these methods excessively focus on global features, neglecting fine-grained object interactions. Recent attempts like MViTv2 [9] introduce vision transformers but face computational bottlenecks for long videos.

2.2 Multimodal Fusion Techniques

Existing fusion paradigms fall into three categories:

- Early Fusion (e.g., VATT [10]): Concatenates raw features for efficiency but amplifies noise.
- Late Fusion (e.g., CLIP [11]): Merges unimodal decisions but fails to capture fine-grained cross-modal alignments.
- Hybrid Fusion (e.g., ViLBERT [12]): Employs cross-modal attention at the cost of high parameters and pretraining dependency.

For event relations, VidSitu adopts late feature concatenation, leading to semantic misalignment. OME incorporates object trajectory features but uses naive average pooling, failing to bridge global-local contextual gaps. Recent work MM-DFN [13] applies graph networks yet ignores video-specific spatiotemporal continuity.

2.3 Event Relation Extraction

Text-based Event Relations are well-studied:

- Rule-based methods (e.g., TimeML [14]) require linguistic priors and generalize poorly.
- Neural models (e.g., JMEE [15]) use GCNs to model event graphs but cannot transfer to multimodal settings.

Video-Text Event Relations remain nascent:

- The VidSitu benchmark first introduced causality/enabling/reaction taxonomies for video-text pairs.
- OME improved relation recognition via object motion features but achieves $< 35\%$ accuracy in complex scenes.
- Causal-Vid [16] incorporated causal inference but relies on manually constructed causal graphs.

2.4 Research Gaps and Our Positioning

Table 1. Limitations of Prior Work and Our Solutions.

Category	Representative Work	Key Limitation	Our Countermeasure
Video Features	SlowFast	Ignores object interactions	GCN-based global-local fusion
Multimodal Fusion	OME	Crude feature aggregation	Text-guided cross-modal screening
Event Modeling	VidSitu	Shallow decision fusion	Temporal-aware event-pair encoding

Table 1 shows three critical gaps:

- Feature Discrepancy: Isolated global scene and local object representations.
- Modality Misalignment: Inadequate semantic matching between text and video.
- Temporal Fragmentation: Neglect of chronological ordering in event pairs.

Our M3FERE framework systematically addresses these gaps through unified architecture design.

3 Methodology

3.1 Hierarchical Unimodal Feature Extraction

Text Feature Encoding. In event analysis, argument roles are constituted by textual sequences describing entities and their states. This work leverages a RoBERTa [17] model based on the Transformer architecture to extract textual features, thereby capturing contextual information within event argument descriptions. Given the structured representation of event arguments, each argument is parsed into marker tokens formatted as " <ArgX> " (where X denotes an integer starting from 0). These tokens are then composed into a coherent paragraph describing the event, which is subsequently fed into the RoBERTa model to obtain its encoded representation, as illustrated in Fig. 1

Fig. 1. Text Feature Encoding.

Video Feature Encoding. As illustrated in Fig. 2, this work employs a graph-structured representation to model visual features of events and their candidate arguments, utilizing Graph Convolutional Networks (GCNs) for visual feature aggregation. Within this graph, global features are directly connected to all candidate object features, whereas no direct connections exist between object features themselves. To preserve potential inter-object relationships, we first derive dual-relation-aware video features through the graph, then leverage GCNs to fuse global and local features.

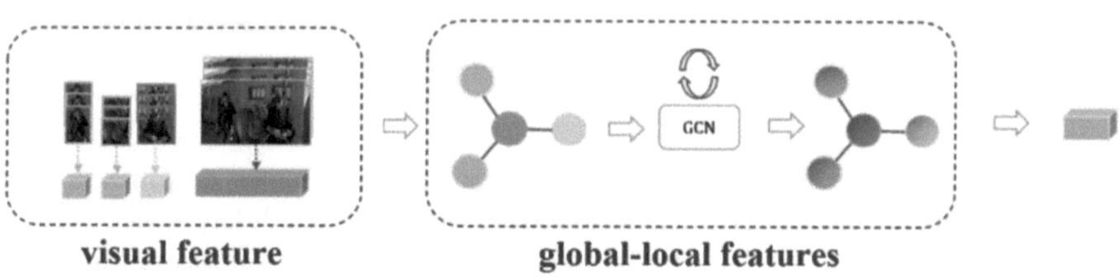

Fig. 2. Graph-Structured Global-Local Feature Fusion for Video Representation.

Let N be the number of candidate objects. The total number of visual features is $N + 1$ (including the global video feature and all candidate object features). The feature representation is formalized as:

$$F_g = [f_1, f_2, \ldots, f_{N+1}] \in R^{(N+1)\times d_f} \tag{3}$$

where d_f denotes the dimensionality of visual features.

A p-layer Graph Convolutional Network (GCN) is employed to fuse global and local visual features. The graph convolution at the p-th layer is implemented as:

$$F_g^{(p)} = \sigma\left(G_g F_g^{(p-1)} W^{(p)}\right) \tag{4}$$

where:

- $W^{(p)} \in R^{(N+1)\times d_f}$: Trainable parameter matrix at layer p p
- $F_g^{(p)} \in R^{(N+1)\times d_f}$: Hidden feature representation at layer p ($F_g^{(0)}$ denotes input features)
- $\sigma(\cdot)$: : Non-linear activation function (e.g., ReLU)

The adjacency matrix $G_g \in R^{(N+1)\times(N+1)}$ is computed based on the topological configuration of the graph, encoding connectivity between nodes.

3.2 Feature Fusion for Multimodal Events and Event Pairs

Multimodal Event Feature Fusion. In multimodal event relation extraction tasks, textual features serve as the ground truth representation of event argument roles, providing precise semantic information. However, direct reliance on video features may introduce significant noise due to the inherent misalignment between candidate objects in videos and textual argument roles.

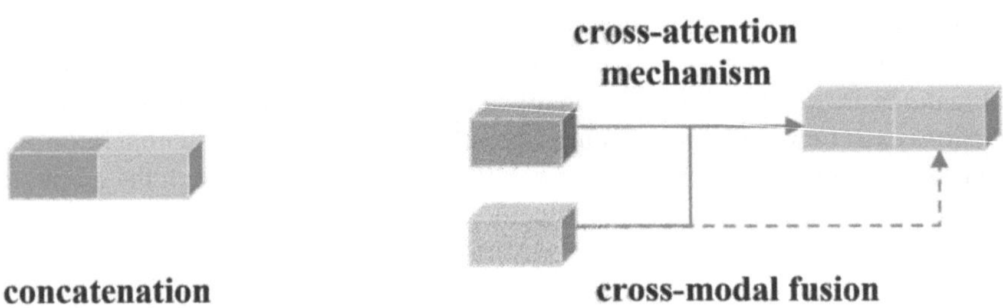

Fig. 3. Feature-Filtered Multimodal Fusion.

To effectively filter event-relevant visual features, this paper employs a cross-attention mechanism to model deep interactions between candidate object features and textual features (Fig. 3). The fused multimodal feature F_m—representing noise-suppressed visual features—is computed as:

$$F_m = \sigma\big(\text{MultiHead}\big(F_t, F_g, F_g\big)\big) \tag{5}$$

where F_g denotes visual features obtained through a global-local strategy, F_t denotes textual features, and $\sigma(\cdot)$ is the activation function.

The final multimodal representation F concatenates F_m and F_t:

$$F = [F_m; F_t] \tag{6}$$

Multimodal Event Pair Feature Fusion. The overall framework for relation extraction of multimodal event pairs, each comprising two events, is depicted in Fig. 4. Within this framework, each event undergoes a unified process involving unimodal feature extraction

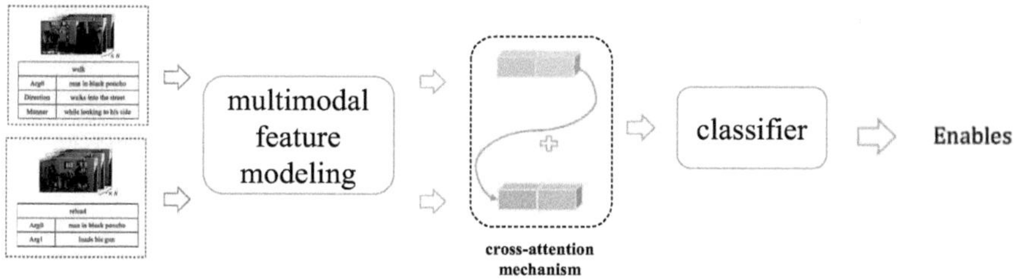

Fig. 4. Overall Framework for Multimodal Event Relation Extraction.

and multimodal fusion: features are first extracted independently from video and text modalities, followed by the fusion of visual and textual features through cross-attention mechanisms to form multimodal representations.

Due to the vast scale of video datasets, Sadhu et al. [1] simplified the multimodal event relation extraction task to identifying relations among five events within the same video (primarily focusing on relations between other events and the central event of the video, i.e., Event 3, as illustrated in Fig. 5). When processing an event pair composed of a given event and Event 3, the temporal relationship between events must be considered. Specifically, Event 3 is positioned at the midpoint of the entire video segment, while the other four events occur at sequential timestamps either preceding or succeeding Event 3. To effectively incorporate temporal order into feature acquisition, special attention must be paid to the relative temporal position between the target event and Event 3 during multimodal feature concatenation. When concatenating features, the features of an event occurring before Event 3 should be prepended to the sequence, while those of an event occurring after Event 3 should be appended. This approach enables the model to leverage temporal cues for improved understanding of event relations, thereby enhancing the accuracy of relation extraction.

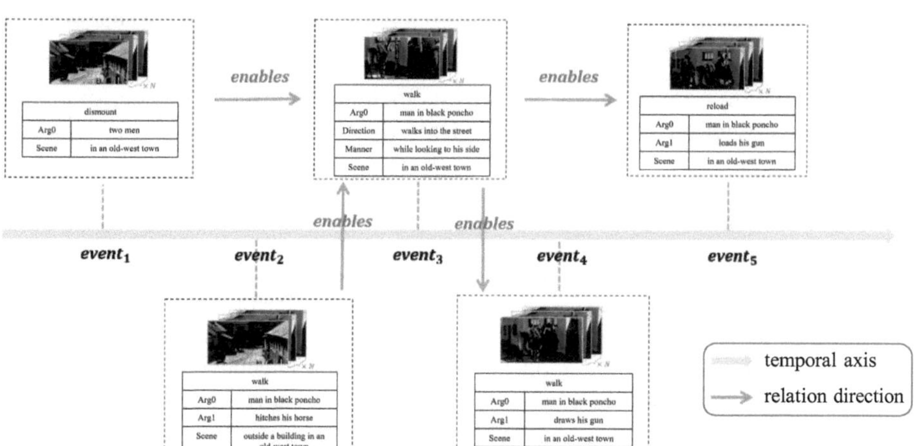

Fig. 5. Multimodal Relation Extraction Task Example.

4 Experiments

4.1 Experimental Setup

Dataset. The experiments utilized the VidSitu video event recognition dataset, comprising approximately 130k video clips lasting 2 s each, with each video consisting of five segments depicting events. As detailed in Table 2 (where "#" denotes corresponding quantities), the dataset is partitioned into a training set of approximately 118k clips, a validation set of about 6.6k clips, and a test set of approximately 6.6k clips for the multimodal event relation extraction task.

Table 2. Statistics of Event Relation Extraction in the VidSitu Dataset.

	Training Set	Validation Set	Test Set
# Videos	23,626	1,326	1,317
# Clips	118,130	6,630	6,585
# Verbs	118,130	66,300	65,850
# Argument Roles	118,130	19,890	19,755

Metrics. Multimodal event relation extraction is a four-class classification problem, where the relationship between each event pair is categorized into four distinct classes. To evaluate model performance, employing macro-averaged top-1 accuracy (Macro-Acc@1) serves as an appropriate metric. During this evaluation process, the top-1 accuracy for each class is first calculated—specifically, the number of correct predictions made by the model for that class divided by the total number of samples in the class. Subsequently, the Macro-Acc@1 is derived by summing the top-1 accuracies of all four classes and dividing the sum by 4. This macro-averaging approach remains unaffected by the sample sizes of individual classes, making it suitable for imbalanced datasets and thus providing a comprehensive and robust evaluation of model performance.

Hyperparameter. The data batch size was set to 8. Model training was performed for 10 epochs on a single A100 GPU, with the learning rate set to $r = 10^{-4}$.

4.2 Main Results

As shown in Table 3, the model proposed in this study achieves the best performance on the multimodal event relation extraction task, reaching 36.07% in Macro-Acc@1, which demonstrates its effectiveness. In the experimental results table, underlined numbers indicate results from suboptimal models, while bold values denote optimal results. The specific configurations for the Feature and Model columns are detailed below:

- Features:
- "Text Sequence Features" refer to text sequences formed by concatenating event arguments.

- "SlowFast" denotes video features directly extracted from the SlowFast model.
- "OME" represents video object features based on object tracking.
- Models:
- RoBERTa is the pre-trained language model used to obtain text features.
- TxEnc denotes a linear mapping layer for processing text features.
- VidEnc denotes a linear mapping layer for processing video features.

Table 3. Performance Comparison on Multimodal Event Relation Extraction Task.

Features	Model	Macro-Acc@1(%)
Textual Sequence Features	RoBERTa	25.00
Textual Sequence Features	TxEnc	25.00
SlowFast (Video Features)	VidEnc	34.54
OME (Object Motion Embeddings)	VidEnc	35.78
SlowFast + Textual Features	Vid TxEnc	34.15
OME + Textual Features	Vid TxEnc	35.59
Ours (Cross-Modal Fusion)	Ours	36.07

4.3 Experimental Analysis

Global-Local Fusion Strategy for Visual Feature Representation. To demonstrate the effectiveness of visual representations that comprehensively integrate global and local video features, ablation studies on this module were conducted under the following configurations:

(1) Candidate object features were sourced from OME, i.e., features directly obtained from object detection and tracking modules;
(2) Candidate object features were derived from the relation-aware module, where argumentative role relationships were considered before global-local feature fusion.

Experimental results are presented in Table 4. Note that the subsequent feature filtering module was excluded during these experiments.

Table 4. Ablation Study on Global-Local Fusion Module Effectiveness.

Features	Model	Macro-Acc@1 (%)
OME	Concatenation	35.78
	Global-Local Fusion	35.80
Dual Relation Awareness	Concatenation	35.28

(*continued*)

Table 4. (*continued*)

Features	Model	Macro-Acc@1 (%)
	Global-Local Fusion	35.23
OME + Textual Features	Concatenation	35.59
	Global-Local Fusion	35.85
Dual Relation Awareness + Textual Features	Concatenation	35.03
	Global-Local Fusion	35.42

Multimodal Feature Fusion Based on Feature Selection. To reduce the proportion of event-irrelevant information in the visual features of candidate objects, this paper employs precise argumentative role features for visual feature selection. Disregarding the aforementioned global-local fusion strategy, an ablation study is conducted on this feature selection module. By comparing the experimental results using concatenation versus cross-modal filtering, the effectiveness of feature selection is demonstrated, as detailed in Table 5.

Table 5. Ablation Study on Cross-Modal Feature Selection Module.

Features	Model	Macro-Acc@1 (%)
SlowFast + Textual Features	Concatenation	34.15
	Cross-Modal Selection	34.64
OME + Textual Features	Concatenation	35.59
	Cross-Modal Selection	35.87
Argument Relation Awareness + Textual Features	Concatenation	35.03
	Cross-Modal Selection	35.45

5 Conclusion and Future Directions

This study develops a hierarchical framework for multimodal event relation extraction, achieving competitive performance (36.07% Macro-Acc@1) on the VidSitu benchmark. Key contributions include:

- A graph-based strategy integrating global-local video features, demonstratingconsistent improvements (+0.26% with OME + Text features in Table 4);
- A cross-modal feature selection module reducing visual noise, which enhanced OME + Text fusion accuracy by 0.28% (Table 5). These modest yet effective designs validate the importance of spatiotemporal modeling and modality-specific filtering.

Future work will explore:

- Computational Efficiency: Simplifying graph convolutions and attention mechanisms for resource-constrained scenarios.
- Temporal Refinement: Incorporating frame-level alignment (e.g., optical flow) to supplement coarse event sequencing.
- Cross-Domain Adaptation: Testing the framework on emerging datasets beyond conventional action recognition.
- Future work will include comparisons with newer generic models (e.g., MM-DFN) adapted to our task-specific constraints.

References

1. Sadhu, A., Gupta, T., Yatskar, M., Nevatia, R., Kembhavi, A.: "Visual semantic role labeling for video understanding. In: Proceedings of the IEEE/CVF Conference on Computer Vision and Pattern Recognition, pp. 5589–5600 (2021)•
2. Huaizu, J., Misra, I., Rohrbach, M., Learned-Miller, E., Chen, X.: In defense of grid features for visual question answering. In: Proceedings of the IEEE/CVF Conference on Computer Vision and Pattern Recognition, pp. 10267–10276 (2020)
3. Christoph, F., Fan, H., Malik, J., He, K.: Slowfast networks for video recognition. In: Proceedings of the IEEE/CVF International Conference on Computer Vision, pp. 6202–6211 (2019)
4. Alexander, K., Marszałek, M., Schmid, C.: A spatio-temporal descriptor based on 3d-gradients. In: BMVC 2008–19th British machine vision conference, pp. 275–1. British Machine Vision Association (2008)
5. Rister, B., Horowitz, M.A., Rubin, D.L.: Volumetric image registration from invariant keypoints. IEEE Trans. Image Process. **26**(10), 4900–4910 (2017)
6. Karen, S., Zisserman, A.: Two-stream convolutional networks for action recognition in videos. Adv. Neural Inf. Process. Syst. **27** (2014)
7. Du, T., Bourdev, L., Fergus, R., Torresani, L., Paluri, M.: Learning spatiotemporal features with 3d convolutional networks. In: Proceedings of the IEEE International Conference on Computer Vision, pp. 4489–4497 (2015)
8. Joao, C., Zisserman, A.: Quo vadis, action recognition? a new model and the kinetics dataset. In: Proceedings of the IEEE Conference on Computer Vision and Pattern Recognition, pp. 6299–6308 (2017)
9. Yanghao, L., et al.: Mvitv2: improved multiscale vision transformers for classification and detection. In: Proceedings of the IEEE/CVF Conference on Computer Vision and Pattern Recognition, pp. 4804–4814 (2022)
10. Akbari, H., et al.: Vatt: transformers for multimodal self-supervised learning from raw video, audio and text. Adv. Neural. Inf. Process. Syst. **34**, 24206–24221 (2021)
11. Alec, R., et al.: Learning transferable visual models from natural language supervision. In: International Conference on Machine Learning, pp. 8748–8763. PmLR (2021)
12. Jiasen, L., Batra, D., Parikh, D., Lee, S.: Vilbert: pretraining task-agnostic visiolinguistic representations for vision-and-language tasks. Adv. Neural Inf. Process. Syst. **32** (2019)
13. Dou, H., Hou, X., Wei, L., Jiang, L., Mo, Y.: MM-DFN: Multimodal dynamic fusion network for emotion recognition in conversations. In: ICASSP 2022–2022 IEEE International Conference on Acoustics, Speech and Signal Processing (ICASSP), pp. 7037–7041. IEEE, 2022

14. Pustejovsky, J., et al.: TimeML: robust specification of event and temporal expressions in text. New Dir. Question Answering **3**, 28–34 (2003)
15. Xiao, L., Luo, Z., Huang, H.: Jointly multiple events extraction via attention-based graph information aggregation (2018). arXiv preprint arXiv:1809.09078
16. Y., Xu, Zhang, H., Qi, G., Cai, J.: Causal attention for vision-language tasks. In: Proceedings of the IEEE/CVF conference on computer vision and pattern recognition, pp. 9847–9857 (2021)
17. Yinhan, L., et al.: Roberta: a robustly optimized bert pretraining approach (2019). arXiv preprint arXiv:1907.11692

COLA-GEC: A Bidirectional Framework for Enhancing Grammatical Acceptability and Error Correction

Xiangyu Yang and Xinying Qiu(✉)

Department of Computer Science, School of Information Science and Technology, Guangdong University of Foreign Studies, Guangzhou, China
xy.qiu@foxmail.com

Abstract. Grammatical Error Correction (GEC) and grammatical acceptability judgment (COLA) are core tasks in natural language processing, sharing foundational grammatical knowledge yet typically evolving independently. This paper introduces COLA-GEC, a novel bidirectional framework that enhances both tasks through mutual knowledge transfer. First, we augment grammatical acceptability models using GEC datasets, significantly improving their performance across multiple languages. Second, we integrate grammatical acceptability signals into GEC model training via a dynamic loss function, effectively guiding corrections toward grammatically acceptable outputs. Our approach achieves state-of-the-art results on several multilingual benchmarks. Comprehensive error analysis highlights remaining challenges, particularly in punctuation error correction, providing insights for future improvements in grammatical modeling.

Keywords: GEC · COLA

1 Introduction

Grammatical Error Correction (GEC) and grammatical acceptability judgment (COLA) represent two fundamental tasks in natural language processing that directly address language proficiency needs of second-language learners [10]. GEC focuses on automatically identifying and correcting grammatical errors in text, while COLA aims to determine whether a given sentence adheres to the grammatical rules of a language. These capabilities have significant implications for educational applications and linguistic research.

In recent years, substantial progress has been made in both areas separately. For COLA, Warstadt et al. [21] established the Corpus of Linguistic Acceptability (CoLA) for English, inspiring similar resources for other languages including Italian [19], Russian [14], Japanese [18], and Chinese [7]. Meanwhile, GEC research has evolved from rule-based approaches to sophisticated neural models based primarily on Sequence-to-Sequence and Sequence-to-Edit architectures.

X. Ding and Y. Dong (Eds.): CLNLP 2025, CCIS 2775, pp. 207–218, 2026.
https://doi.org/10.1007/978-981-95-4788-3_19

Despite their shared foundation in grammatical knowledge, these research areas have developed largely in isolation. The fundamental connection remains underexplored: a GEC system implicitly requires the ability to distinguish between grammatical and ungrammatical sentences, which is precisely the capability modeled by COLA systems. Similarly, COLA datasets typically contain minimal pairs of grammatical and ungrammatical sentences, while GEC datasets contain error-correction pairs that implicitly encode similar contrasts [31].

This paper addresses these gaps by establishing a bidirectional enhancement framework between GEC and COLA tasks. First, we enhance COLA models by incorporating GEC data, transforming error-correction pairs into acceptability judgment instances. Our GEC-enhanced COLA models achieve state-of-the-art performance across Chinese, English, German, and Arabic. Second, we integrate COLA into GEC models through an innovative architecture that evaluates candidate corrections and provides grammaticality signals to guide the GEC model toward more acceptable outputs. This approach achieves new state-of-the-art performance on multiple GEC datasets across languages. Finally, our comprehensive error analysis identifies specific grammatical phenomena—particularly punctuation errors—that present difficulties, providing valuable insights for future research in grammatical error correction systems. We provide our codes at: https://github.com/YXY2gdufs/colagec-project.

2 Related Research

2.1 Grammatical Acceptability Judgment

Research in grammatical acceptability judgment has developed along two main paths. First, large-scale annotated corpora have been established, beginning with Warstadt et al.'s [21] Corpus of Linguistic Acceptability (CoLA) for English, which collected examples from linguistics textbooks. This approach has been replicated for Italian [19], Russian [14], Japanese [18], and Chinese [7], with most corpora containing binary judgments distinguishing grammatical from ungrammatical sentences. Modeling approaches initially utilized RNNs and LSTM swith various word embeddings, while recent work has leveraged pre-trained language models, with Mikhailov et al. investigating multilingual capabilities using XLM-R and RemBERT.

Second, researchers have developed methods to generate contrastive examples automatically. Warstadt et al. [22] and Xiang et al. [23] created BLiMP and CLiMP benchmarks respectively using grammatical templates with specific constraints. Nielsen [15] extended this approach by automatically generating ungrammatical sentences through word deletion or swapping for Scandinavian languages.

2.2 Grammatical Error Correction

Early GEC methods relied on rules and targeted classifiers, but struggled with complex errors involving multi-word dependencies. Current approaches primarily use Sequence-to-Sequence (Seq2Seq) or Sequence-to-Edit (Seq2Edit) architectures. The Seq2Seq approach treats GEC as a translation task, evolving from statistical machine translation to sophisticated neural architectures. Yuan and Felice [26] pioneered the application of neural machine translation (NMT) to grammatical error correction (GEC). More recent innovations include the introduction of the Transformer architecture, dynamic masking to enhance generalization [30], the integration of pre-trained masked language models [9], decoding interventions guided by external critics [31], and incorporating explanations into GEC systems to improve interpretability and performance [6]. Several studies have also investigated comparative performance of GEC techniques in learner writing, particularly in educational settings [16].

Despite their shared foundation in grammatical knowledge, COLA and GEC research has developed separately. A GEC system implicitly requires the ability to distinguish between grammatical and ungrammatical sentences—precisely what COLA models do—while COLA datasets contain minimal pairs that parallel the error-correction pairs in GEC data. This suggests significant potential for bidirectional knowledge transfer, which we address in this paper.

3 Methodology

3.1 Enhancing Grammatical Acceptability Models with GEC Data (G-Cola Model)

Current grammatical acceptability judgment (COLA) models evaluate whether a sentence adheres to the grammatical rules of a language. We propose to enhance COLA corpora by augmenting linguistic theory-based datasets with processed GEC datasets.

Corpora Construction. For all languages, we use only the training set and the validation set of the GEC datasets to augment COLA corpora. The complete data statistics are provided in Table 1. We discuss model training and implementation in Sect. 4.

Chinese COLA Corpus: We build upon CoLAC [7], which contains 7,495 sentences from Chinese grammar textbooks, linguistics journals, and The Handbook of Chinese Linguistics. Following, we use crowd labels as ground truth (where "1" indicates grammatical acceptability and "0" indicates unacceptability). We incorporate sentence pairs from three Chinese GEC datasets: MuCGEC [27], FCGEC [24], and NaSGEC [28], yielding 1,059, 7,862, and 4,115 high-quality sentence pairs, respectively. For each pair, corrected sentences are labeled as grammatically acceptable (1) and error-containing sentences as unacceptable (0). The resulting corpus contains 6,072 sentences from CoLAC and 10,700 sentences from GEC datasets.

Table 1. Statistics of the Multilingual Corpus of Linguistic Acceptability judgments

Language	Train	Dev	Test
English(en)	36,551	2,400	516
Chinese(zh)	16,772	2,928	931
Russian(ru)	7,869	1,483	2,341
Italian(it)	7,801	946	975
German(de)	19,621	2,803	402
French(fr)	500	521	521
Spanish(es)	500	321	322
Japanese(jp)	7,419	1,378	694
Arabic(ar)	14,330	2,413	313
Icelandic(is)	500	1,194	1,194
Norwegian(no)	8,030	1,000	1,000
Swedish(sw)	7,682	890	888

English COLA Corpus: We apply a similar approach to the original CoLA corpus [21], which contains 9,594 sentences from syntax textbooks, verb classification resources [11], and papers on syntactic movement. We augment this with filtered sentence pairs from W&I+LOCNESS [2], FCE [25], and NUCLE [4], selecting 10,312, 9,706, and 9,855 sentence pairs, respectively. The enhanced corpus contains 8,551 sentences from CoLA and 28,000 sentences from GEC datasets.

German and Arabic COLA Corpora: For German and Arabic, we started with theoretical linguistics textbook examples collected by Zhang et al. [29]. We enhanced the German corpus with sentence pairs from the Falko and MERLIN learner corpora, and the Arabic corpus with sentence pairs from QALB-2014 and QALB-2015 datasets.

Multilingual COLA Corpus: Building on the MELA corpus, which covers 10 languages, we incorporate additional languages and GEC data. We enhance the Japanese portion with JCoLA [18], add Norwegian [8] and Swedish [20] acceptability corpora, and augment multiple languages with their respective GEC datasets. The final corpus covers 12 languages with standardized binary labels.

3.2 COLA-Guided Training for Grammatical Error Correction (G-Cola GEC Model)

We now present our approach for integrating grammatical acceptability signals into GEC training, addressing limitations in current GEC models.

Framework Overview: As illustrated in Fig. 1, our framework integrates a COLA model to evaluate and guide the GEC training process through the following components:

- We train a BART-based Seq2Seq GEC model that transforms ungrammatical input sentences into corrected versions
- We add GEC data to enhance pretrained COLA model using corpora discussed in Sect. 3.1.
- We implement a Dynamic loss based on Label Confidence Weighted Learning (LCWL) mechanism [17] that incorporates COLA model judgments into the GEC model's loss function. We name our GEC model G-Cola GEC.
- We plug in our G-Cola GEC model to the GEC-di model (which is a dual-critc model achieving SOTA performances on English and Chinese GEC tasks). The G-Cola GEC-di model performs inference on GEC test sets.

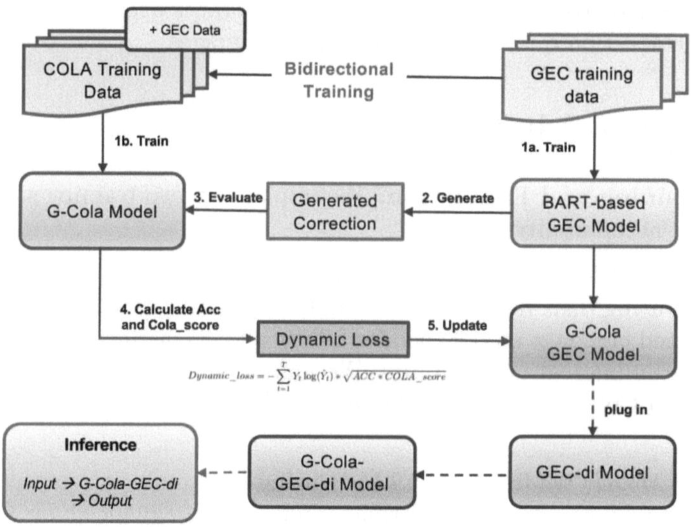

Fig. 1. Bidirectional Framework of COLA-GEC

Incorporating COLA Judgements Into GEC Training: The COLA model evaluates corrected sentences from the GEC model by producing scores for two categories: "0" (grammatically unacceptable) and "1" (grammatically acceptable). We transform these using a sigmoid function:

$$COLA\_score = \frac{1}{1 + e^{-(Logits\_0 - Logits\_1)}} \tag{1}$$

where Logits_0 and Logits_1 represent scores for categories 0 and 1 respectively. When $\text{Logits}_0 > \text{Logits}_1$ (indicating grammatical unacceptability), the score increases, signaling grammatical errors in the correction.

To integrate COLA judgments into GEC training, we adapt the Label Confidence Weighted Learning (LCWL) approach [17]. We modify the GEC cross-entropy loss to incorporate COLA scores:

$$Dynamic\_loss = -\sum_{t=1}^{T} Y_t \log(\hat{Y}_t) * \sqrt{Acc * COLA\_score} \tag{2}$$

where T is sequence length, Y_t is the ground truth at time step t, $\hat{Y}_t$ is the model's prediction, and Acc is the COLA model's accuracy. This formulation weighs the loss according to grammatical acceptability, with higher penalties for grammatically problematic corrections.

Through this integrated approach, we develop G-Cola GEC, a grammatical confidence-guided error correction model that leverages acceptability judgments to improve correction quality across multiple languages.

4 Training and Implementation

G-Cola Training and Evaluation. We implement two training strategies for grammatical acceptability judgment:

Monolingual Models: We fine-tune RoBERTa-based models for English, Chinese, and German using their respective GEC-enhanced datasets. Each model consists of a pre-trained language model encoder followed by a classification layer predicting binary grammatical acceptability. We name our monolingual COLA model G-Cola-EN, G-Cola-CN, and G-Cola-DE.

Multilingual Model: We fine-tune XLM-R using our combined corpus of 12 languages, with Chinese, English, German and Arabic enhanced by GEC data. This leverages cross-lingual transfer learning, enabling knowledge sharing across languages. We name this model G-Cola-Multi.

We compare our two strategies with MELA [29] , which is the current SOTA COLA model, and vanilla RoBERTa or XLM-R based COLA model without GEC data augmentation. All models are evaluated using accuracy (ACC) and Matthews correlation coefficient (MCC).

G-Cola GEC Training and Evaluation. Our GEC models were trained on substantial corpora with high error rates. The Chinese model used Lang8 (590K sentences, 89.5% error rate) and HSK (157K sentences, 60.8% error rate) for pre-training, followed by fine-tuning on FCGEC, MuCGEC, and NaSGEC datasets. The English model pretrained on Clang8 (2.37M sentences, 57.8% error rate) and fine-tuned on W&I+LOCNESS, FCE, and NUCLE datasets. The German model used Falko (11K sentences, 65.5% error rate) for pretraining and MERLIN (10K sentences, 78.7% error rate) for fine-tuning.

Chinese Implementation: Our Chinese GEC model used BART-large-Chinese as the base architecture. Following Zhou et al. [31], we employed a two-stage training strategy:

1. Pre-training on Lang8 corpus (split 8:2 for training/validation)
2. Fine-tuning on HSK, MuCGEC-dev, FCGEC train and dev, and NaSGEC-Exam train and dev. We name this model G-CoLA-GEC-CN.

The resulting G-CoLA-GEC-CN model was further combined with GECdi-CN (a dual-critic framework [31]) to create G-CoLA GECdi-CN, which was evaluated on MuCGEC and FCGEC test sets. We compare our performances with GEC di [31] , MrGEC [13], and EPOGEC [12].

English Implementation: We used BART-large for English GEC and implemented a three-stage training approach:

1. Pre-training on Clang8 corpus
2. First fine-tuning on W&I+LOCNESS
3. Second fine-tuning on FCE, NUCLE, and BEA-19-dev to adapt to diverse error types. We name this model G-CoLA-GEC-EN.

The resulting G-CoLA GEC-EN was also combined with Zhou's dual-critic framework [31] to create G-CoLA GECdi-EN, evaluated on CoNLL-14 and BEA-19 test sets. We compare our model's performance with GEC di [31] , MultimodelGEC [5], EPOGEC [12], Unsupervised GEC [3].

German Implementation: For low-resource German, we based our model on Hugging Face's Bart-German We pretrained on Falko and finetuned on MERLIN. This model was enhanced with our G-Cola-DE model because it performs better than G-Cola-Multi on German dataset. Furthermore, since there is no dual-critic GEC model [31] for German, we trained GEC-Di-DE as follows:

1. We train a language model critic (LM-Critic) based on German-GPT2, fine-tuned on 9,000 sentences from German Wikipedia articles on social and cultural topics
2. We train a target-side grammatical error detection critic (Target GED Critic) based on Bart-German, to identify specific error types using ERRANT-computed error annotations
3. We combined the above two step to implement Gecdi-DE (i.e. adapting the dual-critic mocel [31] for German).

The resulting Gecdi-DE model was combined with the G-Cola-DE and evaluated on the Falko-MERLIN test set. We name this model G-CoLA GECdi-DE and compare with MultimodelGEC [5], and WikiGerman GEC [1].

All models were evaluated using language-specific metrics: ChERRANT for Chinese and ERRANT for English and German, with performance measured through Precision (P), Recall (R), and F0.5 score.

5 Results and Analysis

5.1 G-Cola Model Results

We distinguish between baseline models (CoLA) trained without GEC corpus data and our enhanced models (G-CoLA) incorporating GEC corpus data. As shown in Table 2, G-CoLA models consistently outperform their CoLA counterparts across all languages, with substantial improvements in both accuracy and MCC metrics. The Chinese G-CoLA model improved by 4.13% in accuracy and 0.59 in MCC, while the Englishe412 model showed improvements of 2.59% and 2.11 respectively. For lower-resource languages, German and Arabic G-CoLA models demonstrated similar gains, confirming the effectiveness of our approach across diverse languages. Table 2 indicates that our multilingual G-CoLA model surpasses MELA (current state-of-the-art) across all languages, with an average MCC improvement of 2.22. Notably, performance improved not only for languages with directly added GEC data, but also for typologically related languages, suggesting beneficial cross-linguistic transfer effects, particularly within language families.

Table 2. G-Cola Model Performance Comparison

Model	**Chinese**		**English**		**German**		**Arabic**	
	ACC	MCC	ACC	MCC	ACC	MCC	ACC	MCC
MELA(2024)	-	54.94	-	60.64	-	26.72	-	14.12
CoLA	81.30	56.61	85.51	63.49	62.90	37.74	60.67	36.30
G-CoLA	**85.43**	**57.20**	**88.10**	**65.60**	**66.42**	**41.81**	**64.90**	**42.24**
G-CoLA-Multi	77.95	55.37	83.2	61.93	42.92	29.55	40.1	18.33

Table 3. G-Cola GECdi Performance Across Languages

Model	**Chinese** (MuCGEC)			**Chinese** (FCGEC)			**English** (CoNLL-14)			**English** (BEA-19)			**German** (Falko-MERLIN)		
	Pre	Rec	F0.5	Pre	Rec	F0.5	Pre	Rec	F0.5	Pre	Rec	F0.5	Pre	Rec	F0.5
GECdi (2023)	56.74	31.0	48.61	-	-	-	79.2	46.8	69.6	77.4	59.9	73.1	-	-	-
MultiModal (2023)	-	-	-	-	-	-	75	53.2	69.3	77.1	66.7	74.8	78.50	68.40	76.30
MrGEC (2024)	56.37	29.12	47.47	65.71	37.78	57.22	-	-	-	-	-	-	-	-	-
EPOGEC (2025)	-	-	-	66.67	**41.93**	**59.63**	76.71	52.56	70.26	78.16	68.07	75.91	-	-	-
Unsupervised (2023)	-	-	-	-	-	-	75	**53.8**	69.6	**78.8**	**68.5**	**76.5**	-	-	-
WikiGerman(2018)	-	-	-	-	-	-	-	-	-	-	-	-	45.22	51.99	29.73
G-CoLA GECdi	**57.12**	**33.9**	**49.91**	**67.1**	39.05	58.6	**79.55**	49.04	**70.84**	77.33	61.67	74.03	71.93	62.47	70.80

5.2 G-Cola GECdi Results

We evaluated our G-CoLA GECdi models across multiple languages as shown in Table 3. For Chinese, G-CoLA GECdi-CN achieved state-of-the-art results on MuCGEC, with the highest scores across all metrics. On FCGEC, our model achieved the highest precision (67.11%) but slightly lower F0.5 than EPOGEC. For English, G-CoLA GECdi-EN achieved the highest precision (79.55%) and F0.5 (70.84%) on CoNLL-14, exceeding GEC di by 0.35 and 1.24 points respectively, though its recall was lower than some competitors. On BEA-19, our model performed competitively but below Unsupervised GEC. For German, G-CoLA GECdi-DE substantially outperformed WikiGerman GEC (70.80 vs 29.73 F0.5) but remained below MultimodelGEC (76.30 F0.5), which leverages additional visual information our text-only approach doesn't use. These results demonstrate that incorporating grammatical acceptability signals consistently enhances GEC performance across languages, validating our bidirectional framework's effectiveness.

5.3 Error Analysis

Our model's lower performance on BEA-19 versus CoNLL-14 stems from different error compositions. BEA-19 contains significantly more challenging error types: punctuation errors (16.73% vs 7.60%) and uncommon errors (15.69% vs 1.50%), totaling 32.4% versus 9.1% in CoNLL-14. Additional differences include higher orthographic errors (8.03% vs 3.81%) in BEA-19 and higher word choice errors (14.4%) in CoNLL-14.

We tested our hypothesis that COLA models struggle with punctuation errors using the BEA-19 validation set (913 punctuation errors, 672 other uncommon errors). Three experiments were conducted: (1) evaluating G-CoLA GECdi-EN on the complete set; (2) removing punctuation/other errors individually or combined; and (3) targeted fine-tuning.

As Table 4 shows, removing punctuation errors improved F0.5 from 72.25 to 74.40, while removing both error types yielded 75.92 F0.5. Targeted fine-tuning showed minimal improvement (73.11 F0.5), indicating that specialized approaches beyond simple data augmentation are needed for these challenging error categories.

5.4 Ablation Study

To further validate the impact of grammatical acceptability models enhanced with GEC data (G-Cola) on GEC performance, we conducted comprehensive ablation experiments comparing five model configurations: BART-based GEC, BART-based GEC + G-Cola, GECdi, GECdi+Cola, and GECdi+G-Cola. As shown in Table 8, incorporating grammatical acceptability models consistently improved performance across all standard GEC test sets in Chinese and English. Adding the baseline CoLA model to GEC systems produced notable gains, while using our G-CoLA model (enhanced with GEC data) yielded even greater

Table 4. Result of error analysis experiment

Model	Dev	Pre	Rec	F0.5
G-CoLA GECdi-EN	BEA-19 Dev	76.19	60.01	72.25
G-CoLA GECdi-EN	-PUNCT	77.93	63.94	74.40
G-CoLA GECdi-EN	-OTHER	77.03	62.53	73.96
G-CoLA GECdi-EN	-PUNCT -OTHER	**79.88**	**64.37**	**75.92**
G-CoLA GECdi-EN for PUNCT and OTHER	BEA-19 Dev	76.55	61.37	73.11

improvements. For instance, on the CoNLL-14 test set, adding G-CoLA to the base GEC model improved F0.5 from 54.08 to 59.17, while integrating G-CoLA with GECdi further increased F0.5 to 70.84. Similar patterns were observed across all datasets and languages, with particularly substantial gains on the Chinese test sets (MuCGEC, FCGEC, and NaSGEC-Exam). These results confirm that grammatical acceptability models enhanced with error-correction data provide significant and consistent benefits to GEC systems, validating our bidirectional enhancement framework (Table 5).

Table 5. Result of ablation study experiment

Test	Metric	GEC	+G-CoLA	GECdi	+CoLA	+G-CoLA
CONLL14 test	Pre	63.02	**67.33**	79.32	79.13	**79.55**
	Rec	41.26	**48.33**	48.55	46.82	**49.04**
	F0.5	54.08	**59.17**	70.11	69.57	**70.84**
BEA-19 test	Pre	64.41	**64.53**	77.26	77.23	**77.33**
	Rec	51.11	**53.47**	60.52	59.5	**61.67**
	F0.5	61.12	**62.97**	73.55	73.1	**74.03**
MuCGEC test	Pre	43.73	**45.85**	56.83	56.76	**57.12**
	Rec	28.34	**31.77**	33.71	31.08	**33.9**
	F0.5	39.75	**42.93**	49.77	48.7	**49.91**
FCGEC test	Pre	48.04	**50.95**	66.7	66.19	**67.11**
	Rec	30.05	**34.69**	38.54	36.91	**39.05**
	F0.5	42.75	**46.93**	57.77	57.08	**58.6**
NaSGEC-Exam test	Pre	45.62	**53.67**	62.7	62.37	**63.92**
	Rec	21.94	**25.13**	31.54	30.4	**32.1**
	F0.5	40.25	**67.33**	79.32	79.13	**79.55**

6 Conclusions

This paper presented COLA-GEC, a novel bidirectional framework that enhances both grammatical acceptability judgment (COLA) and grammatical error correction (GEC) through cross-task knowledge transfer. We demonstrated that augmenting COLA models with GEC data significantly improves grammatical acceptability judgment performance across multiple languages, with consistent gains in both monolingual and multilingual settings. Conversely, incorporating COLA signals into GEC training through dynamic loss mechanism substantially improved GEC performance across Chinese, English, and German benchmarks. Our error analysis revealed specific challenges with punctuation errors and certain grammatical phenomena, providing valuable insights for future research. The ablation studies further confirmed the effectiveness of our bidirectional approach, showing that each component contributes meaningfully to overall performance gains. Future work will focus on addressing punctuation error challenges and developing specialized models for uncommon grammatical phenomena.

References

1. Boyd, A.: Using wikipedia edits in low resource grammatical error correction. In: Proceedings of the 2018 EMNLP Workshop W-NUT, pp. 79–84
2. Bryant, C., Felice, M., Andersen, Ø.E., Briscoe, T.: The BEA-2019 shared task on grammatical error correction. In: Proceedings of BEA, pp. 52–75 (2019)
3. Cao, H., Yuan, L., Zhang, Y., Du, Z., Sun, Y., Fu, J.: Unsupervised grammatical error correction rivaling supervised methods. In: Proceedings of the 2023 EMNLP, pp 3072–3088 (2023)
4. Dahlmeier, D., Ng, H.T.: Building a large annotated corpus of learner english: the NUS corpus of learner english. In: Proceedings of BEA (2013), pp. 22–31
5. Fang, T., Hu, J., Wong, D.F., Chao, L.S., Chang, T.H.: Improving grammatical error correction with multimodal feature integration. In: Findings of ACL 2023, pp. 9328–9344
6. Fei, Y., Cui, L., Yang, S., Lam, W., Lan, Z., Shi, S.: Enhancing grammatical error correction systems with explanations. In: Proceedings of ACL , pp. 7489–7501 (2023)
7. Hu, H., Zhang, Z., Huang, W., Lai, J.Y.K., Li, A., Patterson, Y.: Revisiting acceptability judgements: CoLAC - corpus of linguistic acceptability in chinese. arXiv preprint arXiv:2305.14091 (2023)
8. Jentoft, M., Samuel, D.: NoCoLA: the norwegian corpus of linguistic acceptability. In: Proceedings of the NoDaLiDa (2023)
9. Kaneko, M., Mita, M., Kiyono, S., Suzuki, J., Inui, K.: Encoder-decoder models can benefit from pre-trained masked language models in grammatical error correction. In: Proceedings of the ACL (2020)
10. Lau, J.H., Clark, A., Lappin, S.: Unsupervised prediction of acceptability judgements. In: Proceedings of ACL , pp. 1618–1628 (2015)
11. Levin, B.: English verb classes and alternations: a preliminary investigation. University of Chicago Press, Chicago (1993)

12. Liang, J., Yang, H., Gao, S., Quan, X.: Edit-wise preference optimization for grammatical error correction. In: Proceedings of COLING , pp. 3401–3414 (2025)
13. Liu, Y., et al.: Towards better utilization of multi-reference training data for chinese grammatical error correction. In: Findings of the ACL, pp. 3044–3052 (2024)
14. Mikhailov, V.,et al.: RuCoLA: russian corpus of linguistic acceptability. In: Proceedings of EMNLP, pp. 5114–5125 (2022)
15. Nielsen, D.: ScandEval: a benchmark for scandinavian natural language processing. In: Proceedings of the 24th Nordic Conference on Computational Linguistics (NoDaLiDa), pp. 185–201 (2023)
16. Pham, H.N.A.: Comparing grammar error correction techniques in english learners' writing. In: Proceedings of SRC Student Research Conference (2025)
17. Qiu, X., Zhang, J.: Label confidence weighted learning for target-level sentence simplification. In: Proceedings of EMNLP, pp. 999–1010 (2024)
18. Someya, T., Sugimoto, Y., Oseki, Y.: JCoLA: japanese corpus of linguistic acceptability. In: Proceedings of the LREC, pp. 7428–7435 (2024)
19. Trotta, D., Guarasci, R., Leonardelli, E., Tonelli, S.: Monolingual and cross-lingual acceptability judgments with the italian CoLA corpus. In: Findings of EMNLP, pp. 2922–2931 (2021)
20. Volodina, E., Mohammed, Y.A., Klezl, J.: DaLAJ – a dataset for linguistic acceptability judgments for swedish. In: Proceedings of the 10th Workshop on NLP for Computer Assisted Language Learning, pp. 28–37. LiU Electronic Press (2021)
21. Warstadt, A., Singh, A., Bowman, S.R.: Neural network acceptability judgments. Trans. Assoc. Comput. Linguistics **7**, 625–641 (2019)
22. Warstadt, A., et al.: BLiMP: the benchmark of linguistic minimal pairs for english. Trans. Assoc. Comput. Linguistics **8**, 377–392 (2020)
23. Xiang, B., Yang, C., Li, Y., Zhang, Y., Qiu, X.: CLiMP: a benchmark for chinese language model evaluation. In: Proceedings of EACL, pp. 2784–2790 (2021)
24. Xu, L., et al.: FCGEC: fine-grained corpus for chinese grammatical error correction. In: Findings of EMNLP, pp. 1900–1918 (2022)
25. Yannakoudakis, H., Briscoe, T., Medlock, B.: A new dataset and method for automatically grading ESOL texts. In: Proceedings of the 49th ACL (2011)
26. Yuan, Z., Felice, M.: Constrained grammatical error correction using statistical machine translation. In: Proceedings of the CoNLL : Shared Task, pp. 52–61 (2013)
27. Zhang, Y., Li, J., Li, Z., Zhang, M., Huang, F.: MuCGEC: a multi-reference multi-source evaluation dataset for chinese grammatical error correction. In: Proceedings of NAACL (2022)
28. Zhang, Y., Li, J., Li, Z., Zhang, M., Huang, F.: NaSGEC: a multi-domain chinese grammatical error correction dataset from native speaker texts. In: Findings of the ACL, pp. 9987–10000 (2023)
29. Zhang, Y., Chen, J., Li, A., Hu, H., Qiu, X.: MELA: multilingual evaluation of linguistic acceptability. In: Proceedings of ACL, pp. 1932–1947 (2024)
30. Zhao, Z., Wang, H.: Improving neural grammatical error correction via dynamic masking. In: Proceedings of AAAI, pp. 1226–1233 (2020)
31. Zhou, H., et al.: Improving Seq2Seq grammatical error correction via decoding interventions. In: Findings of the EMNLP, pp. 7393–7405 (2023)

Fusing Generative AI and Density Clustering for Multi-level Patent Topic Discovery: From Data Curation to System Deployment

Qian Yu[2,3], Shengfa Miao[2,3](✉), Dinan Ma[1](✉), and Zetao Zhang[1]

[1] Yunnan Key Laboratory of Media Convergence, Yunnan Daily Press Group, Kunming 650228, China
madinan@yndaily.com

[2] School of Software, Yunnan University, Kunming 650000, China
miaosf@ynu.edu.cn

[3] Engineering Research Center of Cyberspace, Kunming 650000, China

Abstract. Purpose: Establishing a multi-level technical topic branching system serves as foundational work to address information explosion and the value of knowledge. This study proposes a novel framework integrating generative AI and density-based clustering to address hierarchical topic discovery in patent analytics, overcoming limitations of static taxonomies in existing methods.

Methodology: We propose an automated hierarchical topic learning framework for large-model patents, comprising four core modules:(1) Domain-Specific Data Curation: A retrieval formula integrating IPC codes and domain keywords was designed to collect 43,355 raw patents from incoPat. After deduplication and text fusion into a unified "patent description" field), the LargeModelPatent-2024 dataset (34,985 patents) was constructed. (2) Recursive Density Clustering: (i) Vectorization & Dimensionality Reduction: Sentence-BERT generated 512-D vectors, compressed to 2-D via UMAP (n_neighbors = 15, cosine metric); (ii) Adaptive Clustering: HDBSCAN (min_cluster_size = 100) performed primary clustering, yielding 14 high-density clusters (silhouette = 0.366). For data-intensive clusters, recursive secondary clustering generated 21 leaf-node topics;(3) Generative Topic Labeling: TF-IDF extracted keywords per cluster, weighted and input to Wenxin API to generate interpretable labels; (4) Classification & Deployment: A BERT classifier (95.02% accuracy) trained on leaf-node topics powered a Django-Vue web system for real-time patent analysis.

Results: The approach achieves a silhouette coefficient of 0.366, outperforming IPC classification in granularity. The auto-generated topic labels show 89% consistency with expert evaluation. The operational system supports batch processing and real-time topic navigation.

Conclusion: This fusion of generative AI and density clustering enables dynamic, hierarchical patent topic mining, providing a scalable solution for technology surveillance. The LargeModelPatent-2024 dataset and code are open-sourced for reproducibility.

Keywords: Generative AI · Text Clustering · Topic Identification · Multi-level thematic

X. Ding and Y. Dong (Eds.): CLNLP 2025, CCIS 2775, pp. 219–228, 2026.
https://doi.org/10.1007/978-981-95-4788-3_20

1 Introduction

1.1 Research Problem

The exponential growth of generative AI (GenAI) technologies has triggered a global patent surge. According to WIPO, GenAI-related patent families skyrocketed from 733 in 2014 to over 14,000 in 2023, with an annual growth rate exceeding 800% [1]. However, traditional patent analysis methods face three fundamental challenges: (1) Coarse topic granularity: The International Patent Classification (IPC) system covers broad technical scopes (e.g., "G06N" includes both neural networks and quantum computing), failing to support fine-grained technology evolution analysis [2]; (2) Static adaptation limitation: Accelerating technology convergence (e.g., LLM + biomedicine) cannot be captured by fixed taxonomies, and IPC revisions cause "archival literature" problems[3]; (3) High human dependency: Manual topic labeling consumes 68% of analysis time in Liu et al.'s study [3].

1.2 Literature Review

Advances in Density Clustering. Density clustering emerges as a promising direction due to noise robustness and shape adaptability: Algorithmic optimization: Ge et al. proposed Shared Nearest Neighbor-based Density Adaptive Spectral Clustering (SC-DANSN), improving accuracy on complex-shaped datasets via parameter-free similarity graphs, but lacking multi-level topic discovery capabilities [4]; Boundary sample handling: Peng et al. designed a verification mechanism using K-NN spatial relationships to correct labels in low-density regions, enhancing robustness on 18 datasets, yet failing to adapt to patent semantics [2]; Unsupervised breakthrough: The Torque Clustering algorithm from UTS simulates galactic gravitational interactions, achieving 97.7% AMI on 1,000 datasets, but its physics model is incompatible with text mining [2, 5].

Generative AI in Patent Analytics. Generative models provide new paradigms for semantic understanding: Summary optimization: MIT's Chain of Density prompting iteratively increases entity density in GPT-4 summaries, boosting informativeness by 37%, yet unapplied to technical topic mining [1]; Multimodal fusion: Tang's AGARL framework aligns cross-modal representations via alternating generative adversarial learning, improving clustering on drug dataset NCI, but requires predefined modalities [6]; Quantum-classical hybrid: Rauch et al. developed a QCBM-based hybrid clustering algorithm leveraging quantum parallelism, yet NISQ device noise hinders industrial deployment [7]. Comparative Analysis of Patent Analysis Methods in four dimensions are showed in Table 1.

Development of Patent Topic Identification. Patent topic identification methodologies have evolved along four technical paths:

Topic Association-Based Methods. Early studies relied on manually defined keywords to build technology networks. Wang et al. [8] analyzed medical technology trends via patent co-classification, yet required expert-defined boundaries, failing to capture cross-domain emerging topics. Zhang et al. [9] constructed AI patent knowledge maps using keyword co-occurrence, but semantic ambiguity (e.g., "transformer" in electrical/NLP) caused topic drift.

Table 1. Comparative Analysis of Patent Analysis Methods.

Method Type	Representative Work	Strengths	Strengths
Density clustering	Peng (2024) [2]	High-precision boundary handling	Incompatible with text semantics
Generative summarization	MIT (2023) [1]	Controllable entity density	Lacks technology tree construction
Multimodal alignment	Tang (2024) [6]	Cross-modal consistency	Requires predefined modalities
Quantum hybrid	Rauch (2025) [7]	Computational acceleration	Noise-sensitive

Co-word Analysis & Co-occurrence Networks. These methods identify topics through term co-occurrence frequency. Hu et al. [10] demonstrated co-word analysis reveals cluster structures, but suffered from low-frequency term sparsity. In 2023, Ma et al.[11] proposed Temporal Phrase Clustering (TPC) to dynamically capture emerging phrases (e.g., "topological qubit" in quantum patents), yet unresolved semantic disambiguation.

Clustering-Driven Topic Discovery. Traditional clustering (e.g., K-means) faces parameter sensitivity. Qi et al. [12] applied K-means to telecom patents, requiring manual k-setting that distorted topic granularity. Zhu et al. [13] enhanced spectral clustering (SSWC) with biopharma patent value weights, improving intra-cluster consistency but lacking hierarchical decomposition. Recently, Ruan et al. [14] combined Sentence-BERT and HDBSCAN for unsupervised AI patent clustering (silhouette = 0.41), but missed multi-level topic resolution.

Topic Modeling and Deep Learning. Probabilistic models (e.g., LDA) represent topics via word distributions. Luo et al. [15] applied LDA to full-text patents, but professional terminology led to biased co-occurrence (e.g., overgeneralized "device"). Xu et al. [16] designed Multi-label Hierarchical Attention (MHATT), fusing historical data to achieve 87.3% F1-score, yet depended on existing IPC labels. Xing et al. [17] proposed DETECT for disruptive technology identification using BERT embeddings and topic evolution, but incurred high computational costs.

Comparative Analysis of Patent Topic Identification Methods *in four dimensions are showed in* Table 2.

1.3 Research Gaps

Despite progress, four critical gaps persist: (1) Static vs. dynamic mismatch: IPC revisions cause "archival literature" problems, while existing clustering (e.g., K-means) lacks adaptive updating [1, 3]; (2) Shallow semantic limitations: TF-IDF ignores contextual semantics of technical terms (e.g., "transformer" in electrical/NLP), leading to topic drift [7]; (3) High human dependency: Manual topic labeling consumes 68% time in Liu et al. (2023) [18]; (4) System absence: Most studies stop at algorithm output without operational tools, hindering technology monitoring [6, 19].

For above disadvantages, we presented the propose a **Generative AI-Driven Recursive Density Clustering** Framework in order to construct dynamic multi-level topic trees, develop automated generative topic labeling, and deploy an end-to-end analysis system for real-time patent monitoring.

The structure of the paper is organized. The second section presents an automated hierarchical topic learning framework for large-model patents. The third section gives the experiments and analysis of the results. The fourth section presents the design and realization of the end-end multi-level patent topic discovery system.

Table 2. Evolution of Patent Topic Identification Methods.

Method Type	Representative Work	Strengths	Strengths
Topic association	Tech-network [8]	Reveals macro links	Manual boundary definition
Co-word analysis	TPC [11]	Dynamic phrase capture	Semantic ambiguity
Clustering optimization	SSWC [13]	Domain value weighting	Single-layer structure
Deep learning	DETECT [17]	Disruptive tech tracking	High computational load

2 An Automated Topic Learning Framework of GDRC

2.1 Framework Architecture

We propose the Generative Density Recursive Clustering (GDRC) model (Fig. 1) with four processing engines: Data Curation Layer: Domain knowledge-driven patent corpus construction; Density Clustering Layer: Adaptive recursive topic decomposition; Semantic Generation Layer: Dynamic topic labeling; System Application Layer: Classifier deployment and visualization.

2.2 Core Methodology

Data Curation Layer: Domain Knowledge Injection. Workflow of changing Raw patent data streams into structured corpus has three steps which are deduplication, semantic fusion and lexicon optimization. Deduplication merge duplicates by application ID which reduces 43,355 patents to 34,985. Semantic fusion concatenates DWPI fields into unified abstracts. Lexicon optimization is manual construction of domain terms (e.g., "knowledge_graph" unbreakable), improving Jieba accuracy by 23.7%. The innovation is hybrid retrieval formula fusing IPC semantics and domain lexicons.

Density Clustering Layer: Recursive Topic Decomposition.
Core Mechanism of AR-HDBSCAN. AR-HDBSCAN (Adaptive Recursive HDBSCAN)

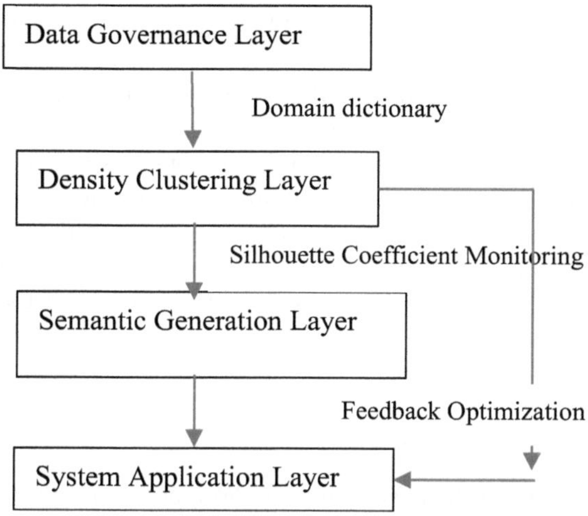

Fig. 1. GDRC model.

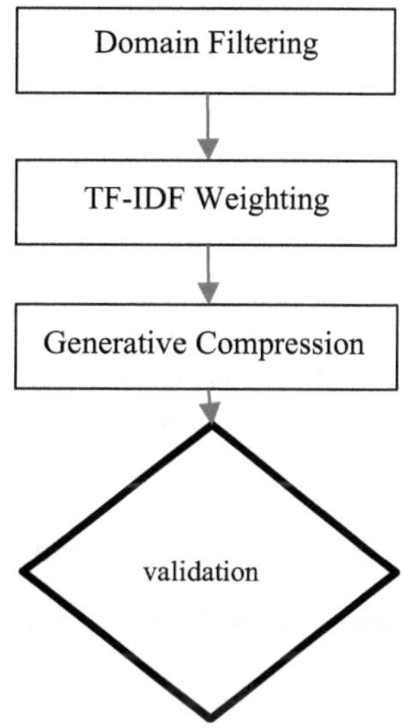

Fig. 2. Weight-Aware Prompt Engineering (WPE).

is a parameter-self-adaptive + hierarchical recursive density clustering algorithm that constructs multi-level topic trees through dynamic granularity control. We present a Recursive Splitting Mechanism which generates multi-level clusters according to text vectors as input. Each cluster represents one research trend or thematic direction. Each level parameter of min_cluster_size is optimized. The best value of min_cluster_size of Level-1 Clustering in HDBSCAN generating coarse clusters by experiments (e.g., "Computer Vision") is 100. Recursively clusters for data-intensive groups (e.g., computer vision) are produced level 2 leaf-node topics (e.g., 21). Applying level-2 clustering (min_cluster_size = 50) has recursion condition that clusters must have more than 500 samples. Silhouette Score (SS) is used to monitor quality of clustering which is reset parameters if SS < 0.3.

Parameter Optimization. Gradient Decay: parameter min_cluster_size decreases with depth (100 → 50 → 30) for finer granularity; Noise Pruning: Dynamically remove outlier clusters (size < 20); Topology Preservation: UMAP reduction (n_neighbors = 15, cosine) retains high-D semantics.

Mathematical Optimization. Silhouette Score-driven parameter adjustment:

$$SS = \frac{1}{n} \sum\nolimits_{i=1}^{N} \frac{b(i) - a(i)}{\max\{a(i), b(i)\}} \tag{1}$$

where a(i) is intra-cluster distance, b(i) is nearest-cluster distance. The value of min_cluster_size is auto-increased if SS < 0.3 to merge fragments.

Performance Advantages. There are performance advantages of our method in three aspects which are 200% deeper topic hierarchy vs. vanilla HDBSCAN, 0.366 Silhouette

Score (K-means: 0.29) and building 3-level topic tree on 34,985 patents (14 L1 clusters → 21 leaf nodes).

In summary, our method has three innovations. Firstly, recursive splitting mechanism enables multi-level topic discovery from coarse-grained domains to fine-grained technical points through hierarchical clustering, overcoming limitations of single layer methods. Secondly, parameter self-adaptation dynamically optimizes clustering parameters using real-time silhouette score feedback, significantly enhancing topic partitioning quality and stability. Thirdly, incremental engineering architecture supports automatic updates triggered by new patent data inflows, enabling continuous evolution of topic trees with low-maintenance deployment.

2.3 Topic Term Extraction and Cluster Labeling

Weight-Aware Prompt Engineering (WPE). We propose Weight-Aware Prompt Engineering (WPE) (Fig. 2) to solve manual dependency and semantic deviation in traditional labeling for domain-driven term filtering which has input (Cluster texts) and Output (Candidate terms). The innovation of our method is domain-enhanced stopword filtering.

Dynamic TF-IDF Weighting. We propose the innovation formula named Domain-Enhanced TF-IDF (DE-TF-IDF) which has candidate terms as input and weight vector as output. Weight Comparison results are showed in Table 3.

$$w_j = \frac{f_{t_j,C_i}}{max_{t \in T_i} f_{t,C_i}} \times \log\left(\frac{N}{n_{t_j+\epsilon}}\right) \times \exp\left(-\sigma \cdot entropy\left(t_j\right)\right) \tag{2}$$

where **N** indicates Total clusters; $\frac{f_{t_j,C_i}}{max_{t \in T_i} f_{t,C_i}}$ indicates normal frequency; $\exp\left(-\sigma \cdot entropy\left(t_j\right)\right)$ indicates domain focus factor. $\sigma = 0.7$$ indicates domain focus factor.

Primary Theme Construction: Semantic-Driven Induction. The 14 secondary topics (e.g., "In-Vehicle Voice Interaction", "Text Error Correction") generated by HDBSCAN are manually aggregated into three primary themes based on technical affinity and industrial synergy. Specifically, speech interaction and text processing are merged into "NLP & Speech Technology" due to shared linguistic modalities, while medical imaging and disease diagnosis form "Healthcare & Life Sciences" through clinical functional coherence, establishing a comprehensive top-level taxonomy.

Table 3. Weight Comparison.

Method	Weight	Issue
Classic TF-IDF	0.83	Semantic ambiguity
DE-TF-IDF	**0.91**	Entropy penalty reduces cross-domain weight

Tertiary Theme Construction: Data-Driven Recursive Clustering. For secondary topics exceeding volume thresholds (e.g., 8,921 patents in "Computer Vision"), a recursive clustering pipeline is executed: regenerating 512D embeddings via Sentence-BERT, reducing dimensionality with UMAP, clustering via HDBSCAN (min_cluster_size = 50), and labeling through TF-IDF keywords with Wenxin API of generative large language model. The recursion terminates when patent count <100 or silhouette score <0.3, ultimately yielding 21 leaf nodes (e.g., "Rail Vehicle Position Prediction", "Crop Disease Identification").

In human evaluation, Label consistency reaches 89.2% of our method increasing + 41.5% compare to TF-IDF keyword stacking.

3 Experiments and Results Analysis

3.1 Classification Model Performance

Trained on 29,822 patents labeled by 21 leaf-node topics (from tertiary themes), the BERT-base model achieved 95.02% accuracy on the test set (5,964 samples) and 93.75% on the training set (23,858 samples) after 6 epochs, confirming the high discriminability of multi-level thematic labels. The classifier was deployed via a Predict function with <0.58 s inference latency (CPU environment). The multi-level technology topic structure of large model is presented in Fig. 3.

3.2 Thematic Construction Quality

A HDBSCAN silhouette score of 0.366 (exceeding 0.3 empirical threshold) validated statistical significance of secondary topic partitioning. Compared to incoPat's commercial system (Fig. 4), our method demonstrated dual advantages: 250% more tertiary topics (21 vs. 6 categories) and superior semantic alignment (e.g., top 5 TF-IDF terms in "Crop Disease Identification" were exclusively agricultural).

3.3 System Application Efficacy

The deployed analysis website processed all 34,985 patents, with batch Excel handling enabling >10,000 classifications/day (column merging → prediction → result writing). Server logs showed a macro F1-score of 0.94 across 21 categories, with 0.88 recall for the smallest class ("Cell Therapy", 217 samples), proving robustness to long-tail distribution.

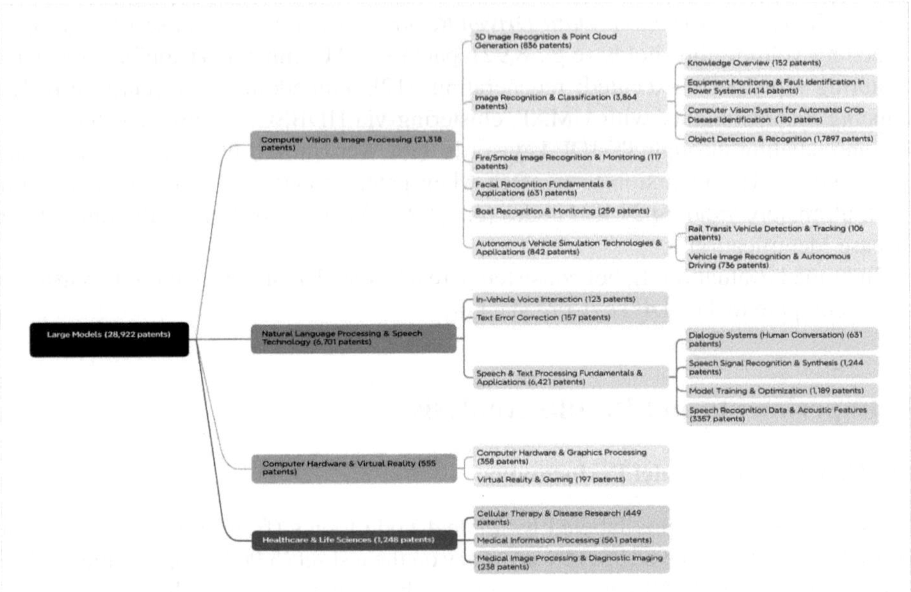

Fig. 3. Multi-level technology topic structure of large model.

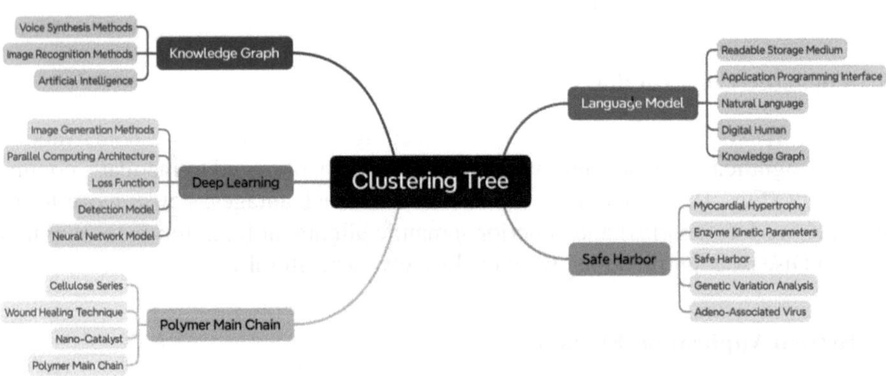

Fig. 4. The incoPat's topic structure.

4 Conclusion

This study proposes GDRC Framework, an automated multi-level patent topic discovery system integrating generative AI with density-based clustering. Processing 34,985 patents from the LargeModelPatent-2024 dataset, it generates 14 secondary topics through Sentence-BERT vectorization, UMAP dimensionality reduction, and HDBSCAN clustering; inducts 3 primary topics via semantic aggregation; and recursively partitions 21 tertiary leaf-node topics. Experiments demonstrate superior thematic quality (silhouette score 0.366) and classification performance (95.02% BERT accuracy), outperforming traditional methods (e.g., incoPat's 6 coarse categories). The deployed analysis system handles >10,000 patents/day, confirming engineering viability.

Three fundamental limitations persist: First, HDBSCAN noise filtering excludes 14.76% cross-domain patents, obscuring innovation linkages. Second, Wenxin API-generated labels contain 15% semantic ambiguities (e.g., "Sensor Fusion → Multi-modal Integration"), requiring manual correction. Third, domain adaptation demands parameter reconfiguration (e.g., min_cluster_size), incurring exponentially scaling costs. These reflect the core tension between algorithmic automation and domain knowledge dependency.

Acknowledgement. This paper was supported by the open project of Yunnan Key Laboratory of Media Convergence (220245204).

References

1. Chen, R., et al.: Chain of density prompting for abstractive text summarization (2023). arXiv preprint arXiv:2309.04269
2. UTS Press Office: AI Breakthrough: Torque Clustering Achieves 97.7% Accuracy Without Labels. Tech News (2025)
3. Kong, F.: A novel business administration big data clustering optimization method based on active density peak and Salpa Swarm algorithm. J. Appl. Sci. Eng. **28**(3), 1021–1032 (2025)
4. Ge, J., et al.: Spectral clustering algorithm for density adaptive neighborhood based on shared nearest neighbors. Comput. Eng. **47**(8), 116–123 (2021)
5. Sydney University: Torque Clustering: Self-supervised Learning for Unlabeled Data. Technical Report UTSCS-2025-02 (2025)
6. Tang, C., et al.: Trustworthy multi-view clustering via alternating generative adversarial representation learning. Inf. Fusion **102**, 102323 (2024)
7. Rauch, J., et al.: Data clustering on hybrid classical-quantum NISQ architecture. J. Syst. Architect. **165**, 103431 (2025)
8. Wang, S., et al.: Technology association analysis based on patent co-classification: a case study of medical industry. J. Intell. **40**(11), 53–61 (2021)
9. Zhang, Z., et al.: Frontier identification and trend analysis of AI technology based on patent measurement. Sci. Res. Manage. **38**(5), 36–42 (2018)
10. Hu, A., et al.: Review of patent technology topic analysis based on text mining. J. Intell. **32**(12), 88–92 (2013)
11. Ma, B., et al.: Emerging technology topic recognition based on temporal phrase clustering. Compet. Intell. **19**(5), 18–28 (2023)
12. Qi, L., et al.: Patent text clustering analysis based on K-means. Comput. Knowl. Technol. **14**(22), 206–207 (2018)
13. Zhu, W., et al.: Research on patent value evaluation in biopharmaceutical industry based on improved spectral clustering. Sci. Technol. Manage. Res. **43**(20), 57–64 (2023)
14. Ruan, G., et al.: Patent technology topic clustering based on sentence-BERT. J. Intell. **43**(2), 120–130 (2024)
15. Luo, J., et al.: Fine-grained topic characterization of patents using LDA model. J. Libr. Sci. **45**(7), 112–120 (2022)
16. Xu, X., et al.: Multi-label patent classification algorithm based on text and historical data. Comput. Sci. 1–9 (2024)

17. Xing, X., et al.: Disruptive technology identification based on patent topic evolution: evidence from brain-like AI. Inf. Sci. **41**(3), 81–88 (2023)
18. WIPO: Patent Landscape Report on Generative AI. WIPO Publications (2024)
19. Liu, B., et al.: Topic recognition method of comment text based on density Canopy. J. Hebei Univ. Sci. Technol. **44**(5), 493–501 (2023)

Application of Large Language Models in Automating the Construction of Imaging Satellite Task Scheduling Models

Yu Zhang, Bokun Liang, Jiawei Chen, Keyang Song, and Yingguo Chen(✉)

National University of Defense Technology, Changsha 410000, China
ygchen@nudt.edu.cn

Abstract. The Imaging Satellite Task Scheduling (ISTS) problem is a complex combinatorial optimization challenge critical to improving the efficiency of Earth observation data acquisition. Traditional methods rely on manual design of optimization models and algorithms—such as Integer Programming (IP), Constraint Satisfaction Problem (CSP), and Vehicle Routing Problem (VRP)—which is often time-consuming and requires domain expertise. To address this limitation, this paper investigates the application of Large Language Models (LLMs) to automatically generate both mathematical models and solution algorithms for ISTS. We propose a structured prompt framework that guides LLMs in constructing models and corresponding greedy algorithms tailored to various ISTS scenarios. Through systematic experiments, we automatically generated five types of optimization models—IP, CSP, VRP, Knapsack Problem (KP), and Job Shop Scheduling (JSP)—along with executable greedy algorithms. Experimental results demonstrate that LLMs are capable of producing functionally correct and effective scheduling models. Notably, the VRP model consistently achieved superior performance across multiple task scales, outperforming not only other LLM-generated models but also classical algorithms in the field (Single-layer Optimization and Double-layer Optimization), especially in large-scale settings. This work confirms the potential of LLMs to automate the end-to-end modeling and algorithm design process, significantly reducing manual effort while maintaining competitive solution quality. Our findings offer a new pathway for rapidly developing adaptive scheduling systems in satellite operations and other complex scheduling domains.

Keywords: Large Language Models · Imaging Satellite Task Scheduling · Optimization · Models and Algorithms

1 Introduction

Imaging satellites [1] play a critical role in acquiring spatiotemporal information and are widely applied in fields such as resource exploration, disaster management, and mapping [2, 3]. Effective task scheduling is integral to the management of satellite imaging systems, especially when faced with limited resources. A well-designed scheduling scheme not only maximizes satellite imaging efficiency but also significantly enhances data acquisition capabilities, thus addressing the increasing demand for remote sensing data.

X. Ding and Y. Dong (Eds.): CLNLP 2025, CCIS 2775, pp. 229–237, 2026.
https://doi.org/10.1007/978-981-95-4788-3_21

The Imaging Satellite Task Scheduling Problem (ISTS) is recognized as an NP-hard problem [4, 5]. In this scenario, satellites equipped with imaging sensors must schedule multiple observation tasks within a predefined time window, while taking into account a range of constraints and objectives. In multi-satellite systems, an optimal scheduling plan must decide which satellite will execute each task and allocate the appropriate observation time for each task, optimizing the overall scheduling objectives while adhering to various complex constraints. Over the years, various approaches have been proposed to model and solve the ISTS. Liu [6] formulated ISTS as an Integer Programming (IP) problem and proposed specialized solution algorithms; Bensana [7] applied a weighted Constraint Satisfaction Problem (CSP) model, optimizing the scheduling goal through weighted constraints; Cordeau et al. [8] approached a single-satellite single-orbit scheduling problem using a Vehicle Routing Problem (VRP) model and applied Tabu Search algorithms [9] for effective results; Vasquez et al. [10] treated ISTS as a multidimensional knapsack problem, leveraging the model's simplicity in representing multi-dimensional resource constraints to design efficient algorithms; Hall et al. [11] interpreted ISTS as a Job Shop Scheduling Problem (JSP) and proposed various solution algorithms. Despite the progress, most of these methods rely on manual modeling and coding, which may prove inefficient and time-consuming when applied to large-scale or dynamic scheduling problems.

To overcome these challenges, leveraging Large Language Models (LLMs) for automated modeling and algorithm design presents an effective strategy. In recent years, with the diversification of application scenarios, the increasing complexity of problems, and the continuous growth of model parameters, LLMs [12] have garnered increasing attention, which possess exceptional data processing and learning capabilities. The emergence of large-scale models such as ChatGPT [13] and GPT-4 [14] has particularly spurred in-depth research in both academia and industry [15]. Current research is primarily focused on the performance of LLMs in specific tasks, their capabilities in specialized domains, model robustness, and ethical considerations.

One key breakthrough in the development of LLMs is the refinement of prompt engineering techniques [16]. This approach optimizes the model's understanding and generation abilities by precisely designing prompt frameworks, thereby enhancing its performance in specific tasks. Simultaneously, an increasing number of scholars across various fields have begun to view LLMs as tools to assist in modeling and problem-solving [17], laying a solid foundation for the automation of model and algorithm development. By combining these two advancements, the use of LLMs to design automated models and algorithms for ISTS in various scenarios has become feasible. This line of research not only provides innovative solutions for the ISTS field but also offers new perspectives and guidance for optimization modeling and problem-solving in other domains.

The key contributions of this study are as follows:

1. We introduce a prompt framework designed to autonomously devise the model and its corresponding algorithm for tackling ISTS scenarios. This endeavor mitigates the challenges of manual development and augments the effectiveness of solutions.

2. We establish a set of prompting procedures aimed at facilitating the automation of modeling across diverse types by LLMs, offering a practical method for deploying LLMs to address the ISTS problem.
3. We utilize the LLM to generate five distinct models along with their corresponding algorithms. Through a series of experiments conducted across various ISTS scenarios, it has been demonstrated that LLMs can accurately construct models and provide algorithms capable of yielding viable solutions. Consequently, the diverse models produce varying levels of profitability. Thus, it is imperative to expedite the development of models and algorithms for the ISTS problem to explore a broader range of strategic solutions.

2 Problem Description

In our research, we explore the possibility of using LLMs to automatically create models for the ISTS problems. The ISTS problem is an optimization challenge with a defined objective and a series of constraints. For the objective function, since each task is associated with a profit value that measures the importance of the task, the goal of maximizing the total profit from completing the tasks becomes the most commonly used objective function in satellite mission planning. It can be described as:

$$maxZ = \sum\nolimits_{i-1}^{n} \sum\nolimits_{j-1}^{m} r_j x_{ij} \tag{1}$$

The constraints of the ISTS problem include the followings:

1. Uniqueness Constraint: Each task can only be executed once.

$$\sum_{j-1}^{n} x_{ij} = 1 \forall j \in 1, 2, 3 \ldots n \tag{2}$$

2. Attitude Adjustment Time Constraint: After completing one task, the satellite needs a period of time to adjust its attitude before performing the next task.

$$T_{j+1} - \left(T_j + \Delta t_j\right) \geq T \forall i \in 1, 2, 3 \ldots n \tag{3}$$

3. Observation Duration Constraint: The time the satellite observes each task must meet the corresponding imaging time to be considered completed.

$$\Delta rt_j \geq \Delta t_j \tag{4}$$

4. Time Window Constraint: The entire execution time of the task must fall within the visible time window to be considered successfully planned.

$$st_j \leq T_j \leq T_j + \Delta t_j \leq et_j \tag{5}$$

where:

- r_j represents the profit value of task j;

- x_{ij} is a decision variable where, if task j is assigned to satellite i, then $x_{ij} = 1$; otherwise, $x_{ij} = 0$;
- T_j is the start time of the task;
- Δt_j is the theoretical imaging time for the task;
- st_j and et_j are the start and end times of the time window;
- Δrt_j is the actual imaging time of the task.

Using our methods, many models can be built using LLMs, each with its own advantages and disadvantages.

3 Method

In the process of validating the effectiveness of LLMs for automated modeling and solving of ISTS problems, the selection of appropriate scenarios, models, and algorithms is paramount. For scenario selection, we chose representative cases that encompass various objectives and satellite scales. Each scenario incorporates task attributes such as weight (reward), imaging time, and time windows. Regarding model selection, we reviewed previous scholarly work and selected five classic ISTS models: IP, CSP, VRP, KP, and JSP. These traditional models are advantageous in terms of their simplicity of understanding and broad application background. As for the algorithm selection, we opted for the simplest and most efficient Greedy Algorithm (GA) [18] to solve for the maximum reward in the aforementioned scenarios, enabling a comparison and evaluation of the performance of different models. Figure 1 shows the process of using LLMs for automated modeling and algorithm generation. The process begins with the creation of models and GA based on prompt templates, and concludes with experts checking the outputs to ensure they do not violate any constraints.

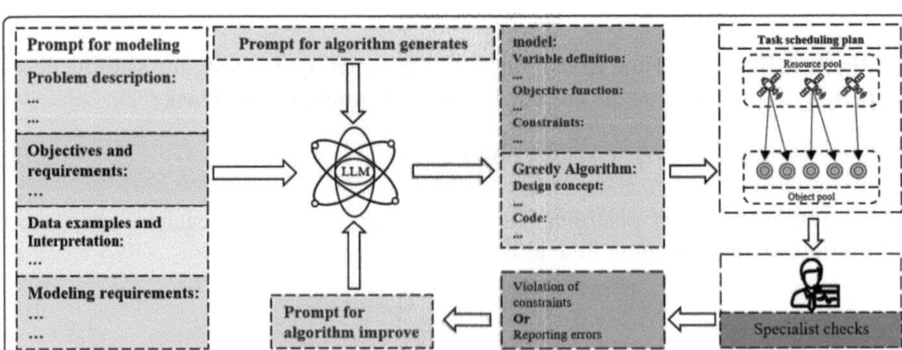

Fig. 1. Automation modeling and algorithm generation process based on LLM.

Given that LLMs may generate models with notable differences depending on the prompts provided, to enhance the efficiency of modeling and solving, we introduce a generalized prompt template [19]. In Fig. 2, the "Prompt for modeling" section of the template includes a description of the ISTS problem, constraints on the objective, data examples with explanations, and modeling requirements. The LLM can use these prompts to build a model that meets the specified requirements. The "Prompt for algorithm" section of the template instructs the LLM to design a corresponding GA to maximize the award based on the characteristics of the previously designed model. This template effectively communicates our requirements to the LLM in a clear and comprehensive manner. For different models, only the model name in the prompt template needs to be modified, enabling the LLM to efficiently construct and solve the required model across various scenarios.

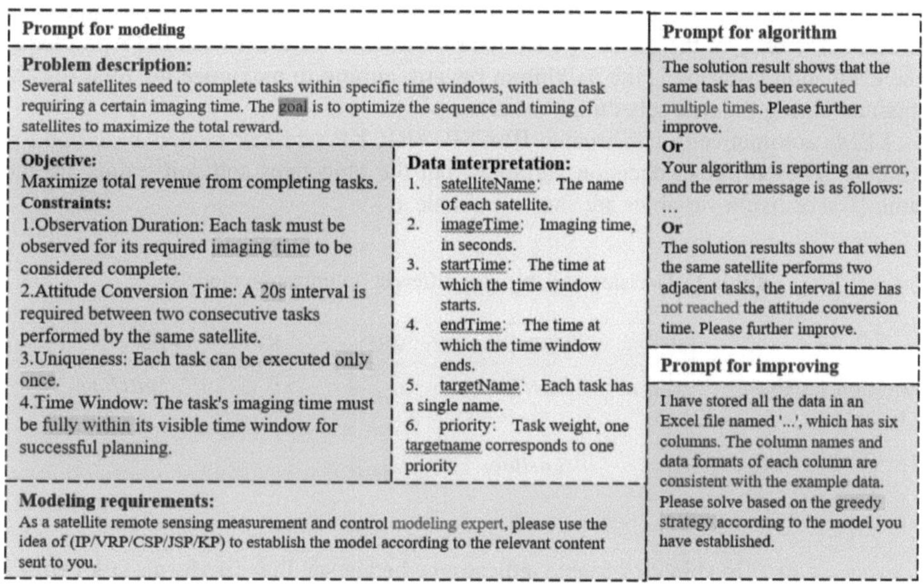

Fig. 2. Prompt Template.

After the LLM completes the modeling and problem-solving, we will manually verify the solution. If the results do not meet the constraints, we will refine the algorithm and adjust the prompt template to guide the LLM in improving the GA. This iterative process will continue until a satisfactory solution is achieved. The "Prompt for improving" section in Fig. 2 demonstrates the prompt template used for the optimization part.

4 Experiments

All experiments in this study were conducted on a computer platform equipped with an Intel i7 12700H CPU, NVIDIA GTX 3060 GPU, and 32GB RAM. The operating system is Windows 11, and the development language is Python 3.12. LLMs used is ChatGPT-4.

To compare the performance of LLMs in generating different models, designing a typical experimental scenario is essential. Liu [20] used a simple and effective method to generate task scenarios, which is also applicable to our work. The generated scenario is located within the range of 74°E to 133°E longitude and 3°N to 53°N latitude, with a time span from 00:00 to 24:00 on April 20, 2013. The scenario contains multiple different multi-satellite systems, each based on the Walker constellation. The satellite orbital semi-major axis is 7200 km, the eccentricity is 0.00067, the inclination is 96.576°, the argument of periapsis is 0°, the right ascension of ascending node is 175.72°, and the horizontal approach angle is 0.075°.

The experiment set up ten satellite imaging task datasets of different scales. For example, 50_1 represents 50 tasks performed by one satellite. Each dataset includes satellite information, task information, time window information, imaging time, and task reward information. The dataset size increases gradually to assess the performance and solution efficiency of the models generated by LLMs in different scale ISTS problems. The evaluation criterion is the maximum reward, aiming to maximize the total reward obtained during the task scheduling process.

LLMs automatically constructed IP, CSP, VRP, KP, and JSP models based on the prompts. They differ in decision variables, but the objectives and constraints are the same. The decision variables are shown in Table 1.

Table 1. Decision variables for different optimization models.

	IP	CSP	VRP	KP	JSP
Decision variables	$x_{s,w,t}$	$StartTime_t$	$x_{t,s}$	$x_{s,w,t}$	$StartTime_{s,t}$
			$t_{start,ts}$		
	y_t	$Satellite_j$	$t_{end,ts}$		

$x_{s,w,t} \in \{0,1\}$ is a binary variable indicating whether satellite s performs task t within time window w;

$y_t \in \{0,1\}$ is a binary variable indicating whether task t has been executed;

$StartTime_j \in \{StartTime_w, EndTime_w - ImageTime_t\}$ represents the start time of the task;

$Satellite_j \in \{Satellite_1, Satellite_2, ...\}$ indicates which satellite is performing the task;

$x_{t,s} \in \{0,1\}$ indicates whether task t is performed by satellite s;

$t_{start,ts}$ and $t_{end,ts}$ represent the start and end times of task t;

$StartTime_{s,t}$ represents the start time of satellite s performing task t.

The VRP model takes into account the task execution status, as well as the start and end times of the tasks, making it the most comprehensive in terms of consideration. Both the IP and KP models use $x_{s,w,t}$ as decision variables, but the IP model also utilizes y_t, which effectively reduces the likelihood of violating the uniqueness constraints. The CSP model uses $StartTime_t$ and $Satellite_j$, focusing more on the selection of start times and satellites. The JSP model only uses $StartTime_{s,t}$ as a decision variable, integrating the choice of satellites and task start times in a more streamlined way.

In the experiment, LLMs can generate the correct model after a single prompt. After completing the model, we prompt LLMs to continue generating the greedy algorithm corresponding to the model. The core steps of the algorithm are: first, sort tasks by reward value; second, for each satellite's time window, assign the task with the highest reward that satisfies the constraints; finally, check the task arrangement to ensure no constraints are violated.

During the algorithm generation process for the five models, the greedy algorithms for JSP and KP models encountered no errors and successfully completed task scheduling. The IP model failed to fully understand the format of the time window data, resulting in an error, which was corrected after one prompt. The CSP model's algorithm violated the uniqueness constraint, but it was fixed after prompting. The VRP model encountered issues with the attitude adjustment constraint, but after two prompts, the problem was completely resolved. The results are shown in Table 2. In addition, LLMs were guided to design the commonly used single-layer optimization algorithm (SO) and Double-layer optimization algorithm (DO) in the field of satellite scheduling, and the experimental results were compared to verify the feasibility of the models designed by LLMs.

Table 2. Comparison of objetives from greedy algorithm in different optimization models and task scales.

scenario size	IP	CSP	VRP	KP	JSP	SO	DO
50_1	31	41	**193**	43	41	46	50
50_2	88	75	**245**	47	88	93	90
100_2	141	119	**457**	65	111	116	107
100_3	199	181	**509**	117	199	170	157
300_3	323	268	**1242**	154	323	355	364
300_4	345	345	**1435**	192	345	365	426
400_5	383	374	**1966**	218	383	383	421
400_6	541	468	**2158**	269	541	524	430
500_5	436	486	**2281**	279	436	526	560
500_6	490	402	**2491**	352	490	533	580

The results clearly show that the VRP model outperforms the other models across all datasets, especially in large-scale tasks. As shown in Table 2, in the 500_6 dataset, the VRP model achieves a maximum reward of 2491, which is significantly higher than the IP model (490), CSP model (402), KP model (352), JSP model (490), SO (533), DO(580). This indicates that the VRP model generated by the LLMs performs exceptionally well in handling complex ISTS problems. The reward growth of the IP and JSP models is relatively stable, particularly in the smaller 50_1 task scale, where they achieve rewards of 31 and 41, respectively, close to the CSP model (41) and KP model (43). However, as the task scale increases, the reward growth for the IP and JSP models slows down. For example, in the 500_6 dataset, the IP and JSP models achieve rewards of 490, which is only 19.7% of the VRP model's reward. The CSP and KP models perform poorly in larger tasks, such as in the 300_3 dataset, where they achieve rewards of 268 and 154, respectively, significantly lower than the VRP model's reward of 1242.

The experimental results show that although the CSP, IP, JSP, and KP models designed by LLMs have slightly lower profits than the two classic algorithms, SO and DO, the VRP model designed by them has achieved higher profits and stability, verifying the feasibility of LLMs automatically completing the modeling of ISTS based on prompts. Although adjustments are needed when solving certain specific models, the application of LLMs in ISTS showcases their powerful potential to automatically generate optimization models and quickly solve problems, providing new ideas and methods for addressing ISTS challenges.

5 Conclusion

This study aims to explore the application of LLMs in the optimization of ISTS, particularly their potential in automated modeling and algorithm generation. The experimental results demonstrate that LLMs can effectively generate various optimization models, such as IP, CSP, VRP, KP, and JSP, and successfully solve ISTS problems of different scales based on given prompts. Across ten datasets of varying scales, the VRP model consistently excels in terms of maximum reward, particularly in handling large-scale tasks. And compared with the two classic algorithms in the field of satellite scheduling, SO and DO, it also shows significant advantages, It can be seen that the models and algorithms designed by LLMS have demonstrated strong adaptability and problem-solving capabilities.

Despite the significant advantages of LLMs in generating optimization models, especially in the generation of VRP models, some models still require adjustments during the solution process to meet all constraints. Particularly when dealing with complex constraints or large-scale tasks, there remains room for improvement in model performance. Future research will continue to optimize the model generation capabilities of LLMs, refine prompt design, and explore their application in larger-scale scenarios with more constraints, in order to further examine the accuracy and efficiency of LLMs in automated modeling for ISTS.

References

1. Xie, P., Du, Y., Yao, F., et al.: Literature review for autonomous scheduling technology of agile earth observation satellites. J. Astronaut. **40**(2), 127–138 (2019)
2. Shimada, M., Tadono, T., Rosenqvist, A.: Advanced land observing satellite (ALOS) and monitoring global environmental change. Proc. IEEE **98**(5), 780–799 (2009)
3. Wang, S., Zhao, L., Cheng, J., et al.: Task scheduling and attitude planning for agile earth observation satellite with intensive tasks. Aerosp. Sci. Technol. **90**, 23–33 (2019)
4. Chen, J., Wang, F., Chen, Y., et al.: A generalized bilevel optimization model for large-scale task scheduling in multiple agile earth observation satellites. Knowl. Based Syst. **309**, 112809 (2025)
5. Peng, G., Song, G., Liu, X.: Agile earth observation satellite scheduling with time-dependent profits. Oper. Res. Manag. Sci. **33**(8), 1–7 (2024)
6. Liu, X., Xu, Y., He, R., et al.: Satellite-oriented on-orbit service mission planning method. J. Natl. Univ. Defense Technol. **42**(5), 143–150 (2020)
7. Bensana, E., Lemaitre, M., Verfaillie, G.: Earth Obs. Satell. Manag. **4**(3), 293–299 (1999)

8. Cordeau, J., Laporte, G.: Maximizing the value of an earth observation satellite orbit. J. Oper. Res. Soc. **56**(8), 962–968 (2005)
9. Cordeau, J., Laporte, G., Mercier, A.: A unified tabu search heuristic for vehicle routing problems with time windows. J. Oper. Res. Soc. **52**(8), 928–936 (2001)
10. Vasquez, M., Hao, J.: A 'logic-constrained' knapsack formulation and a taboo algorithm for the daily photograph scheduling of an earth observation satellite. Comput. Optim. Appl. **20**(2), 137–157 (2001)
11. Hall, N., Magazine, M.: Maximizing the value of a space mission. Eur. J. Oper. Res. **78**(2), 224–241 (1994)
12. Wang, Y., Li, Q., Dai, Z., et al.: Current status and trends in large language modeling research. Chin. J. Eng. **46**(8), 1411–1425 (2024)
13. OpenAl. ChatGPT[EB/OL], https://openai.com/chatgpt, last accessed 2025/1/23
14. GPT-4 technical repor[EB/01], https://arxiv.org/abs/2303.08774, last accessed 2025/1/23
15. A survey on evaluation of large language models[EB/01], https://arxiv.org/abs/2307.03109v2, last accessed 2025/1/23
16. Huang, J.: From prompt engineering to generative artificial intelligence for large models: the state of the art and perspective. Chin. J. Intell. Sci. Technol. **6**(2), 115–133 (2024)
17. Chen, S., Liu, D., He, J.: CodeBERT-based language model for design pattern. Chin. J. Intell. Sci. Technol. **50**(12), 75–81 (2023)
18. Sun, H., Li, H., Zhao, M.: Selection of agile satellite observation period based on greedy-linear programming algorithm. Radio Eng. **48**(9), 803–809 (2018)
19. Wang, D., Lu, F., Zhang, B.: Survey on prompt engineering in large language model. Comput. Syst. Appl. **34**(1), 1–10 (2025)
20. Liu, X., Laporte, G., Chen, Y., et al.: An adaptive large neighborhood search metaheuristic for agile satellite scheduling with time-dependent transition time. Comput. Oper. Res. **86**, 41–53 (2017)

Classifying Disaster Tweets Using Natural Language Processing and Machine Learning

XueQi Wang[1] and Shengkun Xie[2(✉)]

[1] Data Science and Analytics, Toronto Metropolitan University, Toronto, ON M5B 2K3, Canada
kami.wang@torontomu.ca

[2] Global Management Studies, TRSM, Toronto Metropolitan University, Toronto, ON M5B 2K3, Canada
shengkun.xie@torontomu.ca

Abstract. Social media and its network data play an important role in modern life, particularly as a key platform and data resource for emergency response. Using machine learning models, this work aims to classify tweets as disaster-related or irrelevant, addressing the critical challenge of filtering genuine disaster information from noisy content on Twitter. The research integrates advanced feature extraction techniques, including Word2Vec and GloVe, with a hybrid approach combining Bidirectional Encoder Representations from Transformers (BERT), Support Vector Machine (SVM), and bagging techniques to enhance classification accuracy. It also compares classification performance across different feature extraction methods and machine learning classifiers. To ensure the reliability of the classification results, model performance is rigorously evaluated using a 5-fold cross-validation approach, with key model performance metrics like accuracy, precision, recall, as well as F1-score. The findings obtained from this study demonstrate that BERT as a feature extraction method effectively captures contextual information, SVM achieves strong performance in high-dimensional feature spaces, and bagging improves model robustness, resulting in superior classification performance for the data set we considered. The study show that the proposed approach outperforms other model combinations, achieving significant improvements in accuracy, recall, and F1-score. The proposed method also significantly enhances the reliability of social media information, providing emergency responders with accurate, real-time data during disasters, thus facilitating timely and effective response efforts.

Keywords: Machine Learning · Natural Language Processing · Disaster Tweets · Text Mining · Social Media

1 Introduction

Social media platforms such as Twitter (now rebranded as X, but referred to as Twitter in this document for consistency) have become integral to global communication, particularly during crises and disasters. With its real-time updates

X. Ding and Y. Dong (Eds.): CLNLP 2025, CCIS 2775, pp. 238–245, 2026.
https://doi.org/10.1007/978-981-95-4788-3_22

and extensive reach, Twitter serves as a valuable tool for disseminating information and enhancing situational awareness during emergencies. However, the immense volume of data generated on the platform every second poses a significant challenge in distinguishing genuine disaster-related information from irrelevant content. Accurately classifying disaster-related tweets is crucial, as timely and reliable information can save lives, allocate resources efficiently, and support effective decision-making by authorities. Conversely, the misclassification of tweets can cause the spread of wrong information, inducing panic and potentially resulting in misguided emergency responses. This underscores the necessity for robust and dependable machine learning models capable of identifying the content related to disaster accurately, amidst the vast and dynamic flow of social media posts.

Recent development within the areas of machine learning (ML) and natural language processing (NLP) have introduced innovative approaches to address the challenges of disaster-related tweet classification [1,2]. Techniques such as Word2Vec and GloVe [3] have transformed how textual data is represented and processed, enabling improved understanding of linguistic nuances and context. Furthermore, BERT (Bidirectional Encoder Representations from Transformers) [4], as typical deep learning models, when integrated with architectures like GRU (Gated Recurrent Units) [5], have demonstrated significant potential in various text mining, including the identification of disaster-related tweets. Despite these advancements, the classification of disaster tweets remains a complex task due to several factors. The informal nature of social media communication—characterized by slang, abbreviations, and emojis—poses significant challenges for traditional NLP techniques. Moreover, the context-dependent nature of disaster-related content further complicates the classification process. Multilingual content adds another layer of complexity [6], as disasters often have global implications, eliciting responses in multiple languages. Beyond technical challenges, ethical considerations play a critical role in this domain. The sensitive nature and inherent biases in disaster-related information raise important questions about privacy, consent, and the ethical use of social network data for research and emergency response [7]. Resolving these challenges necessitates a balanced approach that not only advances technical capabilities but also ensures responsible and ethical practices in leveraging social media for disaster management.

This research aims to address the challenges of classifying disaster tweets by evaluating and enhancing machine learning models. Through the use of NLP techniques and the integration of novel model architectures, this study seeks to improve the accuracy and reliability of disaster-related information extracted from social media. Specifically, it focuses on combining Support Vector Machines (SVM) with BERT models, building upon the foundational work in [8] and other recent advancements in the field. The research contributes to a deeper understanding of how social media, as a widely accessible public platform, can be effectively utilized during disasters. By developing robust tools, this study seeks to support emergency responders and researchers who rely on social media data for disaster management and response. The findings have the potential to enhance the use of social media data as a critical resource, facilitating more effective and timely disaster responses and ultimately improving outcomes during emergencies.

2 Methods and Materials

The dataset we considered in this work, sourced from Kaggle's "Natural Language Processing with Disaster Tweets" competition, consists of 10,876 hand-labeled tweets. It is partitioned into a training set containing 7,613 entries and a testing set comprising 3,263 entries. Each tweet entry includes an ID, keyword, location, text, and a target label indicating whether the tweet is related to a disaster (1) or not (0). The training set, which contains nearly twice as many entries as the testing set, provides a robust foundation for developing a reliable model. Within the training data, the target variable is relatively balanced, with 3,271 tweets classified as disaster-related and 4,342 as non-disaster-related, ensuring adequate representation of both classes for model training. Figure 1 shows distribution of top 10 locations for both training and test data sets.

This study aims to evaluate machine learning models for accurately classifying tweets as either related to real disasters or unrelated ones. By leveraging advanced NLP techniques and machine learning methods, this research seeks to enhance the reliability and efficiency of information dissemination during disaster events. To achieve this, three different algorithmic model combinations will be evaluated to address the linguistic complexities [9] of tweets, including slang and informal expressions. The performance of these models will be statistically analyzed to identify the suitable approach for classifying disaster-related tweets. The experimental process consists of four key stages: data preprocessing, feature extraction, model development, and model evaluation.

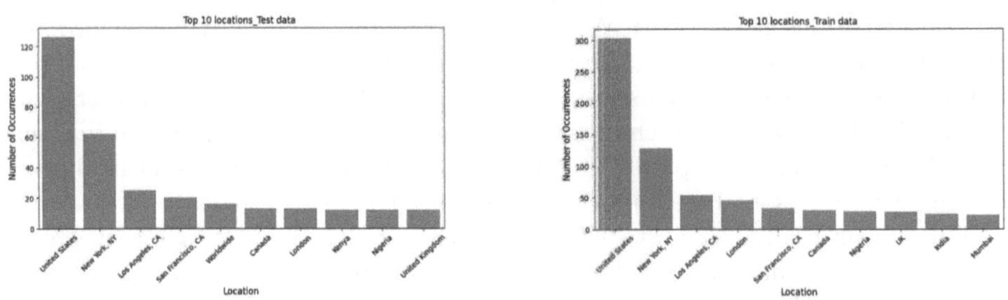

a)Training Data Top 10 Locations b)Testing Data Top 10 Locations

Fig. 1. Top 10 Locations from Training & Testing data

2.1 Data Preprocessing

In this stage, several text-cleaning techniques are applied to improve the quality of the dataset. First, noise such as URLs is removed and replaced with a designated <URL> token to preserve sentence structure. All text is converted to lowercase to maintain consistency. Next, text normalization techniques are implemented, including the replacement of emojis with corresponding tokens and the application of stemming or lemmatization to reduce words to their base forms. Additionally, the PySpellChecker library is used to correct misspelled words, further enhancing text quality for model training.

To ensure robust experimental results, the dataset is randomly partitioned into training and testing sets, with 80% of data allocated for training and 20% of data reserved for testing. Within the training set, a 5-fold cross-validation approach is used to ensure model stability and reliability of the results. This technique involves dividing the training set into five subsets, where each subset is used once as a validation set while the remaining subsets form the training data (Leave one out approach). The model is trained on these subsets iteratively, ensuring a more generalized and reliable classification performance.

2.2 Feature Extraction

To represent disaster-related tweets effectively, multiple feature extraction techniques are explored: Term Frequency-Inverse Document Frequency (TF-IDF) [10], Word2Vec, GloVe, and BERT embeddings. These methods differ in their ability to capture contextual relationships and semantic meaning within text data. TF-IDF is chosen for its effectiveness in representing text-based frequency patterns, but it lacks the ability to capture contextual relationships between words. Word2Vec and GloVe are included because of their ability to capture semantic relationships and contextual dependencies within text, making them suitable for understanding conversational data in tweets. BERT embeddings are considered due to their superior contextual understanding and pre-training on large-scale datasets, making them highly effective for complex text classification tasks. To optimize feature extraction, text preprocessing parameters are systematically varied. The goal is to identify the best combination of feature engineering and preprocessing techniques that maximize classification performance.

2.3 Model Development

In the initial experiment, three classifiers, SVM,Long Short-Term Memory (LSTM) networks, and Gated Recurrent Units (GRU), are trained. This selection combines classical machine learning models and deep learning architectures. SVM is chosen due to its strong performance on small to medium-sized datasets, making it a robust baseline. GRU and LSTM are considered for their ability to capture dependencies in sequential text data, particularly in handling long-term contextual relationships within tweets. However, these models are computationally more expensive compared to traditional approaches. To further enhance model robustness, ensemble learning techniques are explored. Bagging and boosting methods are investigated to leverage the strengths of different classifiers while reducing variance and bias. Bagging involves model training using subsets of the dataset and averaging their predicted values, thereby reducing variance and improving model stability. Boosting, in contrast, trains models sequentially, where each model corrects the errors of the previous one, leading to improved overall performance but potentially increasing computational cost.

For this study, bagging is selected due to its effectiveness in reducing variance and mitigating overfitting model risks. By combining multiple classifiers (SVM, GRU, and LSTM) within an ensemble framework, the final model aims to achieve improved generalization and reliability in disaster tweet classification.

2.4 Model Evaluation

The performance of the classifiers in distinguishing disaster-related tweets is assessed by key evaluation metrics, including accuracy, precision, recall, and F1-score. To analyze classification results, a confusion matrix, measuring the number of true positives, false positives, true negatives, and false negatives, is employed. To ensure a fair and reliable comparison of different algorithms, a consistent data-splitting strategy is applied. Additionally, 5-fold cross-validation is performed within the training set to improve the reliability and robustness of the results. Each model is trained using the training data and subsequently evaluated on the test dataset, based on the defined performance metrics. Finally, the results are systematically analyzed to identify the model that best meets both performance and practical requirements for disaster tweet classification. In the next section, the findings are comprehensively summarized to facilitate clear communication and interpretation of the outcomes.

3 Results and Analysis

We first compare the performance of four feature extraction methods, with the results summarized in Table 1. The analysis reveals that GloVe performed well in terms of accuracy (i.e., 0.780) and precision (i.e., 0.813). However, BERT achieved the best overall balance across all metrics (i.e., accuracy of 0.783 and F1-score of 0.740). BERT's outstanding performance may be due to its deep bidirectional architecture and pre-training on large text corpora, which enable it to capture contextual nuances and semantic relationships more effectively than other methods. This ability allows BERT to understand complex language patterns and generalize well to our specific classification task. Given its strong performance across all metrics, particularly its high recall and F1-score, BERT emerges as the most suitable choice for tweets classification.

In order to find a better classifier for further model development, we start from using several classifiers, including SVM, GRU, and LSTM.

The results of applying each classifier to the training dataset are presented in Table 2. Accuracy measures the overall correctness of the model, while precision indicates the proportion of predicted positive cases that were actually correct. Recall reflects the proportion of actual positive cases, and the F1-score provides a balanced measure. To ensure the reliability and robustness of the model, these four metrics were computed using a 5-fold cross-validation approach. This

Table 1. Performance of Feature Extraction Techniques With SVM Classifier

	TF-IDF	Word2Vec	GloVe	BERT
Accuracy	0.726	0.641	0.780	0.783
Precision	0.785	0.595	0.813	0.764
Recall	0.503	0.519	0.634	0.719
F1-score	0.610	0.554	0.712	0.740

Table 2. Classifier Performance With BERT Embedding.

	SVM	LSTM	GRU
Accuracy	0.821	0.792	0.775
Precision	0.857	0.800	0.792
Recall	0.700	0.689	0.647
F1-Score	0.771	0.740	0.712

method helps assess the model's stability, reducing the risk of performance fluctuations due to data partitioning. The results presented in Table 2 clearly indicate that SVM outperforms both LSTM and GRU. With an accuracy of 0.821, SVM demonstrates the highest classification correctness among the three models. Additionally, SVM achieves a precision of 85.7%, meaning that 85.7% of the samples predicted as positive are indeed positive, which is also the highest among the models. In terms of recall, SVM attains a score of 0.700, correctly identifying 70% of actual positive samples. While LSTM and GRU are effective in capturing long-term dependencies in text data, their overall performance in this dataset is slightly lower than that of SVM. Table 3 shows the bagging method perform better than boosting when it come to a ensemble model with BERT and SVM. The overall model performance comparison is presented in Fig. 2. These findings suggest that while deep learning models like GRU and LSTM may benefit from additional training data, SVM is the most effective model for the data we considered.

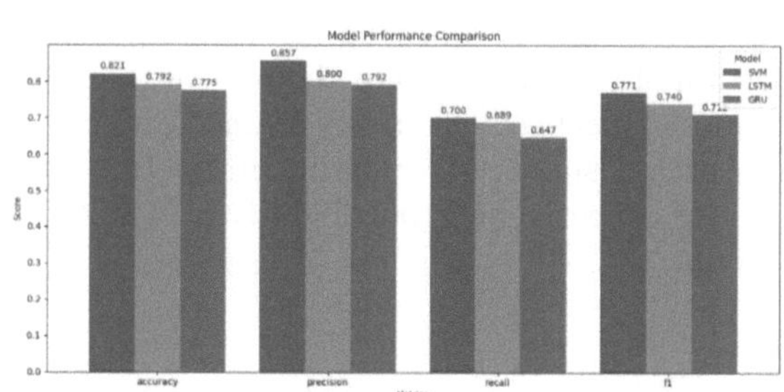

Fig. 2. Model Performance Comparison with three Models.

Table 3. Performance of Ensemble Model With BERT and SVM Classifier

	Bagging	Boosting
F1-Score	0.776	0.747

After comparing the models, we evaluated whether bagging or boosting would be the most effective enhancement technique. Our results indicate that a hybrid model combining SVM with bagging outperforms other approaches across all four evaluation metrics. SVM provides strong classification capabilities, while bagging enhances generalization and robustness, leading to improved performance—particularly in classifying disaster-related social media tweets. Although BERT demonstrated advantages in processing complex text and capturing contextual meaning, prior literature suggests that SVM combined with bagging has a higher potential for optimal performance in this specific task. Considering all evaluation metrics, particularly the high recall and F1-score, we selected SVM with bagging as the most suitable approach for disaster-related tweet classification. This model not only achieves high accuracy but also effectively handles large datasets while maintaining reliability and stability.

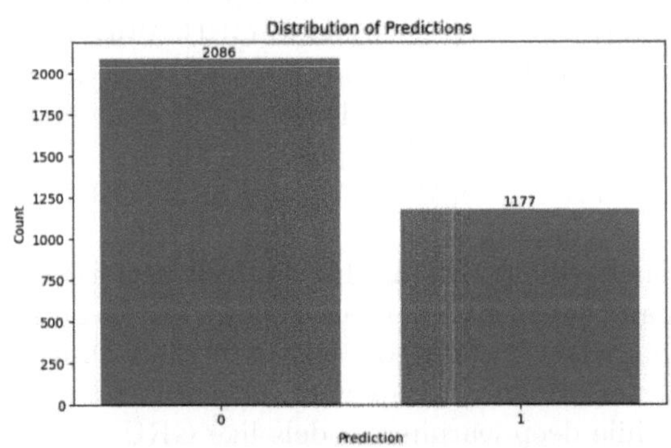

Fig. 3. Distribution of Predictions for Testing data

Figure 3 presents the results of applying the combined model to the testing dataset. The proportion of test data closely aligns with that of the training data, suggesting that the model has been effectively trained and performs consistently. This alignment indicates a successful experimental setup, providing a reliable assessment of the model's effectiveness, particularly in classifying disaster-related content on social media.

4 Conclusion

In this study, we explored and evaluated different machine learning models for classification of tweets data as either disaster-related or not. By leveraging machine learning models and natural language processing techniques, we improved the efficiency and reliability of processing and disseminating disaster-related information on social media. Our findings indicate that the combination of BERT embeddings, SVM, and bagging techniques outperform other combination of methods that we considered. This hybrid approach not only outperformed other models in classifying disaster-related tweets but also demonstrated greater robustness, making it applicable for real-world applications, particularly in event detection and disaster response systems. For future research, the proposed method can be extended to other social media platforms or applied to different types of textual data beyond disaster-related content, allowing for broader applicability.

References

1. Parilla-Ferrer, B.E., Fernandez, P.L., Ballena, J.T.: Automatic classification of disaster-related tweets. In: Proceedings International Conference on Innovative Engineering Technologies (ICIET), vol. 62 (2014)
2. Xukun, L., Caragea, D.: Improving disaster-related tweet classification with a multimodal approach. In: ISCRAM 2020 Conference Proceedings–17th International Conference on Information Systems for Crisis Response and Management (2020)
3. Rakshit, P., Sarkar, A.: A supervised deep learning-based sentiment analysis by the implementation of word2vec and glove embedding techniques. Multimedia Tools Appl., 1–34 (2024)
4. Alaparthi, S., Mishra, M.: Bidirectional encoder representations from transformers (BERT): a sentiment analysis odyssey. arXiv preprint arXiv:2007.01127 (2020)
5. Dey, R., Salem, F.M.: Gate-variants of gated recurrent unit (GRU) neural networks. In: 2017 IEEE 60th International Midwest Symposium on Circuits and Systems (MWSCAS), pp. 1597–1600. IEEE (2017)
6. Gracia, J., Montiel-Ponsoda, E., Cimiano, P., Gómez-Pérez, A., Buitelaar, P., McCrae, J.: Challenges for the multilingual web of data. J. Web Semant. **11**, 63–71 (2012)
7. Townsend, L., Wallace, C.: The ethics of using social media data in research: a new framework. In: The Ethics of Online Research, pp. 189–207. Emerald Publishing Limited (2017)
8. Horne, L., Matti, M., Pourjafar, P., Wang, Z.: GruBERT: a GRU-based method to fuse bert hidden layers for twitter sentiment analysis. In: Proceedings of the 1st Conference of the Asia-Pacific Chapter of the Association for Computational Linguistics and the 10th International Joint Conference on Natural Language Processing: Student Research Workshop, pp. 130–138 (2020)
9. Dahl, Ö.: The growth and maintenance of linguistic complexity (2004)
10. Christian, H., Agus, M.P., Suhartono, D.: Single document automatic text summarization using term frequency-inverse document frequency (TF-IDF). ComTech: Comput. Math. Eng. Appl. **7**(4), 285–294 (2016)

A Survey on Retrieval-Augmented Generation Technology in Large Language Models

Jiaqi Guo(✉), Heyu Yang, and Qianyi Liu

China Mobile Digitization Technologies, Beijing 100080, China
guojiaqi2@cmdi.chinamobile.com

Abstract. In recent years, Retrieval-Augmented Generation (RAG) technology has effectively mitigated the "hallucination" phenomenon and knowledge obsolescence issues in Large Language Models (LLMs) caused by reliance on static training data through dynamic integration of external knowledge bases. This paper systematically reviews the core advancements and challenges in RAG tecnology. First, we clarify the fundamental theoretical framework of RAG, which consists of collaborative retrieval and generation modules: The retrieval module dynamically extracts relevant knowledge from heterogeneous data sources through semantic mapping, query optimization, and multi-strategy retrieval, while the generation module leverages pre-trained language models combined with re-ranking, context compression, and fusion strategies to produce high-quality text based on retrieval results. Second, we conduct in-depth analyses of critical technical challenges and solutions in the retrieval module, including data chunking techniques, query optimization methods, and retrieval strategies. Concurrently, we explore recent progress in retrieval result optimization and fusion mechanisms within the generation module. Finally, we identify current challenges in RAG technology, including insufficient retrieval-generation synergy, limited multimodal support, and privacy biases. Future research directions should focus on end-to-end joint optimization, multimodal expansion, and robustness enhancement. This paper provides theoretical references and practical guidance for systematic research and applications of RAG technology.

Keywords: Retrieval-Augmented Generation · Large Language Models · Knowledge Retrieval · Generation Optimization

1 Introduction

In recent years, the rapid development of deep learning and natural language processing technologies has driven technological innovations in LLMs, demonstrating exceptional capabilities in text generation, translation, and conversational tasks. However, the knowledge of LLMs primarily originates from static information encoded in training parameters, which imposes limitations in terms of restricted knowledge coverage and inadequate adaptability to dynamic domains. This reliance on static knowledge not only fails to meet the demand for real-time knowledge updates but also tends to

X. Ding and Y. Dong (Eds.): CLNLP 2025, CCIS 2775, pp. 246–265, 2026.
https://doi.org/10.1007/978-981-95-4788-3_23

generate erroneous or fabricated information, manifesting as the "hallucination" phenomenon. To address these challenges, RAG technology introduces external knowledge bases and efficient retrieval modules to provide dynamic knowledge support for LLMs, fundamentally mitigating their hallucination tendencies. The RAG architecture typically comprises two core components: a retrieval module responsible for dynamically extracting query-relevant information from external knowledge bases, and a generation module that synthesizes contextually appropriate, high-quality text based on retrieved results. This collaborative mechanism effectively achieves dynamic knowledge supplementation, demonstrating superior performance over standalone LLMs in both knowledge coverage and generation accuracy.

With the continuous advancement of research on RAG technology, scholars have proposed various improvement approaches, including data source selection, chunking strategies, and retrieval strategies for the retrieval module, as well as deep integration strategies between retrieval and generation. However, current research exhibits fragmented and diverse characteristics, lacking systematic summarization and analysis. This paper systematically organizes the theoretical framework and latest developments of RAG technology, conducts in-depth analysis of core technologies in both retrieval and generation modules, and explores their advantages and challenges. First, based on RAG's dual-module architecture, we elaborate key technical pathways including knowledge base construction, semantic retrieval, and query optimization. Second, we conduct comparative analyses of cutting-edge methods in the generation module such as re-ranking, context compression, and cross-modal fusion. Finally, we clearly identify the current limitations of RAG technology and propose perspectives on its future development trends and potential improvement directions.

2 RAG Technical Framework and Core Advantages

The core architecture of a RAG system primarily consists of two key components: a retrieval module and a generation module. These two components work collaboratively through efficient interaction mechanisms to complete the "retrieve-generate" workflow (see Fig. 1).

The retrieval module aims to accurately retrieve the most relevant information from extensive external knowledge bases based on user input queries, thereby providing real-time and dynamic knowledge support for the subsequent generation module. Its implementation process can be meticulously divided into the following steps:

1. **Knowledge Base Construction**: This phase involves preprocessing raw data, chunking the processed data, and building efficient information indexes to facilitate rapid retrieval operations.
2. **Semantic Mapping**: Vector models are employed to encode both input queries and knowledge base content into vector representations.
3. **Query Optimization**: Techniques such as semantic expansion or query rewriting are adopted to enhance query coverage and accuracy.
4. **Retrieval Strategy**: Efficient retrieval algorithms are designed to support real-time information retrieval.

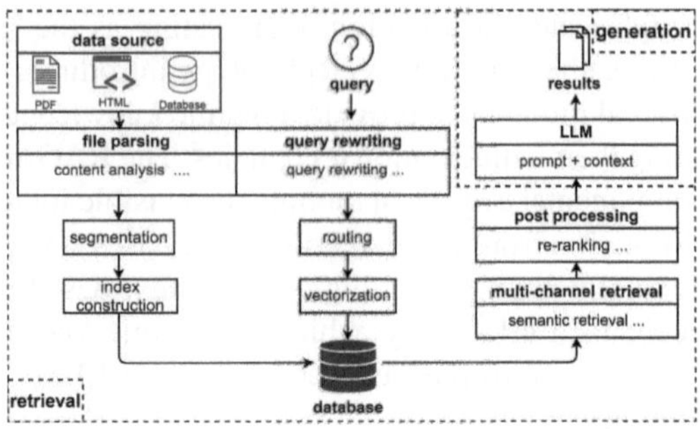

Fig. 1. Workflow diagram of a RAG system.

The generation module is responsible for synthesizing user queries with retrieval results to produce logically coherent and high-quality textual content. To achieve this, the generation module typically employs pre-trained generative models based on the Transformer architecture [1] (e.g., GPT-4 [2], Qwen [3], Gemini [4]) as its core generation engine. These models are widely applied to various text generation tasks due to their exceptional language comprehension and generation capabilities. To improve the accuracy of generated content, the generation module first performs reranking and compression filtering on retrieved results to further optimize the relevance and precision of input information. Additionally, researchers have explored multiple strategies to effectively integrate retrieved knowledge, including direct concatenation [5, 6] and cross-attention mechanism fusion [7].

Compared to standalone LLMs, RAG demonstrates significant technical advantages across multiple dimensions. First, in terms of knowledge breadth and real-time currency, RAG dynamically retrieves from external knowledge bases during content generation, enabling real-time integration of the latest and most relevant information. In contrast, LLMs are constrained by the timeliness and coverage limitations of their training data, making such real-time updates unattainable. Second, RAG exhibits marked improvements in content accuracy and credibility, as its retrieval mechanism provides high-quality information that effectively mitigates the risk of "hallucination" phenomena in generated content. Furthermore, RAG demonstrates exceptional scalability and flexibility - its external knowledge bases can be easily updated or expanded without requiring retraining of the generative model itself, which significantly enhances the system's adaptability and practical utility.

3 Key Technologies and Challenges of the Retrieval Module

In RAG systems, the retrieval module is tasked with precisely and efficiently identifying the most relevant information segments from vast external knowledge bases to provide foundational support for subsequent text generation tasks. This process relies on a series of sophisticated models and algorithms to ensure accurate comprehension of user query intent, thereby enabling swift and precise localization of pertinent information. Technically, the core components of the retrieval module encompass multiple critical aspects including data source selection, document chunking, query optimization, and retrieval strategies. This chapter conducts an in-depth examination of these key technical elements while systematically organizing the relevant literature pertaining to retrieval modules, as illustrated in Fig. 2.

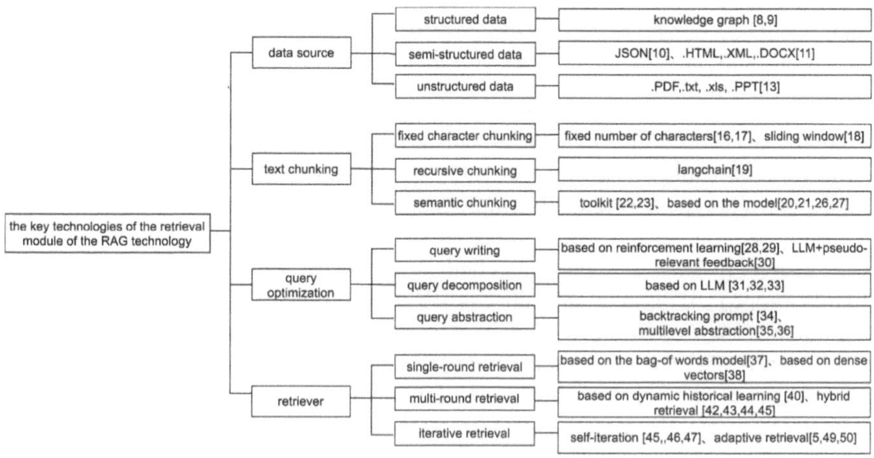

Fig. 2. Literature on key technologies of the RAG retrieval module.

3.1 Data Source

The integrity and quality of data sources directly impact the breadth of domain-specific knowledge coverage and information accuracy in RAG systems. Based on the organizational format and characteristics of textual data, data sources can be categorized into three primary types: structured, semi-structured, and unstructured. Selecting high-quality and appropriate data sources constitutes a fundamental step in enhancing the performance of RAG systems.

Structured Data. Structured data refers to information organized in highly standardized formats, typically stored in relational databases and efficiently retrievable through structured query languages like SQL. Particularly suitable for RAG applications requiring precise matching and rapid response, this tabular-organized data features columns representing specific fields (e.g., user ID, product name, date) and rows denoting individual records. While facilitating analysis, management, and efficient indexing/search operations - commonly seen in product databases, user repositories, and transaction records - its tabular format presents limitations in encapsulating complex nonlinear information, thus constraining complex QA task capabilities. Knowledge Graphs (KGs) offer an effective solution by transforming document information into entity-relationship networks for enhanced information connectivity. Darren Edge et al. [8] proposed a Graph RAG methodology that first extracts entities and relationships from source documents to construct a knowledge graph, subsequently partitioning it into tightly interconnected "communities." Leveraging LLMs to generate community summaries, this approach identifies relevant communities during user queries and utilizes corresponding summaries as contextual input for LLM-generated responses, thereby addressing the limitations of tabular data and existing RAG models in processing complex, globally-scoped queries. Guan X et al.'s [9] KGR method integrates LLMs with KGs to achieve automated fact verification and answer refinement without additional human intervention. Experimental results demonstrate KGR's effectiveness in reducing hallucination rates across three datasets and three distinct LLMs, significantly enhancing factual QA performance.

Semi-Structured Data. Semi-structured data is a flexible yet partially organized data form commonly represented in formats such as JSON and XML, capable of storing complex information while remaining efficiently processable through parsing tools. In RAG systems, this data type is frequently employed to store logs, emails, API responses, etc., which after parsing can provide comprehensive contextual information for generative models. However, such data presents challenges due to the absence of unified schema standards: preprocessing may introduce noise, and complex JSON parsing risks semantic loss or misinterpretation, ultimately affecting generation quality. Michael J. Mior et al. [10] proposed enhancing semantic parsing through LLMs and manually curated JSON Schema corpora, yet the high cost of manual annotation limits its scalability for large datasets. Hang Yang et al. [11] addressed multi-format processing challenges by integrating multiple open-source API parsing tools to convert formats including.html and.xml into.docx. Through a pipeline combining detectron2-powered element detection (titles, text, images, tables), cleaning functions, HTML storage, and GPT-4 Vision API-generated image descriptions, their approach effectively resolves heterogeneous format processing issues, providing high-quality data sources for RAG systems.

Unstructured Data. Unstructured data (text, images, audio, video, etc.), as the predominant information form on the internet, provides RAG systems with rich knowledge and real-time information [12]. However, their processing entails high complexity, requiring reliance on Natural Language Processing (NLP), Computer Vision (CV), and audio processing technologies. Taking PDF documents as an example, their diverse content elements and non-standardized layouts significantly increase information extraction complexity. S.S. Manathunga et al. [13] investigated the extraction of textual data from multi-source unstructured information through LLMs and embedding into vector spaces, thereby enhancing information retrieval efficiency. Nevertheless, critical challenges persist in RAG technology, including addressing semantic ambiguity in data, interpreting visual content, handling heterogeneity of data sources, as well as achieving accurate rapid processing and enabling large-scale applications amidst exponential data growth.

3.2 Text Chunking Technology

When processing large-scale semi-structured and unstructured textual data, chunking techniques effectively enhance system retrieval and generation efficiency by decomposing data into smaller, more content-focused segments(see Fig. 3). This approach simultaneously alleviates the context window [14, 15] limitations of LLMs, strengthening their capacity to capture and respond to information within constrained scopes. However, practical implementations face challenges including chunk size optimization, maintenance of cross-chunk information coherence, and boundary effect management. These require the development of chunking algorithms that account for textual characteristics and application scenarios to achieve optimal performance.

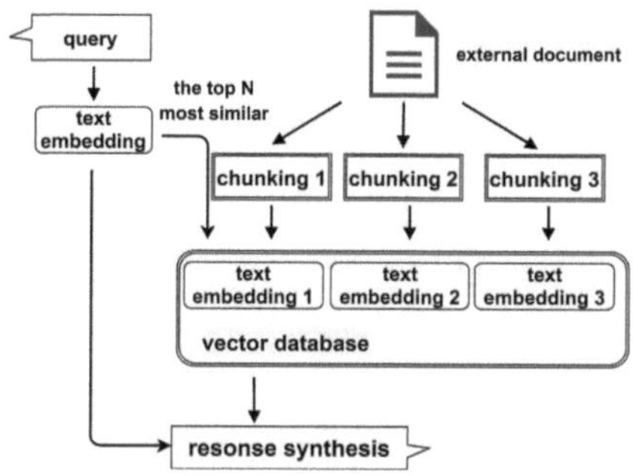

Fig. 3. The process of the chunking technology.

Fixed Character Chunking. The fixed-length chunking strategy [16, 17] divides text based on predefined character/word counts, often incorporating a sliding window mechanism with overlapping regions [18] to maintain contextual coherence and minimize information loss, as illustrated in Fig. 4. While this approach demonstrates implementation simplicity and supports parallel processing - making it particularly suitable for rapid handling of large-scale textual data - it presents notable limitations. The strategy tends to disregard semantic boundaries, potentially fragmenting coherent semantic units. The sliding window implementation introduces redundant information, increasing computational and storage overhead. Furthermore, when processing linguistically complex structures or texts with strong cross-chunk dependencies, it struggles to adequately capture global semantic context. Practical applications therefore require careful consideration of task-specific requirements to balance these trade-offs.

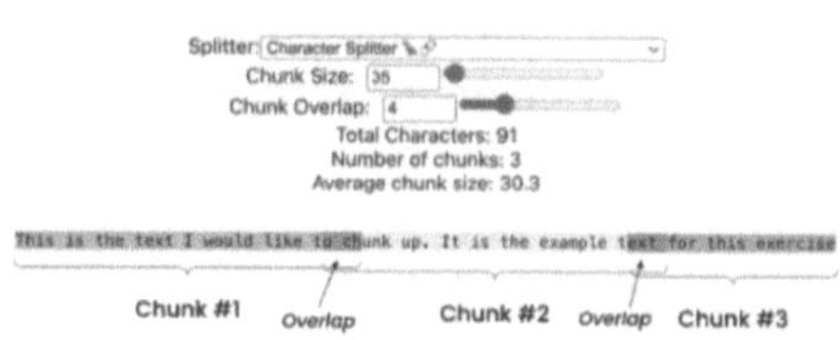

Fig. 4. Example of fixed character chunking with a sliding window.

Recursive Chunking Strategy. Recursive-based chunking strategy [19] recursively decomposes text by applying preset and alternative delimiters layer by layer until generating chunks that meet predefined size or structural criteria, as illustrated in Fig. 5. The primary advantage of this strategy lies in its effective preservation of semantic consistency and contextual coherence within text chunks. However, challenges persist including uneven chunk sizes potentially compromising system processing efficiency, and the risk of semantic fragmentation when handling complex long-form texts. The critical trade-off between maintaining textual logical continuity and optimizing processing efficiency remains to be further refined.

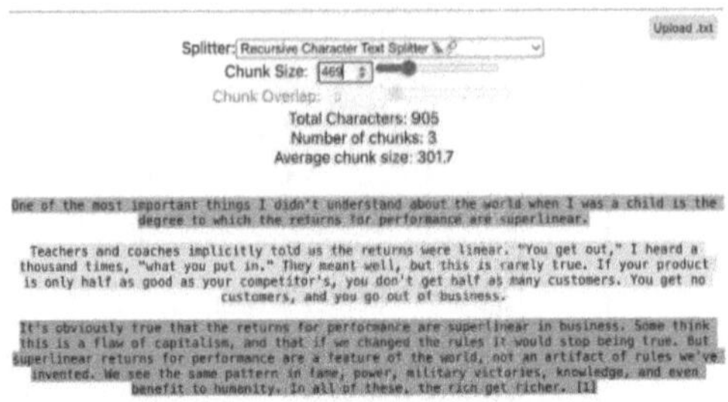

Fig. 5. Example of recursive chunking.

Structural Chunking Strategy. Structure-based chunking strategies are primarily employed to process text files with specific structural or syntactic features, including but not limited to HTML, Markdown, LaTeX, and Python code. These chunking approaches rely on format-specific identifiers or structural tags to preserve both structural integrity and logical coherence of segmented content. For instance, in Markdown documents, elements such as headers (#), list items (-), and blockquotes (>) can serve as chunking delimiters. This strategy effectively leverages inherent structural information within documents - including section headings, paragraphs, and lists - to define chunk boundaries, thereby ensuring maximal logical continuity and semantic consistency in text segmentation.

Semantic Chunking Strategy. Semantics-based chunking strategies [20, 21] ensure independent and coherent semantic units in text segmentation through two primary approaches. The first method employs natural paragraph segmentation using NLP tools like NLTK [22] and SpaCy [23] for automated processing. However, when handling long documents, this approach may compromise contextual coherence by neglecting cross-paragraph semantic connections. The second approach utilizes semantic similarity segmentation, where pre-trained word embedding models such as Word2Vec [24] and BERT [25] map text to high-dimensional semantic spaces for relationship analysis, more effectively preserving semantic consistency and contextual relevance. Furthermore, Michael Günther et al. [26] proposed a delayed chunking method that first converts long texts into token-level vector representations before segmentation, subsequently generating chunk vectors through average pooling - an approach that considers full-text information. LLM-based agent chunking strategies leverage the semantic parsing capabilities of LLMs to identify natural segmentation points, ensuring semantic coherence and information integrity while maintaining flexibility for complex texts. Jihao Zhao et al. [27] introduced "meta-chunking," an intermediate granularity between sentence and paragraph levels that groups semantically related sentences. This method dynamically adjusts chunk size and boundaries by combining LLMs with perplexity analysis techniques. Nevertheless, this strategy faces challenges including substantial computational resource consumption and ongoing model performance optimization requirements.

3.3 Query Optimization

Query optimization techniques refer to the process of refining the expression of user's original queries to enhance their precision or broaden their semantic coverage, which proves crucial for improving the quality of retrieval outcomes.

Query Rewriting. Query rewriting serves as a fundamental query optimization technique. At the basic level, it enhances the consistency and parsability of user queries through error correction, standardized terminology adoption, and supplementary contextual information expansion. For instance, rewriting "global warming causes" to "main causes of global warming and their impacts" enables access to broader research materials. On a more sophisticated level, this technique emphasizes contextual comprehension and deep learning technologies to decode user intent for query refinement. Ma et al. [28] developed a reinforcement learning feedback framework for training language model rewriters, implementing a two-phase approach: pseudo-dataset pre-training followed by policy gradient reinforcement learning optimization. Their reward mechanism incorporates both answer accuracy and hit rate metrics from language models, though limitations persist when applied to retrieval-augmented generation tasks. Yujing Wang et al. [29] proposed a dense reward feedback-based reinforcement learning method for rewriter optimization, with experimental validation demonstrating more stable and satisfactory generation outcomes. The HTGQE [30] approach, integrating LLMs with pseudo-relevance feedback technology, significantly enhances query effectiveness in open-domain question answering systems, particularly demonstrating superior performance in addressing long-tail problem resolution.

Query Decomposition. When handling complex user queries, decomposing them into simple answerable subproblems constitutes a critical strategy for enhancing retrieval accuracy. As illustrated in Fig. 6, the process involves three key steps: first leveraging LLMs to derive subquestions from the original query, then independently executing the RAG pipeline for each subquestion, and ultimately synthesizing subproblem solutions into a comprehensive response. In related research: Denny Zhou et al. [31] proposed decomposing original queries through LLM-prompted question parsing, progressively incorporating prior Q&A contexts into current prompts during subproblem resolution to achieve progressive problem-solving. Zhaorun Chen et al. [32] developed the self-supervised framework AutoPRM, which integrates a question decomposition model with reinforcement learning to achieve granularity-controllable decomposition and iterative optimization of primary queries. Chi-Min Chan et al. [33] end-to-end trained a 7B Llama2 model capable of dynamically decomposing, rephrasing, and disambiguating queries based on their complexity and semantic structures, significantly improving retrieval precision.

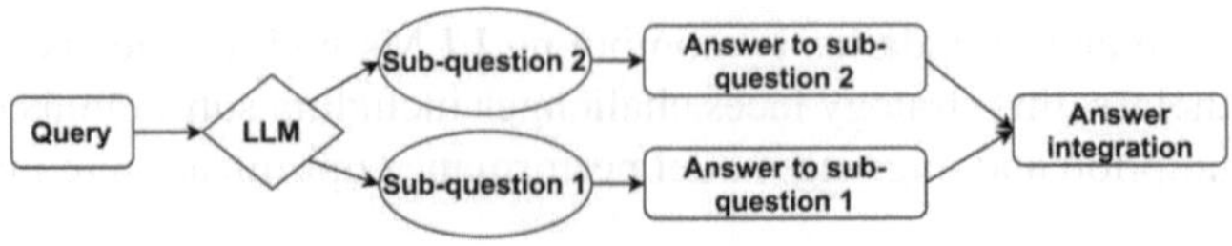

Fig. 6. Sub-problem query strategy.

Query Abstraction. When handling complex multi-step queries, simply decomposing the problem sequentially often fails to yield accurate solutions. Researchers typically adopt a more macroscopic perspective by abstracting problems to higher cognitive levels, thereby reducing error risks in intermediate processing stages [34]. For instance, backtracking prompting constructs high-level questions encompassing background knowledge to guide models' attention to essential aspects, subsequently combining original queries to enable LLMs to respond within appropriate theoretical frameworks. Huaixiu Steven Zheng et al. [34] developed the "Step-Back Prompting" technique, which prompts LLMs to first derive high-level conceptual questions and retrieve relevant factual knowledge, then reason about original problem solutions based on these established facts. Silin Gao et al. [35] employed fine-tuned LLMs to generate reasoning chains containing abstract placeholders, subsequently invoking external tools to acquire domain-specific knowledge for placeholder substitution before materializing the reasoning process. Ruixin Hong et al. [36] proposed the "Abstraction-of-Thought (AoT)" method that explicitly integrates multi-level abstractions in reasoning, prompting LLMs to engage in abstract-level contemplation before concrete problem-solving.

3.4 Retriever

In RAG systems, complex tasks impose higher demands on the accuracy and flexibility of information acquisition, necessitating the development of more intelligent and efficient retrieval strategies. Retrievers can be categorized into three strategic types based on their operational mechanisms: single-step, iterative, and multi-round retrieval. Each approach demonstrates distinct advantages in enhancing the relevance and depth of retrieved information, with specific comparative analyses presented in Table 1.

Single-Round Retrieval. Single-round retrieval necessitates the identification of all relevant information within a single query iteration. As it eliminates the need for multi-round interactions, this approach imposes higher demands on retrieval algorithms in terms of precision and recall. The BM25 [37] algorithm, grounded in the bag-of-words model, computes similarity rankings through statistical features such as term frequency (TF) and inverse document frequency (IDF). While it excels in keyword matching scenarios, it suffers from inherent limitations including lexical mismatch and constrained semantic comprehension. To address these challenges, dense vector-based retrieval strategies have emerged. For instance, DPR [38] employs dual-tower encoders to encode queries and documents into dense vector representations, achieving semantic relevance matching through cosine similarity computation and efficient nearest neighbor search [39]. This paradigm enables semantic similarity-based retrieval even in the

Table 1. Comparison and summary of retrieval strategies.

Method	Advantage	Weakness
Single-round retrieval	1. Simple to implement and convenient for rapid deployment 2. Fast response and is suitable for time-sensitive scenarios 3. Low cost and occupies few computing power resources	1. The accuracy is relatively low when dealing with complex and ambiguous queries 2. The capabilities of deep semantic understanding and information integration are limited
Multi-round retrieval	1. Can solve complex or multi-level queries 2. Enhance the comprehensiveness and relevance of the generated results 3. Combine the characteristics of different retrieval intensities, and the retrieval method is flexible	1. Capable of solving complex or multi-level queries 2. Retrieval results with different granularities increase the difficulty of information screening 3. The system design and implementation are complex, which increases the computational overhead
Iterative retrieval	1. Dynamically adjust the retrieval strategy and intelligently determine the retrieval timing 2. Filter out irrelevant documents and enhance the precision of the generated content 3. Avoid unnecessary frequent retrievals and reduce the response time	1. Requires complex algorithms and additional computing resources 2. The effect depends on the model's accurate understanding of the context 3. Inaccurate retrieval judgment may lead to the omission of key information

absence of keyword matches, demonstrating superior performance in practical RAG system development.

Multi-round Retrieval. Multi-round retrieval enhances search accuracy through interactive mechanisms, yet faces challenges including retrieval deviation caused by shifting user intent and error accumulation. To address these issues, Feiyuan Zhang et al. [40] proposed the DH-RAG model, which achieves efficient retrieval through two core modules and a dynamic database: The Historical Learning Query Reconstruction Module enriches queries by integrating standard knowledge bases with dynamic historical information, subsequently feeding enhanced queries to LLMs for response generation. Post-interaction, the Dynamic Historical Information Update Module refreshes the database with new responses to adapt to evolving user intent. Hybrid retrieval methods [41–43] dynamically adjust retrieval granularity for enhanced flexibility: Structured queries employ fine-grained strategies to maintain precision, while complex natural language queries utilize coarse-grained approaches to capture deeper semantics. Exemplified by the GPT-FedRec system [44], this approach combines ID-based retrieval for tracking user behavior and identifying long-term preferences with textual retrieval for semantic element parsing. Through its multi-tiered framework, the system effectively balances persistent interests with immediate needs, delivering personalized and precise retrieval outcomes.

Iterative Retrieval. Iterative Retrieval [45, 46] is a method that automatically optimizes retrieval results through multiple search iterations, focusing on system-internal optimization rather than user interaction. This approach proves particularly effective in scenarios with suboptimal initial query outcomes or when precise information needs to be extracted from massive datasets. The core of this approach lies in determining the optimal timing and content for retrieval. For instance, Guangzhi Xiong et al. [47] developed the i-MedRAG method, which leverages LLMs to iteratively generate subsequent queries based on historical information. These queries are processed through a RAG system, enabling progressive refinement of both retrieval accuracy and answer generation quality, thereby significantly enhancing performance in complex medical question-answering tasks. Traditional RAG systems that integrate all retrieved documents for generation exhibit inherent limitations (as not all documents contribute value) [48]. Moreover, given that LLMs inherently possess substantial knowledge reserves, not all queries require retrieval augmentation. To address the latency issues caused by excessive retrieval operations, researchers have proposed adaptive retrieval strategies: Shi-Qi Yanet al. [5] introduced CRAG to assess relevance scores and categorize retrieval outcomes; Zhengbao Jiang et al. [49] designed an active retrieval strategy that employs prediction models to generate potential sentences as dynamic queries; Weihang Su et al. [50] developed the DRAGIN framework, which adaptively determines retrieval timing and methods based on LLMs' real-time requirements. These innovations collectively optimize the collaborative efficiency between retrieval and generation processes.

4 Key Technologies and Challenges of the Generation Module

The generation module produces high-quality text based on the query input and knowledge retrieved by the retrieval module, whose performance directly impacts the accuracy and coherence of generated results, as well as the practical application effectiveness of RAG technology. This chapter discusses the topic from two key perspectives - critical technologies and main challenges - while systematically reviewing relevant literature (as illustrated in Fig. 7).

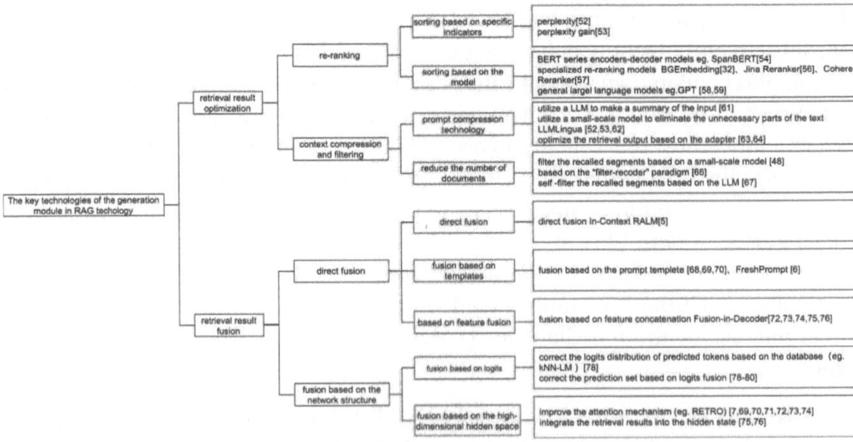

Fig. 7. Literature on key technologies of the generation module.

4.1 Retrieval Result Optimization

Re-ranking. As knowledge bases scale up, redundant information can interfere with the generation outcomes of LLMs, while excessively long contexts may lead to the "lost-in-the-middle" phenomenon [15]. Constrained by the capabilities of text embedding models, the quality of retrieved semantic vector segments may degrade. Moreover, during vector knowledge base construction, text embeddings typically lack query context and only generate generalized average embedding representations, which fail to fully capture the specific semantic requirements of queries. To address these challenges, reranking techniques have been introduced into retrieval workflows. These methods enhance LLMs' comprehension of relevant content and generation quality through secondary analysis and reordering of preliminary retrieval results [51].

RAG systems require filtering and reranking after acquiring the top-k text chunks: Rule-based reranking methods rely on domain knowledge and expert-defined rules, offering high interpretability and controllability. However, their effectiveness is constrained by rule quality and applicability. While most systems rank documents using retriever relevance scores, some studies employ metrics like perplexity and perplexity gain as criteria [52, 53].

Model-based reranking approaches leverage machine learning/deep learning techniques to identify complex interaction patterns between queries and documents through historical training data, enabling more accurate relevance assessment. These include BERT-family models like SpanBERT [54], BGEmbedding [55], Jina Reranker [56], Cohere Reranker [57], and GPT-based solutions [58, 59]. Consequently, hybrid systems often combine rule-based and data-driven methods to enhance flexibility, adaptability, and retrieval performance.

Concurrently, LLM-based reranking has emerged as a prominent trend, with current methodologies focusing on three key aspects: 1) Supervised fine-tuning of LLMs for specialized reranking tasks; 2) Implementation of prompt optimization strategies to guide task execution; and 3) Utilization of LLM-generated data to augment training sets and improve model capabilities.

Context Compression and Filtering. In RAG scenarios, lengthy inputs lead to significantly increased processing costs for LLMs. Prompt compression techniques aim to shorten input length while preserving critical information, thereby reducing inference costs and improving efficiency. Relevant research includes: Gilbert et al. [60] demonstrated that compressed text can still enable LLMs to effectively reconstruct source code while maintaining functional accuracy; Alexis Chevalier et al. [61] proposed using LLMs to convert long texts into compact summaries or vector representations as input; LLMLingua [53, 62, 63] employs smaller language models to detect and remove insignificant tokens, achieving a balance between textual integrity and compression ratio; Other studies utilize LLMs to assess text chunk utility, optimizing retrieval outputs through reward mechanisms, while RECOMP trains information condensers through contrastive learning [64].

On the other hand, reducing document quantity can enhance model answer accuracy [65]. Related research improves recall quality by pretraining specialized small language models (SLMs) to filter erroneous retrieval texts; Ma et al. [66] proposed a "filter-then-rerank" paradigm that combines SLMs for filtering with LLMs for reranking complex samples, significantly enhancing performance in information extraction tasks. Additionally, enabling LLMs to evaluate retrieved content before generating answers proves to be a simple yet effective approach. For instance, in Chatlaw [67], LLMs assess the relevance of cited legal provisions through self-suggestion mechanisms.

4.2 Retrieval Result Fusion

Direct Fusion. Directly concatenating retrieved results with input queries serves as a simple yet effective fusion strategy, termed "In-Context RALM" by Ori Ram, Yoav Levine et al. [5]. This method prepends retrieved documents to the language model input sequence without requiring additional training or model modifications. It demonstrates significant performance improvements across various model scales and corpora, achieving effects equivalent to increasing model parameters by 2–3 times. However, challenges persist regarding information redundancy, noise accumulation, and compromised generation efficiency/quality caused by excessive input length. Another direct fusion [68–70] approach employs carefully designed prompting strategies. For instance, Tu Vu et al. [6] developed the FreshPrompt method, which standardizes retrieved information formatting while providing demonstration examples. The Fusion-in-Decoder framework [71] concatenates encoded retrieval results with input features as generator input. Subsequent studies [72–76] have further optimized knowledge representation through joint adjustment of retrievers and encoders [77]. Although these straightforward fusion methods offer implementation convenience and easy integration, they face inherent limitations including redundant information propagation, noise accumulation, and potential truncation of valuable content due to sequence length constraints.

Fusion Based on Network Structure. The retrieval fusion methods based on network architectures primarily include logits-based fusion and high-dimensional hidden space fusion. In logits-based fusion, generative models incorporate retrieval information through logits during decoding, with common approaches involving either simple summation of logits or model-assisted calculation of generation probabilities. For instance, the kNN-LM [78] model combines pre-trained language models with k-nearest neighbor search, where it retrieves k relevant neighbors from a datastore when generating candidate words and probability distributions, thereby enhancing the output. Related studies [78–80] have demonstrated that integrating the logits of retrieved knowledge into prediction sets improves model generalization and robustness. Regarding high-dimensional hidden space fusion, the attention-based fusion methodology in RAG technology achieves enhanced integration by combining retrieval results with contextual information from the generative model through sophisticated attention mechanisms. This approach significantly improves the relevance and quality of generated content, particularly demonstrating superior performance in handling complex problem-solving scenarios.

The attention fusion mechanism based on the Transformer architecture fundamentally integrates retrieval module information flow into the generation process. While traditional self-attention mechanisms solely focus on intra-sequence correlations, this approach enables generative models to simultaneously attend to both current context and retrieved content. A seminal implementation is the RETRO model proposed by Sebastian Borgeaud et al. [7] which employs chunked cross-attention to incorporate external text segments. This design enhances temporal efficiency through linear time complexity relative to retrieval volume while improving text generation quality.

Subsequent studies [81–85] have expanded this paradigm through diverse methodologies: One research direction introduces external knowledge via novel attention modules. For instance, LiLi et al. extended RETRO by decoupling contextual encoding from model reasoning, while Wu [85] and Wang [86] implemented external memory systems for attention key-value storage and retrieval. Alternative approaches adopt lightweight weighted summation strategies. Fevry's "Entities as Experts" model [87] integrates top-k entity embeddings into hidden states, whereas Wu and Xiong et al. [88] explored knowledge integration through retrieval re-ranking mechanisms.

Network-based retrieval fusion architectures demonstrate three principal advantages: efficient information extraction from retrievals, dynamic attention intensity modulation, and enhanced knowledge sharing/transfer in multi-task learning. However, challenges persist in computational complexity (escalating costs with long documents/large-scale retrievals) and information processing optimization (mitigating attention misallocation from noise/redundancy), necessitating advanced solutions for information filtering and weight allocation.

5 Future Prospects

RAG technology significantly enhances the generation accuracy and knowledge coverage of LLMs by dynamically integrating external knowledge bases. However, as application scenarios grow increasingly complex and diverse, RAG still faces critical challenges in multiple dimensions that demand breakthroughs.

End-to-End Joint Training. Currently, the retrieval module and generation module in RAG systems are typically designed independently, relying solely on loose interfaces for information transfer. This disjointed architecture makes it challenging to align their objective functions, potentially resulting in mismatches between retrieved results and generation requirements. For instance, the retrieval module might overemphasize keyword matching while neglecting the semantic coherence required by the generation module; conversely, the generation module may fail to fully utilize critical information from retrieved results. Therefore, end-to-end joint optimization emerges as a crucial research direction. Future efforts should focus on developing a unified end-to-end training framework that jointly optimizes the objective functions of retriever and generator. This can be achieved through shared encoders or interactive decoders for deep semantic alignment, along with dynamic collaborative mechanisms enabling real-time information exchange between modules during training, thereby enhancing overall model consistency and generation quality.

Robustness Enhancement. The performance of a RAG system highly depends on the quality of the external knowledge base and the accuracy of the retrieval algorithm. However, in practical applications, such systems often face multiple challenges, including noisy data and adversarial attacks, which impose higher demands on the model's robustness. Noisy data typically originates from non-malicious data defects, such as text recognition errors, missing information, or unstructured noise. In contrast, adversarial attacks involve maliciously introduced semantic perturbations or spelling alterations aimed at deliberately misleading the retrieval and generation processes. Although these two types of disturbances differ in motivation and manifestation, both can lead to reduced relevance in retrieval results and diminished credibility in generated content.

To enhance the system's stability in complex environments, it is necessary to collaboratively design robustness enhancement mechanisms at both the training and inference stages. On one hand, adversarial sample augmentation techniques can be introduced during the training phase by injecting noise patterns such as semantic interference words, spelling variations, or syntactic perturbations, thereby improving the model's tolerance and generalization capability for unconventional inputs. On the other hand, a credibility assessment module should be integrated during the inference process to perform multi-dimensional fact verification on retrieval results. For instance, a lightweight fact-checking classifier can be employed to filter extracted texts based on confidence levels, combined with a multi-source evidence cross-verification mechanism to identify potential anomalies. Additionally, constructing a retrieval architecture based on semantic consistency, which reduces over-reliance on bag-of-words models or surface-level features, can also help improve retrieval quality in adversarial environments.

Privacy Protection and Bias Mitigation. The utilization of large-scale external knowledge bases in RAG systems may potentially trigger ethical and privacy risks, including user privacy breaches and amplification of data biases. Across diverse application scenarios, ensuring fairness and reducing biases in both retrieved and generated content becomes paramount. This can be achieved through implementing federated retrieval technology, which enables cross-domain knowledge queries without sharing raw data, while incorporating fairness constraints and privacy-preserving strategies during the retrieval phase.

Computational Efficiency Optimization. The real-time performance of RAG systems is constrained by large-scale knowledge base retrieval and the high computational costs of generative models. As system scales continue to expand, the development of efficient computational frameworks oriented towards lightweight and edge deployment has emerged as a critical direction for expanding RAG application scenarios. For instance, leveraging knowledge distillation techniques enables transferring the capabilities of large models to lightweight counterparts, effectively reducing inference latency while maintaining performance.

Multimodal Extension. Current RAG systems primarily focus on textual data, yet the demand for multimodal information fusion has become increasingly prominent in domains such as medical imaging analysis, intelligent customer service (including voice interactions), and virtual reality. The core challenges facing cross-modal RAG systems lie in constructing a unified cross-modal semantic-aligned vector space, achieving embedding alignment for heterogeneous data (text, images, audio, etc.) through technologies like contrastive learning. Concurrently, there is a need to develop output adaptation mechanisms for multimodal generative models, ensuring logical consistency and semantic coherence during cross-modal knowledge fusion.

6 Conclusion

RAG technology addresses the limitations of traditional LLMs' static knowledge dependency by dynamically integrating external knowledge bases with LLM generation capabilities, effectively mitigating "hallucinations" while enhancing knowledge timeliness and generation accuracy. This paper systematically reviews the theoretical framework and key technological advancements in RAG: In the retrieval module, strategic designs including data chunking strategies, query optimization methods, and diversified retrieval mechanisms lay the foundation for efficient and accurate information extraction; In the generation module, technological explorations such as re-ranking, context compression, and cross-attention fusion further optimize the collaborative efficiency between retrieval results and generative models. However, current RAG systems still face challenges including insufficient retrieval-generation synergy, limited multimodal support, and privacy/bias concerns. Future research directions may focus on end-to-end joint optimization, enhanced system robustness, expanded multimodal fusion capabilities, lightweight deployment exploration, and privacy preservation mechanisms. This paper summarizes RAG's technical pathways and cutting-edge directions, providing valuable references for academia and industry to advance the development of more efficient, reliable, and universal RAG systems.

References

1. Vaswani, A., Shazeer, N., Parmar, N., et al.: Attention is all you need. Adv. Neural Inf. Process. Syst. **30** (2017)
2. Achiam, J., Adler, S., Agarwal, S., et al.: Gpt-4 technical report (2023). arxiv:2303.08774
3. Bai, J., Bai, S., Chu, Y., et al.: Qwen technical report (2023). arxiv preprint arxiv:2309.16609
4. Team, G., Anil, R., Borgeaud, S., et al.: Gemini: a family of highly capable multimodal models (2023). arxiv:2312.11805
5. Ram, O., Levine, Y., Dalmedigos, I., et al.: In-context retrieval-augmented language models. Trans. Assoc. Comput. Linguist. **11**, 1316–1331 (2023)
6. Vu, T., Iyyer, M., Wang, X., et al.: Freshllms: refreshing large language models with search engine augmentation (2023). arxiv preprint arxiv:2310.03214
7. Borgeaud, S., Mensch, A., Hoffmann, J., et al.: Improving language models by retrieving from trillions of tokens. In: International Conference on Machine Learning, pp. 2206–2240. PMLR (2022)
8. Edge, D., Trinh, H., Cheng, N., et al.: From local to global: a graph rag approach to query-focused summarization (2024). arxiv:2404.16130
9. Guan, X., Liu, Y., Lin, H., et al.: Mitigating large language model hallucinations via autonomous knowledge graph-based retrofitting. Proc. AAAI Conf. Artif. Intell. **38**(16), 18126–18134 (2024)
10. Mior, M.J.: Large language models for JSON schema discovery (2024). arxiv:2407.03286
11. Yang, H., Guo, J., Qi, J., et al.: A method for parsing and vectorization of semi-structured data used in retrieval augmented generation (2024). arxiv preprint arxiv:2405.03989
12. Thulke, D., Daheim, N., Dugast, C., et al.: Efficient retrieval augmented generation from unstructured knowledge for task-oriented dialog (2021). arxiv preprint arxiv:2102.04643
13. Manathunga, S.S., Illangasekara, Y.A.: Retrieval augmented generation and representative vector summarization for large unstructured textual data in medical education (2023). arxiv:2308.00479

14. Kaddour, J., Harris, J., Mozes, M., et al.: Challenges and applications of large language models (2023). arxiv:2307.10169
15. Liu, N.F., Lin, K., Hewitt, J., et al.: Lost in the middle: How language models use long contexts. Trans. Assoc. Comput. Linguist. **12**, 157–173 (2024)
16. Yih, S.: Retrieval-augmented generation for knowledge-intensive NLP tasks. In: Conference on Neural Information Processing Systems, Vancouver, Canada (2020)
17. Finardi, P., Avila, L., Castaldoni, R., et al.: The chronicles of rag: the retriever, the chunk and the generator (2024). arxiv preprint arxiv:2401.07883
18. Safjan, K.: From fixed-size to NLP chunking-a deep dive into text chunking techniques. Krystian's Safjan Blog (2023)
19. Langchain: Recursively split by character (2023). https://python.langchain.com/docs/modules/dataconnection/documenttransformers/recursivetextsplitter
20. Greg Kamradt, Semantic chunking (2023). https://github.com/FullStackRetrieval-com/RetrievalTutorials/tree/main/tutorials/LevelsOfTextSplitting
21. Duarte, A.V., Marques, J., Graça, M., et al.: Lumberchunker: long-form narrative document segmentation (2024). arxiv preprint arXiv:2406.17526
22. NLTK: Natural Language Toolkit (2023). https://www.nltk.org/
23. Spacy (2016-2024). https://spacy.io/
24. Mikolov, T., Chen, K., Corrado, G., et al.: Efficient estimation of word representations in vector space (2013). arxiv:1301.3781
25. Devlin, J., Chang, M.W., Lee, K., et al.: Bert: pre-training of deep bidirectional transformers for language understanding (2018). arxiv:1810.04805
26. Günther, M., Mohr, I., Williams, D.J., et al.: Late chunking: contextual chunk embeddings using long-context embedding models (2024). arxiv preprint arxiv:2409.04701
27. Zhao, J., Ji, Z., Qi, P., et al.: Meta-Chunking: learning efficient text segmentation via logical perception (2024). arxiv preprint arxiv:2410.12788
28. Ma, X., Gong, Y., He, P., et al.: Query rewriting for retrieval-augmented large language models (2023). arxiv:2305.14283
29. Wang, Y., Zhang, H., Pang, L., et al.: MaFeRw: query rewriting with multi-aspect feedbacks for retrieval-augmented large language models (2024). arxiv preprint arxiv:2408.17072
30. Zhu, W., Zhang, X., Zhai, Q., et al.: A hybrid text generation-based query expansion method for open-domain question answering. Future Internet **15**(5), 180 (2023)
31. Zhou, D., Schärli, N., Hou, L., et al.: Least-to-most prompting enables complex reasoning in large language models (2022). arxiv preprint arxiv:2205.10625
32. Chen, Z., Zhao, Z., Zhu, Z., et al.: Autoprm: automating procedural supervision for multi-step reasoning via controllable question decomposition (2024). arxiv preprint arxiv:2402.11452
33. Chan, C.M., Xu, C., Yuan, R., et al.: RQ-RAG: learning to refine queries for retrieval augmented generation (2024). arxiv e-prints arxiv:2404.00610
34. Zheng, H.S., Mishra, S., Chen, X., et al.: Take a step back: evoking reasoning via abstraction in large language models (2023). arxiv preprint arxiv:2310.06117
35. Gao S, Dwivedi-Yu J, Yu P, et al. Efficient tool use with chain-of-abstraction reasoning (2024). arxiv preprint arxiv:2401.17464
36. Hong, R., Zhang, H., Pan, X., et al.: Abstraction-of-thought makes language models better reasoners (2024). arxiv preprint arxiv:2406.12442
37. Robertson, S., Zaragoza, H.: The probabilistic relevance framework: BM25 and beyond. Found. Trends® Inf. Retrieval **3**(4), 333–389 (2009)
38. Karpukhin, V., Oguz, B., Min, S., et al.: Dense passage retrieval for open-domain question answering. In: EMNLP (1), pp. 6769–6781 (2020)
39. Xiong, L., Xiong, C., Li, Y., et al.: Approximate nearest neighbor negative contrastive learning for dense text retrieval (2020). arxiv preprint arxiv:2007.00808

40. Zhang, F., Zhu, D., Ming, J., et al.: DH-RAG: a dynamic historical context-powered retrieval-augmented generation method for multi-turn dialogue (2025). arxiv preprint arxiv:2502.13847
41. Ren, Y., Cao, Y., Guo, P., et al.: Retrieve-and-sample: document-level event argument extraction via hybrid retrieval augmentation. In: Proceedings of the 61st Annual Meeting of the Association for Computational Linguistics (Volume 1: Long Papers), pp. 293–306 (2023)
42. Ye, L., Lei, Z., Yin, J., et al.: Boosting conversational question answering with fine-grained retrieval-augmentation and self-check. In: Proceedings of the 47th International ACM SIGIR Conference on Research and Development in Information Retrieval, pp. 2301–2305 (2024)
43. Zhong, Z., Liu, H., Cui, X., et al.: Mix-of-granularity: optimize the chunking granularity for retrieval-augmented generation (2024). arxiv:2406.00456
44. Zeng, H., Yue, Z., Jiang, Q., et al.: Federated recommendation via hybrid retrieval augmented generation (2024). arxiv:2403.04256
45. Shao, Z., Gong, Y., Shen, Y., et al. : Enhancing retrieval-augmented large language models with iterative retrieval-generation synergy (2023). arxiv preprint arxiv:2305.15294
46. Jiang, Z., Xu, F.F., Gao, L., et al.: Active retrieval augmented generation. In: Proceedings of the 2023 Conference on Empirical Methods in Natural Language Processing, pp. 7969–7992 (2023)
47. Xiong G, Jin, Q., Wang, X., et al.: Improving retrieval-augmented generation in medicine with iterative follow-up questions. In: Biocomputing 2025: Proceedings of the Pacific Symposium, pp. 199–214 (2024)
48. Yan, S.Q., Gu, J.C., Zhu, Y., et al.: Corrective retrieval augmented generation (2024). arxiv:2401.15884
49. Jiang, Z., Xu, F.F., Gao, L., et al.: Active retrieval augmented generation (2023). arxiv:2305.06983
50. Su, W., Tang, Y., Ai, Q., et al.: Dragin: dynamic retrieval augmented generation based on the real-time information needs of large language models (2024). arxiv:2403.10081
51. Zhuang, S., Liu, B., Koopman, B., et al.: Open-source large language models are strong zero-shot query likelihood models for document ranking (2023). arxiv preprint arxiv:2310.13243
52. Jiang, H., Wu, Q., Lin, C.Y., et al.: Llmlingua: Compressing prompts for accelerated inference of large language models (2023). arxiv preprint arxiv:2310.05736
53. Jiang, H., Wu, Q., Luo, X., et al.: Longllmlingua: accelerating and enhancing LLMS in long context scenarios via prompt compression (2023). arxiv preprint arxiv:2310.06839
54. Joshi, M., Chen, D., Liu, Y., et al.: Spanbert: improving pre-training by representing and predicting spans. Trans. Assoc. Comput. Linguist. **8**, 64–77 (2020)
55. BGEmbedding: Bilingual and Crosslingual Embedding for RAG. https://github.com/netease-youdao/BCEmbedding
56. Jina Reranker (2020-2024). https://jina.ai/reranker/
57. Cohere (2024). https://cohere.com/rerank
58. Blagojevi, V.: Enhancing rag pipelines in haystack: introducing diversityranker and lostinthemiddleranker[EB/OL] (2023)
59. Gao, Y., Sheng, T., Xiang, Y., et al.: Chat-rec: towards interactive and explainable LLMS-augmented recommender system (2023). arxiv preprint arxiv:2303.14524
60. Gilbert, H., et al.: Semantic compression with large language models (2023). arXiv preprint arXiv:2304.12512
61. Chevalier, A., Wettig, A., Ajith, A., et al.: Adapting language models to compress contexts (2023). arxiv:2305.14788
62. Anderson, N., Wilson, C., Richardson, S.D.: Lingua: addressing scenarios for live interpretation and automatic dubbing. In: Proceedings of the 15th Biennial Conference of the Association for Machine Translation in the Americas (Volume 2: Users and Providers Track and Government Track), pp. 202–209 (2022)

63. Yang, H., Li, Z., Zhang, Y., et al.: PRCA: fitting black-box large language models for retrieval question answering via pluggable reward-driven contextual adapter (2023). arxiv preprint arxiv:2310.18347
64. Xu, F., Shi, W., Choi, E.: Recomp: improving retrieval-augmented LMS with compression and selective augmentation (2023). arxiv preprint arxiv:2310.04408
65. Gao, Y., Xiong, Y., Gao, X., et al.: Retrieval-augmented generation for large language models: a survey (2023). arxiv preprint arxiv:2312.10997
66. Ma, Y., Cao, Y., Hong, Y.C., et al.: Large language model is not a good few-shot information extractor, but a good reranker for hard samples! (2023). arxiv preprint arxiv:2303.08559
67. Cui J, Li Z, Yan Y, et al. Chatlaw: Open-source legal large language model with integrated external knowledge bases. CoRR, 2023
68. Fabbri A R, Ng P, Wang Z, et al. Template-based question generation from retrieved sentences for improved unsupervised question answering (2020). arxiv preprint arxiv:2004.11892
69. Li, X., Lv, K., Yan, H., et al.: Unified demonstration retriever for in-context learning (2023). arxiv preprint arxiv:2305.04320
70. Wang, S., Xu, Y., Fang, Y., et al.: Training data is more valuable than you think: A simple and effective method by retrieving from training data (2022). arxiv preprint arxiv:2203.08773
71. Izacard, G., Grave, E.: Leveraging passage retrieval with generative models for open domain question answering (2020). arxiv preprint arxiv:2007.01282
72. De Jong, M., Zemlyanskiy, Y., FitzGerald, N., et al.: Pre-computed memory or on-the-fly encoding? A hybrid approach to retrieval augmentation makes the most of your compute. In: International Conference on Machine Learning. PMLR, pp. 7329–7342 (2023)
73. Guo, Z., Cheng, S., Wang, Y., et al.: Prompt-guided retrieval augmentation for non-knowledge-intensive tasks (2023). arxiv preprint arxiv:2305.17653
74. Izacard, G., Lewis, P., Lomeli, M., et al.: Atlas: few-shot learning with retrieval augmented language models. J. Mach. Learn. Res. **24**(251), 1–43 (2023)
75. Liu, S., Cho, H.J., Freedman, M., et al.: Recap: retrieval-enhanced context-aware prefix encoder for personalized dialogue response generation (2023). arxiv preprint arXiv:2306.07206
76. Singh, D., Reddy, S., Hamilton, W., et al.: End-to-end training of multi-document reader and retriever for open-domain question answering. Adv. Neural. Inf. Process. Syst. **34**, 25968–25981 (2021)
77. Wu, S., Xiong, Y., Cui, Y., et al.: Retrieval-augmented generation for natural language processing: a survey (2024). arxiv preprint arxiv:2407.13193
78. Khandelwal, U., Fan, A., Jurafsky, D., et al.: Nearest neighbor machine translation (2020). arXiv preprint arXiv:2010.00710
79. Khandelwal, U., Levy, O., Jurafsky, D., et al.: Generalization through memorization: nearest neighbor language models (2019). arXiv preprint arXiv:1911.00172
80. Xiong, Y., Yang, X., Liu, L., et al.: EARA: improving biomedical semantic textual similarity with entity-aligned attention and retrieval augmentation. In: Findings of the Association for Computational Linguistics: EMNLP 2023, pp. 8760–8771 (2023)
81. Cai, D., Wang, Y., Li, H., et al.: Neural machine translation with monolingual translation memory (2021). arXiv preprint arXiv:2105.11269
82. De Jong, M., Zemlyanskiy, Y., FitzGerald, N., et al.: Mention memory: incorporating textual knowledge into transformers through entity mention attention (2021). arXiv preprint arXiv:2110.06176
83. Li, Z., Guo, R., Kumar, S.: Decoupled context processing for context augmented language modeling. Adv. Neural. Inf. Process. Syst. **35**, 21698–21710 (2022)
84. Wang, Z., Nie, W., Qiao, Z., et al.: Retrieval-based controllable molecule generation (2022). arXiv preprint arXiv:2208.11126

85. Wu, Y., Rabe, M.N., Hutchins, D.L., et al.: Memorizing transformers (2022). arXiv preprint arXiv:2203.08913
86. Wang, W., Dong, L., Cheng, H., et al.: Augmenting language models with long-term memory. Adv. Neural Inf. Process. Syst. **36** (2024)
87. Févry, T., Soares, L.B., FitzGerald, N., et al.: Entities as experts: sparse memory access with entity supervision (2020). arXiv preprint arXiv:2004.07202
88. Wu, S., Xiong, Y., Cui, Y., et al.: Improving natural language understanding with computation-efficient retrieval representation fusion (2024). arXiv preprint arXiv:2401.02993

Text Sentiment Analysis Based on Word2Vec: A Comparative Study of SVM and Deep Learning Models

Shutong Cao[1(✉)], Zhitong Liu[1], Ziyuan Wang[2], and Hao Tang[3]

[1] School of Intelligent Rail Transit, Dalian Jiaotong University, Dalian 116028, China
3167059968@qq.com

[2] School of Software, Henan Normal University, Zhengzhou 451191, China

[3] School of Computer Science, Zhongyuan University of Technology, Zhengzhou 451191, China

Abstract. Text sentiment analysis is a fundamental task in natural language processing, with extensive applications in social media monitoring, market research, and public opinion analysis. This study systematically investigates the performance of classical and deep learning models for this task. The methodology begins by employing Word2Vec technology to convert textual data into dense word vectors, effectively capturing semantic relationships within the data. These generated embeddings are then used as input for four distinct classification algorithms: Support Vector Machine (SVM), Recurrent Neural Network (RNN), Long Short-Term Memory network (LSTM), and Gated Recurrent Unit (GRU).

Comparative experiments were conducted on a unified dataset to ensure a fair evaluation of each model's efficacy in text classification. The results demonstrate a clear trade-off: the SVM model delivers robust and computationally efficient performance on smaller-scale datasets, serving as a strong baseline. In contrast, the more complex LSTM and GRU models excel on larger datasets. Their gated architectures are specifically designed to overcome the limitations of simple RNNs by effectively capturing long-range contextual dependencies and temporal features within sequences, which significantly enhances classification accuracy.

The analysis concludes that model selection is highly dependent on data scale and computational resources. Furthermore, it proposes promising future optimization directions, suggesting that hybrid approaches which integrate the feature extraction strengths of SVMs with the sequential modeling power of advanced recurrent networks like LSTM could potentially yield superior performance.

Keywords: Text Sentiment Analysis · Support Vector Machine · Long Short Term Memory Network · Recurrent Neural Network · Gated Recurrent Unit

1 Introduction

According to the 53rd Statistical Report on the Development of Internet in China released by the China Internet Network Information Center (CNNIC) in March 2024, by December 2023, the number of Internet users in China had reached 1.092 billion [1].

X. Ding and Y. Dong (Eds.): CLNLP 2025, CCIS 2775, pp. 266–272, 2026.
https://doi.org/10.1007/978-981-95-4788-3_24

Traditional machine learning methods such as SVM can utilize text features for sentiment classification, while deep learning models such as LSTM can better capture the contextual relationships of text. Therefore, SVM and LSTM methods play a significant role in sentiment polarity analysis of short and long review texts [2]. Reference [3] analyzes and organizes the application of topic mining techniques in sentiment analysis, mainly pointing out the problems and difficulties in traditional sentiment analysis, and the shortcomings of current research in comprehensively considering the adaptability of different models and data conditions. Some studies are limited to specific data sets to optimize a single model, lacking comprehensive consideration of the two models under broad data conditions [4]; Reference [5] focuses on the research of deep learning text sentiment analysis technology. However, some of the theoretical research results in this study are difficult to effectively implement in practical application scenarios due to insufficient consideration of the complexity of actual data. Reference [6] introduces the application of natural language processing technology in text sentiment analysis, providing technical reference for improving the accuracy of sentiment analysis using different text features in this paper.In terms of social media text sentiment analysis, reference [7] proposes an adaptive sentiment analysis method that analyzes social media posts and extracts users' viewpoints in real-time, providing relevant practical references for this study. Reference [8] uses deep learning models for visual sentiment analysis of social media data, and its experience in model application and data processing can also provide reference for text sentiment analysis. Reference [9] uses the topic distribution generated by the topic model as a feature to perform sentiment analysis on documents, providing a new perspective for this paper when processing text data with different features. Reference [10] conducted research on Chinese text sentiment information recognition based on CNKI.

2 Basic Knowledge

2.1 Traditional Methods of Sentiment Analysis

Dictionary based methods, such as sentiment lexicon and rule matching, rely on predefined sentiment lexicons to analyze the sentiment polarity of sentiment words contained in the text. This type of method is simple and easy to use, but it cannot capture subtle emotional differences in context very well.

2.2 Word2Vec

Word2Vec is a distributed word representation (word vector) that learns context words via neural networks. It gains word semantics by predicting context words, with common training methods like Skip-gram and CBOW. Skip-gram predicts other context words using a central word, and its goal (given a central word) is to maximize the following conditional probabilities:

$\mathrm{P}(w_{t-k}, ..w_{t+k}|w_t) \approx \sum_{i=t-k}^{t+k} \mathrm{P}(w_i|w_t)$ (1).

Among them, P is the contextual word around the central word, which represents the probability of the word appearing under the given conditions of the central word.

Text Feature Representation. In sentiment analysis tasks, text is typically composed of multiple words. To convert the text into a fixed length vector representation, take the mean of the word vectors in each text. In this way, the word vectors corresponding to each word in the text will be aggregated into one text vector:

$$\underset{v}{\rightarrow}(T) = \frac{1}{|T|}\sum_{i=1}^{|T|} \underset{v}{\rightarrow}(w_i) \tag{2}$$

3 Emotion Analysis Algorithm

This article proposes the use of four algorithms, namely Support Vector Machine (SVM), Recurrent Neural Network (RNN), Long Short Term Memory Network (LSTM), and Gated Recurrent Unit (GRU), to classify and analyze the generated word vectors. The working principles of these algorithms are introduced below.

3.1 Support Vector Machine (SVM)

SVM is a supervised classifier that maps data to a high-dimensional space via kernel functions, finds the hyperplane with maximum margin, and relies on support vectors to perform linear or nonlinear separation; it excels with high-dimensional, small-sample data.

3.2 Recurrent Neural Network (RNN)

RNN (Recurrent Neural Network) is a network structure proposed by John Hopfield in 1982, specifically designed for deep learning models that process sequential data. By introducing a fully connected cyclic structure, the network is endowed with memory capabilities, enabling it to handle tasks related to time series. The unfolding diagram of RNN is shown in Fig. 1.

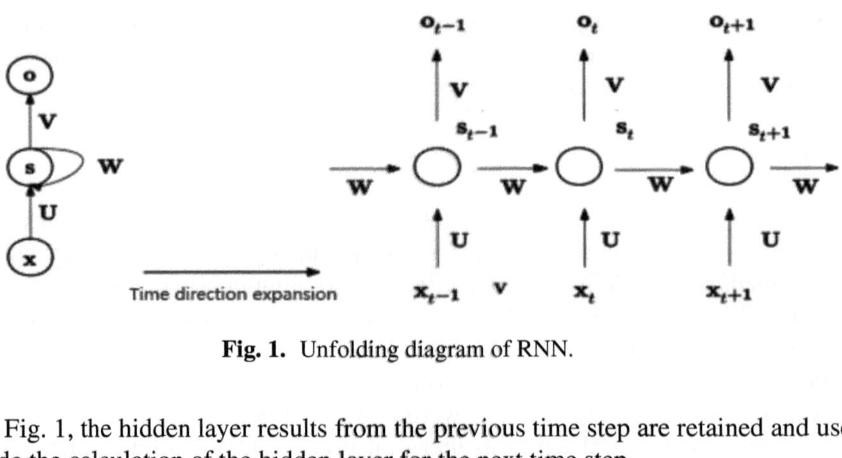

Fig. 1. Unfolding diagram of RNN.

In Fig. 1, the hidden layer results from the previous time step are retained and used to guide the calculation of the hidden layer for the next time step.

3.3 Long Short Term Memory Network (LSTM)

The essence of the LSTM model is its innovative gating mechanism, composed of three core elements: input gate, forget gate, and output gate. The working diagram of LSTM's internal structure is shown in Fig. 2.

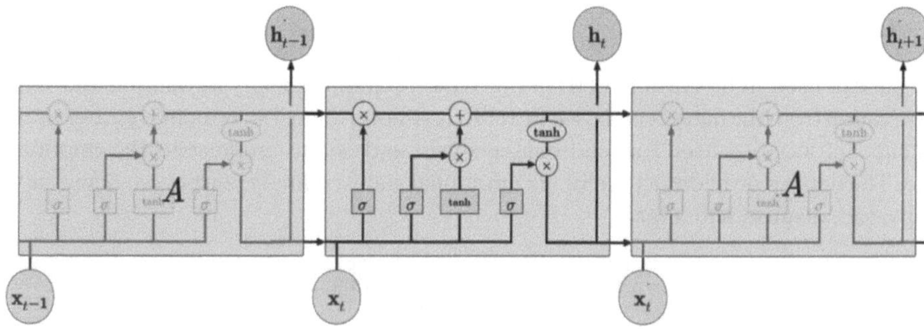

Fig. 2. Internal working diagram of LSTM.

As shown in Fig. 2, each time step receives one more dimension of input than traditional recurrent neural networks (RNNs), making them better at processing and memorizing long-term dependency information.

3.4 Recurrent Gated Unit (GRU)

GRU uses two core gates—Update Gate and Reset Gate—to regulate information flow: the update gate determines cell state updates and retains previous memory, while the reset gate filters past irrelevant information (letting the model "forget" it at each time step) to better capture long-term data dependencies. The overall result is shown in Fig. 3.

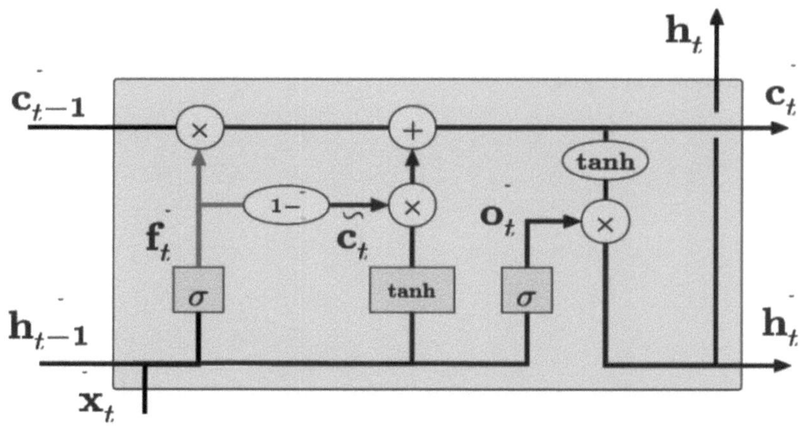

Fig. 3. Overall GRU results.

GRU innovates by merging LSTM's forget and input gates into an update gate (plus a reset gate). This cuts parameters while keeping gating advantages, so only the current time step's cell state update formula is modified.

4 Experiments

4.1 Dataset

The dataset used in this article is from the Weibo sentiment analysis dataset, and some information from the dataset is shown in Table 1. Among them, "statement" represents the sentence information used for sentiment analysis, and "status" represents the emotional state. The dataset provides a total of six emotional states, namely: surprised, depression, happy, sad, disgust, and angry.

Table 1. Dataset information.

id	statement	status
0	@You can't escape like that! Be tied to me for the rest of your life. [Hehe]	Happy
1	If we meet again someday! Are we still like before? [Tears]	sad
2	All wrong, back off dear, forward doubt. Stay in a restless and restless place	Depression

4.2 Experimental Environment

Experimental environment: Intel i7-9700K, RTX 3060 12 GB, 32 GB RAM, Win 10 64-bit; Python 3.8, TensorFlow 2.4, Scikit-learn 0.24, NLTK 3.5.

4.3 Experiment and Results Analysis

This section compares and analyzes the performance of four models, SVM, LSTM, RNN, and GRU, in sentiment classification tasks.the visualization results of performance indicators are shown in Fig. 4.

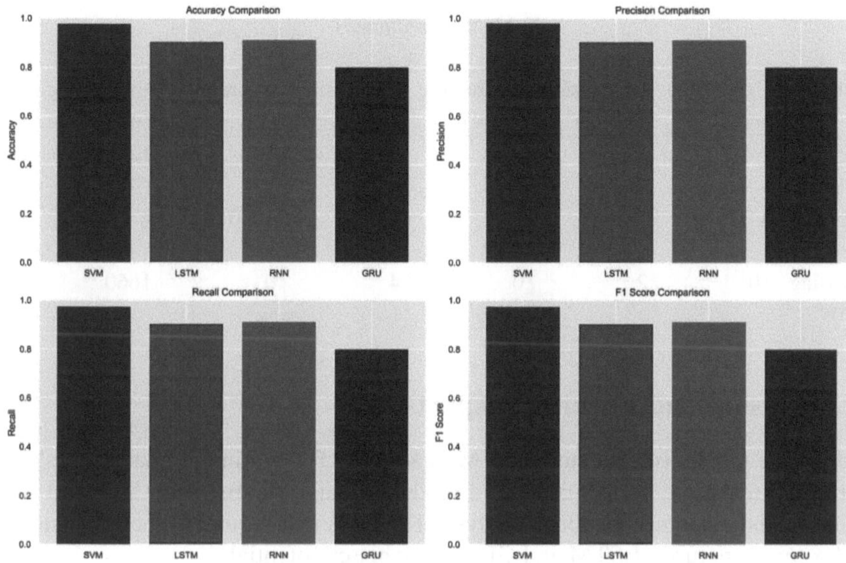

Fig. 4. Bar chart of performance indicators for four models.

Figure 4 show that SVM clearly outperforms the others, with accuracy, precision, recall, and F1 all ≈ 0.98. LSTM and RNN follow closely (≈ 0.91), while GRU lags at ≈ 0.80.

As shown in Table 2, the confusion matrix of the SVM classification results demonstrates the model's performance across six emotional categories: expressing happiness, sadness, disgust, anger, fear, and surprise. The table displays the number of correct and incorrect predictions, with the diagonal values representing correct classifications. For instance, out of 4115 instances labeled as "Expressing happiness," 4090 were correctly classified, while the remaining were misclassified into other emotion categories. Similarly, high true positive counts are observed for "Expressing surprise" (1660 correct out of 1676) and "Expressing fear" (1010 correct out of 1033), indicating strong classification accuracy for these emotions. Overall, the confusion matrix reveals that the SVM model achieves high precision for most emotion classes, with relatively few misclassifications across the board.

Table 2. Confusion matrix of SVM.

True\Pred	Expressing happiness	Expressing sadness	Expressing disgust	Expressing anger	Expressing fear	Expressing surprise	Total
Expressing happiness	4090	10	1	5	1	8	4115
Expressing sadness	12	2503	7	5	5	7	2539
Expressing disgust	6	7	707	12	1	10	743

(*continued*)

Table 2. (*continued*)

True\Pred	Expressing happiness	Expressing sadness	Expressing disgust	Expressing anger	Expressing fear	Expressing surprise	Total
Expressing anger	7	23	9	953	14	12	1018
Expressing fear	4	7	0	8	1010	4	1033
Expressing surprise	10	2	0	4	0	1660	1676

5 Conclusion and Future Prospects

Based on the results of this study, SVM is suitable for sentiment analysis tasks that require high real-time performance and moderate data volume, such as social media monitoring and customer feedback analysis. For tasks that require higher precision and complex text structures, LSTM and GRU show better potential.

However, this study has certain limitations. The current experiments are only based on the Weibo sentiment analysis dataset. Although the SVM model performs well on this dataset, the generalization ability of the model still needs to be further verified. Future research can consider applying SVM to other real-time datasets, such as news comments and e-commerce platform user reviews.

References

1. The 53rd Statistical Report on China's Internet Development was released. News Forum, **38** (02): 17 (2024). https://doi.org/10.19425/j.cnki.cn15-1019/g2.2024.02.025
2. Sheng, M., Ma, S., Gu, M., et al.: Online drama review analysis model based on SVM and LSTM. Mod. Comput. **30**(02), 60–65 (2024)
3. Zhu, X., Song, J., Zhang, X.: A review of text sentiment analysis based on theme mining technology. Intell. Theory Pract. **42**(11), 156–163 (2019). https://doi.org/10.16353/j.cnki.1000-7490.2019.11.025
4. Li, Y.: Research on the construction method of dynamic sentiment dictionary based on bidirectional LSTM and text sentiment analysis. Zhengzhou University (2019)
5. Ji, L.: Research on Text Sentiment Analysis Technology Based on Deep Learning. Beijing University of Posts and Telecommunications (2019)
6. Zhang, Y., Wang, H.: Application of Python natural language processing methods in text sentiment analysis. Comput. Knowl. Technol. **16**(36), 87–88 (2020). https://doi.org/10.14004/j.cnki.ckt.2020.3692
7. El Alaoui, I., Gahi, Y., Messoussi, R., Chaabi, Y., Todoskoff, A., Kobi, A.: A novel adaptable approach for sentiment analysis on big social data. J. Big Data **5**(1), 1–18 (2018). https://doi.org/10.1186/s40537-018-0120-0
8. Ganesh, C., Naaji, A., Gabor, A., et al.: Visual sentiment analysis using deep learning models with social media data. Appl. Sci. **12**(3), 1030 (2022)
9. Pearce, D., Pinto, S.H., Blair, J.S., et al.: Sentiment classification of social media content with features generated using topic models. Front. Artif. . Appl. **284**, 155–166 (2016)
10. Liu, B.: Research on Chinese Text Emotion Information Recognition Based on CNKI. Beijing University of Posts and Telecommunications (2009)

Author Index

X. Ding and Y. Dong (Eds.): CLNLP 2025, CCIS 2775, pp. 273–274, 2026.
https://doi.org/10.1007/978-981-95-4788-3

MIX
Papier aus verantwortungsvollen Quellen
Paper from responsible sources
FSC® C105338
FSC
www.fsc.org

If you have any concerns about our products,
you can contact us on
ProductSafety@springernature.com

In case Publisher is established outside the EU,
the EU authorized representative is:
Springer Nature Customer Service Center GmbH
Europaplatz 3, 69115 Heidelberg, Germany

Printed by Libri Plureos GmbH
in Hamburg, Germany